Rethinking the Economics of War

Rethinking the Economics of War
The Intersection of Need, Creed, and Greed

Edited by
Cynthia J. Arnson
and
I. William Zartman

Woodrow Wilson Center Press
Washington, D.C.

The Johns Hopkins University Press
Baltimore

EDITORIAL OFFICES

Woodrow Wilson Center Press
Woodrow Wilson International Center for Scholars
One Woodrow Wilson Plaza
1300 Pennsylvania Avenue, N.W.
Washington, D.C. 20004-3027
Telephone: 202-691-4029
http://www.wilsoncenter.org

ORDER FROM

The Johns Hopkins University Press
Hampden Station
P.O. Box 50370
Baltimore, Maryland 21211
Telephone: 1-800-537-5487
www.press.jhu.edu/books

Printed in the United States of America on acid-free paper ∞
9 8 7 6 5 4 3 2 1

Library of Congress Cataloging-in-Publication Data

Rethinking the economics of war : the intersection of need, creed, and greed / Cynthia J. Arnson and I. William Zartman, editors.
    p. cm.
  Includes index.
  ISBN 0-8018-8297-4 (hardcover: alk. paper)—ISBN 0-8018-8298-2 (pbk: alk. paper)
  1. War—Economic aspects—Developing countries. 2. Civil war—Economic aspects—Developing countries. 3. Developing countries—Economic conditions. 4. Developing countries—Politics and government. I. Arnson, Cynthia. II. Zartman, I. William.
HB195.E3533 2005
355.02'18'09172409045—dc22

2005015117

To Gerry, Zack, Jeannie, and Micah,
and to Danièle, Alex, and Susan,
with faith, hope, and love

Contents

Tables and Figures   x

Acknowledgments   xi

1. The Political Economy of War: Situating the Debate   1
   Cynthia J. Arnson
2. Trafficking, Rents, and Diaspora in the Lebanese War   23
   Elizabeth Picard
3. The Evolution of Internal War in Peru: The Conjunction
   of Need, Creed, and Organizational Finance   52
   Cynthia McClintock
4. The Criminalization of the RUF Insurgency in Sierra Leone   84
   Jimmy D. Kandeh
5. Resource Wealth and Angola's Uncivil Wars   107
   Philippe Le Billon
6. The Democratic Republic of the Congo: Structures of
   Greed, Networks of Need   140
   Erik Kennes
7. Economic Resources and Internal Armed Conflicts:
   Lessons from the Colombian Case   178
   Marc Chernick
8. Surviving State Failure: Internal War and Regional
   Conflict in Afghanistan's Neighborhood   206
   Paula R. Newberg
9. Economic Factors in Civil Wars: Policy Considerations   234
   David M. Malone and Jake Sherman
10. Need, Creed, and Greed in Intrastate Conflict   256
    I. William Zartman

Index   285

Tables and Figures

Tables

4.1. Average Annual Growth Rate of Sierra Leone's Economy,
1980–90 and 1990–95   95

7.1. Phases of Conflict in Colombia, 1946–2003   183

Figures

5.1. Interim Peace Consolidation Tax and Budgetary Regime   137

7.1. Price per Pound of Colombian Coffee, 1930–70   187

7.2. Deaths Caused by La Violencia in Colombia, 1948–60   187

7.3. Price per Pound of Colombian Coffee, 1957–2001   188

7.4. Colombia's Oil Fields and Gas Pipelines   193

7.5. Colombia's Petroleum Exports, 1941–75 and 1986–2001   194

7.6. Andean Net Coca Cultivation, 1991–2000   196

Acknowledgments

We have gathered many debts during the three and a half years of researching and editing this book. Numerous colleagues at the Woodrow Wilson Center—especially Gil Khadiagala, professor of African Studies at the Paul H. Nitze School of Advanced International Studies at the Johns Hopkins University and former director of the Wilson Center's Africa Project, as well as Joseph Dresen, Haleh Esfandiari, Robert Hathaway, Robert Litwak, Blair Ruble, Anita Sharma, Joseph Tulchin, and Michael Van Dusen—provided valuable guidance and suggestions for an initial conference on the economics of war, held at the Wilson Center on September 10, 2001. We are deeply grateful to Karen Ballentine, David Malone, and Jake Sherman, stewards of the International Peace Academy's path-breaking project on economic agendas in civil wars, for their expert advice and cosponsorship of the original conference. We are also grateful to Paul Collier, Kathleen Collins, Terry Karl, Charles King, Anatol Lieven, Eric Schwartz, and Ricardo Soberón, whose thoughtful comments enriched the discussion on which this inquiry is based.

Latin American Program interns Allison Werner and Kristen Jancuk, and Andreas Hipple of the Nitze School of Advanced International Studies, provided outstanding research assistance. Shawnetta Jackson and Theresa Simmons of the Nitze School and Trisha Fields of the Woodrow Wilson Center provided excellent overall support and management of budgets and persons. Joseph Brinley and Yamile Kahn of the Woodrow Wilson Center Press and Alfred Imhoff lent their professionalism and high standards and helped guide the manuscript through all phases of review and production.

Finally, we wish to thank the Woodrow Wilson Center and the Ford Foundation, without whose generous financial support this book would not have been possible.

Cynthia J. Arnson
I. William Zartman
Washington
March 2005

Rethinking the Economics of War

1

The Political Economy
of War: Situating the Debate

Cynthia J. Arnson

Contrary to prediction as well as hope, the end of the Cold War and of superpower competition in the developing world witnessed not less armed conflict but new and deadlier forms of civil war. To be sure, some conflicts deeply penetrated by a Cold War logic—Cambodia, El Salvador, Guatemala, and Mozambique are notable examples—came to an end through politically negotiated settlements. But in such places as Afghanistan, Angola, Colombia, Somalia, and Zaire, long-running conflicts pitting a variety of rebel

Cynthia J. Arnson is deputy director of the Latin American Program at the Woodrow Wilson International Center for Scholars. She is the editor of *Comparative Peace Processes in Latin America* (Stanford University Press and Woodrow Wilson Center Press, 1999) and the author of *Crossroads: Congress, the President, and Central America 1976–1993* (Pennsylvania State University Press, 1993). Before joining the Woodrow Wilson Center in 1994, she was associate director of Human Rights Watch/Americas, taught at American University, and worked in the U.S. Congress on Latin America, human rights, and foreign assistance issues. She thanks Allison Werner, a Latin American Program intern, for outstanding research assistance.

movements against weak or collapsing states intensified, even as former Cold War patrons receded or took on new roles. Elsewhere, places such as Rwanda and the Balkans erupted into ethnic conflicts of catastrophic proportions. The British political scientist Mary Kaldor has drawn a sharp distinction between the "old wars" of the Cold War era and the "new wars" of the 1990s. Such "new wars," she argues, could be understood only in the context of political, economic, military, and cultural globalization; they have blurred the distinction between war and organized crime, are at once local and dependent on transnational connections, and have fostered a war economy that is built on plunder, black market transactions, and external assistance and is sustained through continued violence.[1]

In some ways, surprise over the failure of internal armed conflict to decline with the end of U.S.–Soviet competition reflected an exaggerated emphasis on the role of superpower patrons in financing and sustaining civil wars. At the risk of oversimplification, much of the struggle over how to understand civil wars at the height of the Cold War era involved the degree of emphasis accorded to the strategic dimensions of conflict (focusing on the external sponsorship and aims of the Soviet Union and its proxies, including Cuba), and the emphasis accorded to the internal historical, political, and socioeconomic factors that generated the grievances that sparked political rebellion.

The fullest explanations for violent conflict most often contained some element of both perspectives, but what is notable about them is their shared attention to the political and ideological motivations of conflict, whether ascribed to national or international actors. To the extent that economic considerations entered the mix, it was in terms of the ways that poverty and inequality constituted or contributed to underlying grievances that fueled rebellions with quintessentially political aims. These political rebellions did need economic resources, and rebel movements engaged in a wide variety of predatory behavior—kidnapping for ransom, extortion, theft, plunder, the diversion of aid supplies (at times facilitated by corrupt government officials), and primitive forms of taxation—to obtain them, frequently exacting a heavy toll on the civilian population. The quest for resources nonetheless served principally as a *means* to an end that was defined in political terms: replacing an existing regime and/or substituting a new form of political order in all or part of the nation's territory.

---

[1]Mary Kaldor, *New and Old Wars: Organized Violence in a Global Era* (Stanford, Calif.: Stanford University Press, 1999, 2001), 1–12.

The study of resources as an issue defining the objectives or *ends* of violent internal conflict emerged in the middle to late 1990s, largely as scholars as well as practitioners took a harder look at the peculiarities of central Africa's devastating wars and attempted to identify the complex mix of incentives and disincentives needed to assist in the transition from war to peace.[2] In countries such as Angola, Sierra Leone, and Liberia, the income from natural resource commodities such as diamonds and oil appeared to play a unique role not only in financing ongoing and ever-higher levels of violence by rebel and state forces but also in redefining the very purposes of struggle. That is, while economic resources (as apart from intangible assets such as loyalty, commitment, and popular support) had always been vital to sustain these conflicts, what appeared new was the degree to which the resources themselves emerged not as a means to an end but as the very *object* of struggle. Control of territory and populations was transformed into an economic rather than purely military or strategic objective, and the pursuit of war into a highly rational enterprise aimed at the enrichment of particular elites or factions.

One of the first thinkers to capture this dynamic was the British political scientist David Keen, who in a seminal study titled *The Economic Functions of Violence in Civil Wars* noted that "war is not simply a breakdown in a particular system, but a way of creating an alternative system of profit, power and even protection."[3] In discussing cases from the former Yugoslavia to Rwanda, Keen warned that not all civil wars in the post–Cold War era were driven by economic agendas. Nonetheless, he argued, some civil wars that began with political motivations had "mutated into conflicts in which short-term economic benefits are paramount." He urged attention to "the emerging political economy" of conflict, arguing that because "there is more to civil wars than simply winning," conflict resolution strategies had to account for the ways that contending forces often had more to gain from a continuation of conflict than from peace.[4]

---

[2]See chapter 9 of this volume by David Malone and Jake Sherman.

[3]David Keen, *The Economic Functions of Violence in Civil Wars*, Adelphi Paper 320 (London: International Institute for Strategic Studies, 1998), 11.

[4]Keen, *Economic Functions of Violence in Civil Wars*, 12, 17, 71–72. There is a growing body of literature on the role of "spoilers" opposed to the settlement of internal armed conflicts. See, for e.g., Stephen John Stedman, "Peace Processes and the Challenge of Violence," and Marie-Joelle Zahar, "Reframing the Spoiler Debate in Peace Processes," both in *Contemporary Peacemaking*, ed. John Darby and Roger MacGinty (New York: Palgrave Macmillan, 2003), 103–13, 114–24.

Keen and Mats Berdal, an Oxford University researcher, similarly emphasized that the efforts by the international community to design and implement peace agreements would be more successful if greater attention
were paid to the political economy of civil wars and "the variety of 'functions' which violence may perform."[5] Referring to Sierra Leone and resurgent conflict in Cambodia after the signing of the 1990 peace accord,
Berdal and Keen argued that "defeating the enemy or bringing the fighting
to an end appears to have become less important for key parties involved
than securing the benefits from the continuation of conflict." Understanding
the economic motives driving the behavior and attitudes of elites and combatants, and deciphering "the *interaction* of political and economic agendas" (emphasis in the original) was critical if the international community
was to contribute to conflict resolution as well as postwar economic and
political stability in war-torn societies.[6]

Perhaps no thinker more influenced the emerging scholarship on the subject of economic agendas in civil wars than the economist Paul Collier of
the World Bank's Development Research Group. Using the tools of analytic
economics, Collier and Anke Hoeffler, an Oxford University colleague,
began to search for those factors most consistently correlated with the probable outbreak and duration of civil wars. In a 1998 study, Collier and Hoeffler
determined that four variables—per capita income, natural resource endowments (the share of primary exports in gross domestic product), population size, and ethnolinguistic fractionalization—were powerfully linked
to the risk of civil war. Contrary to the prevailing wisdom about ethnic conflict, they concluded that the two extremes—either highly fractionalized
societies or homogeneous ones—were unlikely to experience war, attribut-
ing the danger of conflict to polarization among groups rather than the extent of ethnic division per se.[7]

Collier and Hoeffler entered the terrain of what has come to be characterized as a debate over "greed versus grievance" in two subsequent articles,
which extrapolated issues of motivation and causation from the various statistical correlations emerging from their econometric model. In a 1999 paper
titled "Justice-Seeking and Loot-Seeking in Civil War," they described rebel-

---

[5]Mats Berdal and David Keen, "Violence and Economic Agendas in Civil Wars:
Some Policy Implications," *Millennium Journal of International Studies* 26, no. 3
(1997): 796.

[6]Berdal and Keen, "Violence and Economic Agendas," 803, 808, 800.

[7]Paul Collier and Anke Hoeffler, "On Economic Causes of Civil War," revised
January 1998, available at http://www.worldbank.org/research/conflict/papers.htm.

lions as *motivated* by "a blend of an altruistic desire to rectify the grievances of a group, and a selfish desire to loot the resources of others." The strongest statistical correlations, however, emerged for a motivation interpreted to be based on greed, in that the share of gross domestic product composed of primary commodity exports "significantly and strongly" affected the risk of war.[8]

In a 2000 study, Collier and Hoeffler went a step further, concluding that conflict was *caused* by "opportunities for primary commodity predation" and that "objective grievance is not a powerful primary cause of conflict."[9] Linking rebellions principally to the capture of resources (diamonds in Angola and Sierra Leone, timber in Cambodia, drugs in Colombia), they allowed for interdependence between greed and grievances, in that conflicts motivated by greed could themselves generate grievances. Indeed, according to Collier and Hoeffler, a narrative of grievance was useful and necessary to maintain military cohesion as well as garner international sympathy and induce diaspora communities to finance further conflict. But the authors found little statistical correlation between conflict and the factors that have long been considered the mainstays of grievances: political repression and economic inequality (measured in terms of both income and land ownership.) Indeed, of the categories they measured relating to objective grievances,[10] only domination by an ethnic majority was determined to add to the explanatory power of greed as a cause of rebellion.[11]

In subsequent works, Collier extended his thesis, maintaining that grievance-based explanations for civil war were "seriously wrong" and that, because certain groups benefit economically from conflict, they have an interest in initiating and sustaining it.[12] He continued to emphasize primary commodity exports as the principal source of lootable resources (other sources of financing included diaspora remittances and, during the Cold

---

[8]Paul Collier and Anke Hoeffler, "Justice-Seeking and Loot-Seeking in Civil War," revised February 17, 1999, available at http://www.worldbank.org/research/conflict/papers/justice.htm, 1, 15–16. In the article, the authors also argue that the severity of objective grievances did not increase the risk of conflict.

[9]Paul Collier and Anke Hoeffler, *Greed and Grievance in Civil War*, Policy Research Working Paper 2355 (Washington, D.C.: World Bank, 2000), 26–27.

[10]These included: hatreds engendered by ethnic and religious differences or domination by an ethnic majority, vengeance (a product of previous conflicts), income and land inequality, and democracy and the openness of political institutions.

[11]Collier and Hoeffler, *Greed and Grievance in Civil War*, 26.

[12]Paul Collier, "Doing Well Out of War: An Economic Perspective," in *Greed and Grievance: Economic Agendas in Civil Wars*, ed. Mats Berdal and David M. Malone (Boulder, Colo.: Lynne Rienner, 2000), 96.

War, foreign powers). He found that the risk of civil war was positively correlated with primary commodity exports and a high proportion of young men in a society, and negatively correlated with levels of education. Indirectly confirming the thesis of Ted Robert Gurr and others that relative deprivation rather than poverty per se contributed to conflict, Collier found that the only grievance factor that appeared to have an impact on the incidence of conflict was a previous period of economic decline.[13] In Collier's model, the objective of rebellion was not to achieve "victory over the government" but rather "to loot natural resource rents[14] on a continuing basis."[15]

Collier's concern with identifying the most salient risk factors behind violent conflict was aimed, among other things, at predicting which societies might be the most prone to civil war, and therefore at devising the best strategies for conflict prevention. These policies included fostering development that lessened a country's dependence on commodity income and commercial policies that limited or infringed upon combatants' ability to trade in lootable resources.[16] His thesis had obvious relevance for explain-

---

[13]Collier, "Doing Well Out of War," 93–98; Ted Robert Gurr, *Why Men Rebel* (Princeton, N.J.: Princeton University Press, 1970).

[14]The concept of rent pervades the economics of war literature. For classical economists of the eighteenth and nineteenth centuries such as Adam Smith, Thomas Malthus, and David Ricardo, rent referred to the return to owners of land, the dominant form of capital asset. In modern economics, rent refers to an income-generating payment to the owner of any kind of productive factor. See William J. Barber, *A History of Economic Thought* (Baltimore: Penguin Books, 1967); and Richard F. Muth, "Rent," in *International Encyclopedia of the Social Sciences*, ed. David L. Sills (New York: Macmillan and Free Press, 1968), 454–61.

[15]Paul Collier, "Rebellion as a Quasi-Criminal Activity," *Journal of Conflict Resolution* 44, no. 6 (December 2000): 840–41. Collier noted that rebellion and crime, especially organized crime, were analogous but not identical.

[16]The political scientist Michael Ross drew the distinction between "lootable resources" such as gemstones, timber, and coca, which were easily transportable by small groups of people, and "unlootable resources" such as oil and natural gas, which depended on heavier capital investments and were harder to transport. Ross correlated different kinds of commodities with different types of internal armed conflict. Unlootable resources, he said, tended to produce separatist conflicts, whereas lootable resources produced those of a nonseparatist nature.

The cases in this book do not support Ross's thesis. In both Colombia and Angola, oil rents supported nonseparatist conflicts, providing income to the Popular Movement for the Liberation of Angola government, and, through extortion of the oil sector, providing millions of dollars in revenue to Colombia's Ejército Nacional de Liberación (National Liberation Army). See Michael L. Ross, "Oil, Drugs, and Diamonds: The Varying Roles of Natural Resources in Civil Wars," in *The Political Economy of Armed Conflict: Beyond Greed and Grievance*, ed. Karen Ballentine and Jake Sherman (Boulder, Colo.: Lynne Rienner, 2003), 47–70.

ing Africa's degraded and intractable wars, as well as the intensification of conflict in such places as Colombia and Afghanistan due to armed actors' access to income from the illegal narcotics trade.

Not surprisingly, however, Collier's initial near-categorical rejection of grievances as a root cause of rebellion stirred up the intellectual pot, provoking at times a furious response from scholars insisting on the continued relevance of history and politics. Some of the critique of Collier—including the chapters in this book—has to do with the extent to which statistical correlations indicating a risk or probability of conflict permit a methodological leap into the realm of causation, as well as the difficulties of discerning rebel motivation and objectives from observable practices or patterns of rent-seeking behavior. Over time, Collier adjusted his thesis, moving away from the discussion of causation or motivation and focusing instead on those attributes that make conflict "feasible" or durable.[17] In other words, objective grievances were present in many societies, but not all of them were at war and only a few possessed the wherewithal to sustain rebellion.[18] But by setting an analytic pendulum swinging radically toward economic or greed-based explanations of civil war, he invited the academic and policy community to push it back toward equilibrium—a merging, of sorts, of economic, political, social, and historical explanations of civil conflict and thus, perhaps, of integrated approaches to its resolution.

This book represents an attempt at such a synthesis, drawing on the path-breaking work of Collier and others on the role of resource income, greed, and predation in fueling and sustaining conflict, and combining those insights with more long-standing, grievance-based explanations. The case studies presented here, far from an inventory of civil conflict worldwide, have been chosen precisely because in all of them, economic resources derived princi-

[17]Jake Sherman, rapporteur, *The Economics of War: The Intersection of Need, Creed, and Greed* (Washington, D.C., and New York: Woodrow Wilson International Center for Scholars and International Peace Academy, 2002), 28. See also Paul Collier, Anke Hoeffler, and Mans Soderbom, "On the Duration of Civil War," World Bank Policy Research Working Paper WPS2681, photocopy, September 30, 2001, in which the authors claim that "rebellions are initiated where they are viable . . . regardless of the prospects of attaining post-conflict goals" and "persist unless circumstances change."

[18]In a 2003 book, Collier and others offer a much more nuanced argument about the relationship among grievance, greed, and ethnicity issues, distinguishing between root causes (that can include such political factors as the nature of institutions) and forces that perpetuate conflict. The authors argue that "the key root cause of conflict is the failure of economic development." Paul Collier et al., *Breaking the Conflict Trap: Civil War and Development Policy* (New York: Oxford University Press for the World Bank, 2003), 53.

pally from primary commodities—lootable and nonlootable—have played an important and observable role in the nature, duration, and intensity of conflict, even if the role of economic resources in the outbreak of conflict remains less constant, and, in certain cases, absent altogether. The following chapters on Afghanistan, Angola, Colombia, the Democratic Republic of the Congo (DRC), Lebanon, Peru, and Sierra Leone thus provide an opportunity to apply and contextualize the notion of economic agendas, fitting them into a broader framework of complementary or alternative explanations.

Our effort owes a large debt to the New York–based International Peace Academy, whose publications constitute the single most extensive source of literature on the issue of economic agendas in civil war,[19] and which cosponsored the Woodrow Wilson Center's conference on which this volume is based.

In their seminal book *Greed and Grievance: Economic Agendas in Civil Wars*, for example, Mats Berdal and David Malone emphasized the ways that economic considerations have shaped the strategies and calculations of parties to conflict, "giving rise to a particular *war economy*" in which the traditional objective of war—to defeat the enemy militarily—is "replaced by economically driven interests in continued fighting and the institutionalization of violence at what is for some clearly a profitable level of intensity."[20] According to this formulation, civil wars previously defined as political rebellions (to which the state responds through counterinsurgency) need to be understood in terms of the interests of rebels, warlords, or armed gangs who benefit from violent economic activity and therefore have incentives to prolong conflict as well as sabotage peacemaking efforts.

Efforts to expand the theoretical understanding of the role of economic resources in war[21] have highlighted the extent to which civil wars are not static; initial rebel objectives, such as capturing state power or secession,

---

[19]See, e.g., Berdal and Malone, eds., *Greed and Grievance*; Ballentine and Sherman, eds., *Political Economy of Armed Conflict*; Charles Cater, rapporteur, "The Political Economy of War and Peace," IPA Seminar Report based on an International Peace Academy conference, New York, May 2002; Jake Sherman, rapporteur, "Policies and Practices for Regulating Resource Flows to Armed Conflict," conference report, International Peace Academy, New York, 2002; Alexandra Guáqueta, rapporteur, "Economic Agendas in Armed Conflict: Defining and Developing the Role of the UN," International Peace Academy, New York, March 2002; and Heiko Nitzschke, rapporteur, Conference on Transforming War Economies: Challenges for Peacemaking and Peacebuilding, International Peace Academy, New York, December 2003.

[20]Mats Berdal and David M. Malone, "Introduction," in *Greed and Grievance*, 2.

[21]See, e.g., the December 2000 issue of the *Journal of Conflict Resolution* 44, no. 6, devoted to the economic analysis of civil conflict.

can change over the duration of a conflict, as economic calculations interact with underlying grievances or overtake them as motives of violence.[22] The availability of resource wealth and the pursuit of greed, in turn, has a profound impact on rebel movements, fostering fragmentation and the breakdown of centralized leadership, command, and control and, in periods of rapid growth or expansion in the number of rebel troops, impeding the ideological formation of recruits.[23]

Economic motives and objectives are not the unique purview of rebel forces, but can also include those of personalistic rulers of corrupt "shadow states," who maximize the use of violence to "manage their own economic environments," siphoning off state resources for personal enrichment and the establishment of patronage networks, instead of providing public goods such as security and economic governance.[24] Describing the central African states of Angola, Sierra Leone, and Zaire/Congo in such terms, for example, the political scientist William Reno has portrayed how leaders have based personal power and derived individual wealth from the overt and clandestine manipulation of markets, at times with the connivance of foreign investors in natural resource enclaves such as oil.[25]

The role of globalization in facilitating the aims of warring parties has emerged as an important aspect of the political economy of civil war literature. As Mary Kaldor and others have indicated, the capacity of conflict actors (state, "shadow state," and nonstate) to realize income from legal and illegal primary commodities depends on transborder and international commercial relationships, including those of a criminal nature.[26] Deregulation

[22]David Keen, "Incentives and Disincentives for Violence," in *Greed and Grievance*, ed. Berdal and Malone, 19–41.

[23]Charles Cater, "The Political Economy of Conflict and UN Intervention: Rethinking the Critical Cases of Africa," in *Political Economy of Armed Conflict*, ed. Ballentine and Sherman, 35; and Karen Ballentine, "Beyond Greed and Grievance: Reconsidering the Economic Dynamics of Armed Conflict," in *Political Economy of Armed Conflict*, ed. Ballentine and Sherman, 270.

[24]William Reno, "Shadow States and the Political Economy of Civil Wars," in *Greed and Grievance*, ed. Berdal and Malone, 55. Reno defines "shadow state" as a concept explaining "the relationship between corruption and politics." Shadow states are "the product of personal rule, usually constructed behind the façade of de jure state sovereignty" (p. 45).

[25]Reno, "Shadow States," 43–68. Elsewhere, Reno and others have described such governments as "kleptocracies."

[26]The failure to address the regional linkages of war economies has heightened the difficulties of achieving peace settlements. See Michael Pugh, Neil Cooper, and Jonathan Goodhand, *War Economies in a Regional Context: Challenges of Transformation* (Boulder, Colo.: Lynne Rienner, 2004).

and liberalization in the global era have made it easier for armed actors to establish the market and other linkages necessary for economic survival.[27] In other words, the deregulated transnational relationships and networks that sustain legal commerce can also be exploited in ways that enhance the self-financing capacity of conflict entrepreneurs, constituting what some scholars have described as the "dark side of globalization."[28] A number of the policy responses to conflict in which resource income is present have been aimed precisely at curbing or limiting the free hand of the market in generating revenue for the warring parties. As David Malone and Jake Sherman's indicate in chapter 9 of this volume, these strategies include coercive, exemplary, financial, and rhetorical measures, even if regulatory regimes constructed to influence governmental as well as corporate behavior have neither been comprehensive nor uniformly applied.[29]

The most crucial insights to have emerged as scholars grappled with Collier's greed thesis include not only that conflict's economic and political drivers are interrelated and change through time but also that questions of political and economic *governance* mediate the risk of civil war where commodity wealth is present. As noted by Karen Ballentine, "The relative capacity of the state to perform core functions, including the provision of security, effective governance throughout its territory, and the equitable distribution of public goods, has a direct bearing on the incidence of armed conflict."[30] Weak or failing states, or those "captured" by a kleptocratic elite, lack these capacities as well as the legitimacy that accrues to the state from the fulfillment of its core functions. Failures of governance generate grievance and, just as important, contribute to the "opportunity structure that makes violent challenge militarily and economically feasible."[31]

[27]Mark Duffield, "Globalization, Transborder Trade, and War Economies," in *Greed and Grievance*, ed. Berdal and Malone, 73–74.

[28]Karen Ballentine and Jake Sherman, "Introduction," in *Political Economy of Armed Conflict*, ed. Ballentine and Sherman, 1–3; Cater, "Political Economy of War and Peace," 3.

[29]See chapter 9 of the present volume. See also Sherman, "Policies and Practices for Regulating Resource Flows to Armed Conflict"; and Nitzschke, Conference on Transforming War Economies.

[30]Karen Ballentine, "Introduction," in *Political Economy of Armed Conflict*, ed. Ballentine and Sherman, 9.

[31]Ballentine, "Introduction," 9. On questions of governance and legitimacy and their relationship to civil war, see Mohammed Ayoob, "State Making, State Breaking, and State Failure," in *Turbulent Peace: The Challenges of Managing International Conflict*, ed. Chester A. Crocker, Fen Osler Hampson, and Pamela Aall (Washington, D.C.: United States Institute of Peace Press, 2002), 37–51.

The following chapters in this book aim to expand the understanding of the interplay between armed conflict's economic, political, and socio-historical dimensions, adding new perspectives on the central African cases (Angola, Sierra Leone, the DRC) that originally sparked interest in the economics of war issues, and incorporating lesser-known cases (Afghanistan, Colombia, Lebanon, and Peru) into the economics of war literature. Specifically, the chapters in this book address a continuum of what I. William Zartman has called issues of "need, creed, and greed," in which grievances ranging from political repression to economic deprivation ("need"), generalized belief and identity feelings ("creed")—and particularly, selective deprivation and discrimination based on those beliefs and identities—and personal or factional ambitions of private gain ("greed") combine to produce conflicts with multiple, overlapping collective as well as private motives.[32]

Zartman's need-creed-greed formulation was aimed at addressing the principal obstacles to mediating ethnic or creed-based conflicts. But in focusing on conflict resolution, he identified a key distinction: Though need- and creed-based conflicts seek redress of grievances and hence solutions to problems, greed-based conflicts (including those steeped in the discourse of need or creed) seek just the opposite—the continuation of war as an avenue to self-enrichment. The obvious implication is to prevent or resolve need- and creed-based conflicts before issues of greed fundamentally and perhaps irrevocably alter the cost-benefit analysis of warring parties. In Zartman's words, "It is better to deter entrepreneurs at the beginning of the adventure than be faced with the need to remove them at the end."[33]

It is notable than none of the conflicts explored in this book started as a greed-based rebellion. Contrary to Collier's earlier predictions, neither greed nor the existence of lootable, resource-based wealth was an important cause or trigger of conflict. Rather, greed was a product or later stage of wars started for other reasons. This attention to the sequencing of need,

---

[32]See chapter 10 of this volume by I. William Zartman. And see I. William Zartman, "Managing Ethnic Conflict," First Perlmutter Lecture, *Foreign Policy Research Institute Wire* 6, no. 5 (1998): 1–2; Zartman, "Mediating Conflicts of Need, Greed, and Creed," *Orbis* 44, no. 2 (Spring 2000): 255–66; and I. William Zartman, "Sources and Settlements of Ethnic Conflicts," in *Facing Ethnic Conflicts: Toward a New Realism*, ed. Andreas Wimmer, Richard Goldstone, Donald Horowitz, Ulrike Joras, and Conrad Schetter (Lanham, Md.: Rowman & Littlefield, 2004).

[33]Zartman, "Mediating Conflicts," 263.

creed, and greed supports the findings of other students of the economics of war; that is, that resources are central in the duration of conflict as well as in its intensity, but grievances and identities—political factors—are still central to understanding the roots and objectives of war. That said, in virtually all the cases explored in this book, resource income became a key—but not insurmountable—aspect of a conflict's intractability, or definitively shaped a postwar economic order based on the corrupt and personalistic networks and relationships forged during the conflict era. Put another way, resources may add to the opportunity for war, but war also creates economic opportunities. Such opportunities create incentives for war's continuation or, in the event of a settlement, shape, distort, and pervert the establishment of the postwar economic order.

Need, Creed, and Greed Revisited: Contextualizing the Resource Debate

In chapter 2, on Lebanon, Elizabeth Picard brings the resource literature into the creed discussion, arguing that the characterization of the 1975–90 civil war as an identity conflict between hostile religious communities (Muslim and Christian) is "not inconsistent with other explanations of the Lebanese civil war that refer to need and greed factors and, more broadly, to economic variables." Though the role of external actors in Lebanon was paramount, and a settlement was possible when the dominant regional and international powers (the United States and Syria) agreed on it, Picard reexamines the Lebanese case in light of "material realities too easily hidden under ideological discourse and cultural superstructures."[34] The shift in analytic emphasis in understanding the Lebanese conflict's economic rationales, she argues, is due not only to Paul Collier's work but also to the difficulties encountered by multilateral institutions in promoting the country's postwar economic recovery.[35] Picard illustrates how the kind of economy that evolved in the postwar period reflected processes at work during

[34]See chapter 2 of the present volume by Elizabeth Picard.

[35]Picard also indicates two ways in which specifics of the Lebanese case run counter to Paul Collier's findings. First, Lebanon's extreme ethnic and religious fragmentation was destabilizing, not stabilizing. Second, Collier found that a period of rapid economic decline increases the risk of conflict. In Lebanon, however, the 1960s and 1970s were periods of rapid economic growth. The key issue during this period was that the benefits of growth did not accrue to all sectors, and least of all to the middle class.

the conflict, in that "economically motivated violence gave way to a new unprecedented peacetime corruption."

Picard discusses Lebanon's three main resources—drugs, land, and labor power—as they relate to the history, social logic, and political processes that contributed to civil war. The drug economy (hashish and poppy production), for example, existed before the war, but as a result of it underwent quantitative and qualitative changes infused with questions of political and social power, financial accumulation, and the exercise of violence. Levels of drug trafficking increased as new actors entered the trade, enabling militia groups to live off the looting of territories under their control. In addition, wartime emigration produced a huge diaspora community that sent millions of dollars to those who remained in the country, providing yet another source of militia income and extending militia control over diaspora assets remaining in Lebanon.

Most significant for the reinterpretation of Lebanon's civil war were the ways that activities such as the drug trade, the importation and distribution of crude oil, and speculative real estate transactions fostered a set of wartime economic relations based on transcommunal and interregional cooperation *between* militias. In Picard's analysis, "greed in the defense (or promotion) of creed could not have been satisfied if it had not been for the cooperation of individuals willing to trust one another beyond apparently intractable identity and ideological differences." Understanding the underlying economic logic of such relationships converts what previously appeared as anomalous and contradictory behavior by antagonists into exceedingly rational conduct. Economically driven war agendas did not prevent the end of Lebanon's civil war when regional and international dynamics changed; rather, distortions in the organization of the postwar Lebanese economy owed much to the transactions and relationships established during the conflict.

Peru's war against the Sendero Luminoso (Shining Path) insurgency resembles the Lebanese case to the extent that an armed conflict was substantially brought to an end despite significant commodity income available to the guerrilla movement. In chapter 3, Cynthia McClintock shows how, by the late 1980s, Sendero was earning $20 to $40 million per year from the coca trade in Peru's Upper Huallaga River Valley, at the time the largest coca-growing region in the world. Sendero used the money to pay salaries to its fighters and bolster its organizational and military capacity; at its height in the late 1980s and early 1990s, the movement controlled approximately 25 percent of the country's municipalities and boasted some

25,000 militants. Nonetheless, between 1992 and 1995, Sendero was decimated following the capture of its charismatic and doctrinaire leader, a
former philosophy professor named Abimael Guzmán. Fragments of armed
Senderista bands continued to operate in the Upper Huallaga in the early
years of the new millennium, but their capacity to garner widespread support
appeared minimal.

McClintock traces the confluence of grievances, ideology, and commodity income from coca in explaining Sendero's origins and the reasons
for its spectacular growth in the 1980s. The movement first took root in
the early 1970s in Peru's southern highlands, the poorest region of the
country. Peasants in these areas had largely failed to benefit from a 1968
agrarian reform declared by the central government; at the same time, other
government policies affecting prices, credit, and public investment led to
drastic declines in already-meager farm income. Remarkably for Peru, the
sharp drop in living standards—between 1971 and 1990, per capita income
dropped 2 percent a year—was coupled with the vast expansion of educational opportunities due to other government reforms. Children from peasant families began to graduate not only from high school but also from the
university, only to be frustrated by their subsequent inability to find employment or meaningful professional opportunities.

Sendero's Maoist ideology and Marxist principles made sense of this
poverty and inequality, basing an appeal on class, not ethnicity. This latter
aspect is also remarkable, in that, as McClintock indicates, the vast majority of people living in Peru's southern highlands were dark skinned and of
indigenous descent. Though fierce discrimination was undoubtedly linked
to the poverty and marginalization of indigenous areas, grievances were not
articulated in ethnic terms.

Sendero's support spread to urban centers as Peru experienced an un-
paralleled economic decline in the 1980s that was extreme even by Latin
American standards. Over the course of the decade, for example, the real
minimum wage lost more than 75 percent of its value. Even middle-class
professionals found it difficult to feed their families, and schoolteachers
came to constitute a bulwark of Senderista support. Meanwhile, opportunism,
not ideology, led to burgeoning Sendero support among coca-growing peasants in the Upper Huallaga Valley, who, like their counterparts subsequently
in Colombia, turned to the guerrillas to protect their livelihoods against
government-sponsored eradication programs.

In explaining how it was possible to achieve the "strategic defeat" of
Sendero despite the role of coca income in Sendero's numerical expansion

and operational capabilities, McClintock emphasizes that economic resources in the Peruvian case served as a means to political ends; that is, the conflict never entered the "greed" phase in which the pursuit of drug-based wealth itself became an objective of armed struggle. She cites several factors contributing to Sendero's decimation following the September 1992 capture of Guzmán, including the meticulous work of a special police intelligence unit, which carried out painstaking investigations to break up urban guerrilla cells; the savagery and fanaticism of Sendero itself, which eventually turned the peasant population against the guerrillas and led to the success of peasant-based armed rural patrols known as *rondas*; changes in Peru's antiterrorist legislation, which combined plea-bargaining leniency with draconian and repressive special courts that denied due process to terrorism suspects; heavy government investment in social programs benefiting poor people, as Peru's government in the 1990s gained resources from the privatization and sale of state-owned corporations; and plunging income from the coca trade, as traffickers relocated cultivation principally to Colombia. Although armed Sendero bands have regrouped, primarily in coca-growing regions, few predict that the movement will again pose a significant threat to the Peruvian state.

In chapter 4, Jimmy Kandeh distinguishes between greed as a cause of rebellion and greed as a motive for it, arguing that in the case of Sierra Leone, both are relevant to the "origins and character" of the Revolutionary United Front rebellion. Greed as cause relates to the social impact of predatory rule and accumulation by the political class and its role in provoking state collapse, while greed as motive refers to the activities of those who took up arms in order to loot the country's diamond wealth. According to Kandeh, Sierra Leone's rebellion was set in motion by a combination of elite and popular grievances rooted in political exclusion and disenfranchisement, lack of access to state resources and offices, declining living standards, and shrinking opportunities for mobility. Sierra Leone's conflict—which was characterized initially by youthful idealism as university students took up arms against a corrupt, one-party government—was "hijacked by criminal and opportunistic elements" domestically and abroad (and eventually including members of international peacekeeping missions) that sought to make huge profits from the illegal diamond trade.

Kandeh argues that the significance of diamonds in Sierra Leone lay not in the mere fact of their presence but rather in the manner of their exploitation, management, and social distribution. Otherwise put, greed became a factor in grievances. Predatory accumulation by state elites created central problems of governance, including the nondelivery of basic services and other public goods, while also generating grievances among sectors of the elite excluded from the benefits of diamond wealth. If grievances were divisible between elite and popular sectors, they also encompassed many of the issues Collier identifies as proxies for greed-based rebellions. That is, in Kandeh's view, the high proportion of young men in Sierra Leone's population was less relevant in the outbreak of conflict than their lack of opportunity. Moreover, contrary to Collier's assertion that low levels of education are correlated with a high risk of conflict, in the case of Sierra Leone, the combination of high levels of education with little or no opportunities for employment contributed to rebellion. In this respect, the Sierra Leonean and Peruvian cases are similar.

The regional aspects of Sierra Leone's war help explain its degeneration from a "legitimate political struggle" into a form of "criminal adventurism by warlords, lumpens, and fortune seekers." According to Kandeh, the Liberian leader Charles Taylor used Sierra Leone's diamonds to finance his own war machine, absorbing some elements of the Revolutionary United Front as an auxiliary military force and dumping excess Liberian combatants into Sierra Leone's diamond fields to raise money and profit from the diamond trade. The Liberian connection made it possible for that country to export ten times the diamonds it was capable of producing, enriching members of Taylor's family and his corrupt business and political associates. Ultimately, however, Kandeh argues that a lasting settlement of the conflict in Sierra Leone must extend beyond controlling diamond wealth and address the injustices and deplorable social conditions that constitute the core of grievances in the country.

Like Kandeh, in chapter 5, Philippe Le Billon sees the relationship between resources and war in Angola as mediated by key questions of governance, including the failure or degeneration of political systems, the withdrawal of the formal state and public services, counterproductive state violence, and sectarianism. The interposition of external powers following Angola's 1975 war of independence transformed an anticolonial struggle into a protracted stalemate, in which the United States, the Soviet Union, Cuba, China, South Africa, and Zaire backed, variously, the National Liberation Front for Angola, the Popular Movement for the Liberation of Angola (MPLA), and the National Union for the Total Independence of Angola (UNITA) in pursuit of strategic interests defined by the Cold War. As foreign backing began to dwindle in the early 1990s, resources (oil for the MPLA government and diamonds for UNITA) significantly influenced the course of the conflict, prolonging the war by "providing the means and rewards of fighting," and providing strong disincentives for compromise in reaching a sustainable peace agreement. Thus, Le Billon views resources as neither the cause nor the sole motivation for war, but as something that gave each contender the means "to sustain a hegemonic and militaristic attitude" that was central to the continuation of conflict.

As in Sierra Leone, the initial availability of resource rents—in Angola's case from the foreign-dominated oil sector—distorted the country's political life and institutions, allowing elites to impose themselves by force because, as Le Billon argues, "they could afford" to do so, while also fostering high levels of rent seeking and corruption and contributing to an overreliance on fiscal revenues and disincentives for economic diversification. Le Billon illustrates how the process of transforming resource endowments into tradable commodities in Angola was deeply political, creating entitlements and inequalities defined along lines of ethnicity, class, kinship, and religion, thereby fostering issues of identity-based grievances. Issues of identity were especially important in explaining the support for the UNITA leader Jonas Savimbi, whose earnings from diamonds were estimated at $3 to $4 billion between 1992 and 2000, and who successfully articulated (and manipulated) Ovimbundu aspirations. Ultimately, Savimbi's death in 2002 paved the way for a peace settlement, in part because UNITA had become a spent military force despite its fabulous diamond wealth. The Angolan case thus illustrates that the availability of resource income need not be a formula for war without end, in that internal armed conflicts can be brought to resolution for reasons that transcend the war-promoting qualities of commodity revenues.

War in the Democratic Republic of the Congo, formerly Zaire, illustrates the regional dimensions of conflict's economic agendas. According to Erik Kennes in chapter 6, the principal actors triggering the armed conflicts of 1996–97 and 1998–2003 were foreign, and the "struggle for regional hegemony" leading to and following the 1997 implosion of the Mobutu Sese Seko regime was as much an economic as a strategic affair. Factions of the Congolese rebel movement received, at various times, the support of Rwanda, Uganda, Angola, Zimbabwe, and Namibia, with the former two in particular competing for direct or indirect control of portions of the Congo's territory in order to exploit diamond and other resource wealth.

Kennes links the formal and informal political and economic relationships that flourished under the Mobutu regime to questions of state weakness and, ultimately, state collapse. Structures of control by a "predatory politico-commercial elite," he argues, were founded on informal, clientelistic networks that gradually emptied the state of its substance, spawning internal factional conflict and the privatization of state functions. Kennes compares the nation's economy to a tree, arguing that the "ruthless plundering" of state resources by members of the politico-economic elite, including members of the armed forces, robbed the economy not only of its leaves but also of its trunk and roots; the state eventually came to resemble a "consumed termite hill" that crumbled under military pressure from the forces of the rebel leader Laurent Kabila. The new elites that took control under Kabila, however, lacked even the rudimentary clientelistic linkages to civil society that had characterized the previous regime, siphoning off what money was left from the state and contributing to grievances that ultimately undermined Kabila's rule.

Kennes demonstrates the continuity between the war economy that emerged during the 1998–2003 conflict and the peacetime networks and relationships in the DRC's mining and minerals sector. State revenues from mining that had serviced Mobutu's personal and clientelistic networks evaporated as major mining companies withdrew in the chaotic environment under Kabila. In their place, a local, artisanal economy emerged, forged out of previously existing informal networks and dependent as ever on international linkages that were increasingly dominated by regional as well as criminal interests. Both Rwanda and Uganda entered the Congolese war for motives of greed as well as regional politics, redirecting gold and diamond trading for the benefit of foreign armies and profiting as well from the trade in coltan (columbite tantalite),[36] the exploitation of which started during the war. The formal withdrawal of the Congo's neighbors and the signing of a peace agreement among belligerents has modified, but not ended, the competition for Congolese resources; the very lack of internal cohesion among the various components of the DRC's national unity government, meanwhile, invites continued struggles for sectoral benefit, rather than national or more amply distributed social gain.

In chapter 7, on Colombia, Marc Chernick explores the transformation and expansion of a long-running internal armed conflict by income from the burgeoning trade in illegal narcotics, weighing the relative contributions of greed and grievances as explanatory factors in the conflict's origins and prolongation. He traces a half-century of conflict and its relationship to com-

---

[36]Coltan is an ore rich in tantalum, used in the manufacture of mobile telephones; jet engines; fiber optics; and capacitors, a component of computer chips.

modity booms and busts (first coffee, then coca and oil), arguing that political actors, regions affected by violence, and political grievances of opposition groups have shown great continuity even as the resource base for war
has changed over the decades. He argues that the drug trade has played a
major role in the final phase of the conflict dating from the mid-1980s,
transforming the guerrillas, especially the Fuerzas Armadas Revolucionarias de Colombia (Revolutionary Armed Forces of Colombia), from a small
peasant insurgency into a significant fighting force, of which a sizable percentage are dedicated to criminal pursuits rather than military strategy or
politics. State weakness or absence from portions of Colombia's territory
facilitated narco-trafficking as well as guerrilla expansion. At the same
time, the drug export boom created a new class of rural landowning elites
closely tied to right-wing paramilitary groups, which became a significant
actor in the internal armed conflict. Additional revenues in the mid-1980s
came from a petroleum boom, which provided resources to the state as well
as a lucrative source of extortion for the Ejército de Liberación Nacional
guerrillas.

Chernick questions Collier's emphasis on the availability of lootable
resources in understanding violent internal conflict in Colombia and elsewhere, pointing to a large body of social science literature dealing with
the historical, sociological, political, and economic dimensions of conflict.
The Colombian experience, he argues, suggests that grievances, ideology,
leadership, and international factors (particularly the role of the United
States), not just resource mobilization or greed, explain the origins and
duration of the war. Though acknowledging that the line between armed
insurgency and organized crime has blurred in the post–Cold War, post–
September 11, 2001, world, Chernick emphasizes the Colombian conflict's
social and political roots, dimensions that, he argues, must be addressed in
any enduring solution.

War in Afghanistan, and questions of state weakness and failure, bear
resemblance to Colombia only in that trafficking in illicit drugs, not legal
commodities such as diamonds or timber, stand at the heart of a war economy that has had a profound impact on state capacity. Beyond that, the sim-
ilarities are few. The October 7, 2001, attack on Afghanistan by an international Coalition led by the United States ultimately removed the Taliban
from power, weakening but perhaps not dismantling its ties to international
terrorist organizations such as al Qaeda. As described by Paula Newberg
in chapter 8, however, Afghanistan's transitional government has failed to
establish its authority adequately beyond the confines of Kabul, and the

country remains enveloped in conflicts fueled by a burgeoning opium trade that threatens the long-term viability of the state. Given Afghanistan's place in a complex web of international financial relationships that support global terrorism, Newberg sees the dismantling of Afghanistan's war economy as central to the effort to weaken and defeat international terrorism.

Newberg argues that the Afghan war can only be understood in the context of three decades of internal and regional conflict, which is rooted in deep-seated problems of governance and economic development and symbolized by the Kabul administration's ongoing struggles with tribal leaders and warlords in the periphery. In the twenty years before the Taliban took power, these same tribal leaders enjoyed international backing to wage war against their own leaders as well as an occupying Soviet army, capitalizing on the country's porous borders to move fighters, war materiel, and money in support of rebellion. As in Sierra Leone and the Congo, Newberg argues that the same factors that led to war in Afghanistan (including struggles over who would run the state, how, and on behalf of whom) promoted and deepened state failure, while the very existence of a failed state became an essential characteristic of, and fostered more, war. Indeed, part of Afghanistan's ongoing conflict arises from the violent rejection of the very notion of a central state by those for whom a power vacuum is convenient and profitable, including local and regional interests engaged in the poppy and opium trade.

The international and regional dimensions of Afghanistan's long-running conflict have been paramount. The country's internal conflicts, built on fragmentation along tribal, ethnic, ideological, and regional lines, became what Newberg calls "proxies for multinational interests." Neighboring states such as Pakistan and Iran, foreign donors including the United States, and non-state actors including transnational Islamist movements have sustained and nurtured local disputes, providing cross-border and global transfers of money, equipment, and personnel. The multinational effort to undercut the Soviet occupation of 1979–89—one of several phases of Afghanistan's successive wars—not only helped dissolve the Soviet Union but, according to Newberg, also set the stage for regional insecurity, weakening Afghanistan's neighbors economically and politically, contributing to tensions throughout central Asia, and spawning actors implicated in a wide range of global threats.

Newberg argues that the narcotics trade that thrived within and contributed to Afghanistan's failed state poses a formidable challenge to the consolidation of the post-2001 invasion's Coalition government, compromising the state's capacity to regulate economic activity and establish the rule of law. The ultimate conundrum in establishing central authority is posed by the following: Afghanistan's powerful regional warlords provided critical support for the Coalition effort to eradicate al Qaeda and at once control the trade that produces as much as 75 percent of the world's opium supplies.

Ultimately, and in the face of such formidable challenges, one is left to ponder how and whether it is possible to end or in some measure attenuate internal armed conflicts fueled and sustained by the trafficking in legal and illicit commodities. In chapter 9, David Malone and Jake Sherman address the array of policy instruments available to individual governments, multi-national coalitions, international organizations, and private-sector entities, which, if imperfect, constitute the evolving response of the international community to questions of economic agendas in civil wars and related humanitarian, anticrime, antiterrorist, and postconflict peacebuilding issues. The vested interests in perpetuating conflict, their exploitation and furtherance of weak and fragmented states, and the criminalization of wartime economic relations make efforts to end the fighting and address underlying causes of conflict both more urgent as well as more complicated.

According to Malone and Sherman, economic sanctions and arms embargoes remain the most frequently employed regulatory instrument, but other frameworks—the suppression of money laundering, combating narco-trafficking, and minimizing the negative impact of private-sector activities—have evolved in response to war as well as the efforts to combat corruption and international organized crime. Certification and warranty systems for commodities such as diamonds and timber seek to identify the source of natural resources and prevent revenues from them from profiting actors in armed conflict, while voluntary, statutory, and (at times) legally binding codes of corporate responsibility seek to regulate the international private sector in extractive, financial, and insurance industries.

Malone and Sherman point to the many trade-offs facing policymakers in resource-consuming countries, from the difficulties of curbing the overseas activities of private firms that generate jobs at home to the norms of secrecy that govern banking and other monetary transactions in the world's leading financial centers. They discuss ineffective and uneven enforcement of sanctions, and the lack of progress in devising legal instruments to punish international white-collar crime (as opposed to war criminals) as further obstacles to limiting or eliminating war profiteering. Ultimately, they argue for more foresighted policies to address underlying causes of conflict, including those that support legitimate and inclusive governance as well as poverty reduction. In addition, Malone and Sherman argue for the establishment of international legal regimes and institutions to address large-scale international economic crimes, similar to the evolving international instruments to prosecute war crimes, crimes against humanity, and genocide.

Refocusing the Debate

For centuries, a cornerstone of liberal ideology has held that free trade, open markets, and the interdependence fostered by mutually beneficial commerce was conducive to peace. As paraphrased by the international relations scholar Richard K. Betts, "If peace is the path to profit, greed should discourage war rather than promote it."[37] The chapters that follow turn such ideology on its head, demonstrating how economic motivations and greed have sustained and intensified internal armed conflict, *and* that a liberal international trading order has facilitated war profiteering by those trafficking in legal as well as illegal commodities. At the same time, these chapters caution against an almost neo-Marxian tendency to reduce war and conflict to its economic dimensions and motivations, showing that some conflicts fueled by resources can end despite opportunities for continued commodity wealth, even if the prior existence of war economies has a profoundly distortionary effect on the postwar order. The chapters in this book illustrate the ongoing relevance of economics, politics, and history to the understanding of internal armed conflict, including those suffused with a regional or international logic. In fact, only by appreciating the complex interplay of such dimensions can one hope to identify the factors that sustain war as well as the issues that might contribute to its resolution.

[37]Richard K. Betts, ed., *Conflict after the Cold War: Arguments on Causes of War and Peace* (New York: Macmillan, 1994), 174.

2

Trafficking, Rents, and Diaspora in the Lebanese War

Elizabeth Picard

Economics against Culture:
A Lebanese Controversy

The civil war in Lebanon took place between 1975 and 1990, nearly a quarter-century before the wave of low-intensity conflicts that plagued numerous countries in Africa, Southern Europe, and the Middle East. Even a decade and a half after the adoption of the Taif agreement that put an official

Elizabeth Picard is research director at the Institut de Recherches et d'Études sur le Monde Arabe et Musulman, Centre National de la Recherche Scientifique, in Aix-en-Provence, France. She lived and worked in the Middle East for several years and directed the French research center in Beirut and Amman from 1997 to 2000. She has written extensively about security and identity politics in the Middle East and is the author, among other works, of *Lebanon: A Shattered Country* (Holmes and Meier, 2002) and *La nouvelle dynamique au Moyen-Orient* (L'Harmattan, 1993). She thanks Kathleen Collins, assistant professor at the University of Notre Dame, for her stimulating comments on an earlier version of this chapter.

end to the fighting,[1] specialists on Lebanon remain divided between two schools of analysis. Some see the Lebanese civil war as a portent of the "war of cultures" that underlies international relations in the age of globalization.[2] Others insist on its economic dimensions and on the strategies of rational actors taking advantage of the breakdown of the rule of law.[3]

The first group relies on convincing arguments. Because of Lebanon's unique character in the Middle East—its population more or less evenly distributed between Muslims and Christians on the eve of the war, its cultural attachment to Western and at the same time to Arab norms and values, and its adoption of consensus democracy ensuring the domination of a multisectarian oligarchy[4]—tensions between identities, between beliefs, and between ideologies played a major role in igniting the conflict as well as in spreading it by means of antagonistic martial propaganda. From the start, the leaders of the warring parties described their enemy in essentialist terms (it was a war between Islam and the West) and interpreted the war using cultural concepts (ethnic antagonism, or a conflict between "traditional authoritarian" and "modern democratic" values). Their explanations received a large popular echo because the shared culture of Lebanese society in the mid-twentieth century was permeated by the memory of past intercommunal hostility, making groups vulnerable to ideological provocation and strategic mobilization. An ahistorical interpretation gained ground, fed by the repressed collective memory of intercommunal massacres in the 1860s.[5] Among each of the seventeen sectarian groups that made up the Lebanese nation, a view began to prevail that religious creed and the survival of minorities were threatened by hostile ethnic groups. In a sweeping dichotomization, the war was deemed a Muslim *jihâd*, or a Christian

---

[1]Having been summoned to a conclave in Taif, Saudi Arabia, in October–November 1989, fifty-eight of the ninety-nine members of Parliament adopted, under heavy regional (mainly Syrian) and international (mainly American) pressure, the Document of National Reconciliation, which contained various amendments to the constitutional system. See Joseph Maila, *The Document of National Reconciliation: A Commentary*, Prospects for Lebanon 4 (Oxford: Centre for Lebanese Studies, 1992).

[2]For an example of this school, see Walid Phares, *Lebanese Christian Nationalism: The Rise and Fall of an Ethnic Resistance* (Boulder, Colo.: Lynne Rienner, 1995).

[3]See, e.g., the famous Lebanese economist Kamal Hamdan, *Le conflit libanais* (Geneva: United Nations Research Institute for Social Development, 1997).

[4]Elizabeth Picard, *Lebanon: A Shattered Country* (New York: Holmes and Meier, 2002).

[5]Leila Tarazi Fawaz, *An Occasion for War: Civil Conflict in Lebanon and Damascus in 1860* (London: I. B. Tauris, 1994).

crusade, for the promotion of the "true" faith on the Lebanese land, by expelling (in the first case) or subjugating (in the second case) the believers of the other faith who, in turn, thought they were rightly defending themselves against such a threat.

Needless to say, several characteristics of the war belied this rigid identity framework of analysis; namely, the frequent occurrence of intracommunal divisions and intercommunal alliances and cooperation. For example, Shiite Muslims, often depicted as *the* unanimously frustrated Lebanese religious community, deemed to form the bulk of insurgency,[6] were divided into many regional subgroups and as many ideological factions. Some chose to stay in Christian-dominated areas; several notables of the community remained opposed to the insurgency and preferred to abide by the old intersectarian elite pact; moreover, among the Shia, the mainstream opposition movement split between the rival Islamist movements of Amal and Hizbollah. While Amal fought the Palestinian guerrillas based in the country and tried to put up with the Israeli occupation of South Lebanon after 1982, Hizbollah supported the Palestine Liberation Organization (PLO) and led the resistance, under Syrian and Iranian patronage, against the Israeli Defense Force. In the end, both factions waged a direct intracommunal war in Beirut's southern suburbs that only ended with a Syrian diktat in December 1990.

Similarly, the internal history of the Christian camp during the war was punctuated by rivalries and fratricidal conflicts that culminated in a two-year war between the Christian fraction of the national army commanded by General Michel Aoun and the main Christian militia group (the Lebanese Forces) in 1989–90, until their common subjugation by Syria. To make the picture more complex, each Christian faction established alliances within the opposite camp. Thus, the Lebanese Forces, whose project was to establish a Christian-dominated state and expel the Palestinians from Lebanese soil, helped PLO fighters to land in the area they controlled in order to go on fighting Amal Shiite militia forces in the 1980s. At the same period, they organized a shared control of Beirut's southeastern suburbs with Hizbollah, ideologically their worst enemy. If it is assumed that the rationale for conflict is to win and that belief and collective identity were the central stakes of the war, much of the behavior on all sides seems unconvincing, not to say bizarre.

---

[6]Augustus R. Norton, *Amal and the Shi'a: Struggle for the Soul of Lebanon* (Austin: University of Texas Press, 1987).

In spite of all the qualifications and difficulties in understanding the Lebanese war as a "war of cultures," the fact remains that creed was a powerful driving force during the fifteen years of fighting. This was all the more important given the fact that the leaders of the warring parties declared creed to be central in their strategic choices and that the populace in each camp saw it at the heart of their commitment.

However, as convincing as "creed" may be in analyzing the Lebanese war, the notion is not inconsistent with other explanations of the Lebanese civil war that refer to need and greed factors and, more broadly, to economic variables. Like any other human being, the Lebanese is an homo economicus as much as a political animal. It is necessary to take into account the material realities too easily hidden under ideological discourse and cultural superstructures in order to reconcile the apparent contradictions of the war. In the two decades before the outburst of violence, rapid growth benefited a limited monopolistic upper class, which contrasted with the proletarianization of masses of rural migrants. At the same time, a large range of middle-class employees and independent workers suffered from the deterioration of their working and living conditions.[7] As I have argued elsewhere, the "need" factor in the outburst of the civil war could be analyzed in terms of relative deprivation; economic inequalities became blatant within each sectarian group, in which rich individuals contrasted with a mass of laborers and a large urban subproletariat.[8] Because of the territorialization of religious groups, the contrast between affluence in Beirut and central Lebanon and underdevelopment on the peripheries overlapped with the sectarian divide, allowing an interpretation of social inequalities in terms of religious differences and giving ground to sectarian strife.

Certainly, war did not put an end to economic inequalities and popular frustration—far from it. From the start, the war occasioned systematic economic destruction that affected the population of all regions and com-

---

[7]Salim Nasr, "The Crisis of Lebanese Capitalism," *MERIP* 73 (December 1978). Here, the Lebanese situation diverges from World Bank economist Paul Collier's finding that "a prior period of rapid economic *decline* increases the risk of conflict" (emphasis added). See Paul Collier, "Doing Well Out of War: An Economic Perspective," in *Greed and Grievance: Economic Agendas in Civil Wars*, ed. Mats Berdal and David Malone (Boulder, Colo.: Lynne Rienner, 2000), 97.

[8]See Ted Gurr, *Why Men Rebel* (Princeton, N.J.: Princeton University Press, 1970); and Elizabeth Picard, "The Lebanese Shî'a and Political Violence," in *The Legitimization of Violence*, ed. David Apter (London: Macmillan, 1997).

munities,[9] while the drastic impoverishment of middle classes went hand-in-hand with the accumulation of amazing wealth. Although the model of conflict laid out by Paul Collier—a model privileging motivations of greed—should not be applied to the Lebanese civil war without strong qualification,[10] greed incited warlords and political entrepreneurs to take advantage of the breakdown of state authority, as social insecurity offered growing opportunities for predation by armed groups.[11] Over a period of fifteen years, they imposed a new social and economic order that came to be known as "Lebanization" and was imitated in several civil wars.[12]

Far from being a hiatus of exceptional circumstances, the war was preparation for future economic developments in the country, while economically motivated violence gave way to new and unprecedented peacetime corruption.[13] In the period of reconstruction that followed, not only were agriculture and industry unable to recover the position they had occupied in the prewar Lebanese economy, but the structure of the national economy also showed growing distortions; by 1998, interest represented 23 percent of gross national product (GNP). Two sectors—land and money—monopolized national wealth and imposed their logic on every economic activity, while emigration, mostly of young degree holders, reached the dramatic cumulative figure of 950,000 people between 1994 and 2000 in a country of 3.5 to 4 million.[14]

More than two decades after the end of the Lebanese civil war, scholars have rightly focused attention on the economic rationales underlying identity

---

[9]The destruction of the industrial zones in the eastern and southern Beirut suburbs deprived workers from all religious communities of their salaries and revenues.

[10]The model raises reservations about his periodicization of wars, the social categories it relies on, and its absence of diachronic comparison. See Paul Collier, *Economic Causes of Civil Conflict and Their Implications for Policy* (Washington, D.C.: World Bank, 2000).

[11]Elizabeth Picard, "The Political Economy of Civil War in Lebanon," in *War, Institutions and Social Change in the Middle East*, ed. Steven Heydemann (Berkeley: University of California Press, 2000).

[12]Joyce Starr, "Lebanon's Economy: The Cost of Protracted Violence," in *The Emergence of a New Lebanon: Fantasy or Reality*, ed. Edward Azar (New York: Praeger, 1984); Nasser Saidi, "Economic Consequences of the War in Lebanon," *Bulletin Trimestriel de la Banque du Liban*, 1986, 29–30.

[13]Sena Eken, Paul Cashin, S. Nuri Erbas, José Martinelo, and Adnan Mazarei, *Economic Dislocation and Recovery in Lebanon* (Washington, D.C.: International Monetary Fund, 1995).

[14]Republic of Lebanon, Administration Centrale de la Statistique, *Monthly Bulletin*. 1994–2000.

conflicts. Nevertheless, an analysis of the war based on political economy, which takes into account interests and rational strategies, is not inconsistent with the interpretation of these interests and strategies within what Max Weber would call a "web of meanings" that makes up the culture of the actors.[15] Understanding the Lebanese case involves drawing on both perspectives: Just as the cultural explanation has an economic dimension, so an economic explanation has to rely on a cultural interpretation of the context surrounding competing strategies.[16]

This chapter discusses three wartime economic activities pertaining to Lebanon's main commodities and resources: (1) the trafficking in illegal or legal goods, (2) land speculation, and (3) emigration. Each factor had a particular relation to war making, by provoking, sustaining, or prolonging armed conflict. In paying attention to these economic dimensions, the chapter relates them to issues of political competition and social representation. The aim is to analyze the war not as a mechanical, reified process but rather as a total social fact.[17]

Studying drug trafficking (and oil smuggling), land speculation, and the role of the war émigrés during the war demonstrates, first, that economic interests and rational strategies as well as primordial identities and group solidarities are independent variables that help explain the outbreak, transformation, and prolongation of the war. Second, examining the role of resources suggests that time is at the heart of the interaction between need and greed on the one hand, and creed on the other. Time refers not only to the change in the relative importance of each variable over the fifteen years of war, when need and creed were progressively superseded by the crude and growing greed of the antagonist parties. The concept of time also suggests

[15]Max Weber, "Religious Rejections of the World and Their Directions," in *From Max Weber: Essays in Sociology*, ed. H. H. Gerth and C. Wright Mills (New York: Oxford University Press, 1958), esp. 323–24.

[16]Jean Leca, "L'économie contre la culture dans l'explication des dynamiques politiques," *Bulletin du CEDEJ* (1988): 23.

[17]Ideally, the chapter would also have included a discussion of the banking and financial sectors, as banks turned from surrogates for the collapsed political system into agents suspected of money laundering. However, given the difficulties in obtaining information on this subject in a country protected by banking secrecy, as well as the overly technical dimensions of banking and finance, the subject is left out. Other important aspects of wartime economic activities, such as plundering and looting, are also left aside. On the role of the banking system, see Clement Henry Moore, "Prisoner's Financial Dilemma: A Consociational Future for Lebanon?" *American Political Science Review*, March 1987.

that the reliance on different kinds of goods or commodities to support war expenses implied a different relation to time and, subsequently, inclined various actors to give priority to either their economic interests or their cultural values.

The following discussion of the Lebanese conflict's economic rationales and identity politics in relation to issues of time follows four central arguments. First, because drugs (and oil) were rapidly produced, easily moved, and immediately consumed goods, the enormous profits they generated were threatened by the return of the state and its concomitant imposition of legality and regulations. As these short-time activities became more and more intense, profit became the main driving force behind the fighting, at the expense of political and ideological rationales. Second, a warring party's reliance on land speculation helped maintain a balance between the economic and cultural logics behind the war. On the one hand were the huge financial benefits derived from real estate sales and rentals, as well as from housing construction for refugees who moved back and forth according to the rhythm of battle. On the other hand, however, lay the aspiration for a secure, homogeneous cultural environment and the desire to control land and property in the long term, an aspiration that privileged identity politics. Third, financial support from war expatriates and the Lebanese diaspora helped reinforce the military power of various militia groups, raising the level of fighting and thus immediately aggravating the consequences of the war. This support from abroad, however, was often detached from local strategic, economic, and political priorities, because it stemmed from a timeless utopian perspective born far outside the country's realities. And fourth, the fullest explanation of Lebanon's civil war requires that its ideological and economic dimensions be analyzed within a broader sociological and historical framework.

Trafficking and the Resource of Illegality

The cultivation, commercialization, and consumption of hashish have been part of the habits of Middle Eastern societies for centuries. Though consumers could be found among Lebanese of all social classes, most of the local production was traditionally exported, mainly to Egypt and, since the 1950s, to Israel and Europe. Such trafficking was more than tolerated by the Lebanese state, whose political elite was notoriously involved in hashish smuggling—one of the country's many lucrative trades. In 1974, the head of state himself, President Sleiman Frangieh, had his luggage searched by narcotics agents upon his arrival in New York for the annual meeting of the UN General Assembly. Although the search turned up nothing and caused a diplomatic incident, it was not initiated arbitrarily, because rumors put his son Tony high on the long list of Lebanese drug dealers.[18]

At the time, Lebanon was not in a state of war, and its institutions forbidding drug consumption and punishing related activities had not collapsed. But there was a tacit collusion between its political and even judicial elites to turn a blind eye to the illegal activity for their common benefit. Limitations and sanctions emanated from the international arena only. Hashish, and eventually poppies, were cultivated in remote mountain areas, especially in the north of the Beqaa Valley and in Hermel, regions from which public administration, police, and security services had been noticeably absent since the creation of the state, despite efforts during the presidency of Fuad Shihab (1958–66). The absence of clearly demarcated borders between Syria and Lebanon—a situation that continues to this day—added to the permissive environment in which drug trafficking flourished. The permeable frontier facilitated crossings by a variety of legal and illegal dealers, including gold smugglers from Kurdish tribes.[19] Local Shiite clans prospered thanks to the production and export of hashish, with the complicity of Lebanese as well as Syrian customs and security officers. Such actions contributed to rather than resulted from the eventual collapse of the state.

The civil war brought a quantitative and qualitative modification to the combination of social and political power, financial accumulation, and exercise of violence surrounding illegal drug-related activities. The war did not initiate them, for these activities had existed before. Nor is there any indication that the war was ignited by drug bosses' "greed," for the drug economy had functioned virtually unchecked, leaving drug lords prosperous and, for the most part, safe. What the war did provoke was the entry of new actors and an unprecedented rise in the level of illegal activity. First, there was a rise in Lebanese drug consumption, especially among fighters of all groups, who used narcotics to enhance their faith and morale. War reporters, personal testimonies, and the postwar literature all

---

[18]According to the *Washington Post* correspondent in Beirut ten years later, Tony made $300 million a year through the export of hashish. See Jonathan Randal, *Going All the Way: Christian Warlords, Israeli Adventurers and the War in Lebanon* (New York: Vintage Books, 1984), 157.

[19]E.g., after the spring harvest, nomad sheep breeders from Syria used to wander through the eastern and northern peripheries of Lebanon.

attest to this phenomenon. Second, the disruption of food market networks and the massive and repeated exodus from war zones caused a nearly complete breakdown of traditional agriculture.[20] Neither religious prejudice nor the fear of state police prevented the remaining farmers from turning to more lucrative crops. The rapid development of hashish and poppy production evidenced the distortions of an economy that fulfilled immediate financial needs without taking long-term interests into account. The area used for growing hashish doubled between 1976 and 1984, and did so again in 1988.[21]

Likewise, between 1984 and 1988, and guided by Kurdish experts under the protection of the Syrian army, the area of poppy cultivation increased from 60 to 3,000 hectares. Drug income gave rise to sudden and ostentatious prosperity in rural areas of Hermel and the Beqaa, where Shiite as well as Christian farmers built oversized Riviera-style villas for themselves.[22] This sudden and short-lived prosperity occurred precisely during the period in which several revolutionary movements—the Armenian ASALA, the Kurdish PKK, the pro-Syrian Palestinian Salvation Front, and finally the Lebanese Hizbollah—established barracks and headquarters in this remote area under Syria's umbrella. The drug culture thus developed in a heavily militarized region that was also a political no man's land.

The costs of waging war certainly provided a strong incentive for militia groups to enter into and expand drug activities. At the outset of the war, most militias were only local self-defense organizations formed in response to real or imagined threats. They developed a symbiotic relationship with the population from which they had sprung, sharing its sectarian identity and living off the looting of territories under their control—both the territories they protected and those they attacked. However, as the objectives of the warring parties became more and more obscure, the civilian population suffered a rate of casualties as high as the "combatants," as snipers and

[20]On the eve of the war (1974), the primary sector provided a mere 9 percent of the country's GNP and Lebanon's dependence on imported grains amounted to 76 percent.

[21]Hashish cultivation covered 80 percent of the cultivated surface area in the region of northern Biqaa and Hermel, according to *Al-Nahar*, September 25, 1985.

[22]For a description of this restructuring, see Hassan Makhlouf, *Culture et commerce de drogue au Liban* (Paris: L'Harmattan, 1994). See also "Face à la mafia de la drogue," *Le Commerce du Levant* 5703 (1993); U.S. Department of State, *International Narcotics Control Strategy Report* (Washington, D.C.: U.S. Government Printing Office, 1990). Salim Nasr gives some figures, without citing sources, in "Lebanon's War: Is the End in Sight?" *MERIP* 162 (January–February 1990); the same numbers appeared in *L'Express*, April 30–May 7, 1987, citing the U.S. Drug Enforcement Administration.

raiders targeted mainly civilians. Throughout the 1980s, and culminating with civilian protests in 1987, relations between the minority of combatants that took advantage of the conflict, and the masses that suffered from the war deteriorated.[23]

Relations also worsened as the economic situation grew more dire, as Lebanon became deprived of the two external rents that had sustained domestic consumption during the early years of the war. First, PLO expenditures in Lebanon shrunk from $1 billion a year to a fifth of that following the expulsion of Yasser Arafat and his men from Beirut by Israel in 1982.[24] Second, after 1984, oil prices began to slide on the world market, carrying with them a drastic diminution of financial support from rich Arab countries to the various fighting factions in Lebanon as well as to the Lebanese state. As a consequence of civilian estrangement and economic crisis, the larger militias (the Lebanese Forces among the Christians, the Druze Parti Socialiste Progressiste, and Amal and Hizbollah among the Shia) turned into professional organizations whose members were paid wages. About one-sixth of the male population joined the militias at one time or another during the war, receiving between $60 and $350 a month.[25] Added to the cost of equipment and ammunition, the war cost Lebanon several hundred million dollars a year for fifteen years. Drugs, in some respects, were a direct response of the militias to the extraordinary demands of war making. Yet, in a logic described by Charles Tilly,[26] drugs also provided for massive capital accumulation among leaders and various middlemen, because the profits from drug processing, transport, and commercialization were immeasurable.[27]

[23]Ghassan Slaiby, "Les actions collectives de résistance civile à la guerre," in *Le Liban d'aujourd'hui*, ed. F. Kiwan (Paris: CNRS Éditions, 1993).

[24]After being under siege in West Beirut from June to September 1982, PLO forces left by sea and land under the protection of the Multilateral Force. See Rashid Khalidi, *Under Siege: P.L.O. Decisionmaking during the 1982 War* (New York: Columbia University Press, 1986).

[25]"Liban: L'argent des milices," *Cahiers de l'Orient* 10 (1988); *Al-Hayat*, January 31–February 8, 1990.

[26]Charles Tilly, "War Making and State Making as Organized Crime," in *Bringing the State Back In*, ed. Peter B. Evans, Dietrich Rueschemeyer, and Theda Skocpol (Cambridge: Cambridge University Press, 1985). Some of the Lebanese warlords (among the Christians and the Druze) aimed to build their independent state.

[27]According to Georges Corm, "The War System: Militia Hegemony and Reestablishment of the State," in *Peace for Lebanon: From War to Reconstruction*, ed. Deirdre Collings (Boulder, Colo.: Lynne Rienner, 1994), the figure is $700 million per year; *Le Commerce du Levant*, July 11, 1988, gives a figure of $1 billion.

As described above, the traditional trivialization of hashish growing and drug consumption in the Middle East contributed to decriminalizing the agricultural shift of the war. Financial incentives combined with physical threats easily convinced hesitant farmers to cultivate drug-producing crops. That said, another crucial factor in the dramatic growth of the narcotics economy was the transcommunal and interregional cooperation among militias—cooperation that developed beyond the religious divide. Indeed, the image of ethnic and religious fragmentation of wartime Lebanon should be tempered by the acknowledgment that markets operated not only within but also across newly created territorial boundaries, producing forms of interaction—and even of interdependence and cooperation—that seemed almost out of place given the intensity of violence between highly polarized communities. Such cooperation started as early as the autumn of 1975, when the *souqs* (markets) and port of Beirut were being sacked. At the time, it took the form of various mechanisms of compensation and supervision between regions—mechanisms that depended, ultimately, on personal trust, notwithstanding the national, sectarian, and family affiliations of the parties. Thus, the narcotics trade provided a large opportunity to turn the wartime economy into a strategic resource: Far from being an obstacle to trafficking, the division of Lebanon into several quasi-autonomous statelets increased the rents from the drug trade.

The cooperation among militias was organized around multiple, cross-sectarian economic networks that negotiated specific divisions of labor: taxing farmers, supervising processing and packaging in remote clandestine plants, and carrying the drugs to the many illegal harbors on the Lebanese coast and from there to various intermediary points (such as West Africa) or final destinations. For purposes of drug trafficking, Amal was associated with the Progressive Socialist Party (PSP), and Hizbollah with the pro-Syrian militia of Tripoli, the Lebanese Forces, and even with officers of the Israeli Golani brigade that had occupied the southern region of the country since 1978, notwithstanding the fact that Syrian army and security officers had the upper hand on production areas as well as strategic crossroads and domestic boundaries. Each group performed its share of operations and took its share of the profit. In that sense, there was an indisputable collective interest in protracting the Lebanese war.

Drug networks not only operated across communal and military borders but also were connected to larger international networks. This helps explain why, after the end of the war, drastic measures imposed by Syrian authorities under pressure from the U.S. Drug Enforcement Administration did not succeed in suppressing the lucrative drug business, even though they had a dramatic effect on the peasantry. The brutal reduction of poppy cultivation and the incremental uprooting of hashish produced a long-term economic crisis; whatever the promises of the Lebanese government or the ambitious alternative development projects of international agencies such as the United Nations Development Program, peasants who returned to traditional agriculture were unable to resist competition from imported Syrian and Jordanian fruit and vegetables. About ten years later, it should have come as no surprise that, as several sources indicated, poppy cultivation was back in the Beqaa Valley.[28]

There has been no sign that clandestine laboratories have been closed or drug networks dismantled. They now feed upon external production zones—mainly in southern Turkey and the Caucasus—and are linked to banking circuits in Lebanon and industrial countries.[29] The demobilization of the militia organizations that had fostered and protected local drug networks resulted in the networks' long-term integration into international drug marketing rings. In Lebanon itself, the men who had led the game for fifteen years kept hold of the local segments of the networks, albeit in their new guise as civilian businessmen and political bosses. What postwar official measures induced was not a break from the war economy but its modernization and routinization.

Beyond the significant distinction between legal and illegal products, the same evolution occurred with regard to several public goods. The importation and distribution of crude oil for the two state refineries in Tripoli and Zahrani (Sidon), and the import of oil derivatives for the Dora reservoir near Beirut, escaped state monopoly as early as 1976; at that time, militia groups associated with the Syrian president's brothers began importing without state licenses. After the two refineries (located in Sunni and Shiite zones, respectively) had been destroyed by Christian fire, the minister of industry and oil—who had close links to the Christian militias—deemed it technically impossible to bring them back into use. Almost overnight, storage units in the central Christian regions (Dora, Nahr el-Mott, and Dbayeh) became the country's main supply centers for fuel, supplying other regions on the basis of intermilitia agreements. However, the Caisse des Carburants

[28]*Al-Nahar*, August 13, 2001.

[29]Between 1995 and 1997, the Lebanese authorities announced several arrests of cocaine dealers linked to Brazilian and Colombian networks, while rumors soared about drug-money laundering by local banks.

(State Fuel Fund), whose ledgers had been "accidentally" burned in 1977, kept subsidizing oil products until 1986, even though the militias were openly collecting their own taxes and even reexporting to neighboring countries.[30] Finally, postwar governments resolved to deregulate the oil trade, legalize a dozen private oil terminals established along the coast, and accept the transformation of the state monopoly into an oligopoly of six private companies, each linked to an ex-militia group.

For oil, as for drugs, individual or collective greed helps to explain the development of the war economy; this greed was associated with, or grafted onto, the exceptional financial expenses incurred by the warring militias or their leaders. In return, economic logic contributed to extending and increasing the level of fighting, even at the expense of the security of the civilians associated with each group; this logic took advantage of the discourse of rupture and intersectarian hostility and drew from deeply rooted creed disputes. Greed in the defense (or promotion) of creed could not have been satisfied if it had not been for the cooperation of individuals willing to trust one another beyond apparently intractable identity and ideological differences, in order to maximize their gains. How else could we explain the shelling of the oil terminal of Zahrani by the pro-Israeli South Lebanon army, which overnight in 1988 raised the price of oil imported (and sold) by its local adversary, the Shiite militia Amal? What of the often-told story of Camille Chamoun, the elderly leader of the Christians, coming to his enemy, Bachir Gemayel, in the wake of the crushing defeat of his militia by the young man's Lebanese Forces in 1980, and offering peace "as long as he could keep free use of his illegal harbor at Dbayeh?"[31]

On the whole, there was a direct relation among military escalation, arms expenditures, and the reliance of nearly all militia groups on the trafficking of drugs and various other goods. Progressively, as the legitimacy of the cause eroded among the population associated with each sectarian group and the corresponding resources drawn from civilians ran dry, smuggling and trafficking provided a larger part of militia finances. As years passed and the war went on, these activities tended to develop an economic logic of their own, disconnected from the driving ideal of group mobilization. Consequently, the logic of seeking rapid and uncontrolled profit persisted after the war, even after the demobilization of the militias and the official reconciliation of the warring sectarian groups.

---

[30]The oil bill accounted roughly for 10 percent of nonmilitary imports during the war.
[31]Randal, *Going All the Way*, 139.

From Territorial Illusion to Land Rent

Examining the function of territory and land during the Lebanese civil war sheds another interesting light on the complex relationship between creed and greed as well as on Lebanon's specific political economy. The hegemonic discourse of sectarian groups based their militia strategy on security priorities and an obsession with communal homogeneity; this strategy resulted in several ethnic cleansing operations, although the term was not used at the time. The Christian central regions under the Lebanese Forces and the Druze region under the PSP constituted the most blatant examples of such cleansing, with the heavy use of religious and political symbols to mark homogenized territory, a much publicized discourse of threat (against internal dissidents) and fear (of alien enemies), and the dramatic expulsion of minority groups.[32] In some cases, sectarian nationalism was strong enough within the society, and especially among intellectuals, to nearly lead to secession.[33] In most cases, it led to the creation of separate public administrations and services, the construction of new local infrastructure, and the reshaping of economic activities.

That said, internal feuds within each of the "liberated" statelets and active transsectarian cooperation outside belied the territorial illusions aroused by militia leaderships. After two years of fighting, when the boundaries had been solidly established and the crossing points neatly controlled, kidnapping, car bombs, and gang fighting within each zone caused more civilian losses than did reciprocal shelling.

The behavior of the militia leaders as well as their confessions made obvious the economic rationale behind the territorial fragmentation of the war. Such fragmentation favored the emergence and development of alternative urban and commercial centers, whose prosperity fluctuated according to the economic climate of the moment.[34] The construction of internal frontiers generated revenues in several ways: through the levying of cus-

[32]Elizabeth Picard, "The Dynamics of the Lebanese Christians: From the Paradigm of the *'Âmmiyât* to the Paradigm of Hwayyek," in *Christian Communities in the Arab Middle East*, ed. A. Pacini (Oxford: Clarendon Press, 1998); Judith Harik, "Change and Continuity among the Lebanese Druze Community: The Civil Administration of the Mountain, 1983–1990," *Middle Eastern Studies* 29, no. 3 (1993).

[33]Percy Kemp, "La stratégie de Bachir Gemayel," *Hérodote* (1983): 29–30.

[34]Elisabeth Longuenesse, "Guerre et décentralisation urbaine au Liban: Le cas de Zghorta," in *URBAMA: Petites villes et villes moyennes dans le monde arabe* (Tours: Urbama, 1986); William Harris, "The View from Zahleh: Security and Economic Conditions in the Central Bekaa, 1980–1985," *Middle East Journal*, 39, no. 3 (Summer 1985).

toms duties, the artificial creation of local shortages leading to skyrocketing prices and windfall profits, and even the lengthening of transportation distances that increased transport fees. As the state retreated, the partitioning of Lebanon among militias nearly reproduced the old Ottoman divisions of military-controlled fiscal domains (*iqtâ'*), each with its borders and customs checkpoints: Bater and Monteverde for the PSP, the Awali bridge north of Sidon for the Nasserists, the Qasmieh bridge for Amal, Barbara for the Lebanese Forces, and so on. Each of these crossing points generated significant revenues for the militias that controlled it.

At the leadership level within each territory, ruptures and clashes resulted more from competing interests than from ideological or strategic contention; both factors were not insignificant, however, as illustrated by the competition between Amal and Hizbollah for support from various Iranian centers of power after 1982, or by the strong interest in controlling the racket of the northern cement factories, an objective that motivated the "punitive" expedition of the Lebanese Forces against the fiefdom of their Christian rival, former president Frangieh, in 1978.[35] The same factors were present in the early destruction of downtown Beirut in 1975–76. Though several assailants were motivated by their fury against unfair economic advantages and their fascination with the destruction of the symbols of consensus life,[36] the destruction was accompanied by the systematic looting of shops and harbor warehouses and was followed by the selling of stolen goods all over the country and in Syria.

Thus, economic lust combined with identity mobilization in the destruction of certain districts and in their transformation into long-term disaster areas. Throughout fifteen years of insecurity, luxurious homes, fashionable shops, and expensive leisure establishments such as restaurants and nightclubs deserted the brisk, modern, and confessionally mixed area in west Beirut, and moved to the city's (Christian) eastern part and northern suburbs. As targeted shelling and military roadblocks helped suppress west Beirut's economic life, the rise of fundamentalist religious movements in this Muslim-dominated area motivated Muslim contractors and businessmen to invest preferably in the Christian part of the city and to launch joint

---

[35]About 20 percent of the salaried employees in the cement works of Chekka were "protector-guards," according to local terminology. Rifaat el-Assad, the brother of the late Syrian president, shared the Chekka racket with the family of President Sleiman Frangieh.

[36]This is what Eric Hobsbawm calls a "revolution of destruction," in *Bandits* (London: Weidenfeld & Nicolson, 1969).

ventures with their Christian fellow countrymen; these, in return, welcomed their capital, in spite of the xenophobic discourse of the local religious authorities.[37]

Another illuminating case involves the way the land occupied by Palestinian refugee camps was dealt with during and after the war. From the very beginning of the war, ethnic antagonism lay at the core of the refusal to settle (*tawtin*) Palestinian refugees and their political and military institutions in Lebanon. To Christians as well as to the Shia who fought the Palestinian encroachment of state authority, the Palestinian *fidayin* (guerrillas) and the masses of Palestinian refugees represented the negative and unbearable "other," stirring up powerful popular hostility. As a result, the siege of the refugee camp of Tell ez-Zaatar by Christian militias (1976), the massacre of Sabra and Chatila by the Lebanese Forces (1982), and the war fought by Shiite militias against the southern suburb Palestinian camps in 1985–88 were among the bloodiest and most merciless episodes of the civil war. Hostility did not diminish after the war, and today resentment toward the Palestinians might be the strongest feeling shared by Lebanese of all sects. Underneath this "creed" aspect, however, loomed another dimension, involving private and public maneuvers to get hold of the camps' much coveted land located in the close-in suburbs of Beirut and to resettle the refugees in remote areas or even abroad. The desire for land revenue thus tells another story and sheds a different light on wartime hostilities.[38]

One might perhaps suspect economic premeditation in the treatment of the Palestinians, as in other campaigns of forced displacement (and extermination) that unfolded one after another in an apparent emotional fury of reprisals, affecting one-quarter to one-third of the country's population at one time or another.[39] These military campaigns were related to the high value of land and the heavy demographic pressure on the eve of the civil war in highly disputed zones of the coastal strip, such as Beirut's central dis-

[37]E.g., after the war, Maronite and Greek Catholic clerics continued to forbid the selling of land to *ghuraba* (foreigners to the region), even if they were of Lebanese nationality. The clerics conjured up the specter of the "islamization" of the land.

[38]*Palestinians in Lebanon: Conference Report* (Oxford: Centre for Lebanese Studies, 1996).

[39]According to Ali Faour, *Geography of the Displacement* [in Arabic] (Beirut, Naufal, 1995), 900,000 Lebanese were displaced during the war. The Ministry of the Displaced put the figure at 450,000. See Ministry of the Displaced, *The Question of the Displacement in Lebanon 1976–1990* [in Arabic] (Beirut: Ministry of the Displaced, 1992).

trict and the regions directly north and south of the capital. In these areas—including the Beirut suburbs, the eastern villages surrounding Sidon, and some quarters of Tripoli—the process of expulsion was notably violent and systematic. At the same time, a relative sectarian pluralism persisted in several other regions.

The craving for land did not decline during the war, as militia leaders, surrounded by entrepreneurs and prone to Weberian "economy-oriented" initiative strove to secure and enlarge their territorial and hence economic power.[40] From at least the early 1980s, developers showed an interest in land recovery and reconstruction in the above-mentioned areas. With the agreement of the local militias—and often with their financial participation—they launched a variety of speculative projects, including coastal land reclamation, marinas, high-rise luxury hotels, gated communities, and shopping malls. Some of these projects, such as the line of seaside resorts extending twenty miles north of Beirut in the Christian zone, were completed and operational before the end of the war. Others—such as the Solidere private real estate operation initiated by Prime Minister Rafic Hariri to rebuild Beirut's destroyed central district—could not be implemented because of continuous fighting and were only undertaken after the war.

Wartime constituted an exceptional period and allowed exceptional initiatives to be taken in the domain of land and real estate dealing. In many towns and villages, official registers disappeared in fires and other violent or obscure circumstances. During more than half the war's fifteen years, fighting prevented civil servants from coming to their offices. Although all of them continued to receive their salaries, many, in fact, had joined the militias or left the country. Those who did report to work took orders not from state authorities but from militiamen, who were called at the time "de facto forces."

In this environment, thousands of land transactions took place without registration and without the payment of legal taxes (although hefty "taxes" were paid to the de facto forces). Thousands of houses and apartments were illegally occupied, either after owners had been violently expelled or when displaced persons squatted in vacant buildings.[41] Thousands of acres of

[40]Weber, "Religious Rejections," in *From Max Weber*, ed. Gerth and Mills, 331–33, 366, 382.

[41]After the war, most of the money spent by the governmental Fund for the Displaced ($250,000 in the Beirut Central District alone, according to the private group Solidere) was distributed to squatters in order to make them leave, rather than to the displaced who needed help to return to their homes. The controversy about fictitious squatters raged in the Lebanese press during October and November 1994.

empty land were built up without permits, especially in Beirut's suburbs, where hundreds of thousands of southern villagers took refuge after successive Israeli invasions (1978, 1982). After the war, this type of construction raised the thorny question of regularization.[42] Ministers operating without controls in this chaotic environment enacted exceptional decrees that allowed for local or national infringement of zoning laws,[43] the pillage of natural resources,[44] and the privatization of the public domain and public infrastructures.[45] In a country long famous for its successful laissez-faire policies, sheer violence became the ultimate authority and the shortest road to profit.[46]

Because reliable documentation is lacking, no study has detailed the changes in land and real estate holdings that occurred during and because of the war. Nevertheless, in postwar Lebanon, booming land and real estate speculative transactions contrasted with the steady emigration of labor power and a continuous decline in GNP.[47] This suggests that war transactions

[42]Wafa Charaf ed-Din, "L'habitat illégal dans la banlieue-sud," in *Reconstruire Beyrouth*, ed. Nabil Beyhum (Lyon: Maison de l'Orient, 1991).

[43]Elie el-Achkar, *Réglementations et formes urbaines: Le cas de Beyrouth* (Beirut: Cermoc, 1998).

[44]The Council of the South, a state institution headed since its creation in 1984 by Amal leader Nabih Berri, allowed a Shiite diamond dealer from Sierra Leone to mine sand off the beaches of Tyre. Similarly, large-scale mining of quarries by private entrepreneurs linked to, and protected by, militia groups began during the war and continued during the reconstruction period. The government failed to adopt the regulations called for by environmentalists in the 1990s, for (ex-militia) ministers and members of Parliament had a direct interest in the business. Karam Karam, "Les associations: Défense de l'environnement et recomposition d'un nouvel espace public," in *Reconstruction et Réconciliation au Liban*, ed. E. Huybrechts and C. Douayhi (Beirut: Cermoc, 1999).

[45]Ten years before Prime Minister Hariri granted a concession in central Beirut in 1993 to Solidere, a private group in which he himself was one of the biggest shareholders, President Amine Gemayel (1982–88) authorized private developers related to the Lebanese Forces to embank the shore 15 miles north of Beirut and gave them possession of 80 percent of the reclaimed land. Prime Minister Hariri and Minister of Interior Michel El Murr (himself an ex-member of the Lebanese Forces) insisted on the continuation of the project in the 1990s, despite criticism from the Council of State. See Henri Eddé, *Le Liban d'où je viens* (Paris: Buchet-Chastel, 1997); and Najah Wakim, *The Black Hands* [in Arabic] (Beirut: Sharikat al-Matbu'at lil-Tawzi' wal-Nashr, 1998).

[46]Between 1987 and 1989, the Lebanese Forces dumped toxic chemical wastes from Italy in several mountain and coastal locations in the region they controlled, for which they were paid about $80 million.

[47]Ten years after the war, about half of Lebanon's GNP was immobilized in a fragile construction bubble. See Georges Corm, *Reconstruction and Public Welfare* [in Arabic] (Beirut: Mu'assasat al-Abhath al-Madiniyah, 1996); Natacha Aveline, *Marchés fonciers et immobiliers à Beyrouth* (Beirut: Cermoc, 2000). Such a rent system resulted in a constant rise in costs, as opposed to the stagnation (or reduction) of production.

did not constitute a sui generis process, whatever the superimposed collective rhetoric about the necessity to separate sectarian groups or the underlying financial appetites of the warlords. Rather, such transactions were in accordance with a long historical process that continued throughout the war and accelerated during the reconstruction period, as postwar Lebanon remained a nearly tax-free country for land and real estate investors. Indeed, for centuries during the Ottoman Empire, domination over a community's land and its population, through tax collection in the name of the state and thanks to an exceedingly unequal share of crops, had been the basis for the political power of Lebanese bosses. Land remained the first material source of enrichment and symbolic source of prestige at the time of independence because Lebanon's economy remained driven by rent, derived principally from banking deposits and land.[48]

This history explains why the use of land by warring factions was related to the conservation of, loss of, and struggle for power among the elite and ultimately to the postwar reshuffling of the Lebanese polity. The apparent dichotomy between, on the one hand, ethnic division and hostility and, on the other, a shared, "secular" (nonsectarian) lust for land was resolved on the ground by intersectarian violence and the consequent redistribution of land in Lebanon. The long-term process of land accumulation in Lebanon was accelerated during the war as a result of the deepening of intersectarian distrust as well as of individual strategies of rent seeking.

Emigration, Diaspora, and Sectarian Politics

When dealing with the determinants of the civil war and its prolongation for fifteen years at the expense of all segments of society, one must certainly take into account the human factor. Because of a lack of natural and mineral resources, labor power has always been the main asset of the Lebanese economy, its real capital and comparative advantage in a Middle East region where education and professional skills lagged far behind those of industrial nations. In the two decades preceding the civil war, Lebanon, the "merchant Republic," had taken the best advantage of the rise in Arab oil

[48]Ilya Harik, "The Iqtâ' System in Lebanon: A Comparative Political View," *Middle East Journal*, fall 1965; Arnold Hottinger, "Zu'ama' in Historical Perspective," in *Politics in Lebanon*, ed. Leonard Binder (New York: John Wiley and Sons, 1966); Elizabeth Picard, "Une sociologie historique du *za'im* libanais," in *Histoire, sociétés et pouvoir aux Proche et Moyen Orients*, ed. C. Chartouni (Paris: Geuthner, 2001).

exports and the rapid development of the Gulf countries. Lebanon provided all kind of services, from banking to leisure and health care, to Emirati and Saudi societies, and it also sent hundreds of doctors, engineers, and teachers to fill the expertise gap in the oil-rich monarchies. Several economists argue that Lebanon's comparative advantage in expertise was rapidly decreasing in the late 1960s, and that the much-praised Lebanese miracle was already threatened because of the mediocre record of its educational sector, the growing imbalance in the urbanization process, and the blatant intersectarian inequalities mentioned above.[49]

On the eve of the war, émigrés' remittances, reflecting a historical trend that had already become dramatic at the time of World War I, provided one-third of the country's resources, an exceptionally high level of external dependency.[50] The trend accelerated during the fifteen years of war, as economic destruction and physical danger combined to provoke massive emigration, whether temporary or permanent.[51] But emigration did not stop in the following decade, when stagflation, a high level of unemployment (20 to 30 percent of the active population), and a sharp decline of minimum wages caused the departure of young degree holders.[52] The "Lebanese miracle," if it had existed at all, had disappeared in the upheaval of war. Nor could it be revived, because in the meantime, neighboring Arab countries had become directly absorbed into the world economy.

Observing the effects of emigration on the Lebanese civil war supports need, greed, and creed theories of armed conflict. On the one hand, the Lebanese diaspora became a major source of financial support for the impoverished civilian population as well as for greedy warlords. The emigration removed about $40 billion from Lebanon,[53] and this capital flight was

[49]According to Toufiq Gaspard, an economic consultant for the United Nations Development Program (personal communication, Beirut, May 2001), only 20 percent of the Lebanese prewar degree holders had studied past elementary school. In 1970, 45 percent of the Lebanese were still living in small villages, while 45 others had moved directly to Beirut.

[50]Migrants' remittances accounted for 22 percent of the GNP in 1950, and up to 33 percent in 1975. Gaspard, personal communication.

[51]According to World Bank estimates, about 200,000 professional and skilled Lebanese sought employment in other countries between 1975 and 1990. This is 7.33 percent of the 1974 population. Eken et al., *Economic Dislocation*, 5.

[52]The decline of minimum wages was 80 percent in real terms between 1981 and 1993. Eken et al., *Economic Dislocation*, 17.

[53]Estimation by Merrill Lynch, March 6, 1997. The Lebanese GDP was $8 billion in 1974.

accompanied by the dollarization of the national economy and spiraling inflation, thus drastically diminishing local investments. With production infrastructures destroyed, the goods and labor market dislocated, and the Lebanese pound having lost nearly 1,000 times its value in relation to the dollar, Lebanon's GDP in the early 1990s plunged to 48 percent of its 1974 level.[54] Those who remained in the country—families without resources, the unemployed, and armed groups—relied heavily on expatriates' remittances. The revenues returned from the diaspora were estimated at the time at $1.5 to $2.5 billion a year.[55]

This situation, in turn, helped perpetuate an exceptional economic order sustained by continuous warfare, as militia networks supplanted traditional solidarity channels. Before the war, relations between the homeland and the diaspora were organized along family lines, as blood ties and patriarchal order maintained a mixture of sentimental attachment and sheer materiel interest. Now only the militias were able to grant emigrants access to their local assets, whether in the form of bank deposits or land and real estate. The militias' control of money transactions and foreign currency movements facilitated the laundering of illegal profits. Long after the fighting ceased and security went back to normal, the Lebanese banking system remained plagued by volatile and uncontrolled short-term deposits, a majority of them by nonresidents. In that sense, the civil war not only reflected the economic strategies of various actors; it also generated a new social and economic order, which survived the final cease-fire.

Economic collapse and the dependence on outside resources were aggravated by the number of additional people forced into exile at the end of the war. The demobilization of the militia enforced by the government in 1991 proved a painful time for arm bearers, who in a moment lost their source of revenue and social power.[56] The refusal of the rank and file of Hizbollah to turn back their arms in 1991 and their insistence to go on fighting the Israeli occupation in the South were partly motivated by basic financial needs, as well as by the dictates of their creed. For their part, hundreds of ex-fighters of the Lebanese Forces had no choice but to emigrate as their militia was disbanded and stigmatized as the spoiler of the restored national

---

[54]See Republic of Lebanon, *Estimation des pertes en revenus en raison des agressions israéliennes contre le Liban* (Beirut: Republic of Lebanon, 2000).

[55]Starr, "Lebanon's Economy," 72.

[56]Elizabeth Picard, *The Demobilization of the Lebanese Militias* (Oxford: Centre for Lebanese Studies, 1999).

consensus. Those who left Lebanon became the financial supporters of those who remained in the country. However, the personal and financial investments of war émigrés in their Lebanese homeland were altogether volatile and divisive. After the war, expatriates remained reluctant to invest in their country's economy, beyond the support extended to their kin and community. Those who did invest in Lebanon were often suspected of contributing to the worst side of the Lebanese banking system: dollarization, a dangerous proportion of highly volatile deposits, and the presence of dirty money.[57]

The financial support from the diaspora and new émigrés to fellow citizens at home began to reflect a clear sectarian dimension and involve political aims. Expatriates did not extend their support only for reasons of family, clan, or communal solidarity. Nor did they send their money for the sole purpose of sharing huge, rapid financial gains with greedy local warlords. Their financial support was also a by-product of what can be called a diaspora complex, a phenomenon related to "creed"; it was a mixture of nostalgia and remorse for being so far from the homeland's danger, shortsightedness compensated by the illusions of an invasive memory, ideologization of domestic political stakes, and a violent mobilization discourse to cover up the absence of direct commitment.[58]

Colonies of Lebanese migrants around the world echoed and magnified the conflict at home.[59] A global geography of war mobilization outside Lebanon could be mapped with Amal and then Hizbollah supporters in West Africa, and Lebanese Forces supporters in Australia and the United States, among others. The collection of money was organized on a sectarian basis, thus enrolling every member of the expatriate community in support of a warring sectarian group at home, irrespective of individual convictions. Churches, mosques, and charity foundations played a militant role among scattered Christian and Muslim communities, by collecting funds that were

[57]Economist Intelligence Unit, *Lebanon Country Profile 2000* (London: Economist Intelligence Unit, 2001).

[58]See Robin Cohen, *Global Diasporas* (London: UCL Press, 1997); Aline Angoustures, "Diasporas et financement des conflits," in *Economie des guerres civiles*, ed. François Jean and Jean-Christophe Rufin (Paris: Pluriel, 1996).

[59]Elizabeth Picard, "Les émigrants et leurs nations: Recompositions identitaires et nouvelles mobilisations des Arabes d'Argentine," in *Les communautés syriennes et libanaises en Argentine*, ed. M. Nancy and E. Picard (Aix-en-Provence, France: IREMAM, 1998).

used as much to buy arms and pay militiamen as to bring relief to civilians. On some occasions, diaspora communities even succeeded in mobilizing public opinion and the government of the host country, as did the supporters of General Aoun after 1989 in France.[60] After the Taif agreement of November 1989 had imposed the suspension of hostilities on the ground, tension, acrimony, and the refusal to acknowledge the new balance of power within the restored political system persisted in the diaspora, fed among other things by the growing discrepancy between the sectarian composition of Lebanese society and that of the diaspora.[61]

Seeing war from afar and judging the warring parties according to their own memory of an idealized past, the Lebanese diaspora mobilized around large political issues: relations with Israel, the role of Syria in the Lebanese war and in postwar reconstruction, the (Christian and/or Arab) identity of Lebanon, and the recovery of Lebanese sovereignty. Émigrés divided on these themes (with a few exceptions) along sectarian lines, in accordance to what they understood to be the prevalent division of the society and polity in Lebanon. They saw the war mainly as an issue of sectarian balance and brought their support to the local militias on a sectarian basis. As a consequence, émigrés who retained a rather conservative image of their country reentered the domestic political arena through sectarian solidarities, thus contributing to the reproduction and confirmation of war cleavages. While leading a modern and often secular life in the industrial countries in which they had settled, they preserved an idealized image of Lebanon and cultivated a utopian design for its future. As a result of their special relation to time through distance, they brought an uncompromising creed-based dimension to the civil war and, by their inflexible militancy, helped prolong the fighting.

---

[60]In 1989–90, General Michel Aoun and the faction of the Lebanese army he commanded opposed the Taif reconciliation agreement and the surrendering of all warring factions to Syria. He was militarily defeated and then sent to France by French diplomats. See Antoine Dinimant, "La politique dans la diaspora libanaise à Paris en 1988–1990: Réseau, identité et territoires," *Mémoire de DEA* (Paris: Institut d'Etudes Politiques, 1998).

[61]Although the Christians made up the majority of the Lebanese abroad, they represented about 35 percent of the residents in postwar Lebanon, where the Shia had become by far the largest religious community.

Putting the War in Historical Perspective

Examining the Lebanese economy's three main resources—legal and illegal goods, land, and labor power—in the prolongation of the civil war draws our attention to the variable of time. It also requires us to use sociology and history to come to a full understanding of the respective importance of resources, their interrelation, and change over the course of the war.

On the eve of the war, Lebanon was enjoying economic growth and undergoing rapid social transformation. The potential of its tertiary and service sector was large but had already been weakened by the decline of Lebanon's regional comparative advantage and the new balance of power induced by the peace process between Egypt and Israel. In such an ambivalent situation, there was an undeniable economic dimension to the motivation of the warring parties. The dominant social classes chose to stir up intersectarian conflict to defuse growing social tensions within each community and rally the masses under their patronage; meanwhile, exploited and marginalized groups in search of compensation took aim at public and private wealth, the centers of power, and especially its core—state institutions. Conservatives and leftists fought over the level of salaries and size of profits, the control of the market, and the balance between economic sectors and between regions of the country. Both agendas, the conservative and the revolutionary, became marginalized in the early months of the war, as the productive economy collapsed when Beirut's commercial district and industrial zones were destroyed. From 1976 on, the political economy framework of mobilization lost its momentum, to be replaced by communal and subcommunal factions, each funded by rents from external (foreign state support, emigrants' remittances) or domestic (goods, land, and financial speculation) sources.

Does this mean that the Lebanese civil war lost its economic dimension after two years, or that, after that time, combatants were driven only by sectarian antagonism and political contention—that social need was replaced by sectarian creed as its motive until the end of the war? On the contrary. Observation of the use of "primary" goods during the war—drugs and oil, land, and labor power—reveals their embezzlement and exploitation by new political and economic actors bound to armed groups and belonging neither to the establishment nor the rebels. Most of these men came from the rural or suburban lower middle classes. In the beginning, moved by religious conviction and drawn by personal loyalty, they had seen no alternative to their enrollment in the war. Soon, they became able to impose themselves on the traditional elite and the leaders in the contest, for they had mastered an extra resource: armed violence organized on a large scale and at a high level.

These new militia entrepreneurs seized opportunities to use public means to private ends. They organized the shifting of the Lebanese economy from rent to predation in order to quickly accumulate wealth before being integrated into the state elite at the end of the war: from legal trade to illegal traffic, from securing land rent and émigrés' remittances to looting private and public goods, and from the development of a national market and public space to their replacement by segmented, monopolistic, communal microspaces. Besides external factors (mainly the successive shifts in the Syrian-Israeli balance of power) and other domestic factors (the inability of the traditional elite to agree on constitutional reforms), the protraction of the civil war owed much to the "greed" of militia leaderships.

This appears all the more blatant when one observes that some leaders showed a willingness to go to the negotiation table earlier than others, depending on the wealth they had accumulated much more than on their military gains, as none could claim victory. Though the Shiite leadership of Amal could take pride in having gained powerful governmental and public administration positions, the Druze Parti Socialiste Progressiste had become rather isolated, short of resources, and eager to settle its relation with the state. For their part, the Lebanese Forces stubbornly continued fighting until their defeat, as if they were expecting no postwar benefit—an expectation that would be sadly fulfilled when they were finally outlawed in 1994. Personal tactics and the calculation of relative, rather than absolute, gain certainly delayed the adoption and implementation of the final ceasefire under Syrian patronage in December 1990.

The identification of economic factors and the study of economic mechanisms would be misleading, however, if not related to history, social logic, and political processes. Economics tells us about the ways and means—even the aims—of human activity; politics and political anthropology provide interpretations of the mental representations at the source of human initiative; and history is necessary to understand where opportunities originate, why they changed, and how actors took them into account in a shifting configuration of power. Thus, one needs to explore the social and political institutions underlying and favoring the development and protraction of a "war system," as well as the institutional changes adopted after the war to minimize the revival of conflict.

Militia entrepreneurs did not invent a new Lebanese economy, and even less a "war economy." Rather, they took advantage of the structure of opportunities offered by the Lebanese environment and distribution of power. More precisely, they took advantage of the social institutions of patrimonial domination that traditionally connected the leaders' economic strategies to the logic of their collective identities in the Ottoman period, when power holders struggled to maintain their image of wealth and to ensure its reallocation to diverse social categories in their community.[62] In the Ottoman districts that would become Lebanon in 1920, land, tax collection, and trade were the main sources of wealth—not production. Official administrative procedures were subordinated to private interests and person-to-person agreement. The public space and the market were divided into a multiplicity of sectarian networks. Thus, patrimonial domination found its justification in the reference that structured the whole social life—sectarianism—and found its legitimization and empowerment in the juridical mechanisms and constitutional institutions of the political system.

In the last quarter of the twentieth century, the Lebanese state, although comparatively young, was supposed to have become a "nation-state" rid of patrimonial values and practices, thanks to a modern administration and institutions such as the judiciary and an elected parliament—all aimed at turning Lebanese civilians from "clients" into citizens. Simultaneously, the integration of the Lebanese market into international economic networks (in a pattern that presaged globalization) was supposed to facilitate Lebanon's adoption of the rules and procedures of modern capitalism. However, behind the official discourse and the international optimism celebrating the country's "modernization without revolution,"[63] reality was different. Neither state institutions nor market rules had been the object of prior agreement between rival communal elites to overcome the sectarian divide. Far from withering away, clientelism pervaded democratic institutions and the state bureaucracy. It has lasted because the unequal exchanges on which clientelism rested were quite economically efficient and politically adapted to indigenous representations of ethnic (family or sectarian)

---

[62]See Samuel Eisenstadt, *Traditional Patrimonialism and Modern Neo-Patrimonialism*, Research Paper in the Social Sciences 90-003 (Beverly Hills, Calif.: Sage Publications, 1973); Jean Leca and Yves Schemeil, "Clientélisme et patrimonialisme dans le monde arabe," *International Political Science Review* 4, no. 4 (1983).

[63]This is the title of a book published two years before the war. Elie Salem, *Modernization without Revolution: Lebanon's Experience* (Bloomington: Indiana University Press, 1973).

solidarity. Modernization has meant the reinvention, not the disappearance, of tradition and its adaptation to the nation-state framework. As a consequence, the Lebanese state developed as a nonautonomous arena where the sectarian elites struggled for positions of power to enable redistribution to their clients.[64] Because the economy was altogether externalized and hardly productive, and the domestic market segmented along confessional lines, the Lebanese transition to capitalism was protracted and distorted.[65] No clear demarcation was drawn between the public domain and private interests. Both the state and the market thus functioned in ways quite distinct from what ideal or typical models would suggest.[66]

It was not a halt in the practices inherited from the past and exacerbated by the fighting that was decisive in ending the war, but rather a change in the Syrian–Israeli strategic balance and an improvement in Syrian–American relations. With the restoration of the state after the adoption of the Taif agreement, the political system was reinstated after some minor procedural changes and constitutional modifications.[67] The sectarian division of power was confirmed and strengthened, notwithstanding the radical change in demographics. The political economy followed the same old rules and practices, with indispensable financial help from the diaspora and the new opportunities provided by the business of reconstruction.

After fifteen years of fighting, Lebanon's domestic social and political structures, political sectarianism, and unruly capitalism remained virtually untouched. Political life returned to its prewar factional games, while sectar-

---

[64] An early and lucid analysis is in Michael Hudson, *The Precarious Republic: Political Modernization in Lebanon* (New York: Random House, 1968). Lebanon can be considered a perfect illustration of the "state-in-society" model. See Joel Migdal, "The State in Society: Developing a State-in-Society Perspective," in *State Power and Social Forces: Domination and Transformation in the Third World*, ed. J. Migdal, Atul Kohli, and Vivienne Shue (Cambridge: Cambridge University Press, 1994).

[65] Michael Johnson, "An Incomplete Bourgeois Revolution?" in *Class & Client in Beirut: The Sunni Muslim Community and the Lebanese State, 1840–1985* (London: Ithaca Press, 1986), 216–27.

[66] This idea is borrowed from Reinoud Leenders, "Public Means to Private Ends, State Building and Power in Post-War Lebanon," in *Politics from Above, Politics from Below: The Middle East in the Age of Economic Reform* (London: Saqi Books, 2003). Several of Leenders's remarks also apply to the prewar period.

[67] Such as a parity between Christians and Muslims in state representation and the devolution of executive power to the Council of Ministers. See Joseph Maila, *The Document of National Reconciliation: A Commentary*, Prospects for Lebanon 4 (Oxford: Centre for Lebanese Studies, 1992).

ian bosses dominated the market.[68] More than ever, the Lebanese political system lacked a link between the constitutional references that provided for the security of each sectarian community, and the unifying discourse of civic loyalty to the state. The Taif agreement, like the Constitution of 1926, failed to introduce cross-cutting modes of representation based on sociological categories related to economic resources and need in order to compensate for the flaws of the sectarian-consensus system based on cultural resources and creed. The Second Republic proved unwilling to promulgate a civil personal status code and acknowledge a transsectarian public space, while the ruling elite carefully avoided any kind of political alternation or channels for upward mobility that might challenge its domination.

The incorporation of militia lumpen-elite and new political entrepreneurs into the traditional oligarchy did not represent a breach in the power-sharing logic, but rather its consolidation. The opening of the market to newly enriched factions neither restrained monopolistic and clientelist practices nor limited public corruption. Thus, the civil war can be understood as the military process through which new actors made their way into the spheres of government and wealth, acquiring by force positions of power that were made official in the postwar reconstruction. While physical violence was their main instrument, the process lasted until a new domestic distribution of power was finally established. But there was a major difference: the postwar balance was based less on intra-elite compromise than on crude power competition and an even deeper sectarian divide. Lebanon's war was over, but in the years that followed, the threat of civil strife loomed large.

Conclusion

As this chapter argues, understanding the Lebanese civil war and the connections between its multiple aspects defies explanation based on one single element. Though economic analysis and rational choice theory throw new light on a conflict too often described as a "war of cultures," these ap-

---

[68]See Elizabeth Picard, "Les habits neufs du communautarisme libanais," *Cultures et Conflits*, 1994, 15–16; Guilain Denoeux and Robert Springborg, "Hariri's Lebanon: Singapore of the Middle East or Sanaa of the Levant?" *Middle East Policy* 6, no. 2 (October 1998): 158–73.

proaches do not diminish the importance of the war's subjective dimensions of creed, such as identity, faith, and group solidarity.

The three important economic resources in the war—drugs and oil trafficking, land acquisition, and expatriate remittances—all had financial value for the combatants as well as a concrete effect on the intensification and prolongation of the war. These resources also had a symbolic dimension, influencing the morale, ethics, and pugnacity of the warring parties through the collective representations underlying resource use. Land in particular reflected a material as well as symbolic stake in the war. And beyond providing financial support, the diaspora echoed and amplified the fears and expectations that moved the warring factions at home. Hence, their role in the war as well as in postwar reconstruction is better understood through the perspective of sociological history.

Finally, need, creed, and greed were of different importance at different periods of the war, with greed incrementally superseding need and creed as the war continued. Whether each variable reflected a more economic or more cultural dimension depended on its relation to time. Goods trafficking and financial profits contributed to the intensification of the war's violence, while the competition for land and mobilization in the diaspora tended to protract the war long after the cease-fire had been proclaimed.

3

The Evolution of Internal War in Peru: The Conjunction of Need, Creed, and Organizational Finance

Cynthia McClintock

Peru's Sendero Luminoso (Shining Path) was founded in 1970 at the University of Huamanga in the remote southern highlands town of Ayacucho. The movement's name came from Peru's first prominent Marxist, José Carlos Mariátegui, who had said that "Marxism-Leninism will open the shining path to revolution"; the group's official name, however, was the Communist Party of Peru. Sendero's leader was a Maoist philosophy professor in the education program at the university, Abimael Guzmán. In contrast to most Latin American insurgencies, Sendero was hierarchical,

Cynthia McClintock is professor of political science and international affairs at George Washington University. She is the author of numerous works on Peru, U.S.–Peruvian relations, and guerrilla movements in Latin America, including *Revolutionary Movements in Latin America: El Salvador's FMLN and Peru's Shining Path* (United States Institute of Peace Press, 1998) and *Peasant Cooperatives and Political Change in Peru* (Princeton University Press, 1981). She is the coauthor, with Fabián Vallas, of *The United States and Peru* (New York: Routledge, 2003), and the coeditor of *The Peruvian Experiment Reconsidered* (Princeton University Press, 1983; Spanish version, Instituto de Estudios Peruanos, 1985).

disciplined, and cohesive—a virtual cult—whose deity was Guzmán. The movement shrewdly recruited first among Peru's highland peasants and then among diverse groups nationwide, but many key militants were teachers and university students who felt socially and economically outcast and found meaning and purpose in Sendero. In the late 1980s, Shining Path numbered approximately 25,000 militants, controlled about 25 percent of Peru's municipalities, and was supported by roughly 15 percent of Peruvians.[1] The death toll for the period 1980–2000 was estimated at 69,280, of which Sendero was judged responsible for 54 percent.[2]

This chapter traces Shining Path's expansion and retreat over the course of four Peruvian governments. Sendero began violent attacks in Peru's southern highlands in 1980—anomalously, the same year that a military government was succeeded by the civilian, elected government of Fernando Belaúnde Terry (1980–85). During a second civilian, elected government, led by Alan García (1985–90), the movement continued to expand. It became active in the Upper Huallaga Valley, which was Peru's most important coca-producing area, and also in the central highlands. During the final years of the García government and the first years of the succeeding government of Alberto Fujimori (1990–2000), Sendero was at its strongest, and it posed a severe threat to the Peruvian state. In 1992, however, Guzmán was captured, and the tide of the war turned. His arrest took place amid other counterinsurgency initiatives, and Shining Path was soon decimated. During the Toledo government (2001–), Shining Path remained a shadow of its former self. Guzmán, who turned seventy years old in December 2004, was still imprisoned; he sought to lead the movement from his cell, but his leadership capacity was questioned among the Senderistas themselves. Armed columns operated in only two small areas of the country, both of which were coca-growing areas. However, militants continued to proselytize among university students and teachers, and it remained possible that the movement could resurge.

This chapter examines the factors that gave rise to and sustained Shining Path, distinguishing four stages in its trajectory: first, its initiation in the

---

[1]Cynthia McClintock, *Revolutionary Movements in Latin America: El Salvador's FMLN and Peru's Shining Path* (Washington, D.C.: United States Institute of Peace Press, 1998), 73–81. "Militants" were those prepared to undertake at least elementary military tasks. The line between "militant," "combatant," and "well-armed and well-trained combatant" was difficult to draw; see Carlos Tapia, *Las Fuerzas Armadas y Sendero Luminoso* (Lima: Instituto de Estudios Peruanos, 1997), 111–12.

[2]Comisión de Entrega de la Comisión de la Verdad y Reconciliación, "Informe final: La tragedia de un pueblo" (Lima: Comisión de Entrega de la Comisión de la Verdad y Reconciliación, 2004), 2.

southern highlands, from the 1970s until the early 1980s; second, its dramatic advance and challenge to the state, from the mid-1980s until 1992; third, its decimation and demoralization from 1992 (with the capture of Guzmán) until 2001; and, fourth, its attempt at resurgence, from 2001 to the present.

I argue that the primary factors triggering and sustaining Shining Path during the first two stages—as well as the primary factors impeding the organization in the second two stages—were issues of need and creed. Although Shining Path became active in Peru's coca-producing areas in the mid-1980s and secured substantial income from the cocaine trade, this revenue was used first and foremost to bolster the insurgent organization, not to enrich militants themselves. As Cynthia J. Arnson discusses in chapter 1 of this volume, resources were the means to a political end, not the end itself. Also, in the mid-1990s, Sendero Luminoso was decimated despite its income from the drug trade. Because Sendero was expanding in Peru's cities right up to the moment of its leader's capture, the conflict in Peru never became prolonged or bogged down; as Arnson and also I. William Zartman (in chapter 10) indicate, it is therefore not surprising that greed never become a key Sendero objective.

In this chapter, I draw on both objective data and subjective evaluations. Especially illuminating were thirty-three interviews with Shining Path militants, conducted in the Huancayo area of Peru in 1993—less than a year after Guzmán's capture.[3] Although the procedure for these interviews was

[3]Rodolfo Osores Ocampo led the research team that carried out thirty-three interviews with Shining Path members in the highlands city of Huancayo and its vicinities in April and May 1993. Osores was a Huancayo native and a sociologist trained at the Universidad del Centro in Huancayo, with a postgraduate degree in demography at the Catholic University in Lima. The focus of the questionnaire was upon the reasons why the respondent had joined Shining Path, and what he or she liked and disliked about the movement. Twenty-three of the interviews were carried out by a former Shining Path member ["Pedro Paredes"] who, in the wake of the capture of Guzmán, was trying to extricate himself from the organization. "Pedro Paredes" did not have a permanent job and welcomed the payment for the interviews; he trusted Osores because they were neighbors in the residential area by the Huancayo university, and because Osores had gotten to know one of his relatives at the Ministry of Health in Huancayo. "Pedro" and Osores conducted some of the interviews together. "Pedro Paredes" had completed secondary school but had no university education. The final ten interviews with Shining Path members were conducted in the Huancayo prison, in the cell block for those arrested on charges of terrorism. These interviews were carried out jointly by Osores and Samuel Sosa (a friend of Osores's nephew), who had recently completed legal studies at the Universidad del Centro and was specializing in anti-terrorist law; Sosa had contacts at the Huancayo jail and brought soap, food, and so forth to gain collaboration from the suspected and convicted Shining Path militants. None of the interviewees denied membership in Shining Path.

far from social science standards, they were the most rigorous to be conducted with Shining Path militants about the reasons for their allegiance to the movement.

The First Stage: Shining Path in Peru's Southern Highlands

During the 1970s and early 1980s, Sendero Luminoso emerged and developed in Peru's southern highlands because of both need and creed. Peru's southern highland departments—Ayacucho, Apurímac, and Huancavelica—were its poorest; Sendero grew not because of resources that could be exploited but because of the lack of resources. To many people in the southern highlands, Sendero's Maoist ideology did not seem at odds with reality, and the cultlike organization provided a sense of power and belonging—although, surprisingly in an area where the overwhelming majority of people were of indigenous origin and dark skinned, ethnic grievances were not articulated. During this period, before the government's dispatch of troops to Ayacucho, Sendero's savage side was not yet salient, and support for Sendero was widespread.[4] In mid-1982, for example, a nineteen-year-old Senderista commander, Edith Lagos, died in police custody in Ayacucho; the turnout for her funeral was estimated at 10,000 to 30,000 people, in a city of about 70,000. Hand-carved statuettes of Lagos sold briskly in the Ayacucho market.

Agriculture and livestock were the economic mainstays in Peru's southern highlands, but conditions were adverse. Most of the land in these departments is precipitous, rocky, arid, and—at altitudes surpassing 12,000 feet—windswept; also, it was difficult to market products because of the lack of a direct paved road to Peru's coast. Demographic pressure was increasing at the same time that soil erosion and land exhaustion became more severe—so that the amount of usable land per family was declining.[5] In 1961, agricultural incomes in the southern highlands were less than half of those in the northern and central highlands, and less than one-seventh

[4]Further indicators of popular support for Sendero in the southern highlands were the high percentage of votes for Marxist parties, the high rate of null and blank voting, and researchers' interviews in the area. See Cynthia McClintock, "Why Peasants Rebel: The Case of Peru's Sendero Luminoso," *World Politics* 47, no. 1 (October 1984): 54–58.

[5]José María Caballero, *Economía agraria de la sierra peruana* (Lima: Instituto de Estudios Peruanos, 1981), 59–91.

of those in Lima.[6] Moreover, agricultural incomes in 3 Ayacucho provinces of early core support for Sendero—Huanta, Huamanga, and Cangallo—were lower than for all but 9 of Peru's 155 provinces.[7] In comparison with Peruvians elsewhere, those in the southern highlands were much less likely to be literate or enjoy basic services such as potable water, and they died in their forties rather than their fifties.[8]

In the late 1960s and 1970s, Peruvian peasants' hopes were high that their land scarcity and poverty would be alleviated by an agrarian reform proclaimed by the government of General Juan Velasco. However, the reform primarily benefited peasants on Peru's coast; a substantial majority of southern highlands peasants were not reform beneficiaries at all.[9] Among those peasants who did receive some land, benefits were limited due to the poor quality of the land and to long-standing tensions in Peru's highlands between peasants who lived in traditional communities and those who worked on haciendas.

Not only were the promises of agrarian reform never realized in Peru's southern highlands, but other trends were also adverse. Government policies—in particular the prices for agricultural products, the cost and availability of credit for agricultural families, and public investment in agriculture—were increasingly unfavorable.[10] As a result, incomes were low and falling. By 1980, per capita income among highland farm families had declined roughly 18 percent relative to 1972 and roughly 23 percent relative to 1950 and 1961.[11] Per capita income among peasants in eight communities of the central and southern highlands as of the late 1970s was only about $75 per year.[12]

Ultimately, the subsistence of Peru's southern highlands peasants was threatened.[13] The World Bank reported that, in the rural highlands as a

---

[6]Richard Webb, *Government Policy and the Distribution of Income in Peru, 1963–1973* (Cambridge, Mass.: Harvard University Press, 1977), 119–29.

[7]Webb, *Government Policy and the Distribution of Income*, 119–21.

[8]Carlos Amat y León, *La desigualdad interior en el Perú* (Lima: Universidad del Pacífico, 1981), appendix.

[9]José María Caballero and Elena Álvarez, *Aspectos cuantitativos de la reforma agraria* (Lima: Instituto de Estudios Peruanos, 1980), 63; and McClintock, "Why Peasants Rebel," 60–74.

[10]McClintock, "Why Peasants Rebel," 67–72.

[11]McClintock, "Why Peasants Rebel," 61.

[12]Adolfo Figueroa, *La economía campesina de la sierra del Perú* (Lima: Pontificia Universidad Católica del Perú, 1983), 68.

[13]William P. Mitchell, *Peasants on the Edge: Crop, Cult, and Crisis in the Andes* (Austin: University of Texas Press, 1991), 128; and Orin Starn, "Missing the Revolution: Anthropologists and the War in Peru," *Cultural Anthropology* 6, no. 1 (February 1991): 79–80.

whole, per capita nutritional consumption dropped from 2,085 calories daily in 1972 to 1,971 in 1980—a 5 percent decline.[14] There were reports of consumption of as little as 420 calories a day.[15] These adverse trends were exacerbated in 1982–83 by bad weather during a severe El Niño (warm air in the hemisphere's Pacific coast in the early months of the year, which occurs about once every seven years); drought devastated the southern highlands. Production of the potato, the food staple of the area, plunged by at least 40 percent.[16] The human toll was tragic:

> In the southern Andes, severe drought completely destroyed the harvest, forcing peasants to consume surplus seed intended for this year's planting. Starvation is rampant among subsistence farmers; illness, particularly tuberculosis, has spread alarmingly. . . . News reports documented cases of peasants selling their children for $25.[17]

Peasants were angry. In an informal survey in 1980 in Vilca, a peasant community in the southern highlands department of Huancavelica, twenty-five residents were asked about the community's progress; 84 percent responded that progress had been "bad."[18] Vilca peasants were also asked, "What have been the achievements in your community in recent years?" Despite the optimistic phraseology, 92 percent of the respondents answered, "None." Some peasants raged that government policies caused hunger and therefore the government was guilty of murder:

> Here, they've always forgotten us. There's no help. Exactly the opposite—the cost of everything has risen too much, and that's not the way to help. They're killing the poor people.[19]

[14]World Bank, *Peru: Major Development Policy Issues and Recommendations* (Washington, D.C.: World Bank, 1981), 140.

[15]Raúl González, "Ayacucho: Por los caminos de Sendero," *QueHacer* 19 (September–October 1982), 43, for unspecified southern highlands zone as of approximately 1980.

[16]McClintock, "Why Peasants Rebel," 69.

[17]*Andean Focus* (November–December 1983), 1. See Juan Torres Guevara, "El Niño": Un fenómeo satanizado," *Andenes*, no. 98 (June/July 1997): 14, for a map that shows the close correlation between the zones of drought during El Niño and the southern highlands areas where Sendero was expanding at the time.

[18]This was a nonrandom survey by the Osores research team, primarily of men.

[19]Peasant in the agricultural cooperative María Laura on Peru's north coast near Virú, speaking to the author, 1983.

Simultaneously, for the first time, a considerable number of these peasants' children were attending not only high school but also university. Between 1960 and 1980, the number of university students nationwide multiplied about eight times, versus twenty times in Ayacucho.[20] However, although these new graduates had struggled and sacrificed for their education, subsequently they could not find professional jobs. They often returned as schoolteachers to the peasant communities of their birth—to be frustrated by perceptions of their failure and angry at the grinding poverty of their students.[21] Among the reasons for these young people's difficulties was their ethnicity; most were darker skinned, of indigenous descent, and familiar with Quechua. As Peru's Truth and Reconciliation Commission emphasized, discrimination against this ethnic group remains severe in Peru.[22] In this context, it was especially difficult for the graduates of southern highlands universities to secure professional positions.[23]

In the 1960s and 1970s at the Ayacucho university, Guzmán interacted with students, in particular those in the education program, to develop the creed that would resonate strongly in the southern highlands. The Peruvian anthropologist Carlos Iván Degregori, who taught at the Ayacucho university in the 1970s, has emphasized that it was Sendero's strategic genius to target teachers and, through them, the next generation of students.[24] Guzmán devoted many hours to political meetings and discussions at his home in Ayacucho. Apparently, he listened closely and respectfully to others' arguments, but his views would prevail.

[20]Carlos Iván Degregori, *Ayacucho 1969–1979: El nacimiento de Sendero Luminoso* (Lima: Instituto de Estudios Peruanos, 1990), 253. As data in the annual issues of the World Bank's *World Development Report* show, these increases were considerably greater than in Latin America as a whole.

[21]See, e.g., Vera Gianotten, Tom de Wit, and Hans de Wit, "The Impact of Sendero Luminoso on Regional and National Politics in Peru," in *The State and the New Social Movements in Latin America*, ed. David Slater (Amsterdam: CEDLA, 1985), 190–91.

[22]Comisión de la Verdad y Reconciliación, *Hatun Willakuy: Versión abreviada del informe final de la Comisión de la Verdad y Reconciliación* (Lima: Comisión de Entrega de la Comisión de la Verdad y Reconciliación, 2004), 23.

[23]Rodrigo Montoya, *Al borde del naufagio: Democracia, violencia, y problema étnico en el Perú* (Lima: SUR, 1992), 91.

[24]Carlos Iván Degregori, "Sendero Luminoso: Los hondos y mortales desencuentros," in *Movimientos Sociales y crisis: El caso peruano*, ed. Eduardo Ballón (Lima: DESCO, 1986), 261.

Having visited China several times, Guzmán's ideology was Maoist; he saw the southern highlands through the lens of prerevolutionary China.[25] For Guzmán, just as China was a "semifeudal" and "semicolonial" state characterized by a dysfunctional "bureaucratic capitalism," so was Peru; just as China's "semifeudal" condition required that the peasantry be the key social base of the revolution, so it did in Peru. Also, this class structure made democratic government impossible; all Peruvian governments, whether elected civilian administrations or de facto military regimes, were labeled "fascist" and "reactionary."

Shining Path doctrine did not mention Peru's ethnic cleavages. As Degregori wrote, "In effect, if one reads the documents of the Peruvian Communist Party/Shining Path, one would think that Peru is a society as homogeneous as the Japanese or Scandinavian; not one line alludes to ethnic or racial problems."[26] Nor were there other indications of an ethnic appeal by Shining Path. In posters and drawings, revolutionary figures were not given Indian features; the militants' noms de guerre were Spanish, not Quechua. Nor did the movement show respect for traditional indigenous culture or religion; there is not a word of reverence for nature, earth, or sun in Shining Path publications, despite their importance in Quechua traditions.

To most political analysts, Sendero's ideology was simplistic and inapplicable to Peru, a country that by the 1970s was much more urban, industrialized, and wealthy than China in the 1940s. Most analysts also believed that because Peru's history included the traumatic Spanish conquest of the Incas and its minorities faced continued ethnic discrimination, an ideological appeal to its darker-skinned persons of indigenous descent would have been compelling.

Yet, among the newly educated youth of Peru's southern highlands, Sendero's fundamentalist, class-based ideology resonated strongly. Degregori reported that many students were seeking "truth," and Sendero proposed a "simplified and accessible version of a theory that defined itself as the only 'scientific truth,' and was legitimized through references to the

---

[25]For an example of Senderista ideology, see Partido Comunista del Perú, *Desarollemos la guerra de guerrillas* (Lima: Ediciones Bandera Roja, 1982); for an excellent discussion, see Colin Harding, "Antonio Díaz Martínez and the Ideology of Sendero Luminoso," *Bulletin of Latin American Research*, 7, no. 1 (1988): 65–73.

[26]Degregori, *Ayacucho 1969–1979*, 205.

Marxist classics."[27] For these young people, Guzmán was "the caudillo-teacher . . . and, therefore, truth incarnate, virtue incarnate."[28]

It is important to note that, unusually among Latin American insurgencies, political exclusion was not a grievance that gave rise to or sustained Shining Path. Between 1968 and 1980, a reformist military government led Peru; it carried out a variety of property reforms, including a sweeping agrarian reform. By Latin American standards, the government was not repressive; indeed, it claimed to be seeking to build "a fully participatory social democracy." As noted above, when Sendero began violent attacks in 1980, Peru had just returned to elected, civilian government; at no time between 1980 and 1992 were political leaders excluded from electoral competition.[29] The Marxist left participated without fear. (However, in 1983–84 Peru's military was dispatched to the southern highlands to combat Sendero and was responsible for the deaths of more than 3,500 innocent people, the vast majority of whom were impoverished Quechua-speaking peasants.[30])

The Second Stage: Shining Path Expands to Much of Peru—Including Coca-Producing Areas

In 1983–84, Shining Path began to operate in another area of Peru: the Upper Huallaga Valley, which at the time was the largest coca-growing area not only in Peru but in the world. By the late 1980s, the movement was gaining $20 to $40 million annually from coca-trade activities.[31] However, Sendero's purpose was not the private enrichment of its members but the bolstering of its organization, to facilitate its expansion in other parts of Peru

[27]Carlos Iván Degregori, "A Dwarf Star," *NACLA Report on the Americas* 24, no. 4 (December–January 1990–91): 16.

[28]Degregori, "Dwarf Star," 16.

[29]Information on the incidence of violence was compiled from all relevant publications by the U.S. Department of State Country Reports on Human Rights Practices, Americas Watch, the Instituto de Defensa Legal, Amnesty International, and the Lawyers' Committee for Human Rights. On electoral processes and the incidence of violence against politically salient groups in Peru during this period, see McClintock, *Revolutionary Movements in Latin America*, 108–29.

[30]Comisión de la Verdad y Reconciliación, *Hatun Willakuy*, 207–23.

[31]These sums were common estimates. See Gordon H. McCormick, *The Shining Path and the Future of Peru* (Santa Monica, Calif.: RAND, 1990), 22; José Gonzales Manrique, "Perú: Sendero Luminoso en el Valle de la Coca," in *Coca, cocaina, y narcotráfico: Laberinto en los Andes*, ed. Diego García-Sayan (Lima: Comisíon Andina de Juristas, 1989), 217; *U.S. News and World Report*, September 28, 1992, 49; *Economist*, September 19, 1992, 53.

and ultimately achieve state power. Because Sendero retained most of its original cadres and recruited thousands of new militants throughout the country, need and creed remained the fundamental factors in its appeal.

The Upper Huallaga Valley, which is located in remote northeastern Peru on the slopes between the Andes and the Amazon in the departments of Huánuco and San Martín, was the center of the global coca boom that began in the 1970s. When international demand for cocaine skyrocketed, peasant families in the valley shifted to coca production, and migration to the area increased. As of the late 1980s, the U.S. Department of State estimated that approximately 85,000 hectares of land in the Upper Huallaga Valley were devoted to illicit coca cultivation—a roughly twenty-five-fold increase since the early 1970s, and 85 percent of Peru's total production.[32] Most of the coca or coca paste was transported in traffickers' small planes to Colombia, where it was refined into cocaine.

Sendero's expansion in Peru's coca-producing areas was considerably more difficult than its expansion in the southern highlands.[33] Two problems were particularly salient. First, Sendero competed for coca producers' allegiance with a secondary insurgency, the Movimiento Revolucionario Túpac Amaru (Túpac Amaru Revolutionary Movement, or MRTA). Only after several years and a shoot-out taking more than forty lives in March 1987 was Sendero able to displace the MRTA from the Upper Huallaga Valley. Also, the MRTA remained active to the north.

Second, for the most part, coca farmers were not drawn to the ideology or organization of Sendero Luminoso. To a greater degree than in other parts of Peru, coca farmers (many of whom had left the communities of their birth for an illicit enterprise in what was the equivalent of Peru's frontier) considered Sendero puritanical, fanatical, and abusive.[34] Rather, coca farmers cooperated with Sendero for opportunistic reasons. Because the United States was spearheading the "war on drugs" and the Peruvian government undertook first in 1984 a coca eradication program and then in

[32]"Political Report," *Peru Report* 2, no. 11 (November 1988): 1–8. Peruvian estimates were roughly twice as large as U.S. estimates.

[33]For further detail on the points in the following paragraphs, see Isaías Rojas, "Peru: Drug Control Policy, Human Rights and Democracy," in *Drugs and Democracy in Latin America*, ed. Coletta Youngers and Eileen Rosin (Boulder, Colo.: Lynne Rienner Publishers, 2004), 188–89; and Enrique Obando, "La política norteamericana hacia el Perú: Dos décadas de desencuentros," draft chapter for a manuscript edited by Brian Loveman, San Diego State University, September 2004.

[34]Raúl González, "Coca y Subversión en el Huallaga," *QueHacer* 48 (September–October, 1987), 70; and Raúl González, "El retorno de lo reprimido: El Huallaga, un año después," *QueHacer* 54 (August–September 1988): 46.

1985–89 the interdiction of cocaine laboratories and airstrips, coca farmers allied with Sendero for the protection of their economic interests. Armed, Sendero was able to attack Peru's antidrug police (and also to protect coca producers in their dealings with traffickers). During intervals when coca farmers were not seeking to oust narcotics control personnel, they loosened their ties to Sendero.

Despite these problems, in the late 1980s and early 1990s Sendero was very active in Peru's coca-producing areas, and, as indicated above, these activities were lucrative. During this period, the U.S. and Peruvian governments were heatedly debating narcotics control policy; the U.S. government was pressuring Peru to adopt a more repressive antinarcotics program, while the Peruvian government feared that such a program would only lose more peasants' hearts and minds to Shining Path. Although the Peruvian police worked with the U.S. government toward its antinarcotics objectives, the Peruvian military was skeptical and emphasized that its key objective was counterinsurgency. Amid the political tensions, U.S. antinarcotics aid to Peru was relatively limited, and the total number of hectares in coca cultivation in Peru increased annually between 1989 and 1992.[35] Although the biggest antinarcotics base in the Americas was established at Santa Lucía in the Upper Huallaga Valley in 1989 under the primary auspices of the U.S. Drug Enforcement Administration, the only result was to shift coca cultivation and the Shining Path's cadres to the north of the base.[36]

Shining Path used the $20 to $40 million it received from its activities in Peru's coca-growing regions primarily to bolster its organizational apparatus. Although during the early 1990s it was thought that a considerable sum was deposited in foreign bank accounts, no such evidence has emerged. Perhaps a third of the funds was used for salaries and other kinds of material support for Senderista militants; in my research team's thirty-three interviews with Senderistas near Huancayo, 57 percent said that they received salaries, and another 36 percent that they received food, housing, or money for expenses. By the early 1990s, Sendero was paying approximately $250 to $500 a month to its militants in the highlands and Lima. These were good salaries by Peruvian standards (about five times the salaries of Peru's teachers), although far from the sums necessary to classify as

[35]Cynthia McClintock and Fabián Vallas, *The United States and Peru: Cooperation— at a Cost* (New York: Routledge, 2003), 7, 115. Data are available at http://www. usaid.gov and in the annual reports from the Bureau of International Narcotics Matters and Its successor, the International Narcotics Control Strategy Report.

[36]Obando, "La política norteamericana hacia el Perú," 7.

wealth.[37] In coca-producing areas, salaries likely reached $1,000 a month.[38] Given these salaries and the estimate above of 10,000 Senderista combatants, probably $5 million or more was spent annually on salaries. A similar sum might have been used for militants' expenses. Millions were probably also allocated for weapons purchases. Although Sendero used dynamite stolen from mines more often than any other weapon, it also had machine guns, G-3 and FAL automatic rifles, U.S.-made hand grenades, and mortars.[39]

For their part, Guzmán and his inner circle lived well but not opulently. Their home was not in the Upper Huallaga Valley but in Lima; considerable sums were allocated for state-of-the-art computers, radios, facsimile machines, equipment to intercept police communications, and frequent moves from one safe house to another.[40] Sendero's leaders enjoyed French wines, imported vitamins, and first-class food—but not fancy cars or swimming pools.

As Sendero's organizational capacity grew, need—which had been severe primarily in Peru's rural highlands—extended to most of the country. From the 1970s through the early 1990s, national economic trends in Peru were among the most negative in Latin America. Peru's decline in gross domestic product (GDP) per capita from 1971 to 1990, roughly −2 percent annually, was among the worst in the region; declines were steeper only in Guyana and Nicaragua.[41] During the period 1985–90, Peru's economic trends constituted "one of the worst economic performances in modern history."[42] Accordingly, the Peruvian experience supports Paul Collier's argument that a previous period of economic decline is a significant grievance that has an impact on the incidence of violent conflict.[43]

[37]These figures were suggested in interviews that I conducted in Lima as well as in my research team's interviews in the Huancayo area. An estimate of $500 per month was made in the *New York Times*, June 26, 1991, A8.

[38]Interview 18 by the Osores research team.

[39]See *Expreso*, July 29, 1990, 8; *La República*, May 27, 1992, 22; *Newsweek*, April 24, 1989, 45; *Caretas*, May 30, 1988, 32.

[40]*Expreso*, September 19, 1992, A12.

[41]Inter-American Development Bank, *Economic and Social Progress in Latin America: 1992 Report* (Baltimore: Johns Hopkins University Press, 1992), 286.

[42]Paul Glewwe and Gillette Hall, "Poverty, Inequality, and Living Standards during Unorthodox Adjustment: The Case of Peru, 1985–1990," *Economic Development and Cultural Change* 42, no. 4 (July 1994): 715.

[43]Paul Collier, "Doing Well Out of War: An Economic Perspective," in *Greed and Grievance: Economic Agendas in Civil Wars*, ed. Mats Berdal and David M. Malone (Boulder, Colo.: Lynne Rienner Publishers, 2000), 96.

By the late 1980s, large percentages of Peru's urban sectors were in economic straits. Jobs were very scarce; the percentage of Lima's population considered "adequately employed" plunged from about 50 percent in the mid-1980s to 6 percent in 1990.[44] Peru's real minimum wage, which had declined by almost 20 percent in the 1970s, stood at only 23 percent of its 1980 value in 1989.[45] As of 1990, the monthly minimum wage was a bare $35, the second lowest among the fourteen Latin American countries for which data were available.[46] Average monthly wages in Peru's public sector—where teachers, nurses, and many other traditionally "middle-class" Peruvians worked—fell from $232 in 1980 to $39 in 1990.[47]

In this economic context, hunger was a problem not only in Peru's rural highlands but throughout the country. Negative food consumption trends were reported in many studies.[48] Even middle-class groups such as teachers could not provide their own children with three meals a day.[49] In Lima, child malnutrition and child mortality rates jumped.[50]

During its nationwide expansion, Sendero continued to focus on the university and to advance ideological principles that appealed especially to teachers and students. By the early 1990s, perhaps 30,000 teachers—or 15 percent of all Peru's teachers—were Senderistas.[51] One nine-member ideology and propaganda "support group" for Sendero included two university professors and two primary school teachers, as well as two students and a self-employed public accountant.[52] Among the thirty-three Senderistas interviewed by my research team, four were teachers and nine were students— or, in other words, 33 percent were based at secondary schools or universities.

[44]For Peru, see Cuánto, *Ajuste y economía familiar* (Lima: Cuánto, 1991), 30; for Latin America, see McClintock, *Revolutionary Movements in Latin America*, 164.

[45]On the 1970s decline, see Richard Webb and Graciela Fernández Baca, *Perú en números 1991* (Lima: Cuánto, 1991), 811; on the 1980s, see Inter-American Development Bank, *Economic and Social Progress in Latin America: 1990 Report* (Washington, D.C.: Inter-American Development Bank, 1990), 28.

[46]*Perú Económico* 13, no. 8 (August 1990): 43–44. The figure was lowest in Bolivia.

[47]Cuánto, *Ajuste y economía familiar*, 31.

[48]World Bank and other data are cited in McClintock, *Revolutionary Movements in Latin America*, 83.

[49]*New York Times*, December 8, 1991, E3. See also *Washington Post,* November 27, 1991, 22A; and *New York Times*, December 15, 1991, 21.

[50]John Crabtree, *Peru under García: An Opportunity Lost* (Pittsburgh: Pittsburgh University Press, 1992), 146–47.

[51]This estimate was made in late 1990 by Gloria Helfer, minister of education at the time in the Fujimori government. The estimate was frequently cited.

[52]*La República*, April 14, 1993, 12–16.

At the same time, Sendero broadened its ideological appeal. In particular, it placed more emphasis on the problem of corruption. Amid Peru's economic crisis, the capacity of the state to maintain essential state social services eroded.[53] Although there was no evidence that state agencies were more corrupt than in other Latin American nations, Sendero's charges of corruption resonated; after all, Peru's state was not highly legitimate, and mistrust was common.[54] Also, amid the economic crisis, corruption was often a life-or-death issue; for example, when public hospital administrators stole medicine or soup kitchen managers stole food, the sick or the hungry were more likely to die. For many Peruvians, these deaths in turn justified Sendero's killings.[55]

Although Sendero's savage violence alienated most Peruvians, in some places and at some times it facilitated Sendero's image as an organization that punished wrongdoers and, therefore, "worked." To many Peruvians by the early 1990s, the movement appeared very "strong" and its march to power inexorable.[56] Accordingly, for darker-skinned Peruvians who had felt voiceless and impotent, when they became Senderistas they "were somebody."

In their own explanations for their support of Sendero, militants in Peru's cities in the late 1980s and early 1990s strongly emphasized Peruvians' grievances—in particular, the threat to subsistence. Senderistas described the Peruvian state as *"hambreador"* (making the people hungry) and "genocidal"—intentionally killing the people with hunger.[57] For

---

[53]McClintock, *Revolutionary Movements in Latin America*, 190–99.

[54]For cross-national assessments of corruption, see McClintock, *Revolutionary Movements in Latin America*, 194–99. On the weak legitimacy of Peru's state, see especially David Scott Palmer, "The Revolutionary Terrorism of Peru's Shining Path," in *Terrorism in Context*, ed. Martha Crenshaw (University Park: Pennsylvania State University Press, 1995), 301–3; and Philip Mauceri, *State under Siege: Development and Policy Making in Peru* (Boulder, Colo.: Westview, 1996), especially 6–11.

[55]Sendero's effective exploitation of the corruption problem in Lima's shantytowns was highlighted by Jo-Marie Burt, "Poverty, Violence, and Grassroots Organizing in Urban Peru," paper presented at the Latin American Studies Association meeting, Atlanta, 1994, 14; and by Deborah Poole and Gerardo Rénique, *Peru: Time of Fear* (London: Latin America Bureau, 1992), 92–94.

[56]See, e.g., Michael L. Smith, "Shining Path's Urban Strategy: Ate Vitarte," in *The Shining Path of Peru*, ed. David Scott Palmer (New York: St. Martin's Press, 1992), 29.

[57]See, e.g., the interview with Isidoro Nunja García in *Caretas*, May 30, 1988, 32.

example, in a eulogy for a teenage boy, the Sendero commander of a Lima shantytown said:

> They say we are terrorists because, in this land, he who has the most economic power is he who rules. . . . [But] the terrorists are those who kill us with hunger every day. The terrorists are those who give us a minimum wage that is not even enough to pay for a grave or the most miserable of food; those are the terrorists.[58]

When "Javier," a twenty-three-year-old law student working in a stock-broker's office in Lima, was asked by his mother why he would kill people, he responded:

> The system kills people with hunger. . . . Sixty thousand children die before their first birthday each year in Peru. What's going to help them?[59]

In my research team's interviews, a large majority of the Senderistas— twenty-four of the thirty-three, or 73 percent—said that they had joined Shining Path because they shared its ideological principles; in general, that they wanted to struggle for social change. Only one of the thirty-three said that he had joined because he had been unemployed and needed the $300-per-month salary. Among the remaining respondents, five (15 percent) said that they were recruited by force, two (6 percent) said that they sought to revenge their relatives' violent abuse or death, and one said that, having been wrongly suspected of Senderista sympathies by the police, he had had no choice but to join.

Even though at the time of these interviews (May–June 1993) Guzmán had been captured, these Senderistas remained remarkably enthusiastic about the movement and its leader. Asked what they liked most about Sendero, sixteen (48 percent) said the discipline and leadership of the organization, and fourteen (42 percent) said the struggle for change. Although none of our respondents reported that they had met Guzmán, twenty-seven (82 percent) had a favorable impression of him; they said he was "a teacher and guide,"

---

[58] Félix Cóndor of the Raucana shantytown, cited in Simon Strong, *Shining Path: Terror and Revolution in Peru* (New York: Times Books, 1992), 263.

[59] This is from a young Shining Path member cited by Tina Rosenberg, *Children of Cain: Violence and the Violent in Latin America* (New York: William Morrow, 1991), 148.

a "philosopher whose ideas will live forever," "the most influential man of the century," and *Super Sabio* (Super Sage). Interestingly, despite the lack of reference to Quechua religion in Sendero ideology, four (12 percent) referred to Guzmán as the "red sun" or the "sun," thereby associating Guzmán with the Quechua deity. Further, twenty-seven (82 percent) were optimistic that Sendero would not be definitively defeated by 1995.

In their explanations for having joined Sendero, militants affirmed their creed—their allegiance to Marxist principles—based on their perception of the overwhelming need of Peru's poor. A thirty-five-year-old architect, for example, said:

> I entered Sendero Luminoso because of the need to change our country, which for centuries has been the estate and the property of the rich. The injustices and the abuses committed always against the poor pushed me to enter the ranks of the Communist Party of Peru, the only true director of the popular war, aiming at the conquest of power in order to install the dictatorship of the proletariat.[60]

A sociologist, "Rosa," struck similar chords, adding an emphasis on the urgency of change:

> I entered Sendero Luminoso because I could no longer bear seeing on one side so much hunger and misery, and on the other side wealth and extravagance. The exploitation has to stop. There has been enough injustice and abuses, humiliations and contempt. The discussion has finished. It's the hour for action.[61]

Less-well-educated respondents' answers were less likely to use Marxist concepts but were equally fervent. A militant who had previously been unemployed said: "[I entered] to conquer power for the poor of the world."[62] A former soldier said: "[I entered] to struggle for the peasants . . . not permitting the abuse of the bad authorities."[63] A schoolteacher explained: "[I entered] to combat the oppressor, the assassin of children and women, this Fujimori *hambreador* and *genocida*."[64]

[60]Interview 18 by the Osores research team.
[61]Interview 19 by the Osores research team.
[62]Interview 12 by the Osores research team.
[63]Interview 8 by the Osores research team.
[64]Interview 10 by the Osores research team.

As indicated above, all but two of the Senderistas said that they had received some kind of material support from the organization. Usually, this support was discussed as helpful—"useful for my family"—but not fundamental. Only one respondent (not the person who had joined for financial reasons) was truly enthusiastic about his personal lifestyle, commenting, for example, that "cars were used to move us around, and we stayed at good hotels."[65]

The Third Stage: A Decimated, Demoralized Shining Path

In mid-1992, Sendero was preparing for full-scale insurrection. In July, a truck bomb in a prosperous Lima neighborhood killed 22 and injured 250, heralding a week of attacks against police stations, factories, schools, and stores. The next week, a two-day "armed strike" paralyzed Lima and much of the rest of the country. Despite the Fujimori government's April 1992 *autogolpe* ("self-coup" by the president himself, in which the Congress was closed and the Constitution suspended, purportedly in part so that the state could "get tough" on terrorism), the possibility of a Shining Path victory appeared greater than ever before.[66]

Yet, between September 1992 and 1995, Sendero was decimated; in the conventional phrase in Peru, there was a "strategic defeat" of the movement.[67] The critical turning point was the capture of Guzmán at his Lima hideout on September 12, 1992.[68] As Peru's Truth and Reconciliation Commission concluded, "The capture of Guzmán was catastrophic for PCP-SL [Partido Comunista del Perú-Sendero Luminoso]. The myth of invulnerability of PCP-SL was annihilated."[69] When Guzmán was captured, the "red sun" that had shone so brightly for most Senderistas was dimmed. A creed of certain victory in a war for poor people against a corrupt, ineffective state was undermined.

[65]Interview 28 by the Osores research team.

[66]McClintock, *Revolutionary Movements in Latin America*, 9–10, 73–90.

[67]Comisión de la Verdad y Reconciliación, *Hatun Willakuy*, 168. See also Isaías Rojas Pérez, "Sendero y el MRTA después de la crisis," *Ideele*, no. 98 (1997): 53.

[68]The most authoritative sources are Carlos Reyna, "Cómo fue realmente la captura de Abimael Guzmán," *Debate*, no. 82 (1995): 46–50; Gustavo Gorriti, "El día que cayó Sendero Luminoso," *Selecciones del Reader's Digest*, December 1996, 117–42; Benedicto Jiménez Baca, "Así fue la captura del siglo," *La República*, September 12–14, 1996, 1–6; and Richard Clutterback, "Peru: Cocaine, Terrorism, and Corruption," *International Relations* 12, no. 3 (1995).

[69]Comisión de la Verdad y Reconciliación, *Hatun Willakuy*, 178.

Two other factors were also important to the strategic defeat of Sendero. First, amid an erosion of peasant support for Sendero, the military was able to establish peasant self-defense patrols (*rondas campesinas*). Second, the country's antiterrorism legislation was changed. In the middle and late 1990s, the strategic defeat was consolidated both by a recovering economy, which reduced Peruvians' need, and by a plunging cocaine trade, which reduced the revenue available to the organization.

The capture of Guzmán was the fruit of several years of effort by an elite police intelligence squad called the Grupo Especial de Inteligencia (Special Intelligence Group, or GEIN). GEIN was founded in the final months of the García government and led by Colonel Benedicto Jiménez Baca. It was focused only on the apex of the Senderista hierarchy, and its strategy was to track suspects, hoping for intelligence that would lead to Guzmán. (By contrast, the conventional practice of Peru's police intelligence units was to arrest and interrogate suspects immediately, and often brutally; this strategy was flawed both ethically and strategically, because the location of Guzmán was known to only a few top leaders.) GEIN's first major breakthrough was in June 1990; missing Guzmán by little more than a week, it seized a safe house in the wealthy suburb of Monterrico and secured valuable documents.

In July 1990, when the Fujimori government took office, his intelligence chief, Vladimiro Montesinos, sought to put GEIN under the control of his military intelligence unit, the National Intelligence Service (SIN). SIN constantly prodded GEIN for more "results," more quickly, but GEIN resisted, maintaining its previous leadership and strategies. However, Montesinos did help to increase resources for GEIN from the U.S. Central Intelligence Agency (CIA). By 1991, the CIA was providing GEIN with cash, sophisticated cameras, video recorders, listening devices, and training in surveillance in disguise (e.g., how agents could pretend to be sanitation workers when they examined the trash at possible Guzmán hideouts).[70]

GEIN's second breakthrough was the discovery of a safe house in another wealthy Lima suburb in January 1991. Although the squad again missed Guzmán, it found videotapes showing him inebriated and dancing to Greek music with other Senderista leaders. These videotapes, played and replayed on Peruvian television, tarnished Guzmán's image.

---

[70]Charles Lane, "'Superman' Meets Shining Path: Story of a CIA Success," *Washington Post*, December 7, 2000, A29; and Colonel Benedicto Jiménez, "El contacto era directo con la CIA," *La República*, June 23, 2000, 11.

Eighteen months later, GEIN arrested Guzmán in the house of a Senderista ballet teacher. The neighborhood of the house, and probably the Senderista sympathies of the ballet teacher, had been identified to GEIN by an arrestee, the Senderista logistics chief Luis Arana Franco, who was apparently persuaded to inform under the recently introduced repentance (plea-bargaining) law.[71] GEIN began to observe the safe house; when Jiménez spotted Winston Light cigarettes—Guzmán's brand—in the rubbish bin, he pounced. Surprisingly, Guzmán did not have a significant security force and did not resist.

Guzmán's capture yielded major tangible and intangible benefits. First, at the safe house, GEIN found information on computerized files and diskettes that facilitated many other captures. Within a few weeks, twelve of nineteen Central Committee members had been rounded up. Within six months, hundreds of midranking militants throughout the country had been arrested. By 1993, of Guzmán's inner circle, only the head of Sendero's military apparatus, Oscar Alberto Ramírez Durand ("Feliciano"), remained at large.

More intangibly, Guzmán's image had been badly damaged. Amid a very effective media campaign, he was revealed to be not a deity but a paunchy, middle-aged man with a ragged beard and thick glasses. He was shown on television dressed in a cartoonish striped prison suit and placed in a cage, ranting and raving—looking silly to millions of viewers. There was no indication of the intelligence that almost everyone had attributed to him.

In the year after Guzmán's capture, he continued to be manipulated by the Fujimori government to its advantage.[72] Immediately upon his capture, Guzmán prevailed on his militants to continue the revolutionary struggle; however, after several months of discussions with Peruvian intelligence chief Montesinos, Guzmán called for a "peace agreement" between Sendero and the Fujimori government. To this end, in October 1993, Guzmán addressed two letters to the government; in the second of these, he even praised the government for its counterinsurgency successes. Though Guzmán was able to persuade imprisoned Senderista leaders to follow his new policy, the abrupt and dramatic policy shift was, not surprisingly, disconcerting to his followers. Moreover, it appeared that he was doing the government's bidding to improve his personal living conditions; he was

[71]*Andean Newsletter*, no. 91 (June 27, 1994): 5. Details are not available.

[72]For a comprehensive discussion, see Comisión de la Verdad y Reconciliación, *Hatun Willakuy*, 178–89.

no longer held in solitary confinement but enjoyed conjugal visits with his lover, Elena Iparaguirre. At this time, "Feliciano" and his band repudiated Guzmán and renamed their group Sendero Rojo (Red Path).

Other changes were helpful to Sendero's decimation as well. The most important change in Peru's countryside was the establishment of peasant self-defense patrols against Sendero.[73] Although Sendero was at its apex in Lima in 1992, *rondas campesinas* were operating in considerable swathes of Peru's countryside after 1989. At that time, more peasant groups were turning against Sendero, and soldiers were positioned to win peasants' hearts and minds.

This shift against Sendero went in tandem with political learning by the military and more legitimate and effective state policies in the country-side. In the early 1980s, when the Belaúnde government dispatched the mil-itary to the southern highlands, the campaign was counterproductive. Be-cause the security forces were unfamiliar with the territory and with the Quechua language, they could not identify and locate Senderistas; scared and frustrated, they abused peasants indiscriminately. The year 1984 was the bloodiest of the war: Approximately 5,000 people, most of whom were southern highlands peasants of indigenous origin, were killed by the secu-rity forces; this figure was more than 20 percent of the total number killed by security forces during the entire war.[74] The soldiers' brutality enraged Peruvians and, in many regions, increased support for Sendero.[75]

After his inauguration in 1985, President García immediately took a different approach. He dismissed three of the military's highest-ranking officers on human rights grounds and brought legal charges against nu-merous other security force personnel; the government demanded that sol-diers respect human rights, and the military's human rights performance improved.[76] Also, the government initiated various economic development policies for the southern highlands, such as low interest rates on Agrarian

[73]See especially Carlos Iván Degregori, José Coronel, Ponciano Del Pino, and Orin Starn, *Las rondas campesinas y la derrota de Sendero Luminoso* (Lima: Instituto de Es-tudios Peruanos, 1996); and Carlos Tapia, *Autodefensa armada del campesinado* (Lima: CEDEP, 1995).

[74]Comisión de la Verdad y Reconciliación, *Hatun Willakuy*, graphs between pp. 96 and 97. Figures in the report are for cases reported to the commission, but the commis-sion extrapolated that the actual number of cases was 2.9 times the number of reported cases.

[75]Ronald H. Berg, "Peasant Responses to Shining Path in Andahuaylas," in *Shining Path of Peru*, ed. Palmer, 116.

[76]Comisión de la Verdad y Reconciliación, *Hatun Willakuy*, 38.

Bank loans and new road and irrigation projects. However, these new policies proved problematical. Because military officers were infuriated by the human rights initiative, they refused to send soldiers out of the barracks. Without protection, development officials were attacked by Sendero, and most officials abandoned their projects.

After 1988, a frustrated President García modified his strategy. He developed new initiatives, including the emphasis on police intelligence described above, and the establishment of *rondas campesinas*. At first, concerns about the establishment of *rondas* were intense. Military officers feared that peasants would use their weapons for rather than against Sendero; leftist political leaders feared that peasant communities would be subordinated to military authority. Analysts on all sides of the political spectrum worried that the *ronderos* would be targeted by Sendero and killed. However, the García government argued that peasants had a right to defend themselves in what was first and foremost a war against them.

Ultimately, the *rondas* proved effective. By the late 1980s, peasants in many parts of Peru were turning against Sendero. When Sendero members first entered villages, they attacked authorities and traders whom the peasants considered egregiously exploitative; over time, however, Sendero sought to impose its rigid ideology and authoritarian organization, and it also targeted peasants who did not comply.[77] At the same time, security forces were trying to work with peasants, and they were less abusive. Under Fujimori, *rondas* were promoted even more vigorously. Peasants were given rifles in addition to shotguns. Soldiers distributed food and medicine and undertook civic action projects. As of mid-1993, there were more than 4,000 *rondas* with approximately 300,000 members, to whom roughly 10,000 rifles had been distributed.[78]

Changes in Peru's antiterrorist legislation were also important to the decimation of Sendero. In the 1980s, it was very difficult for Peru's prosecutors and judges to convict and imprison Senderistas. Senderistas guarded their identities carefully, and prosecutors could not secure key evidence. Also, Senderistas often delegated the execution of terrorist attacks to new or forced recruits or even to unsuspecting children, but Peru's antiterrorist law

[77]Among the many sources, see Billie Jean Isbell, "Shining Path and Peasant Responses in Rural Ayacucho," in *Shining Path of Peru*, ed. Palmer, 71–79; and Raymond Bonner, "Peru's War," *New Yorker*, January 4, 1988, 44–45.

[78]Carlos Iván Degregori, "Shining Path and Counterinsurgency Strategy since the Arrest of Abimael Guzmán," in *Peru in Crisis: Dictatorship or Democracy?* ed. Joseph S. Tulchin and Gary Bland (Boulder, Colo.: Lynne Rienner, 1994), 89.

had no provision for the conviction of the "intellectual authors" of terrorism. Further, Sendero bribed, intimidated, and even assassinated judges. For these reasons, of 4,897 terrorism cases tried between 1981 and 1991, 56 percent were dropped due to a lack of evidence; 19 percent resulted in verdicts of not guilty, and only 11 percent yielded convictions.[79] Sentences were often relatively short, and parole was available. Tragically, the rarity of conviction and long imprisonment was one of the reasons behind the security forces' human rights violations; officers feared that released Senderistas would seek revenge, and so they opted to kill.

Although the García government backed various new antiterrorist provisions, they were not implemented.[80] The government provided for the establishment of special civilian tribunals for terrorist cases, offering greater protection for judges. The government also initiated a repentance law, whereby a repentant terrorist would receive clemency in return for information. However, the military and the judiciary were wary of these changes and blocked them. During the 1990 presidential campaign, additional proposals were advanced but subsequently dropped.

Only after the April 1992 *autogolpe* did the Fujimori government introduce new antiterrorist legislation.[81] At that time, without the need for congressional approval, the government decreed legislation that did not meet international democratic standards. Essentially, in cases of terrorism, guilt was presumed and due process denied. Defense rights were drastically reduced. For example, defense lawyers were not allowed to hear the prosecution's evidence or to cross-examine prosecution witnesses; often, they were notified of the time of a trial only a few hours before it began. Also, the powers of the antiterrorist police to investigate and charge suspects were greatly broadened. Judges were fully protected; they were hooded, and

[79]*Caretas,* February 10, 1992, 37. Almost another 1,000 terrorist suspects were released without trial as a result of lack of evidence. See also Richard Clutterbuck, "Peru: Cocaine, Terrorism, and Corruption," *International Relations* 12 (August 1995): 87, and Charles D. Kenney, *Fujimori's Coup and the Breakdown of Democracy in Latin America* (Notre Dame, Ind.: University of Notre Dame Press, 2004), 197–98.

[80]Americas Watch, *Una guerra desesperada: Los derechos humanos en el Perú después de una década de democracia y violencia* (Lima: Comisión Andina de Juristas, 1990); and Alan Riding, "Peru Offers Laws to Combat Terror," *New York Times,* August 21, 1988, 9.

[81]Among the excellent analyses, see Coletta Youngers, *After the Autogolpe: Human Rights in Peru and the U.S. Response* (Washington, D.C.: Washington Office on Latin America, 1994); and Comisión Internacional de Juristas, *Informe* (Lima: Instituto de Defensa Legal, 1994).

trials were secret. Minimum prison sentences of not less than twenty years were mandated.

Further, a "repentance," or plea-bargain, law was enacted to entice Senderistas to surrender. (As noted above, this law was helpful in persuading Luis Arana Franco to betray his Senderista comrades.) By June 1994, more than 4,100 former Senderistas had "repented."[82] However, sadly, to take advantage of the repentance law, terrorists and terrorist suspects often denounced innocent persons who were then convicted. Between April 1992 and late 1993, between 4,500 and 5,000 persons were imprisoned for crimes of terrorism; at least 30 percent were estimated to be innocent.[83] Human rights organizations such as the Instituto de Defensa Legal and Peru's ombudsman office, the Defensoría del Pueblo, calculated that between late 1992 and 2000, 22,000 people were unjustly detained.[84]

Most draconian of all was the decree that the crime of "treason against the mother country" (*traición a la patria*) be tried in military courts. "Treason" was not precisely defined; distributing Shining Path propaganda could be classified as treason. The decision about whether a suspect would be charged with treason or the lesser crime of terrorism was made by the antiterrorist police, not by the courts. Of the suspects charged with treason and tried in military courts, an overwhelming 97 percent were convicted.[85]

The strategic defeat of Sendero was consolidated in the mid-1990s amid two other positive trends. First, Peru enjoyed a period of sustained economic growth, and Peruvians' need was less severe. During the five-year period 1993–97, GDP growth averaged above 7 percent, higher than any other Latin American nation save Chile.[86] The principal engine behind the growth was the privatization of state-owned enterprises and, concomitantly, a surge in foreign investment. Between 1990 and 1998, more than 180 state holdings—spanning from telecommunications to banking, tourism, mining,

---

[82]"Key 'Red Sendero' Leader Captured," *Latin America Weekly Report,* June 9, 1994, 244.

[83]These figures were collected by Ernesto de la Jara of the Instituto de Defensa Legal; they are reported in Coletta Youngers, *Violencia política y sociedad civil en el Perú* (Lima: Instituto de Estudios Peruanos, 2003), 335–36.

[84]Youngers, *Violencia política y sociedad civil,* 336.

[85]Youngers, "After the Autogolpe," 18.

[86]Economic Commission for Latin America and the Caribbean, *Preliminary Overview of the Economies of Latin America and the Caribbean 1998* (Santiago: United Nations, 1998), 83.

transport, and cement—were privatized, for a total sale value of about $6.6 billion.[87] This handsome sum went into the Fujimori government's coffers.

Although some of these revenues went directly into officials' bank accounts, unprecedented amounts were allocated to social programs that benefited Peru's needy. Government expenditures on social programs—a mere $100 million in 1991 and 1992—doubled in 1993 and more than quadrupled in 1995.[88] From only 2.1 percent of GDP in 1990, social expenditures tripled to 5.9 percent in 1995.[89] By the end of 1993 alone, the Fondo Nacional de Compensación y Desarrollo Social (National Compensation and Social Development Fund, or FONCODES) had initiated 10,000 small-scale projects, including especially roads, schools, and health facilities.[90] In part as a result of previous weak support for Fujimori in Peru's disadvantaged rural highlands (also, of course, Sendero's traditional base) and a desire to secure votes there in the 1995 election, the government targeted expenditures to these regions in particular.[91]

Further, international aid to the Fujimori government facilitated its support for poor people. The international development banks were supportive of FONCODES' programs. Whereas the United States was at best cool to the García government, as of 1993 it warmed to Fujimori, and U.S. economic aid was increasing.[92] Of particular importance to Peru's poor people was a jump in U.S. food aid (P.L. 480, or Food for Peace). Whereas in 1989 U.S. food aid was reaching less than 5 percent of Peru's population, it was reaching an estimated 15 percent by 1993.[93]

---

[87]Commission for the Promotion of Private Investment, *Peru: A Country on the Move* (Lima: Commission for the Promotion of Private Investment, 1999), 31.

[88]Kenneth M. Roberts, "Neoliberalism and the Transformation of Populism in Latin America: The Peruvian Case," *World Politics* 48 (October 1995): 103.

[89]John Sheahan, *Searching for a Better Society: The Peruvian Economy from 1950* (University Park: Pennsylvania State University Press, 1999), 125.

[90]Roberts, "Neoliberalism," 103–4. See also Susan C. Stokes, "Economic Reform and Public Opinion in Fujimori's Peru," in *Public Support for Market Reforms in New Democracies*, ed. Susan C. Stokes (New York: Cambridge University Press, 2001), 173.

[91]Carol Graham and Cheikh Kane, "Opportunistic Government or Sustaining Reform? Electoral Trends and Public Expenditure Patterns in Peru, 1990–1995," *Latin American Research Review* 33, no.1: 67–104.

[92]McClintock and Vallas, *United States and Peru*, 6.

[93]U.S. Department of State, "Economic Support for Peru," 1991 memorandum, Washington, D.C., 3.

A second positive trend was the decline in the cocaine trade. The U.S. and Peruvian governments reported that, whereas the number of hectares cultivated in coca hit a record high of 129,100 in 1992, the figure dropped to about 109,000 in 1993–94, and plummeted precipitously thereafter to a low of 34,100 in 2000.[94] Although critics pointed out that these figures exaggerated the extent of success because the amount of coca produced on one hectare was increasing and because U.S. satellite imagery was flawed, no one disputed that the trend was toward a decline. In short, thousands of peasants were shifting to other crops, and the revenue that Sendero had secured from the cocaine trade plummeted.

The reasons for the decline in coca production were various.[95] U.S. and Peruvian officials emphasized the importance of what was called "air bridge denial," or, more recently, "shoot-down." In this aerial interdiction program, CIA contractors in surveillance aircraft provided intelligence on suspicious planes to the Peruvian air force, which then shot down the planes. Although preliminary steps toward air bridge denial were taken as early as 1991, the program was not officially launched until early 1995. The program was effective because at the time Peruvian growers were selling most of their coca to Colombian traffickers flying small planes across the relatively small, remote stretch of land between Colombia and Peru's coca-growing valleys. In 1995, a record 22 aircraft were seized; between 1994 and 1997, the fee demanded by pilots quintupled and the number of flights fell precipitously. Without buyers for growers' coca, at the end of 1995 the price of a kilogram of coca leaf was a scant $0.60, less than one quarter the price at the beginning of the year and no longer sufficient to cover the cost of production.

From the perspective of the Peruvian government, air bridge denial was a helpful policy, because antidrug personnel were confronting a small number of Colombian traffickers rather than a large number of Peruvian peasants. However, the policy was also risky, because its legal foundation was shaky at best and because the possibility of a tragic accident loomed. On April 21, 2001, this accident happened. A U.S. missionaries' plane was shot down, and a missionary and her daughter were killed. Immediately, the air bridge denial policy ended.

[94]Bureau of International Narcotics and Law Enforcement Affairs, *International Narcotics Control Strategy Report 2002* (Washington, D.C.: U.S. Department of State, 2002).
[95]Sources for the figures in this paragraph are available in McClintock and Vallas, *United States and Peru*, 122–27.

Although air bridge denial was important to the decline in coca production in Peru, it was far from the only factor.[96] Probably, the program was
one of several reasons behind Colombian traffickers' decisions to shift coca
production to Colombia. In the early 1990s, Colombia's large trafficking
cartels were being dismantled, and new trafficking groups were emerging;
these traffickers preferred to secure their raw material in Colombia. These
traffickers' decisions were probably affected not only by air bridge denial
but also by cost issues and fears about a fungus (*Fusarium oxysporum*),
which had severely damaged about 30 percent of coca plants in the Upper
Huallaga Valley at the start of the 1990s. In any case, and fortunately for the
Fujimori government, the decline was not a result of eradication or fumi-
gation programs; accordingly, coca growers were not directly confronted by
antidrug personnel and they did not mount protests, which could have been
exploited by Sendero.

The Potential for a Resurgence of Shining Path

As of 2004, the possibility that Sendero would again pose a serious threat
to the Peruvian state appeared remote. The U.S. Department of State estimated that in 2003, Sendero was responsible for the deaths of eight persons
(five police, two *ronderos*, and one community leader)—a smaller number
than in 1980 or 2000.[97] The conjunction of need, creed, and organizational
finance that empowered Shining Path in the late 1980s and early 1990s
was absent. Guzmán and his lieutenants remained imprisoned, their ideological appeal seriously compromised. Armed Senderistas numbered fewer
than 500 and operated almost exclusively in Peru's coca-producing areas;
lacking the large revenues of the late 1980s and early 1990s, they were not
recruiting very successfully. Analysts were most concerned that unarmed
Senderistas were again proselytizing and protesting at universities in Lima
and the southern highlands, but their long-term objectives were unknown.

[96]McClintock and Vallas, *United States and Peru*, 125–27. Scholars are continu-
ing to debate the weight of these various factors in the decline. For example, Obando,
"La política norteamericana hacia el Perú," emphasizes air bridge denial, whereas
Rojas, "Sendero y el MRTA," does not.

[97]U.S. Department of State, *Country Reports on Human Rights Practices: 2003*
(Washington, D.C.: Bureau of Democracy, Human Rights, and Labor, 2004), 3. For figures for 1980 and 2000, see Comisión de la Verdad y Reconciliación, *Hatun Willakuy*,
graph between pp. 96 and 97.

However, though Sendero itself did not appear on the verge of a dramatic resurgence, Peruvians were sorely disappointed by the Toledo government; it was possible that Sendero would evolve in new directions, blend with other protest groups, and ultimately provoke greater political violence in Peru.

By 2004, Shining Path's creed, previously an impassioned call to arms on behalf of Peru's poor, appeared wishy-washy. In 2000, Guzmán formulated a new objective: "a political solution to the problems derived from the war."[98] Advancing this new objective, he stated that several of his previous key ideological arguments about global revolutionary trends were incorrect—corrections that could hardly have been compelling to possible new Sendero recruits. Not surprisingly, Guzmán was unable to engage the government in discussions about what a "political solution" might be.

The primary focus of Guzmán and the other imprisoned Shining Path leaders was on legal issues related to their own incarceration. In 2003, the Fujimori government's antiterrorist legislation, which as noted above violated due-process standards, was ruled unconstitutional by Peru's Constitutional Tribunal; nearly all inmates jailed on terrorism charges (about 2,000 at the time) were eligible for new trials. Subsequently, Guzmán was planning his defense; apparently, he was to argue that he was only the ideological inspiration for Sendero and never participated in attacks.[99] Guzmán and his lieutenants were engaged in other legal maneuvers as well. In August and September 2004, Shining Path filed legal petitions for more than 200 inmates, demanding release because they had been imprisoned for years without a fixed sentence.[100]

Further, the Senderistas were seeking relaxed jail conditions; in mid-2004, Guzmán went on a hunger strike to protest glass interview booths that had been installed for meetings with relatives and lawyers. Despite concerns that Guzmán was trying to direct Sendero strategy from his cell and was exploiting these meetings for strategic purposes, the Senderista leader prevailed.

As of 2004, two armed Shining Path bands continued to operate in Peru. Both were based in the country's coca-growing areas and, in most analysts' views, both seemed motivated primarily by greed, with limited capacity to

[98]Comisión de la Verdad y Reconiliación, *Hatun Willakuy*, 189.
[99]ConsultAndes, S.A., *Monthly Security Indicators*, April 2003, 1.
[100]ConsultAndes, S.A., *Peru Key Indicators*, September 19–26, 2004, 10–11.

secure popular support.[101] However, the two bands' leaders and strategies were distinct.

One armed Senderista faction was led by "Artemio" and professed loyalty to Guzmán, but it did not appear to coordinate with the imprisoned Senderista leadership. Numbering approximately 300 members, this group operated primarily in the Upper Huallaga Valley.[102] Because the valley had become much less important to Peru's cocaine trade than in the early 1990s, the resources available to the "Artemio" band were relatively limited; probably in part for this reason, its capacity to gain popular support was also limited. Heeding Guzmán's call for a "political solution" to Peru's conflict, this faction was not actively launching violent attacks in 2000–2003. Apparently, however, frustrated that the Peruvian government led by President Alejandro Toledo was not answering its requests for a negotiation of the "political solution," in June 2004 the "Artemio" faction attacked a police patrol in the town of Aguaytía.

The second armed Sendero faction, known as Proseguir (In Pursuit), was led by "Alipio" and was not loyal to Guzmán. "Alipio" had assumed the band's leadership after the arrest of Sendero's second-in-command, "Feliciano," in 1999. Numbering 100 to 150 insurgents, Proseguir operated in the Apurímac and Ene River Valley (far south of the Upper Huallaga Valley, to the east of Ayacucho).[103] Although not circumscribed by Guzmán's leadership, "Alipio" had only a third-grade education, and his capacity to build an appealing ideology seemed minimal.[104] Proseguir's resources were derived to some degree from the cocaine trade, and also from extortion against illegal logging. Apparently, possibly with the encouragement of the Colombian guerrilla group known as the Fuerzas Armadas Revolucionarias de Colombia (Revolutionary Armed Forces of Colombia, or FARC), Proseguir

[101]Ricardo Soberón Garrido, "Peru and Coca in the Amazon Region and War over Illegal Natural Resources: From Internal Conflict to Criminality and Violence," unpublished manuscript prepared for the Woodrow Wilson International Center for Scholars, Washington, 2002, 6. Also, with respect to the limited popular support for the faction led by "Artemio," see Luis Pariona Arana, "Cocaleros, narcotráfico y Sendero Luminoso en el Alto Huallaga," *Ideele*, no. 163 (May 2004): 36–40.

[102]On this faction, see Pariona Arana, "Cocaleros, narcotráfico y Sendero Luminoso," 39. Estimates of the number of members are from author's interview with former interior minister Fernando Rospigliosi, in Lima, July 8, 2004, and from "Actuaremos de manera drástic y rápida con SL," *Peru 21*, April 18, 2004, 9.

[103]On this faction, see Rojas, "Sendero y el MRTA," 28.

[104]Eduardo Toche and Martín Paredes (interviewing Sendero expert Carlos Tapia), "Los chinos son más chinos que comunistas," *QueHacer* 148 (May–June 2004), 44.

was responsible for the June 2003 armed kidnapping of 71 workers for the Techint company, who were laying the pipeline for the huge Camisea gas project.[105]

Although both armed groups were small, the government was increasingly worried that they were exploiting coca farmers' anger at its antinarcotics policies. As mentioned above, in 2001 the U.S. government terminated the air bridge denial program; because of the end of this program and the development of new routes for coca transport, the price of coca increased. Indeed, between 1999 and 2002, the price quadrupled—just as the price of coffee and other licit alternative crops was declining—and farmers wanted to grow coca again.[106] The Toledo government was committed to partnership with the United States in the "war on drugs," and the number of hectares in coca cultivation apparently declined during the first two years of his government. According to U.S. figures, the number of hectares in coca cultivation decreased about 15 percent from 2002 to 2003; the 31,350 hectares estimated to be cultivated in coca in 2003 was slightly below the figures for 2000 and 2001.[107] However, many analysts believed that the yield of coca per hectare was increasing, and also that coca growers were hiding their crops more effectively, so that the official data on hectares cultivated in coca were underestimates.[108]

Although the Toledo government repeatedly asked the George W. Bush administration to reinstate the shoot-down program, its requests were denied, and the Toledo government returned to the traditional policy of forced eradication of the coca. In this program, antinarcotics agents confront coca growers directly, often sparking unrest and violence. In April 2003, a federation of 50,000 Peruvian coca growers began major protests.[109] Subsequently, to the coca growers' anger, the group's leader, Nelson Palomino, was imprisoned. In 2004, Senderistas were increasingly entering

[105]Interview with Enrique Obando, July 12, 2004.

[106]James Rudolph and Miguel Ordinola, "The Drug War in Peru: Learning from Failure?" paper presented at the Latin American Studies Association meeting, Las Vegas, 2004, 20. See also McClintock and Vallas, *United States and Peru*, 166–67.

[107]U.S. Department of State, *International Narcotics Control Strategy Report* (Washington, D.C.: Bureau for International Narcotics Control and Law Enforcement Affairs, 2003 and 2004).

[108]See, e.g., "Perú disminuye un 5% superficie de cultivo de coca," *El Comercio*, June 18, 2004.

[109]Hugo Cabieses, "Peru's Cocaleros on the March," *NACLA Report on the Americas* (July–August 2004), 12.

coca-growing areas and pledging to defend coca growers against anti-narcotics agents.[110]

Despite the apparently positive trends in coca cultivation and drug-fueled insurgency in Peru, concerns remained about potential new drug cultivation and new drug-trafficking groups. Especially in Peru's remote northern jungle areas, the growth of poppies (from which heroin is made) was spreading. Also, coca cultivation was apparently increasing along the Napo River on Peru's border with Colombia, possibly but not conclusively under the direction of Colombia's FARC.[111] (Apparently, FARC was not building ties to Sendero but instead to a more traditional Maoist group, the Communist Party of Peru, Patria Roja, for goals that were not entirely clear.[112])

Of greater concern to many political observers than the armed Sendero bands was the resurgence of activity by unarmed Sendero militants.[113] By one estimate, in 2004 about 600 imprisoned Senderistas were seeking to direct the reconstruction of the organization from their cells, while another 1,200 militants were working at the grassroots, primarily proselytizing at universities.[114] Probably, some of these militants were among the 350-odd Senderistas convicted of terrorism circa 1990, who completed their ten- or fifteen-year sentences in 2002–4 and were freed.[115] Senderista "study circles," flyer distribution, and other ideological initiatives were reported at universities in Lima, Huancayo, Puno, Huacho, Huánuco, and Callao. Also, in the poorer regions of Peru, where Sendero was traditionally strong—particularly Ayacucho—cadres were apparently seeking new recruits by participating in public works projects, apologizing for their past violence, and promising to help peasants achieve a better life.

Senderistas likely were seeking to reactivate their traditional bases in Peru's national teachers' union, the Sindicato Único de Trabajadores de la Educación Peruana (Union of Education Workers of Peru, or SUTEP), which embraced nearly 300,000 teachers and has long been at the forefront

[110]See, e.g., "New 'Ultimatum' from Sendero Leader," *Latin American Weekly Report*, no. 16 (April 27, 2004): 5; and Pariona Arana, "Cocaleros, narcotráfico y Sendero Luminoso," 38.

[111]ConsultAndes, *Monthly Security Indicators*, July 2004, 4.

[112]ConsultAndes, *Monthly Security Indicators*, July 2004, 4.

[113]See, e.g., the assessments by Carlos Iván Degregori, "Ayacucho: Un viejo círculo vicioso," *Perú 21*, July 5, 2004, 4; and Carlos Tapia, "Sendero Luminoso quiere captar estudiantes e intelectuales," *La República*, September 28, 2004, 1.

[114]This estimate by Sendero expert Carlos Tapia is reported in *Latin American Weekly Report*, October 5, 2004, 7.

[115]*La República*, May 16, 2004, 14.

of popular protest in Peru. Traditionally, SUTEP has been affiliated with the Communist Party of Peru—Patria Roja (Red Fatherland, a Maoist offshoot of the Communist Party, which opposed Guzmán and his allies in Ayacucho in the 1970s and which, after 1980, participated with some success in Peru's electoral politics). However, in Junín and Ayacucho, a breakaway faction of SUTEP was led by Robert Huaynalaya, who was alleged to be a member of the Communist Party of Peru—Pukallacta, a Maoist party that had been sympathetic to Sendero in the 1980s.[116]

In mid-2004, a rumor that the government was about to abolish free education sparked a teachers' strike in Ayacucho, which escalated into a violent rampage. Government offices were set ablaze and stores and banks vandalized; at the attorney general's office, at least 10,000 court files—mostly on drug trafficking and terrorism cases—were destroyed. Although the government charged that Shining Path infiltrators of SUTEP were responsible, criminal thugs and drug traffickers also appeared complicit—probably to a much greater degree.[117]

Although it was clear that unarmed Senderistas were more active than in previous years, their objectives and even their ideology were unclear. Did they continue to believe in the goal of a violent takeover of the state, or did they now prefer nonviolent strategies of social change? Were they trying to coordinate with Guzmán and were they vigorously pursuing his release, or were they hoping to renew the movement's leadership? These questions were intensely debated by Peruvian experts on insurgency.[118]

Further, in 2004, other factors that had given rise to and sustained Sendero were absent. First, need was not intensifying. Although poverty and unemployment remained severe, they were not dramatically worsening; on the contrary, GDP grew by more than 4 percent annually between 2002 and 2004, and real wages were above the levels of the late 1990s.[119] Also important, whereas in the early 1980s President Belaúnde had been nonchalant about the Sendero threat and then had dispatched soldiers to Ayacucho without significant concern about the abuses that they might perpetrate, the Toledo government appeared to be acting responsibly. For example, police were arresting considerable numbers of Senderista suspects,

[116]ConsultAndes, *Monthly Security Indicators*, July 2004, 2.

[117]Anonymous, "Ayacucho: Sombras nada más?" *Ideele*, no. 164 (July 2004): 85–88.

[118]*Latin America Weekly Report*, October 5, 2004, 8.

[119]*CEPAL news* 24, no. 8 (August 2004): 2; and CEPAL, *Situación y perspectivas: estudio económico de América Latina y el Caribe, 2002–2003*, 45; available at http://www.eclac.org.

and, in coca-growing regions of Peru, fifty-odd counterinsurgency bases were operating—but charges of human rights abuse were scant.[120] Also in contrast to the early 1980s, Lima's media were very concerned about the threat and regularly pressed the government about it.[121]

Although, accordingly, a dramatic resurgence of Shining Path appeared unlikely, Peruvians—like their counterparts in most of the region—were in a sour mood. In 2004, dissatisfaction with the Toledo government was pervasive and protest was rampant. Forced coca eradication was provoking particularly intense confrontations. Though Shining Path itself was not likely to pose a serious threat, it could adapt, mutate, and join with other violent groups, and this new amalgam could prove dangerous.

Conclusion

Sendero Luminoso would not have mounted as severe a threat to Peru's state as it did in the late 1980s and early 1990s if it had not secured funds from the cocaine trade. However, at no time did the control of resources become an objective in itself for Sendero. Rather, its militants' primary goal, shaped by the profound economic crisis in Peru at the time, was, in their words, "to struggle for the poor." The Marxist ideology of Sendero resonated for a surprisingly large sector of Peruvians, many of whom were teachers or students at universities, grappling with the meaning of life in the context of the Peru of the late twentieth century.

Moreover, despite the movement's continuing large revenues from the cocaine trade, it was strategically defeated in 1992–93. Organizational finance abetted Sendero, but it did not make it or break it. After 1992–93, the nexus of need, creed, and organizational finance that had propelled the movement fell apart, and it appeared unlikely to be reestablished.

---

[120]On recent arrests, see the *Latin American Regional Report: Andean Group*, no. 10 (October 5, 2004): 8; on the bases, see Rojas, "Sendero y el MRTA," 28.

[121]Fernando Rospigliosi, "Terrorismo y corrupción?" *QueHacer*, no. 143 (July–August 2003), 31.

4

The Criminalization of the RUF Insurgency in Sierra Leone

Jimmy D. Kandeh

The armed insurgency by the Revolutionary United Front (RUF) in Sierra Leone has been variously portrayed in academic and policy circles as marking the dawn of a "new barbarism" (Kaplan), as a resource or diamond war (Collier), as the outcome of a patrimonial crisis (Richards and Reno), as an urban struggle displaced in the countryside (Mkandawire) and as a conflict rooted in predatory accumulation (Kandeh), youth crisis (Abdullah), and state failures (Opala).[1] In none of these accounts is the role of creed or

Jimmy Kandeh is associate professor of political science at the University of Richmond. He is the author of numerous scholarly works on politics and society in West Africa, including *Coups from Below: Armed Subalterns and State Power in West Africa* (Palgrave Macmillan, 2004). His current research focuses on a comparative study of state failure in Liberia and Sierra Leone.

[1]The references here are to Richard Kaplan, "The Coming Anarchy," *Atlantic Monthly*, February 1994; Paul Collier, "Doing Well Out of War," in *Greed and Grievance: Economic Agendas in Civil Wars*, ed. Mats Berdal and David Malone (Boulder,

youthful populism accorded any explanatory relevance. But the rusticated university students whose original idea it was to take up arms against an oppressive and corrupt one-party government were motivated not by greed but by a combination of need and creed. What started as a rebellion set in motion by grievance and a smattering of populist fancy was later hijacked by criminal and opportunistic elements (domestic and external, elite and lumpen) united by a common pillage agenda. Greed as motivation prolonged the armed conflict in Sierra Leone, but it was not critical to its inception.

The interplay of resource-based greed and need-based grievances highlights some of the limitations of greed-centric and economic explanations of the Sierra Leone conflict. Government greed as the instigating cause of armed conflict must be distinguished from rebels' greed as the motivating factor for continuing the rebellion. Greed as cause refers to the societal impact of predatory rule, whereas greed as motive describes the activities of those who wield arms to loot rather than to right social wrongs or pursue some ideological agenda. Both senses of greed, as grievance-inducing abuse of power and as motive for rebellion, are relevant to understanding the origins and character of the RUF rebellion in Sierra Leone.

Recognizing that diamonds fueled rather than caused the war in Sierra Leone is not to discount or trivialize the centrality of resources in this conflict—indeed, the trajectory of the struggle between successive governments and the RUF was partly but not uniquely shaped by competition over access to diamonds and other resources. The explanatory significance of diamonds, however, ultimately derives from their mismanagement by incumbent political elites. Predatory accumulation by public officials impoverished society, lumpenized the country's youth, devalued education,

Colo.: Lynne Rienner, 2000); Paul Richards, *Fighting for the Rain Forest. War, Youth and Resources in Sierra Leone* (London: Heinemann, 1996); William Reno, *Corruption and Politics in Sierra Leone* (Cambridge: Cambridge University Press, 1995); Thandika Mkandawire, "The Terrible Toll of Post-Colonial Rebel Movements in Africa: Towards an Explanation of the Violence against the Peasantry," *Journal of Modern African Studies* 40, no. 2 (2002); Jimmy Kandeh, "Ransoming the State: Elite Origins of Subaltern Terror in Sierra Leone," *Review of African Political Economy*, no. 81 (1999); Ibrahim Abdullah, "Bush Path to Destruction: The Origin and Character of the Revolutionary United Front (RUF/SL)," *Africa Development* 22, nos. 3–4 (1997) and; Joseph Opala, "Sierra Leone: The Politics of State Collapse," paper presented at Science Applications International Corporation conference on irregular warfare in Liberia and Sierra Leone, Denver, July 30–August 1, 1998.

incapacitated the state, and made Sierra Leone susceptible to armed rebellion. Rather than diamonds, the root cause of Sierra Leone's armed conflict can be traced to the unbridled rapacity of its political class. Elite greed created the grievances that made the RUF insurrection possible and prolonged the insurgency once it got under way.

The criminalization of the RUF insurgency was due to several factors, most notably elite greed and opportunism, the elimination of former university students from the organization, the *sobelization* (the transformation of armed regulars into brigands) of the national army, and the involvement of external patrons and rogue businessmen. Elements of the political class that lost power in 1992 later supported the rebellion out of desperation and rank opportunism, even though it was first launched against them. As President Ahmad Tejan Kabba noted after his reinstatement in 1998, "greed and treachery were the underlying causes" of Sierra Leone's tragedy" and those who collaborated with the RUF "were the very people who presided over this system of corruption and incompetence."[2] It was the greed of political incumbents that also transformed the national army into a rogue outfit dominated by *sobels* (soldiers moonlighting as rebels). The complicity of armed regulars and their officers contributed to the RUF's criminalization. Also, the elimination in 1992 of the last remaining former students in the RUF paved the way for the ascendancy of Foday Sankoh and his retinue of criminal adventurists, whose ideas about the goals and strategies of the insurrection were radically different from the students who founded the movement. The involvement of foreign rogue leaders (Charles Taylor of Liberia and Blaise Compaoré of Burkina Faso) and clandestine foreign business agents also contributed to the transformation of the RUF insurgency into a criminal enterprise.

Even when a resurgent civil society contributed to a democratic renewal symbolized by Sierra Leone's 1996 transfer elections, political elites failed to alter the spoils logic that had characterized the exercise of political power for several decades. The failure of popularly elected President Kabba to tackle long-standing problems of corruption and insecurity contributed to a 1997 military coup, which had the blessing of the RUF leader Sankoh. Ultimately, domestic opposition, international condemnation and sanctions, and a Nigerian-led military offensive forced the junta to relinquish power in 1998, but the RUF continued in its effort to topple the government by force,

---

[2]Reuters, March 10, 1998.

betraying even an internationally brokered power-sharing arrangement that brought some of its leaders into the government.[3]

Periodizing the RUF's criminalization is problematic because the direct involvement of Charles Taylor suggests an element of criminal intent even at the inception of the insurgency. But leaving aside Taylor's role, which grew as the insurgency spread from the border with Liberia to engulf almost the entire country, it can be argued that the RUF began its descent into criminality after the ouster of the All People's Congress (APC) government in 1992. This event delegitimized the insurgency in areas (parts of the eastern and southern provinces) that had been initially supportive and "legitimized" it among sectors (APC politicians) that had been previously opposed to the insurgents.

Both the loss of support for the insurgency in the eastern and southern provinces and the collaboration of APC politicians in helping the RUF destabilize the country marked the beginning of the degeneration of the RUF as a credible insurgent movement. It was after 1992, for example, that the RUF, starved of recruits, began routinely abducting children to fill the ranks of its fighting forces. Targeting innocent civilians also became commonplace after 1992, making it increasingly difficult to distinguish means from ends in the conflict and obscuring the original basis of the insurrection. The more territory the RUF seized, the more brutal and criminal it became, especially from 1997 to 2001, when the insurgents held almost half the country, including the diamond fields of the eastern province.

To understand how the RUF insurgency was criminalized, it is necessary to first trace the origins of the movement from the campus politics of university students in the 1970s and 1980s. Student politics was rooted in deprivation caused by gnawing poverty, corruption, and a weakening state. Student protests against a corrupt and repressive political leadership in the 1970s and 1980s were met with repression. Rather than address student demands for democratization and an end to official corruption, the government jailed scores of student leaders and expelled them from the University of Sierra Leone. The student union governments of Fourah Bay College and Njala University College, at the time the two constituent colleges of the University of Sierra Leone, were also proscribed in an all-out effort to silence the political voice of students. The combination of mass deprivation—as articulated by students and to a lesser degree by workers—and

---

[3]See Jimmy D. Kandeh, "Elections without Rupture: Sierra Leone's Transfer Elections of 1996, *African Studies Review* 41, no. 2 (1998): 91–111.

state repression spawned the deep-seated grievance that later found expression in armed insurgency.

Student Vanguardism and the RUF

Chronic official malfeasance and political repression fomented grievances that provoked a few university students to initiate armed rebellion against the one-party dictatorship of the APC. Although this rebellion later degenerated into a criminal insurgency after the APC was ousted from power in a 1992 coup d'état, aggrandizing calculations were far from the minds of the students who originally plotted the RUF insurgency.

Confrontation between students and a corrupt and repressive APC government first came to a head in January 1977 when Fourah Bay College students staged a demonstration against the government during the larger university's annual commencement ceremonies. A visibly shaken and humiliated President Siaka Stevens, who was in attendance as chancellor of the university, was prevented from finishing his speech, which was drowned out by boisterous calls for his resignation. Less than fifteen hours later, security personnel and armed thugs of the APC (led by Kemoh Fadika) were dispatched to the Mount Aureol campus of the college with instructions to "teach" the students a lesson. The APC leadership's decision to unleash thugs and armed security units on university students incensed secondary school students, who promptly organized a mass demonstration in Freetown against the government and in solidarity with university students. Secondary, postsecondary, and primary school students replicated these demonstrations throughout the country. The labor movement briefly sided with the students, but its leadership was promptly co-opted and silenced by APC bosses. Sensing that it was losing control of a rapidly deteriorating political situation, the government declared a state of emergency, closed all schools and colleges, and detained scores of students.[4]

The 1977 countrywide student demonstrations marked the political coming of age for a generation of young Sierra Leoneans who were becoming increasingly radicalized by social injustice, localized deprivation, and political disenfranchisement. Political awareness among youths found expression in growing student demands for an end to corruption and dictatorship. The restive youths of this period were particularly influenced by the triumphant, irreverent, antisystem lyrics of reggae musicians like Bob

---

[4]The author was a participant observer of the events described.

Marley, Peter Tosh, Jimmy Cliff, Eric Donaldson, and a host of others. Songs with suggestive titles like "System Dread," "Police and Thieves," "Equal Rights and Justice," and "Tenement Yard" (to name a few) pervaded the airwaves, capturing the imagination of both student and lumpen segments of the youth population. The situational relevance of the lyrics of these songs, especially the generalized notion that peace is a function of social justice, helped shape the political outlook and activism of students during the late 1970s and early 1980s. Youths, particularly university students, came to see themselves as agents of political change and as the last bastion of societal opposition to a corrupt and oppressive APC government.

Government response to student political activism and social unrest was to impose a one-party system of government and outlaw student union governments. APC informants infiltrated college campuses, and student organizations (Gardeners, Auradicals, Future Shock) considered radical by college authorities were denied registration. The mass expulsion and suspension of students, including the entire student union executive, in 1985 was meant to disunite students and take away their political voice. These expulsions followed the unopposed election of Ali Kabba as president of Fourah Bay College's Student Union government in February 1985. Ali Kabba, who was instrumental in organizing a training program for potential insurgents in Libya, was well connected to Libyan authorities and was the leader of the Green Book study group on campus. His emergence as student leader sent shock waves through the political and university establishments, as the uncompromising rhetoric and actions of the new student union government threatened to undermine the authority of both university administrators and political leaders. He was later accused of misappropriating funds provided by the Libyan government, but this act alone does not delegitimize the grievances that propelled students to take up arms against the government.[5]

College administrators and political authorities regarded the threat posed by the new student union government to be serious enough that they resolved to shut down the university before the end of the Easter term. Students were instructed to turn in their keys, vacate the campus within twelve hours, and reapply for readmission to the university after signing an agreement renouncing the right to protest against conditions on campus and in the country at large. But the defiant students refused to hand over their keys

---

[5]For an account of Ali Kabba's role in initiating preparations for the military training of potential insurgents in Libya, see Abdullah, "Bush Path to Destruction."

and challenged the authorities to remove them from campus. The college authorities (Koso Thomas, Eldred Jones, and C. P. Foray) responded by calling on the government to send in the dreaded Special Security Division to take care of the situation. Within a few hours, the campus was brutally emptied of all students. Kabba and other student leaders were arrested and detained at the Pademba Road prison, and scores of students were either expelled or suspended from the university. Three university lecturers were relieved of their positions, and university student union governments were abolished.

The student expulsions of 1985 triggered the RUF rebellion. Without these expulsions it is doubtful whether there would have been a rebellion, because upon their release from prison, some of the expelled student leaders—denied any prospect of furthering their education locally—found their way to Libya via Ghana, where they commenced training in 1987 for what was to later become the RUF insurgency. Student grievances played into the hands of the Libyans, who were at the time pursuing a policy of destabilizing states in the region considered pro-West; included on the list of such states were Sierra Leone and Liberia, whose leaders had refused to allow the Libyans to convert their embassies in Freetown and Monrovia into People's Bureaus. Creed and hegemonic aspirations, rather than greed, explain Libyan involvement in the training of dissidents from Sierra Leone, Liberia, Gambia, and other parts of Africa. The agenda of the Libyan leader Mu'ammar Gadhafi, in other words, was not economic but ideological and hegemonic.

One local organization, the Pan-African Union (PANAFU), was instrumental in providing both ideological direction and the first batch of recruits for the insurgent enterprise.[6] The prime movers of PANAFU were Olu Gordon and Cleo Hanciles, former lecturers in the history department at Fourah Bay College, who were among those dismissed from their university positions during the 1985 standoff between students and university authorities. Government propaganda at the time alleged that they were Libyan provocateurs, but PANAFU's origins and ideological leanings lay elsewhere. The organization grew out of the Movement for Progress in Africa (MOPA), an inclusionary, student-based organization founded at Fourah Bay College in 1979 with the goal of championing the struggle for social emancipation and democratic representation in Africa. MOPA—beset by poor organiza-

---

[6]Ebiyemi Ridder, a PANAFU member, recruited Foday Sankoh into the insurgency. For details, see Abdullah, "Bush Path to Destruction."

tion and lack of resources, with the graduation of most of its founding members—moved in a new direction, with greater emphasis on expanding its social composition to include ordinary workers and occasional lumpens. The organization's name was changed to PANAFU so as to broaden its legitimacy, camouflage its domestic focus, and increase its chances of being registered by the government.

The populist rhetoric of the RUF expressed residual vestiges of PANAFU, an organization that placed a high premium on political education and whose members met frequently to discuss political issues. RUF platitudes about social transformation through "a cultural revolution whose main objective will be the liberation of our minds to instill in everyone . . . a high sense of African patriotism" were lifted right out of the PANAFU's founding script.[7] But while the RUF liberally appropriated populist and pan-Africanist rhetoric, neither the Pan-Africanism of PANAFU nor the populism of Gadhafi had much of an impact on the movement. PANAFU was itself divided over the insurgency, with some of its members supporting military training and others opposing it. PANAFU members who took part in the training exercise in Libya were subsequently expelled from the organization upon their return to Freetown. In the end, only a handful of PANAFU activists took part in the insurgency during its initial stages.

The RUF insurgency was, first and foremost, the brainchild of disgruntled and idealistic students who saw their political role in vanguardist terms. Abu Kanu (a former university student, PANAFU activist, and founding member of the RUF) was prompted to take up arms against the APC government not to further a rapacious agenda but to pursue a radical commitment to fight political repression and social injustice. Many former students who trained in Libya shared this commitment, but very few were prepared to follow through with the insurgency. Indeed, the attrition rate among those trained in Libya who declined to participate in the insurrection was very high, with many developing cold feet and opting out of the insurgency before it got under way. The handful of former university students who remained to launch the armed rebellion were marginalized and later eliminated on the orders of Foday Sankoh in 1992. The elimination of these former students, most notably Kanu and Rashid Mansaray, finalized the lumpen displacement of students within the movement's leadership and marked the beginning of the RUF's criminalization. But though the class

[7]See the RUF propaganda document *Footpaths to Democracy: Toward a New Sierra Leone* (Freetown: RUF, 1995), vol. 1, 42–43.

composition of the RUF turned out to be lumpen, its origins and formative influences were found in the petit bourgeois students.

Grievances, Armed Conflict, and the State

Grievances emanating from political exclusion and repression were important factors in both the initiation and the continuation of armed conflict in Sierra Leone. Two types of grievances were relevant—those felt by elites who found themselves out of power and those experienced by popular sectors (peasants, workers, and students). Elite grievances mostly stemmed from greed, political exclusion from their time at the trough of official prebends, and a lack of access to state offices and resources; the grievances of popular sectors, conversely, were rooted in need, social deprivation, and political disenfranchisement.[8]

In many instances, out-of-power elites collaborated with the RUF. It is common knowledge, for example, that the RUF insurrection in its early stages attracted support from Sierra Leone People's Party (SLPP) oligarchs, who were at the time languishing in the political wilderness. Monopolization of power by the APC forced many disaffected politicians to embrace extraconstitutional means of unseating the government. While the grievances of SLPP elites by no means caused the RUF insurgency, they nonetheless made available an elite audience that was potentially receptive, or at least not opposed, to armed struggle against the APC.

Grievances resulting from the loss of power explain the role of elements of the political class in prolonging the RUF insurrection. Some disgruntled SLPP leaders clandestinely identified with the RUF during the first year of the rebellion, and many APC leaders, after the overthrow of their party in 1992, found themselves supporting a rebellion that was originally directed at them. Former president Joseph Momoh (now deceased), against whose government (1985–92) the insurrection was launched, later established the National Forum for the Restoration of Democracy, which was active in promoting dissension in the Sierra Leone army during the National Provisional Ruling Council (NPRC) years (1992–96).[9] The APC leaders,

---

[8]I. William Zartman, ed., *Governance as Conflict Management: Politics and Violence in West Africa* (Washington, D.C.: Brookings Institution Press, 1995).

[9]For a brief account of Momoh's role in destabilizing the state after he was overthrown, see Stephen Riley, "Sierra Leone: The Militariat Strikes Again," *Review of African Political Economy*, no. 72 (1997): 287–92.

who were discredited but unaccustomed to being out of power, stood no chance of making a political comeback through the ballot box. Abass Bundu, a former APC and NPRC cabinet minister and one time secretary general of the Economic Community of West African States, contested and lost the 1996 presidential election. Bundu could only muster 3 percent of the popular vote, and his personalist party, the People's Progressive Party, failed to win a single seat in parliament. Given the poor showing of discredited politicians like Bundu in the 1996 elections, an outcome reinforced by the SLPP's landslide victory in the 2002 elections, it was quite obvious that the chances of APC politicians walking the corridors of power once again lay not with the electorate but with armed subalterns.[10]

In contrast to elite grievances, which derived primarily from political exclusion and competition over access to public resources, disenchantment among popular sectors was rooted in mass deprivation, declining living standards, shrinking mobility opportunities, and state repression. Starting with the 1977 demonstrations, popular sectors found themselves on a collision course with an increasingly rapacious and dictatorial APC elite. The imposition of a one-party Constitution in 1978 criminalized opposition to the APC and disenfranchised many citizens. The legal reclassification of political opposition as a criminal offense and the prolonged absence of a legitimate political order unleashed widespread social discontent, institutional decomposition, and armed insurrection.

The most irrepressible opposition to the APC came from university students. Student alienation from the national political process and attempts by college and political authorities to muzzle their voice created a confrontational setting that invited rebellion. The student expulsions from Fourah Bay College in 1985 added a direct, personal, and subjective element to student estrangement from the political establishment. Though some former students, particularly those affected by the expulsions, resorted to armed struggle, the vast majority moved on to other pursuits or chose to continue the struggle against injustice and dictatorship by other means. And though the APC was arguably more repressive under Stevens (1968–85) than Momoh (1985–92), the country was far more susceptible to armed rebellion with the latter at the helm, illustrating Paul Collier's hypothesis that "severe political repression yields a lower risk of political conflict than partial

[10]For analyses of the 1996 and 2002 elections, see Kandeh, "Elections without Rupture," and "Sierra Leone's Post-Conflict Elections of 2002," *Journal of Modern African Studies* 41, no. 2 (2003): 189–216.

democracy."[11] Indeed, Momoh's deathbed conversion to democracy in 1991 could neither save the APC nor prevent a rebellion caused by the abuses of his party.

Alongside students, the grievances of peasants uprooted from their homes in the Pujehun district motivated some of the RUF's early recruits to take up arms against the government. Most of these peasants fled their homes into neighboring Liberia during the 1983 "Ndorgbowusui" uprising in Pujehun. This uprising was triggered by the efforts of Francis Minah (a top APC leader and one-time vice president) to impose his client as representative of the district in parliament. The confrontation that ensued, which pitted soldiers against machete-wielding peasants, left behind a legacy of death and destruction that was to later haunt the APC. Not only did the uprooted victims of the "Ndorgbowusui" (the local Mende name for this disturbance) uprising join the RUF in large numbers, the district they fled was also by and large rebel friendly during the first year of the RUF insurrection. As the war progressed, however, some peasants in southern Sierra Leone who had been driven by grievances to join the RUF while the APC was in power later reconstituted themselves as Kamajors (local militias) after the APC was overthrown in 1992.

As a source of grievances, government performance devoured the state, alienated popular sectors, and sparked armed insurrection. A Reconciliation Commission chaired by a judge from Trinidad and Tobago concluded in 1996 that former president Momoh "appeared to treat Sierra Leone as his personal fiefdom and felt that he was at liberty to act as if its finances were at his disposal no matter what contrary advice was tendered."[12] As political incumbents "engorged themselves on the country's vast natural resources, . . . the rest of the nation slid to the bottom of the UN charts rating human misery around the world."[13] The cumulative effect of elite aggrandizement was the nondelivery of public services and collective goods, which had a devastating impact on the youth segment of the population. The nonpayment of teachers and the unavailability of basic instructional materials devalued schooling among a whole generation of Sierra Leonean youth. As dropout rates soared, criminal behavior and banditry came to define youth responses to the collapse of meaning and loss of hope in their lives.

[11]Collier, "Doing Well Out of War," 98.

[12]See *Report of the National Commission for Unity and Reconciliation* (Freetown, Sierra Leone: Government Printers, 1996), 8.

[13]Elizabeth Rubin, "An Army of One's Own: In Africa, Nations Hire a Corporation to Wage War," *Harper's Magazine*, February 1997, 46.

Table 4.1. *Average Annual Growth Rate of Sierra Leone's Economy, 1980–90 and 1990–95 (percent)*

Indicator	1980–90	1990–95
Gross domestic product	1.6	–4.2
Agriculture	4.4	–2.8
Industry	5.7	–2.8
Services	–1.1	–5.9
Exports	2.8	–15.2
Domestic investment	–6.5	–20.0

Source: World Bank, *World Development Report 1997* (New York: Oxford University Press, 1997).

The economy was in the doldrums at the time the APC was overthrown by the junior military officers in the NPRC in 1992. Not a single economic sector or activity registered any growth during the first half of the 1990s, with exports showing the sharpest decline (table 4.1). Declining exports were due to the informalization of the economy, diamond smuggling by politicians and their cronies, and the pervasive insecurity created by the RUF rebellion. The decline in export earnings, however, predated and could not be entirely blamed on the RUF rebellion.

As proxies for grievance, ethnic and religious hatred are the least relevant to understanding the RUF insurrection. Some APC politicians initially dismissed the RUF insurgency as a Mende war, but Foday Sankoh, the now-deceased former RUF leader, was Temne and not Mende. Issa Sesay, who replaced Sankoh as interim RUF leader in 2000, is also Temne from the northern province. Ethnicity did not factor into the RUF's grievance narrative, and no ethnic group or region was spared the atrocities committed by its combatants. That the majority of RUF irregulars were from the East and South was largely due to the proximity of these regions to neighboring Liberia, from where the RUF insurrection was launched. John Hirsch, in this regard, misses the proverbial forest for the trees in claiming that "geographically based ethnic tensions between Mendes in the south and Temnes and Limbas in the north, manipulated by politicians, were at the root of the state's progressive collapse in the nearly four decades since independence."[14] Ethnic tensions were epiphenomenal, masking an underlying unanimity of purpose among competing fractions of Sierra Leone's political class. Predatory accumulation, rather than ethnic tensions manipulated

[14]John Hirsch, *Sierra Leone: Diamonds and the Struggle for Democracy* (Boulder, Colo.: Lynne Rienner, 2001), 24.

by opportunistic politicians, was the root cause of armed rebellion and state collapse in Sierra Leone.

Greed and the RUF Insurgency

One of the leading proponents of the view that greed is the primary cause of domestic armed conflicts is Paul Collier. His argument, as originally formulated, is that "a country with large natural resources, many young men, and little education is very much more at risk of conflict than one with opposite characteristics."[15] These variables tend to be good proxies for grievances rather than greed. As Indra de Soysa contends, "The results of empirical analyses that find a strong positive connection between natural resource abundance and conflict may in fact be capturing the grievance effects generated by . . . perverse sociopolitical conditions."[16] David Keen makes a similar point regarding the lack of education as a proxy for need rather than greed; he notes that "the civil war in Sierra Leone cannot really be understood without comprehending the deep sense of anger at lack of good government and educational opportunities."[17]

Primary commodities or lootable resources have always been in abundance in Sierra Leone, but their presence did not generate the type of armed conflict in the past that the country has experienced in recent times. Why, it is pertinent to ask, did primary commodity exports all of a sudden predispose Sierra Leone to armed conflict in the 1990s but not in the 1960s or 1970s? What changed in the intervening period to produce the violence and terror that convulsed the country for the better part of the 1990s? Surely, the absence of armed conflict during the period when diamonds accounted for 70 percent of export earnings and the prevalence of armed conflict following the decline of the mineral economy can tell us something about the role of natural resources, especially their management, in the Sierra Leone conflict.

Botswana, like Sierra Leone, has diamonds but has so far been able to avoid armed conflict over this prized resource.[18] What these contrasting ex-

[15]Collier, "Doing Well Out of War," 97.

[16]Indra de Soysa, "The Resource Curse: Are Civil Wars Driven by Rapacity or Paucity?" in *Greed and Grievance*, ed. Berdal and Malone, 121.

[17]David Keen, "Incentives and Disincentives for Violence," in *Greed and Grievance*, ed. Berdal and Malone, 35.

[18]Alluvial mining in Sierra Leone, as opposed to kimberlite mining in Botswana, may also help explain this contrasting experience with diamonds, but the fact remains that Botswana's exploitation and management of its diamonds have been more transparent and beneficial to ordinary citizens than has been the case in Sierra Leone.

amples may suggest is that it is not the mere presence of natural resources like diamonds that predispose societies to armed conflict but the manner of their exploitation, management, and social distribution. Diamonds by themselves explain nothing; they only begin to enter the narrative of Sierra Leone's despoliation when linked to the "story of flawed leadership and voracious [official] greed."[19] How Sierra Leone's natural patrimony was mismanaged and looted has greater explanatory relevance than the mere presence of diamonds. Natural endowments like diamonds do not make societies conflict prone, but the way these resources are exploited and managed can either increase or reduce the likelihood of armed conflict. Sierra Leone mismanaged its diamond resources to benefit political incumbents and their business associates at the expense of the public. Grievances caused by elite pillage, rather than diamonds, increased the prospects of armed rebellion in Sierra Leone.

The proportion of young men in the population also tends to proxy need rather than greed.[20] Like diamonds among its resources, Sierra Leone has always had a high proportion of young men in its population; indeed, this is a condition generally shared by underdeveloped societies. The critical issue, however, is not the proportion of youths in the population but the existence of opportunities for them to do something positive with their lives. There were no more young men (as a percentage of the population) in the 1990s than the in 1960s and 1970s, but the opportunities for social advancement among youths were relatively more accessible during the earlier than later period. Youths do not inherently represent a problem or predispose societies to armed conflict because of their preponderance; rather, as the case of Sierra Leone suggests, it is the presence of young men with nothing to do that poses the greatest danger. Having a high proportion of young men in the population only becomes a problem when opportunities for their growth and development are arrested, stifled, or nonexistent.

Collier's assertion that "the greater the proportion of young men, the easier it would be to recruit rebels" does not account for the fact that not all rebel groups rely on voluntary enlistment to fill their ranks.[21] In the case of the RUF in particular, abductions were the standard method of replenishing and swelling rebel ranks, especially after the removal of the APC

---

[19]Hirsch, *Sierra Leone*, 13.

[20]Henrik Urdal, *The Devil in the Demographics: The Effect of Youth Bulges on Domestic Armed Conflict, 1950–2000*, World Bank Social Development Paper 14 (Washington, D.C.: World Bank, 2004).

[21]Collier, "Doing Well Out of War," 94.

from power in 1992. This explains why no matter how many rebels were killed, there always seemed to be more left to subdue or eliminate. The RUF relied on voluntary enlistment during the early stages of the insurrection, when motivation was supplied by grievances, than in the latter stages when it became inordinately consumed by the impulse to plunder and brutalize society into submission. Rebels motivated by need appear to have been less inclined to use abduction as a recruitment strategy than rebels instigated by greed, when child-soldiers, not young men, swelled the RUF ranks and combatants were not recruited but abducted.

Low educational levels also proxy grievances more convincingly than greed. Education reduces the risk of conflict by providing income-generating opportunities for young men. This claim, however, holds true only to the degree that employment opportunities are available for the educated. Where employment opportunities are nonexistent, high educational levels may actually increase rather than reduce the risk of conflict. A combination of low educational levels and rapidly declining employment opportunities for the educated few made it possible for the RUF rebellion to spread from the eastern borders of Sierra Leone to the rest of the country.[22] Failure to differentiate need from greed as distinct forms of economic agenda overlooks the significance of low educational levels or education without employment as proxies for grievance. Ultimately, economic agendas rooted in need have less to do with greed than with grievances.

In explaining domestic armed conflicts, greed's primacy over grievances rests on the absence of free riders (the benefits of rebellion are limited to its participants), coordination (rebellion does not have to be large to be predatory), and time-consistency problems (rebel recruits can be paid during the conflict rather than promised rewards later) to contend with in greed-motivated rebellions. But rebels motivated by grievances and who take up arms to right social wrongs are the least likely to be absorbed by calculations of immediate rewards. When security agents of the state indiscriminately target an ethnic group or members of a religious faith, the motives for rebellion cannot be reduced to the expectation of material rewards. Simply getting rid of an oppressive government may be the ultimate reward for insurgents inspired by targeted discrimination and a sense of social justice.

---

[22] Among the early recruits of the RUF were teachers who had not been paid for months. Governments may get away with not paying teachers, but not paying soldiers is quite another thing.

Elite greed and rapacity help explain the RUF insurgency, but those who initially took up arms against the APC were not motivated by their own greed. It became, however, the most important variable in prolonging the war. The RUF rebellion became criminalized when greed displaced the original need- and creed-based motives for continuing the war. This transformation occurred after the elimination of the last remaining students from the organization in the aftermath of the APC's removal from power in 1992. After 1992, with the enlarged role of Charles Taylor in sustaining and profiting from the insurgency, the war in Sierra Leone began to resemble the war in Liberia both in objectives and combat strategies. Abduction became the primary mode of recruitment, and attacks on innocent civilians became widespread following the visibly rapid transformation of the RUF into a criminal outfit.

Beneficiaries of the Sierra Leone Conflict

Politicians, businessmen (local and foreign), uniformed officers, rebels, *sobels*, armed robbers, thugs, and even peacekeepers all benefited in various ways from the RUF insurgency. Though the majority of Sierra Leoneans were victimized by the insurgency, some sought to derive from war and disorder what they could not expect to achieve in peacetime, because war and disorder had become the pervasive condition of the country. Opportunistic politicians (both incumbents and out-of-power politicians) contributed to prolonging the war in Sierra Leone by capitalizing on the misery they created. The war for some provided an opportunity to resurrect spent political careers and pursue delusions of leadership grandeur. Discredited politicians who identified with the RUF cared less about their standing with the public; what mattered to them was making a political comeback, regardless of the desperate or brutal means by which this was done. Successive governments (APC, NPRC, SLPP) saw the war as a convenient excuse to delay elections, while some unscrupulous politicians (Momoh, Bundu, Karefa-Smart) collaborated with armed subaltern insurgents. A few businessmen also did well, as did criminals who were often indistinguishable from rebels and *sobels*.

A few rebel leaders and their families were among the principal beneficiaries of the armed conflict in Sierra Leone. Although he spent much of the 1990s in the bush or in detention, Sankoh was doing quite well before his arrest in May 2000. Documents recovered from his residence confirm the rebel leader's direct involvement and key role in the conflict diamond trade.

There is some confusion, however, regarding Sankoh's control over the diamonds mined by the RUF, with some reports suggesting that Taylor received a greater share of the proceeds from the sale of these diamonds than did Sankoh. Sankoh's Senegalese wife, Fatou Mbaye, was literally purchased by the lure of conflict diamonds, with Taylor performing the role of matchmaker. RUF combatants were also made to believe that Sankoh had stashed away a good quantity of diamonds for their upkeep after the war.[23]

Sam Bockarie (alias Maskita), another assassinated RUF leader, was a short-term beneficiary of the Sierra Leone conflict. Bockarie was a hairdresser in Abidjan before joining Taylor's National Patriotic Forces of Liberia (NPFL) in Liberia. He later linked up with Sankoh and was responsible for some of the worst atrocities committed by the RUF. Bockarie was reportedly proud of the international notoriety he gained through his ruthless exploits and, although he was to later fall out with Sankoh before the latter's arrest and detention in 2000, Bockarie was provided sanctuary in Liberia, where he briefly played a key role in Taylor's Anti-Terrorism Unit and lived the life of a petty warlord, with much cash and many gadgets at his disposal. Bockarie was later indicted on war crimes by the Sierra Leone Special Court but was eliminated on the orders of Taylor rather than be repatriated to Sierra Leone to stand trial. A top RUF commander, Dennis Mingo (alias Superman), alleged in a letter to Sankoh that Bockarie had bought houses in Liberia and France from diamond proceeds.[24] Mingo, a Liberian, was himself at one point in charge of RUF diamond operations in Kono, from where he frequently smuggled gemstones into Liberia via Buedu, an RUF stronghold. One of the main concerns of rebels before they were disarmed by UN peacekeepers in 2001 was the safety of looted items in their possession. Safeguarding looted property and protection against reprisals ranked high among the postconflict concerns of rebels in Sierra Leone.

Among external patrons, Taylor of Liberia was perhaps the most important beneficiary of the RUF insurrection in Sierra Leone. He was instrumental in both launching and prolonging the war in Sierra Leone. Resources looted by rebels found their way into Liberia, which exported ten times the diamonds it was capable of producing during this period. Apart

[23]This information is based on interviews of demobilized RUF fighters by author in Kenema, July 2001.

[24]See *U.N Panel of Experts Report on Diamonds and Arms in Sierra Leone*, http://www.sierra-leone.org, 2.

from some petty grudges against the Sierra Leone government, Taylor's involvement in the Sierra Leone conflict was largely dictated by three main factors: to use the diamonds of Sierra Leone to finance his war machine; to dump excess NPFL combatants in the diamond fields of Sierra Leone, where they could fend for themselves, thereby relieving authorities in Monrovia of a potentially dangerous security problem; and to use the RUF as an auxiliary military force. Taylor's friendship with Jesse Jackson, the Bill Clinton administration's point man on Africa, and Donald Payne, the chair of the U.S. Congressional Black Caucus, and the role of these men in facilitating the discredited Lomé peace agreement of 1999 that brought RUF leaders into the government, led many Sierra Leoneans to conclude that Jackson and Payne were in Taylor and Sankoh's camp.[25]

The beneficiaries of the Sierra Leone conflict also included Taylor's son, Charles Taylor Jr., and a slew of unscrupulous business cronies and political associates. The junior Taylor supervised his father's security apparatus and was known to be a key sponsor and beneficiary of RUF terror in Sierra Leone.[26] Among Taylor's closest business partners who made a fortune out of the RUF insurgency were Talal El-Ndine (a Lebanese businessman and Taylor's clandestine paymaster), Fred Rindle (a retired South African army officer), Leonid Minin (a Ukrainian with many aliases), Victor Bout (a native of Tajikistan and former KGB operative who also uses many aliases), Gus Van Kouwenhoven (a Dutch national with hotel, logging, and diamond interests in Liberia), and Ibrahim Baldeh Bah (a Senegalese national with close ties to Taylor, Blaise Compaoré, and the RUF). El-Ndine handled payments for diamond and weapons transactions, Rindle trained RUF commandos, Bout supplied weapons to embargoed nonstate actors in

---

[25]For a revealing account of the connections between Jackson/Payne and Taylor, see Ryan Lizza, "Sierra Leone: The Last Clinton Betrayal. Where Angels Fear to Tread," *New Republic*, July 24, 2000, available at http://www.thenewrepublic.com. The Lomé agreement went further than the Abidjan accord in not only granting a blanket amnesty to all RUF leaders and combatants but also in providing for the inclusion of rebel leaders in the government. The power-sharing experiment between the government and the RUF lasted for only a few months (1999–2000) before it unraveled in the aftermath of Foday Sankoh's unsuccessful attempt at capturing power by force in May 2000; Kwaku Nuamah and I. William Zartman, "Intervention in Sierra Leone," in *Military Intervention: Cases in Context for the Twenty-First Century*, ed. William Lahneman (Lanham, Md.: Rowman & Littlefield, 2004).

[26]See James Rupert, "Diamond Hunters Fuel Africa's Brutal Wars," *Washington Post*, October 16, 1999, A1, A21, for an investigative account of the involvement of Taylor and his close associates in the RUF insurgency.

exchange for diamonds; Minin was neck-deep in the timber, diamond, and weapons trading; and Kouwenhoven parlayed his logging interests into dealing weapons for diamonds with the RUF.[27]

Another important external patron of the RUF was Blaise Compaoré, the president of Burkina Faso. Taylor and Sankoh reportedly helped Compaoré seize power in Burkina Faso, and Compaoré outsourced fighters to both Taylor's NPFL and Sankoh's RUF.[28] Although his connections to Taylor partly explain Compaoré's involvement with the RUF, the NPFL and RUF were not the only rebel groups to attract the support of the Burkinabe leader. Compaoré was also linked to UNITA in Angola, on behalf of whose leader, Jonas Savimbi, he was accused of running guns and smuggling diamonds. The involvement of West African leaders like Taylor and Compaoré in destabilizing their neighbors was critical in prolonging the armed insurgency in Sierra Leone. Although the conditions that gave rise to armed conflict in Sierra Leone had nothing to do with Taylor and Compaoré, it is doubtful whether the RUF insurgency could have lasted for as long as it did without the active support (sanctuary, training, arms, ammunition, fighters) of these two men.

Politicians in the Côte d'Ivoire were also complicit in the RUF insurgency. Both Presidents Félix Houphouët-Boigny and Henri Konan Bedie allowed the RUF to operate freely out of Abidjan in exchange for what many believe were diamond payments to highly placed Ivoirien officials. Côte d'Ivoire's involvement in the Sierra Leone conflict was tied to its support of Taylor, whose insurgency in Liberia was launched from Ivoirien territory and with the support of its political establishment. Robert Guei, the Ivoirien general who ousted Bedie in 1999, also came to rely on Taylor for his own personal security. Taylor reportedly dispatched Gio (the same ethnic group as Guei's Yakouba) mercenaries from Liberia to protect Guei during the waning days of the latter's disastrous dictatorship. The election of Amara Essy, the former Ivoirien foreign minister and facilitator of the Abidjan accord, as secretary general of the African Union was greeted with disappointment in Sierra Leone, where many still remember Essy's close ties to Foday Sankoh and his role in brokering the Abidjan accord, a 1996 agreement that granted amnesty to RUF leaders and combatants in exchange for ending the war. Though it is virtually impossible to document the RUF's financial transactions, it is public knowledge in both Sierra

---

[27]Rupert, "Diamond Hunters."
[28]*U.N. Panel of Experts Report*, part 2, p. 2.

Leone and Côte d'Ivoire that unscrupulous elements of the Ivoirien political class supported the RUF for the same reasons as their counterparts in Sierra Leone.

A few local businessmen, especially Lebanese and "Marakas" (mainly from Gambia and Mali) also did quite well, albeit in an increasingly high-risk environment. Scores of Lebanese were deported from Sierra Leone for doing business with the RUF, but many found their way back into the country with the connivance of top politicians and bureaucrats. The dramatic upsurge in diamond exports from Gambia, a country that has no diamonds, was largely due to the smuggling activities of Maraka businessmen operating in Sierra Leone. In 1998 alone, Gambia exported 449,000 carats of diamonds valued at $78.3 million, with the bulk (90 percent) of these diamonds originating in Sierra Leone.[29] Stephen Bio, a relative of Maada Bio (the former head of state in the last two months of NPRC rule), ran a local airline company that derived huge profits from diamond smuggling and the closure of most highways in the 1990s due to RUF ambushes. Bio eventually ran out of luck and was gunned down after escaping from prison during the 1999 rebel invasion of Freetown.

Elements of the Sierra Leone Army, especially senior officers and *sobels*, also profited from the war. The perception that senior officers were making money out of the war was a precipitating factor in the 1992 coup. At the time of their execution in 1998, Brigadier Hassan Conteh (chief of defense staff) and Lieutenant Colonel Max Kanga (chief of army staff) had either acquired or were in the process of finishing construction work on palatial homes that were incommensurate with their official emoluments.[30] Before and during the war, senior military officers siphoned rice rations allocated to their men, which were then sold on the market for huge profits. Senior military officers, however, did more than sell rice. The war provided many with the opportunity to engage in diamond mining and smuggling. By the time the NPRC relinquished power in 1996, the army was a virtual mining syndicate as diamond mining took precedence over defense of country among officers and the rank and file. Every NPRC boss had his own paramilitary auxiliary, which was routinely used to mine diamonds and pillage the countryside.

[29] *U.N. Panel of Experts Report*, part 2, p. 9.
[30] This information is based on interviews of soldiers by author in Freetown, July 2001.

Many civil defense commanders and coordinators thrived as a result of the armed conflict. The Kamajors, local militias that fought against the RUF and on the side of the NPRC and SLPP governments, became involved in diamond mining from the onset of the war, with the proceeds going not only to financing the counterinsurgency but also into the private coffers of Kamajor bosses. Hinga Norman, the Kamajor leader, does not conceal the fact that his men were involved in mining diamonds but justifies such activity as the only way local militias can fund their counterinsurgency.[31] Besides digging for diamonds to enrich themselves, Kamajor bosses also became notorious for diverting supplies provided by the government for their men to private use. Kamajor commanders, not unlike their counterparts in the army, also became rice dealers; in many instances, the rice allocated to their units exceeded what was required for their sustenance, with the surplus being routinely sold for private profit. Kamajors also looted and dispossessed ordinary citizens, especially those suspected of rebel collaboration, and a few commanders built impressive homes during the course of the war. Despite the aggrandizing activities of some Kamajor leaders and fighters, it would be inaccurate to view the Kamajors as initially motivated by greed rather than grievances. Like the RUF, the Kamajors were hijacked by elements of the political class who were more interested in power and lining their pockets than ending the insurgency.

Peacekeepers also benefited from the conflict and were in some ways responsible for prolonging the war. Though it is true that many Nigerian soldiers perished in Sierra Leone, a few Nigerian military officers are reported to have made huge profits from the illicit diamond trade. General Kumar Jetley, the first commander of UN troops in Sierra Leone, accused his Nigerian colleagues in the United Nations Mission in Sierra Leone (UNAMSIL) of profiting from the war by collaborating with the RUF in the mining and smuggling of diamonds. Press reports of the troops of the Economic Community of West Africa Monitoring Group (ECOMOG) withdrawing from their positions and leaving behind huge caches of weapons lend credence to allegations of complicity by some ECOMOG officers in the 1999 rebel advance on Freetown.[32] Rebel combatants were known to

[31]Norman was indicted in 2003 by the Sierra Leone Special Court on charges of war crimes and crimes against humanity.

[32]The 1999 rebel invasion of Freetown could also be attributed to the demoralization of Nigerian troops, many of whom were betrayed and killed in cold blood by elements of the Sierra Leone army in Makeni.

brag about their ability to purchase some of their weapons, including tanks, from Guinean troops serving in ECOMOG.

Peacekeepers from India, Nigeria, Guinea, Ghana, Kenya, Zambia, Pakistan, Bangladesh, and Nepal served UNAMSIL. What motivated some of these countries to send peacekeeping troops to Sierra Leone was to make money. Soldiers in UNAMSIL are generally paid higher salaries than those serving at home; and although governments like Kenya and Zambia tend to withhold a portion of these salaries, UNAMSIL soldiers are still better off than their counterparts serving at home. Some peacekeepers deployed in diamond-mining areas found ways to benefit from the illicit diamond trade. In Daru (eastern Sierra Leone), peacekeepers often sold their fuel ration below market price, thereby incurring the wrath of local petrol dealers.[33] Peacekeeping can indeed be a lucrative undertaking for soldiers deployed in resource-rich countries like Sierra Leone—the longer the duration of the assignment. Many former Nigerian ECOMOG officers have, since the end of the war in 2002, returned to Sierra Leone as businessmen.

Local representatives and workers of nongovernmental organizations (NGOs) also received a financial windfall from the protracted war. An army of humanitarian and relief organizations descended on Sierra Leone in the 1990s and early 2000s, providing a wide variety of services in addition to employment for expatriate and local workers. Working for an NGO currently trumps working for the state; NGOs have practically displaced the state as avenue of personal enrichment and class formation. However, the relief provided by these agencies pales in comparison to the benefits provided for their workers and the politically connected. As Chabal and Daloz observe,

> There is little doubt that the present profusion of uncoordinated NGO involvement in Africa is unlikely to lead to sustained development. . . . The spread of NGO activities, allied to the collapse of state resources, is much more eminently favorable to the instrumentalization of disorder than it is to the emergence of a Western-style civil society. . . . Far from strengthening civil society . . . the role of NGOs could well lead to the hijacking of genuinely needed development aid by the same old and well-established political elites.[34]

---

[33]This information is based on interviews of petrol dealers in Kenema in July 2001.
[34]Patrick Chabal and Jean-Pascal Daloz, *Africa Works: Disorder as Political Instrument* (Oxford: James Currey, 1999), 24.

With so many profiting in one form or another from Sierra Leone's criminal insurgency, it is little wonder that this armed conflict defied resolution for so long. Whenever it seemed an end was in sight, the hopes of the public would be dashed by the resumption of hostilities among indistinguishable warring factions. But the reason some rebels were not interested in peace had less to do with benefits that would be lost than with fear of reprisal from local communities. Given the gruesome nature of their crimes, many rebels and *sobels* doubted the capacity of Sierra Leoneans to forgive and reintegrate them into society.

Conclusion

Any political conflict "can become criminal if its legitimacy dissolves," [35] and any rapacious government can bring on civil conflict if its legitimacy dissolves. The RUF insurgency is a perfect example of a legitimate political struggle that degenerated into criminal adventurism by warlords, lumpens, unscrupulous politicians, and fortune seekers. Lacking criminal intent at its inception, the RUF insurrection in time attracted some of the worst criminal elements in society. Urban lumpens, rural drifters, rogue soldiers, discredited politicians, and clandestine businessmen all found common cause with the RUF. What united this motley amalgam of unsavory elements was opposition to the will of the people and a determination to acquire wealth through pillage. The criminalization of the RUF insurgency attracted hordes of disaffected youths, some of whom joined rebel ranks while others freelanced in a variety of criminal pursuits.

Removing the economic incentives for participants in the Sierra Leone conflict without addressing the deplorable social conditions that underpinned it is not likely to yield a lasting solution. Neither the youth problem nor the rapacity of the political class would go away simply because of an international ban on conflict diamonds. Disarming combatants still leaves intact the social injustice that led to the RUF rebellion. Mass deprivation, not greed, predisposes youths to engage in criminal behavior, including banditry. Greed, as both underlying cause and as motive for rebellion, is more descriptive of the role of political elites than youths in the Sierra Leone conflict.

[35]Chabal and Daloz, *Africa Works*, 83.

5

Resource Wealth and Angola's
Uncivil Wars

Philippe Le Billon

With its wealth of natural resources, most notably oil and diamonds, Angola figures among the wealthiest countries with the most needy populations. War is the main factor generally identified for this sharp contrast between the relative wealth of this country and the absolute poverty of most of its people. This ethnically diverse country has indeed been in a perpetual state of war since a national liberation struggle was initiated in the early 1960s. Both "need" and "creed" were prominent in the war for independence as

Philippe Le Billon is assistant professor in the Department of Geography and the Liu Institute for Global Issues, University of British Columbia. Previously, he worked with the International Institute for Strategic Studies in London and the French Ministry of Foreign Affairs, as well as several humanitarian and advocacy nongovernmental organizations and development research institutes in Angola, Cambodia, Sierra Leone, and the former Yugoslavia. He is the author of *Fuelling War: Natural Resources and Armed Conflicts* (Routledge, 2005) and the editor of *Geopolitics of Resource Wars: Resource Dependence, Governance, and Violence* (Cass, 2005).

nationalist movements demanded the economic and political emancipation of "indigenous" populations from the grip of an authoritarian Portuguese colonial regime and a bourgeois *mestiços* elite that grew rich from slave trading and forced labor.

The continuation of war beyond independence in 1975 has often been portrayed as a product of the Cold War and the "frontline state" policy of the South African apartheid regime. The end of the Cold War and the collapse of the South African apartheid regime, however, did not bring an end to continued hostilities. Rather, the independence struggle had long degenerated into a conflict between largely socioethnically based competing nationalist movements in which the "creed" dimension became more divisive while the "greed" of the leadership became itself more obvious. Unbridled by international markets and a seemingly disinterested or powerless international community, a "war without end" financed by oil and diamonds appeared as a possible scenario for Angola in the late 1990s.

In light of vanishing ideological motivations and the massive oil and diamonds revenues at stake in the conflict, hostilities in Angola have been increasingly perceived as motivated by financial greed during the past decade. Such a perspective stressed the importance of curtailing access to diamonds financing National Union for the Total Independence of Angola (UNITA) rebels, while allowing oil revenues to militarily strengthen the government. By oversimplifying the belligerents' motives and actions, this perspective depoliticized the war, and in particular its "need" and "creed" dimensions.

The ensuing strategy enabled the government to successfully isolate the armed branch of the rebel movement from most of its local, regional, and international sources of support, ending more than two decades of conflict through the killing of rebel leader Jonas Savimbi in early 2002. This decisive victory demonstrated how much the war was dependent upon the single-mindedness of a rebel leader. More than two years after the official end of the civil war, however, critics of the Angolan government can still point out that the greed of the elite, rampant racism, and drastic inequalities between social classes, as well as widespread destitution, constitute major injustices and potential factors in future conflicts.

This chapter examines the mutual relations and relative importance of need, creed, and greed in the case of an armed conflict occurring in a resource-rich environment. After a general analysis of the links between wars and resources, the chapter briefly outlines the history of hostilities in Angola, examines political and social ideological motivations among parties, and analyzes the significance of oil and diamond revenues in the course of the conflict. Before concluding, the last section details conflict resolution strategies building upon this understanding.

War in a Resource-Rich Environment

There is growing concern that whereas economic resources were once a means of funding war to serve political ends, war is increasingly becoming the means to pursue economic agendas.[1] In other words, greed—rather than need or creed—would motivate belligerents. Among economic resources, primary commodities are likely to be the main motivation, means, and prize for belligerents. Not only are commodities like timber or minerals often the only valuable resources in poor countries, they are also deemed to be the most easily taxed or looted. In examining contemporary armed conflicts, numerous journalistic and academic accounts have consolidated the idea of war as driven by greed rather than political agendas. Most prominently among economists, Paul Collier argued that greed and opportunism are behind most rebellions, noting that countries that depend on the export of primary commodities faced a higher risk of conflict.[2] The UN Security Council itself singled out the role of natural resources in motivating and financing parties to conflicts in Angola, the Democratic Republic of the Congo, and Sierra Leone.[3]

The role played by natural resources in several contemporary conflicts, mostly in Africa, is inscribed in a long succession of instances of conflictual "resource" exploitation, often associated with violence, to export slaves, rubber, timber, coffee, minerals, petroleum, or diamonds.[4] Not all resource exploitation is associated with conflicts and violence, however, and several factors come into play in this relationship.[5]

---

[1] D. Keen, *The Economic Functions of Violence in Civil Wars* (Oxford: Oxford University Press, 1998); M. Berdal and D. Malone, eds., *Greed and Grievance: Economic Agendas in Civil Wars* (Boulder, Colo.: Lynne Rienner, 2000).

[2] P. Collier, *Economic Causes of Civil Conflict and Their Implications for Policy* (Washington, D.C.: World Bank, 2000). This finding has since been questioned by several political scientists also based on large N-studies, see Michael Ross, "What Do We Know about Natural Resources and Civil War?" *Journal of Peace Research* 41, no. 3 (2004): 337–56; and James Fearon, "Primary Commodities Export and Civil War," forthcoming in *Journal of Conflict Resolution*.

[3] UN Security Council, "Presidential Statement," S/PRST/2000/20, June 2, 2000.

[4] J. C. Miller, *Way of Death: Merchant Capitalism and the Angolan Slave Trade, 1730–1830* (Madison: University of Wisconsin Press, 1988).

[5] For an extended examination, see P. Le Billon, "The Political Ecology of War: Natural Resources and Armed Conflicts," *Political Geography* 20 (2001): 561–84.

First, a high degree of dependence on the valuable resources of societies has distortionary effects influencing the political, institutional, and economic *vulnerability* of societies to conflicts. Resource dependence reflects not only a rich natural endowment but also a historical process associated with a pattern of relation with the global economy, through colonial powers, private transborder commercial interests, and domestic elites. In this respect, dependence on aid shares some commonalities, insofar as it forms an essential pair of local strategies of accumulation and domination (e.g., Rwanda).[6] Resource rents generated by narrow and mostly foreign-dominated resource industries can significantly weaken or distort political life and institutions, notably by inducing ruling groups to overly rely on fiscal revenues and transfers for economic growth and social peace, to dispense with sound economic diversification and statecraft, and—in a worst-case scenario—to impose themselves by a force they can afford.[7] Economically, the vulnerability of countries that are rich in natural resources is related to poor economic diversification, slower growth, brutal price shocks, and high levels of rent seeking and corruption, as well as little social mobility outside state patronage—all factors susceptible of raising grievances among non-beneficiaries.[8]

Second, there can be specific conflicts over resource exploitation and allocation. The transformation of nature into tradable commodities is a deeply political process; involving the definition of property rights, the organization of labor, and the allocation of costs and profits. Although processes of resource extraction and allocation can be peaceful and cooperative, conflicts can arise and violence be deployed, either in the form of physical force or through coercion and domination. Access to the commodity value chain is often closely linked to political and social identities, articulating in particular entitlements and horizontal inequalities according to ethnicity, class, kinship, or religion. If institutionally mismanaged, such political economy risks degenerating into violent conflict, as privileged groups confront forceful initiatives by politico-military entrepreneurs and the broader population motivate seeking to achieve personal ambitions or political and economic reforms. In a context of relative deprivation, po-

[6]P. Uvin, *Aiding Violence: The Development Enterprise in Rwanda* (West Hartford, Conn.: Kumarian Press, 1998).

[7]T. Karl, *The Paradox of Plenty: Oil Booms and Petro-States* (Berkeley: University of California Press, 1997).

[8]For a review, see M. L. Ross, "The Political Economy of the Resource Curse," *World Politics* 51, no. 2 (1999): 297–322.

litical entrepreneurs can successfully mobilize and manipulate the grievances of marginalized people to turn them into supporters—especially if resources can be territorially linked to their identity, thus creating a sense of
despoliation by dominant groups and raising the stakes of separatism.

Third, violence itself may be involved with the extraction or production
of resources, for example, through the appropriation of land and displacement of local populations, human rights abuses conducted to protect resource exploitation projects, or coercive forms of labor control.

Fourth, the lootable character—or lootability—of resources is crucial to
the opportunities offered to belligerents. This lootability arises in part from
the fact that resource rents are often easily accessible to governments and
rebels alike with minimal bureaucratic infrastructure. The greater the distance or difficulty of control by the government, the higher the risk of losing the resource to the adversary. Furthermore, resource extraction activities are, to a greater degree than other economic activities, spatially fixed.
Unlike manufacturing and to some extent agriculture, primary resource
exploitation activities cannot be easily relocated. Resource businesses
thereby generally protect their investments by militarily securing their project area and paying "whoever is in power" or has a chance of grabbing it—
ranging from a few dollars to let a truck pass at a rebel checkpoint, to multi-
million-dollar concession signature bonuses or resource-collaterized loans
paid to belligerents in advance of exploitation. Finally, some types of resource exploitation can be more easily sustained during conflicts than other
economic activities, thereby maintaining a source of finance to belligerents.
This is the case of alluvial diamonds: They require little investment to exploit, are easy to transport, and yield high prices.

Resources and war are mainly associated with the failure or degeneration
of political systems—most generally patrimonial or clientelist—that are
overly reliant on resource rents into "spoil politics," whereby "the primary
goal of those competing for political office or power is self-enrichment."[9] If
left unchecked by nonexistent, circumvented, or biased institutional structures—such as anticorruption mechanisms or politically sensible redistribution schemes—the most predatory practices of "spoil politics" risk turning into "terminal spoils politics." The combination and exacerbation of
competitive corruption, withdrawal of the (formal) state and public services, counterproductivity of state violence, and sectarianism may ultimately

---

[9]C. Allen, "Warfare, Endemic Violence and State Collapse," *Review of African Political Economy* 81 (1999): 377.

result in the outbreak of armed conflict as belligerents find both means and rewards in lootable resources.

Need and Creed: Liberation and Domination in Angola

After sporadic violent opposition to Portuguese colonialism, Angola has been in a quasi-continuous state of war since the early 1960s.[10] The first period was marked by a war of liberation fought until 1975 by competing nationalist movements, including the National Liberation Front of Angola (FNLA), the Popular Movement for the Liberation of Angola (MPLA), and UNITA.[11]

The FNLA, headed by Roberto Holden, had a strong ethnic base of Bakongo who were located in the northwest or had emigrated to Zaire, representing about 15 percent of the national population. Though the leadership of the FNLA initially attempted to recreate the former Kongo kingdom through secession, it later moved to a national independence agenda and received the assistance of Western powers and Zaire.

The MPLA, headed by Agostinho Neto and since his death in 1979 by Eduardo dos Santos, was an elitist movement constituted of *assimilados*—institutionally educated or "civilized" Africans and *mestiços,* some of them linked to the long-established multiracial colonial bourgeoisie—from the capital city. Because the MPLA was linked to Portuguese socialist groups and mobilized local unions, its Marxism attracted the support of the Soviet bloc, including Cuba.[12] Marxism also avoided the pitfall of a racially based nationalist ideology that would conflict with the *mestiços* or white origin of the MPLA's intellectual elite and provided a link to black workers and the poor people of Luanda's slums.[13] Despite rejecting any ethnic or

[10]L. H. Henderson, *Angola: Five Centuries of Conflict* (Ithaca, N.Y.: Cornell University Press, 1979); R. Pélissier, *Les guerres grises: Résistance et révolte en Angola, 1845–1941* (Orgeval, France: Pélisser, 1977).

[11]W. M. James, *A Political History of the Civil War in Angola, 1974–1990* (New Brunswick, N.J.: Transaction Publishers, 1992); F. A. Guimaraes, *The Origins of the Angolan Civil War: Foreign Intervention and Domestic Political Conflict* (London: Macmillan, 1998); A. D. Kwamba, D. M. Casmirio, N. J. Pedro, and L. B. Ngonda, "Angola," in *Comprehending and Mastering African Conflicts: The Search for Sustainable Peace and Good Governance*, ed. A. Adedeji (London: Zed Books, 1999); J. Marcum, *The Angolan Revolution*, vols. 1 and 2 (Cambridge, Mass.: MIT Press, 1969, 1978).

[12]M. Cahen, ed., *"Vilas" et "cidades" bourgs et villes en Afrique lusophone* (Paris: L'Harmattan, 1989).

[13]Guimaraes, *Origins of the Angolan Civil War.*

"tribalist" character, it remained strongly affiliated—most notably through its "popular defense" scheme—with Mbundu populations concentrated in and around the capital city of Luanda and representing 20 percent of the country's population.

UNITA was created by Savimbi and headed by him until his death in February 2002. His personal ambitions and frustration with the two main nationalist parties (FNLA and MPLA) with regard to their proposed official position, leadership, and policy led him to create the movement in 1966. He successively turned to the Portuguese, Chinese, South African, and American governments for assistance in his struggle against the MPLA. Although the movement admitted *mestiços* within its ranks, UNITA essentially consisted of provincial *assimilados* drawn from the central highlands and had a dominant ethnic base of Ovimbundu—the largest group, with 35 percent of the population—from the central highlands (*planalto*).[14]

The war of independence was marked by drastic Portuguese repression, and military fronts remained largely circumscribed to marginal areas on the borders or forested areas. Portuguese settlers continued arriving in Angola, which was experiencing unprecedented economic growth and diversification. Independence came about in 1975, more as a result of the fall of Antonio Salazar's regime in Portugal in 1974 and the proindependence stand of the new Portuguese government than as a victory of any of the three major competing Angolan nationalist parties. The Alvor Accords were signed in 1975 between the post-Salazarist Portuguese government and Angolan nationalist political parties to bring about an independent coalition government before national elections were held. The accords collapsed, however, as the political factions pursued a hegemonic agenda resulting in violent opposition and internecine conflicts. Successive wars have to a large extent maintained an armed and conspiratorial pattern of political engagement, rather than allowing a shift toward more peaceful and open interactions.

The division and competition within and between nationalist movements had major implications for their political radicalism and successive conflicts. Such political (under)development resulted from the repression of the Portuguese authorities, as well as personal ambitions, political ideology, social prejudice, ethnonationalism, and interventionism by regional and world

---

[14] A fourth party, the Cabinda Enclave Liberation Front, headed by Ranque Franque, has a secessionist agenda for the enclave of Cabinda and was not part of future national political accords.

powers;[15] as well as the political economic context made possible by the country's natural wealth. During the colonial period, clandestine work, exile, and the adoption of the armed struggle defined the political development of Angolan organizations.[16] The absence of local civil or labor movements, a free press, public demonstrations, or debate under the regime of Salazar did not prepare citizens for an early transition outside the framework of the competitive nationalist armed movements. Late reforms by the colonial regime in favor of the African population were not integrated by these movements, which imposed their divisions upon the population when a Portuguese power vacuum occurred in 1974–75.

The MPLA held the capital, Luanda, on the scheduled day of independence, and it defeated the Western- and Chinese-backed FNLA and the joint South African–UNITA offensives with the assistance of Cuban troops. Thus the MPLA became the de facto Angolan government. By 1976, the FLNA had been routed militarily, and many Bakongo were exiled in Zaire, coming back to Angola as an entrepreneurial/petty trading class only in the late 1980s. UNITA had also been routed militarily, and the civil war could have ended then. Yet, unlike the FNLA leadership, Savimbi remained in Angola and worked on rebuilding his movement with assistance from local populations in central Angola. Later on, he regained the support of South Africa as well as a number of African countries, including Zaire, and still later that of the United States and other Western powers.[17] The conflictual transition to independence thus turned into a lasting political and military stalemate. Half-hearted disengagement by Cold War patrons and South Africa following the New York Accords on the independence of Namibia and the withdrawal of Cuban and South African troops from Angola and Namibia, respectively, in 1988 (re)initiated the "Angolanization" of the conflict, giving further importance to local economic resources, even though UNITA continued to receive U.S. support.

[15]See C. Messiant, "Angola 1961: Histoire et société, les prémisses du mouvement nationaliste," Ph.D. thesis, École des Hautes Études de Sciences Sociales, Paris, 1983; Messiant, "Angola: The Challenge of Statehood," in *History of Central Africa: The Contemporary Years since 1960*, ed. D. Birmingham and P. M. Martin (London: Longman, 1998), 130–65.

[16]M. da Conceição Neto, "Angola: The Historical Context for Reconstruction," in *Communities and Reconstruction in Angola*, ed. P. Robson (Luanda: Development Workshop, 2001), 25–49.

[17]F. Bridgland, *Jonas Savimbi: A Key to Africa* (London: Hodder & Stoughton, 1988).

Beyond the dividing context of the Cold War, a hegemonic approach to power and deep distrust between MPLA and UNITA leaders undermined two successive peace processes—the 1991 Bicesse Peace Accords and the 1994 Lusaka Protocol—which were based more on tactical accommodation by Angolan parties than on genuine goodwill or international constraints. As explained by a UNITA general formerly in charge of concealing troops and weapons during United Nations–monitored demobilization processes:

> The collective motivation of [UNITA's] superstructure has been Maoist since its foundation, and continues to be so. The doctrine is that power flows from the barrel of a gun and power is indivisible. Agreements and negotiations are tactics for the assault on political power, to take over the power of the state.[18]

The hopes brought by the Bicesse Accords were dashed when Savimbi resumed the war after refusing to acknowledge his electoral defeat in 1992 to President dos Santos's MPLA, and the latter retaliated with indiscriminate killings of UNITA supporters and Ovimbundu people in Luanda—reinforcing the ethnicization of the conflict.[19] The ensuing two years of warfare led to more devastation than had occurred throughout three decades of the independence struggle and Cold War conflict, as the bush war turned into battles for controlling major cities.[20] Now claiming that it retained its arms during the peace process to defend its expected electoral victory from any military reaction of the MPLA, UNITA's military structure had remained ready to strike against a governmental army weakened by demobilizations.[21]

[18]General Diógenes Raúl Malaquias 'Implacável,' interview at the United Nations, 2000.

[19]M. J. Anstee, *Orphan of the Cold War: The Inside Story of the Collapse of the Angolan Peace Process, 1992–93* (Basingstoke, U.K.: Macmillan, 1996); K. Maier, *Angola: Promises and Lies* (London: Serif, 1996). The electoral results were 53.7 percent for MPLA and 34.1 percent for UNITA for the National Assembly and 49.7 percent for dos Santos and 40 percent for Savimbi for the presidency (second turn for necessary majority canceled due to the resumption of war). President dos Santos promised new elections for 2002.

[20]Human Rights Watch, *Arms Trade and Violations of the Laws of War since the 1992 Elections* (New York: Human Rights Watch, 1994); United Nations, *Updated Consolidated Inter-Agency Appeal for Angola* (New York: United Nations, 1996).

[21]Implacavel interview, 2000.

With Luanda as its ultimate military objective, UNITA rapidly extended its territory to control more populations and to secure revenues, through the control of diamond-mining areas, and losses for the government, through the destruction of infrastructure including onshore oil installations. With huge military spending and the assistance of mercenaries enabled by oil-collaterized loans, the MPLA government succeeded in gaining back the control of the most strategic locations in the country, with the exception of important diamond mining areas. Negotiations between the two parties resulted in November 1994 in the Lusaka Protocol, bringing back a relative peace and motivating the United Nations to send a more significant peace-keeping force (known as UNAVEM III).

Following the reluctance of UNITA to abide by the Lusaka Protocol and President dos Santos's decision in December 1998 to resume the war "to save peace," Angola became one of the worst conflict resolution failures of the 1990s. About two-thirds of the half-million war victims died since resumption of the conflict in 1992, the majority due to the collapse of food security and health services. An estimated 1.5 million people were internally displaced, and 330,000 fled the country.[22] Despite military victories by government force over key UNITA strongholds since 1999, the idea of complete victory was initially rejected, even by the armed forces, as UNITA intensified an effective guerrilla war. By 2001, however, the isolation of UNITA forces from most of its sources of support had broken the rebel movement. The forced displacement of local populations in the central eastern provinces cut access to food and labor. The military backing of pro-MPLA governments or policies in the region (including through military interventions in the Democratic Republic of the Congo, the Republic of the Congo, and to a lesser degree in Namibia) cut regional support. Finally, a widespread consensus among Western powers in favor a governmental military victory rather than further negotiations led to a more effective implementation of sanctions.

At a societal level, "the effect of more than twenty years of postindependence wars on national cohesion has been paradoxical. While national awareness grew, national unity weakened."[23] The independence struggle

[22]J.-M. Balancie and A. de La Grange, *Mondes rebelles: Guerres civiles et violences politiques* (Paris: Michalon, 1999); UN Office for Coordination of Humanitarian Affairs, *2000 Mid-Term Review of the UN Consolidated Inter-Agency Appeal for Angola (Jan.–June 2000)* (New York: UN Office for Coordination of Humanitarian Affairs, New York, 2000).
[23]Da Conceição Neto, *Angola*, 38.

and ideology of the two main parties have reinforced the idea of "Angola" and "Angolan's rights." Population movements have reinforced national consciousness through the spread of Portuguese and the mixing of different regions. Yet, the country is militarily divided, the economy remains highly fragmented, and national mechanisms of solidarity have weakened during the past decade as class stratification and inequalities have increased. There are now deeply embedded structural divisions within society, which the dominance of the oil sector and the political economy of the regime have further reinforced. Though many Ovimbundu have moved to the cities, most find themselves among a numerically dominant but politically and economically marginalized group.

MPLA Ideology and Presidential Politics

The MPLA government has faced considerable problems in asserting its sovereignty and legitimacy since independence. Militarily, UNITA progressively took over the hinterland in the 1980s and left the government in control of only the coast and provincial towns, reflecting the duality of political power and claims for legitimacy. Internally, the division between partisans of a populist socialism and the *nomenklatura* led by Neto resulted in a failed uprising in 1977 by the former, purges in the party, and the consolidation of presidential rule.[24] Theoretically a "mass movement" of socialist obedience, the MPLA was fundamentally an elitist movement that turned into a "party apparatus" after co-optation of, or violent confrontations with, competing groups. Though an orthodox "Marxist-Leninist" political line reigned, the personal convictions of party members "were hidden [and] conflicts over policy direction and fights over group interests took the form of silent struggles for posts and privileges."[25] After initial reforms started in 1985, notably under pressure from leading Luanda families eager to develop private business interests, in 1990 the MPLA abandoned its references to Marxism-Leninism and the one-party system.[26]

Despite constitutional changes toward a parliamentarian democracy in the 1990s, the overall political structure remained one of personalistic rule by the president and his entourage, yet less extreme than in the case of UNITA.

[24]Hodges, *Angola: From Afro-Stalinism to Petro-Diamond Capitalism* (Oxford: James Currey, 2001).
[25]Messiant, *Angola*, 153.
[26]Hodges, *Angola*, 12.

Having been nominated by the president, most provincial governors ruled their province as private fiefdoms, embezzling much of the budget through "phantom" civil servants or overbudgeted public projects awarded to their private companies. In the pro-MPLA province of Malange, a former minister of health with a reputation for corruption long remained governor despite accusations of commercial dealings with UNITA and large-scale embezzlement of public resources, before being ousted by presidential decision following widespread opposition among the MPLA, the local population, and the aid community. This gynecologist, who by all accounts was an embarrassment to the regime, had boasted that his presidential protection came from his intimate involvement in the most private aspects of presidential life.[27] Using his presidential position—occasionally extended to that of prime minister—as well as the financial and institutional context created by the centralized control of the oil rent and allocation of state resources, dos Santos acted as the tactical arbiter of a clientelist presidential regime. His relative victory in the September 1992 presidential elections reinforced his legitimacy and power, allowing distancing from the MPLA and the eviction of contenders.

Similarly, the privatization of most sectors of the economy has allowed dos Santos's close relatives and cronies to take up economic stakes, as did his daughter Isabel in ASCORP—a joint venture between the government, private Angolan interests close to the president, and diamond-marketing companies from Belgium and Israel, headed by Lev Levied. People in the immediate presidential entourage were not the only ones, however, to seize economic opportunities. Many generals, in particular, grew increasingly independent through diamonds mining and trafficking, cattle trading, private security firms, the privatization of state farms and real estate, or the import sector. Dos Santos's declaration of nonparticipation in elections that kept being postponed may accelerate reforms and the institutionalization of more democratic politics, but such a prospect also risks a breakdown of an already tenuous political order.

The former socialist ideology and centralism of the Angolan state, as well as its direct control of key sectors of the economy, have placed the government at the heart of Angolan society. Yet the state has been absent, especially in the hinterland, and it has become further disengaged from its role of social services provider as a result of the huge costs of the war and its corrupt profits. The official shift from socialism to a "liberal market democracy"

---

[27]Interviews with anonymous civil society members, Luanda and Malange, 2001.

(in fact, a single-party "petro-regime") further aggravated this disengagement. As was noted by the president of UNITA "Renovada," who integrated the peace process:

> The strength of Savimbi [came] from the state's absence in the hinterland. It is not that Savimbi is strong, but that the state is weak; and it is weak because the state leadership is uninterested [in the population].

Criticism within and against the MPLA has generally been muted, in part through the exile of major players and co-optation; the government finances most "opposition" parties and rewards supportive members of parliament.[28] If there has been some progress during the past decade in more freedom of opinion and public political opposition, arbitrary arrests and repression are still taking place, while populations remain at the mercy of arbitrary rule by a corrupt and politically immune *nomenklatura*.[29]

Savimbi's UNITA

UNITA's history was inextricably linked to that of its leader, Jonas Savimbi. His ambitions and achievements as a political entrepreneur were linked to his personal background, opportunism in securing allies, and the failures of the MPLA regime, as well the ideology and grievances of his core group of supporters among the Ovimbundu and other populations of the hinterland, for which UNITA filled a gap of political representation left by the MPLA and FNLA. Savimbi's grandfather participated in the Bailundo war of 1902, one of the most violent attempt to resist Portuguese domination, and his father joined the Protestant church, gaining through this education the status of *assimilado* and a position of railway stationmaster rarely given to an African. The work of Savimbi's father with the Protestant church participated in setting up an alternate society under Ovimbundu control, through its own schools, churches, clinics, and leadership institutions.[30]

[28]Hodges, *Angola*, 58.

[29]As experienced by the author in July 2001, when arrested and deported following research on a notoriously corrupt provincial governor; a gynecologist who was formerly the minister of health and was reportedly close to, and protected by, President dos Santos for private reasons.

[30]L. M. Heywood, "Towards an Understanding of Modern Political Ideology in Africa: The Case of the Ovimbundu of Angola," *Journal of Modern African Studies* 36, no. 1 (1998): 139–67.

While seeking a role in the independence struggle, Savimbi was apparently hurt by Neto's derogatory remarks toward Southerners and found the FNLA unrepresentative and its leadership, authoritarian, and incompetent.[31] Ideologically, Savimbi was frequently referred to as a Maoist, but though he did train in China and put in practice Mao's guerrilla theories, he did not support Maoist economic ones.[32] Politically, UNITA has been arguing for the "genuine [African] nationalism" against the "tainted [foreign] nationalism" of the MPLA.[33] As such, the movement stood for the "total" independence of Angola—finding beyond the dominance of *mestiços* in the MPLA government a new justification in the Cuban and Soviet presence after the departure of the Portuguese—while pragmatically associating itself with apartheid South Africa.

Throughout the history of the UNITA movement, Savimbi developed opportunistic relationships with a number of external sources as diverse as Portuguese intelligence, China, apartheid South Africa, Saudi Arabia, and the United States. The international diamonds market, or more precisely its intermediaries, was just one more such external source of support. The main difference was that diamond dealers enabled Savimbi to become independent from international public opinion and to a large extent from foreign state allies—at least until the diamond industry came under the light of the media for trading in "conflict diamonds." Even then, according to the president of a dissident UNITA branch now on the government side, "Savimbi [could] hide during two years but foreign diamond dealers [would] still find him to trade."[34] Savimbi's killing on February 22, 2002, by government troops in the pro-vince of Moxico proved otherwise. Isolated in the central eastern province of Moxico, UNITA's leader reportedly died with a sizable stock of diamonds, having no one with whom to trade them even for food and leaving most of his troops starving.[35]

Foreign military and financial support is not sufficient for a rebel group over the long term: UNITA status and continued survival in the late 1980s stemmed "primarily from its long-standing ability to express Ovimbundu

---

[31]Bridgland, *Jonas Savimbi*, 41.

[32]Bridgland, *Jonas Savimbi*, 41.

[33]Heywood, "Towards an Understanding," 148.

[34]Eugenio N'Golo, " 'Manuvakola': President of UNITA 'Renovada,'" personal communication, Luanda, 2001.

[35]Interview with Lopos do Nascimento, citing General "Gato" Lukamba's wife, April 2002.

aspirations and social organization."[36] UNITA would represent something that was Ovimbundu and that Ovimbundu "could be really proud of."[37] Ovimbundu's "ethnic pride" had been sharpened by past abuse and scorn by Portuguese as well as FLNA and MPLA urban *assimilados*. Savimbi held his position in part because of his ability to exploit the legacy of precolonial political ideology that rests on two contrasting forms of leadership: blacksmith kings and hunter kings—the latter more autocratic and violent than the former, but nonetheless as legitimate.[38]

Contrary to the MPLA, which theoretically maintained an "antitribalist" policy, Savimbi also recognized and used customary authorities and powers. In 1993, he recognized the authority of the Zaire-based Lunda paramount titleholder's authority by calling on him to ritually protect and "hide" the main diamond-mining area of UNITA in Cafunfo (in Lunda Norte province), which was threatened by MPLA aerial bombardments. Savimbi subsequently used this for propaganda, while his troops abused the local Lunda population.[39]

Savimbi's main historical grievance and justification for waging a rebellion was that "all the bloodshed and destruction was started by those who destroyed Angola's promised electoral process back in 1975"—referring to the FNLA and MPLA.[40] The foundation of this grievance was, however, bluntly undermined by Savimbi's bellicose attitude during and after such electoral process was finally followed in 1992. According to UNITA supporters, the main obstacles to peace were the corruption of the government and its continued capacity to purchase weapons from oil and diamond revenues.

It is difficult to ascertain whether UNITA's denunciations over the use of "genocidal oil" by the government was given credit by a large part of the population, but some poor people in the capital echoed them, often with xenophobic overtones. For a twelve-year-old street child, the war was about an Angolan, Savimbi, who was trying to expel a group from São Tomé and Príncipe that took power from Neto after his death and that continually stole

[36]L. M. Heywood, "UNITA and Ethnic Nationalism," *Journal of Modern African Studies* 27, no. 1: 47–66; the quotation is on 49.

[37]Amelia Cardozo, cited in Heywood, "UNITA," 52.

[38]Heywood, "Towards an Understanding."

[39]Filip De Boeck, "Postcolonialism, Power and Identity: Local and Global Perspectives from Zaire," in *Postcolonial Identities in Africa*, ed. Richard Werbner and Terence Ranger (London: Zed Books, 1996), 78.

[40]Bridgland, *Jonas Savimbi*, 460.

the wealth of the country ever since—the reason why he was poor.[41] Popular support for Savimbi, however, dropped drastically following increased abuses by UNITA troops after 1992, and while Savimbi's charisma and supporters' self-interest once also motivated adhesion to the movement, coercive means came to play the most significant role as people increasingly doubted their personal project of "self-realization" within and through UNITA.[42] Hopes of financial rewards and privileges to be gained through the UNITA electoral success in 1992 failed to materialize, as did a military victory. In contrast, the MPLA's political accommodation and co-optation, as well as amnesties, offered significant rewards from the government side. Finally, former UNITA members who became critics pointed to the privileges received by Savimbi's children and relatives, arguing that it was in this respect following a path similar to that of dos Santos's presidential rule.

Although sources on the current status and workings of UNITA were limited to defectors and refugees, the overall picture was one of rule through fear. UNITA's security apparatus, the status of Savimbi as "all seeing" among many of the rank and file, as well as severe punishment (including summary executions for such offenses as making or drinking alcohol, stealing diamonds, or disrespecting officers), have long instilled fear and a culture of strict discipline within the ranks and the population.[43] In diamond-mining camps, the internal security harshly imposed through torture and summary executions by UNITA soldiers or Congolese "collaborators" (*artivistes*) explains much about Savimbi's capacity to centralize diamonds trade and revenue, even in his fiefdom of Andulo.[44]

Politically, Savimbi maintained an autocratic rule by murdering dissenters and competitors, occasionally under the pretext of ridding the movement of witches—officials allegedly accused of abusing their power to satisfy their greed and self-interest—a practice legitimated by precolonial Ovimbundu political ideology.[45] Many senior officials left the movement

[41]President dos Santos's father was allegedly from São Tomé and Príncipe; interview, Luanda, 2001.

[42]Abel Chivukuvuku, UNITA member of parliament, personal communication, Luanda 2001.

[43]Interviews with eyewitnesses, Malange, 2001.

[44]Filip De Boeck, "Garimpeiro Worlds: Digging, Dying and 'Hunting' for Diamonds in Angola," *Review of African Political Economy* 28, no. 90: 554–55. Interviews with diamonds buyers, 2001 and 2002.

[45]For a former Ovimbundu slave trader interviewed in 1914, society was disorderly because of the new political situation resulting from the takeover of the state by Euro-

fearing for their life, some after extended periods of incarceration, which led to the integration of UNITA members, such as UNITA Renovada, into the peaceful political process.

Savimbi's death in combat in 2002 marked a watershed in Angola's tragic history by providing the government and the remaining UNITA hierarchy with a unique opportunity to end a twenty-six-year war. His death and that of his second in command, Antonio Dembo, followed a military campaign of depopulation and crop burning in Moxico province aimed at starving local rebel units. The tales of "greed-driven war" did not appear to match the emaciated faces of many hard-line UNITA commanders who could have settled in Luanda, Burkina Faso, or elsewhere with their supposed diamond wealth.[46] Peace is deemed to finally settle in Angola— given the poor morale and military situation of UNITA; a comprehensive cease-fire, disarmament, and reintegration agreement signed by the new UNITA leader, Paulo "Gato" Lukamba; and a general amnesty law for UNITA fighters.

Greed: Diamonds, Oil, and War

Although Angola's natural wealth was likely to constitute a major prize to the winning party and to have played a role in the strategic decisions of the belligerents and foreign backers, there is very little available evidence indicating that a scramble over Angola's resources significantly influenced the early phase of the civil war. Greed, in other words, would not appear as a major factor in starting the conflict. From a Portuguese perspective, the military defense of colonial possessions had as much to do with the imperialist ideology of the Salazarist regime as the growing economic interests provided by the colony. Even fast-rising oil revenues in the context of the 1973 oil crisis did not derail the independence process launched by the new

peans who outlawed traditional practices—among which was the burning of "witches": people accumulating and abusing power for selfish purposes. Abuses of power for selfish motives by the new state and its local agents in this early colonization period for the central highlands included forced labor and apartheid policies, land grabbing, physical abuses, and the undermining of traditional authorities. Heywood, "Towards an Understanding."

[46]The possibility that Savimbi's associates would have turned him in, or even killed him to cut a deal with the government, and possibly enjoy their diamonds wealth, has not been in any way reported.

Portuguese government. Although the nationalist parties undoubtedly realized that controlling the capital was the key to power, Savimbi himself had
underplayed the significance of oil to his supporters by declaring that "the
MPLA controls the capital, but in Luanda they produce only sand. Here [on
the central plateau] we produce food."[47]

At a regional level, while Zaire eyed the oil resources of the enclave of
Cabinda, the necessity of transporting Zairian and Zambian copper on Angolan railways actually dampened the conflict, with both countries withdrawing support for opposition parties in 1976. South Africa's military intervention in Angola was not so much motivated by a resource grab as by
the understanding that the natural wealth of the country, and oil in particular, would provide a communist state with much greater independence
toward Pretoria than it had expected from a country as economically dependent upon South Africa as Mozambique.[48] If the U.S. government did
embargo the oil revenues generated under the MPLA by U.S. companies,
it relaxed this decision in 1976 along with the Clark amendment, which
prohibited funding UNITA until 1985.[49] Finally, the Soviet Union and
Cuba did not undermine U.S. and Western economic interests in the Angolan oil and diamond sectors. Though Cuba's position on the cobalt market may have given it incentives to intervene in favor of the rebellion in
the cobalt-producing province of Katanga/Shaba in Zaire during 1978, allegations by the Mobutu regime and the Jimmy Carter administration were
not demonstrably supported.[50]

Natural resources, however, came to significantly influence the course of
the conflict as foreign backing started to dwindle. Oil funding for the
MPLA and diamond funding for UNITA is a simplistic yet relatively accurate reading of the Angolan war economy. Until recently, this division
over natural resources was reinforced by the war, as the government lost
control over diamonds, while oil remained out of reach of UNITA due to its
mostly offshore location. Throughout the 1990s, this duality and comple-

---

[47]Bridgland, *Jonas Savimbi*, 19.

[48]The South African Defense Force, however, did move into southern Angola to
protect South African investments in the Cunene River hydroelectric dam. Guimaraes,
Origins of the Angolan Civil War, 131.

[49]G. Wright, *The Destruction of a Nation: United States' Policy towards Angola
since 1945* (London: Pluto Press, 1997).

[50]William Blum, *Killing Hope: U.S. Military and CIA Interventions since World
War II* (Monroe, Maine: Common Courage Press, 1995).

mentarity of resources consolidated MPLA's and UNITA's respective political and military terrain. International resource-based business schemes were keys to sustaining capital-intensive armies when foreign state backing ended in the early 1990s, and as such participated in the belligerents' security dilemma and violent drive for power.

Yet, despite UNITA's losing its control of most major mining sites during the past four years and facing difficulties in converting its large diamond stock into fuel and weapons, the war did not end before the death of Savimbi.[51] Instead, UNITA shifted to guerrilla activities in large part sustained by predation over civilians and commercial trade.

UNITA's Diamond Windfall

Although previous support, most notably from South Africa and the United States, had provided UNITA with significant reserves of arms, additional income for rearmament was nevertheless necessary to sustain its military offensive, especially given the intensity of shelling on besieged towns such as Huambo and Kuito.[52] Since the early 1990s, as acknowledged by UNITA's former chief of staff, General Arlindo Pena ("Ben Ben"),

> diamonds are UNITA's lifeblood. Without them UNITA wouldn't be able to maintain its options . . . [such as] military reserves so that the government doesn't destroy us.[53]

Alongside gold, timber, and wildlife products, diamonds were a source of revenue for UNITA starting in the late 1970s.[54] UNITA first concentrated its attacks on existing mines, raiding and racketing companies as well as *garimpeiros* (i.e., freelance diggers). From 1983 onward, UNITA professionalized its diamond operations, training its staff in diamond sorting and investing in mining equipment. It not only stood to benefit financially from

---

[51]UN sanction monitor, personal communication, Luanda, 2001.

[52]A. Vines, personal communication, London, 2000.

[53]Human Rights Watch, *Angola Unravels: The Rise and Fall of the Lusaka Peace Process* (New York: Human Rights Watch, 1999).

[54]R. Reeve and S. Ellis, "An Insider's Account of the South African Security Forces' Role in the Ivory Trade," *Journal of Contemporary African Studies* 13 (1995): 213–33; Bridgland, *Jonas Savimbi*.

such raids, but they also undermined government revenues, which dropped from $221 million in 1981 to $33 million in 1986.[55]

Starting in the second half of the 1980s, commercial activities were extended to a quasi-industrial scale and commercial networks were reinforced as the guerrilla war reached the Lunda provinces in the northeast, in part thanks to U.S. assistance allowing UNITA to set up operations from military sanctuaries in Zaire. By the late 1980s, UNITA had greater control in northern regions and directly exploited mines, as well as recruited, controlled, and taxed many *garimpeiros*, generating several million dollars per month.[56] Following the withdrawal of U.S. and South African support in the early 1990s, UNITA's reliance on diamond revenues increased and further influenced its military strategy.

With the Bicesse Accords in 1991 and the relative halt of hostilities, production had sharply increased following a massive influx of *garimpeiros*, military entrepreneurship, and foreign companies. The military advantage enjoyed by UNITA following the resumption of the conflict in late 1992 allowed it to gain control over vast mining areas and to capture key mines.[57] UNITA's quasi-monopoly on the control of diamond exploitation until mid-1994, which was undermined by mercenary-led government forces' recapture of some mining areas, and the Lusaka Protocol brought about a new period of relative peace, which attracted mining companies and traders to expand exploitation.[58]

As the war started again, both the geographical conditions of access to such a valuable resource and the complacency, if not complicity, of the international diamond industry were key. If diamonds had been available mostly from kimberlite or seabed deposits (e.g., as in Botswana and Namibia, respectively), UNITA would have undoubtedly found their control and exploitation more difficult, if not impossible, due to access and investment problems. The same can be said about a responsive international community and a responsible diamond industry not allowing the trade in "conflict diamonds."

[55]J. Cilliers and C. Dietrich, eds., *Angola's War Economy: The Role of Oil and Diamonds* (Pretoria: International Institute for Strategic Studies, 2000); S. McCormick, *The Angolan Economy: Prospects for Growth in a Postwar Environment* (Washington, D.C.: Center for Strategic and International Studies, 1994).

[56]Bridgland, *Jonas Savimbi.*

[57]F. Misser and O. Vallée, *Les Gemmocraties: L'économie politique du diamant Africain* (Paris: Desclée de Brouwer, 1997).

[58]D. Shearer, *Private Armies and Military Intervention*, Adelphi Paper 316 (Oxford: Oxford University Press, 1998).

UNITA's reluctance to give up its control over much of the diamond sector led to a lengthy process of negotiation with the MPLA over its legalization. In November 1996, the government and UNITA signed a memorandum of understanding granting UNITA "the right to control or to participate in the exploitation of certain diamond areas."[59] Accommodation at the local level between UNITA and MPLA military officers and officials also facilitated diamond extraction and trade. Up until January 1998, some UNITA and MPLA army officers were reported to have struck a "gentlemen's agreement" on the Cuango Valley, through which each side exploited a bank of the river. The situation was not uncommon.[60] Finally, many in the international community saw UNITA's control of diamonds as a necessary counterbalance to the MPLA's control over oil revenue, a position that the Lusaka Protocol had institutionalized by granting UNITA the post of minister of mines and geology.

To increase diamond revenues, UNITA developed transnational business partnerships; the most important with David Zollman, a partner in the Antwerp-based diamond trading company Glasol.[61] In partnership with the current chairman of Gecamines, George Forrest, as well as the backing of late Zairian president Mobutu Sese Seko, Zollman created the Cuango Mining Corporation, the largest UNITA-controlled mining operation before UN sanctions in 1998. The corporation sold licenses, taxed subbuyers, and recruited a large workforce—estimated at 100,000 and from whom UNITA took half the gravel production and best diamonds—from neighboring Zaire through an agreement with Mobutu. To facilitate his operations from Zaire, Zollman reportedly secured and operated through a position as consul of Chile.[62]

With the fall of its allies in Kinshasa and Brazzaville in 1997—in part following the military intervention of the MPLA government in Zaire and the Congo (Brazzaville). UNITA reoriented some of its land-based logistics through Zambia, with Burkina Faso, Côte d'Ivoire, Togo, and Rwanda also providing safe transit and trading places. Furthermore, government offensives

[59]P. Hare, *Angola's Last Best Chance for Peace: An Insider's Account of the Peace Process* (Washington, D.C.: United States Institute of Peace Press, 1998); R. W. Copson, *Angola: Background and Current Situation* (Bethesda, Md.: Penny Hill Press, 1997).

[60]*Africa Confidential* 39, no. 29 (1998): 3; DiamondsWork official, personal communication, London, 2000; Human Rights Watch, *Angola Unravels.*

[61]UN S/2000/1225.

[62]UN sanctions monitor, Luanda, 2001.

put additional pressure on UNITA to abandon its main diamond area—
Luzamba in the southern Cuango Valley—in early 1998, although it reportedly did so only after the most lucrative diamonds had been mined out.
The value of diamonds produced under UNITA's control for the period
1992 to 2000 is estimated at $3 to $4 billion, but the level of profits is unknown. Despite the UN presence and an arms embargo, UNITA's diamond
windfall was used to purchase military equipment, fuel, and other supplies.
This windfall "created premature over-confidence within UNITA, leading
the rebels to commit major military and political errors," including using
conventional warfare tactics that ultimately failed, given the government's
easier access to military hardware, fuel, and monopoly in airpower.[63]

As a result of a government takeover of mines in compliance with the
Lusaka Protocol, the depletion of existing mines in the absence of new investments, and UN sanctions imposed in 1998 against UNITA diamonds
mining and trading, as well as successful governmental offensives, UNITA-
controlled production fell from a peak of $600–760 million in 1996 to
$100–150 million in 2000.[64] The government also set up a diamond-
marketing monopoly controlled by ASCORP as well as improved diamond
certificates of origin to reduce possibilities of UNITA laundering diamonds
through legitimate channels.

However, diamond buying in the provinces was still carried out through
largely unmonitored intermediaries, providing UNITA with the opportunity
to access these channels. Although UNITA retained access to mining sites
and smuggling networks and held an important stockpile of diamonds, it
faced logistical and financial difficulties in translating this wealth into a
military capability. UNITA was therefore limited to guerrilla warfare after
losing its strongholds in 1999, and it largely relied for its supplies on the
predation of local populations and trade. UNITA—tracked by the army in
a province emptied of its population and with little wild food available—
was despite its diamond stock a spent force.

Yet UNITA was not the only belligerent benefiting from diamonds. Government army units and generals greatly benefited from the trade, with or
without the backing of President dos Santos, who used concession licenses

---

[63] Assis Malaquias, "Diamonds Are a Guerrilla's Best Friend: The Impact of Illicit
Wealth on Insurgency Strategy," *Third World Quarterly* 22, no. 3 (2001): 313.

[64] Global Witness, *A Rough Trade: The Role of Companies and Governments in the
Angolan Conflict* (London: Global Witness, 1998); United Nations, "Report of the Monitoring Mechanism on Angola Sanctions Established by Resolution 1295," S/2000/1225.

for patronage politics.[65] Though the MPLA side derives the bulk of its revenues from oil, diamonds were and remain of major importance in the governmental clientelist networks, in particular with regard to the army. Many so-called *garimpeiro* generals have become wealthy through their instrumentalization of war to secure access to diamond mines and through official concessions or informal digging, as well as their participation in trafficking. Diamond-trafficking networks previously linking UNITA mining areas to major import-export companies in Luanda survived and, although flouting regulations and the monopoly imposed through ASCORP, continued to be tolerated by the relevant authorities.

MPLA's Oil Sanctuary

Secure and abundant oil revenue representing an annual average of $2.5 billion helped the Angolan government to resist well-equipped South African and UNITA armies by building up a capital-intensive war machine with the assistance of its Cold War allies. Between 1992 and the end of the conflict in 2002, the government is estimated to have spent $20 billion on military expenditures—about 14 percent of Angola's Gross Domestic Product, with arms purchased mostly from former Warsaw Pact countries, with the financial assistance of oil brokers and Western banks providing the cash-strapped government with oil-collaterized loans.[66] This financial capacity influenced the domestic and regional political behavior of the government in favor of a militaristic approach. A government military officer argued that, in contrast to UNITA, "We always take losses, then recover. . . . If we lose a tank, we pick up the phone and order another one. If UNITA loses one, it is more difficult."[67] This strength also enticed the government to intervene militarily to root out support for UNITA in the Republic of Congo (Brazzaville) and the Democratic Republic of the Congo since 1997, as well as in Namibia in 1999.[68]

Military expenditures—paid from a public budget allocation, oil-collateralized short-term commercial loans, and signature bonuses from foreign companies for oil concessions—not only served security interests but also

[65]Hodges, *Angola*.

[66]IMF staff country reports; Human Rights Watch, *Arms Trade*; Human Rights Watch, *Angola Unravels;* SIPRI, Military Expenditure Database, Stockholm International Peace Research Institute, http://www.sipri.org.

[67]Angolan Armed Forces officer cited in Human Rights Watch, *Angola Unravels*.

[68]C. Gordon and H. French, "Angola Aids Congo to Corral Unita," *Globe and Mail*, October 17, 1997.

provided considerable opportunities for corruption.[69] This military buildup proved unsustainable when oil prices fell in 1998. The financial crisis faced by the government as it launched a new military campaign led to debt rene-gotiations, openings toward the International Monetary Fund, and the allo-cation of oil block shares to small companies largely unknown to the in-dustry and possibly linked to arms dealing.[70] The oil price recovery in 1999 and $900 million in signature bonuses for new oil concessions eased the financial crisis and facilitated arms purchases in 1999.[71]

Politically, the oil and other state rents have allowed the presidency to sus-tain a clientele beyond the military apparatus, building a degree of legitimacy among those rewarded and allowing support or resistance to reforms accord-ing to short-term expediency. This clientelism requires a contractual stabil-ity with foreign oil corporations, ensuring their long-term obedient partici-pation in the system, a stability indeed acknowledged and prized in return by corporations. The preservation of foreign corporate interests has long been rewarding for the government. By avoiding the nationalization of United States–based Gulf Oil (since taken over by Chevron) at independence, and even protecting it with Cuban troops during the 1980s, the government sus-tained oil rents, benefited from commercially driven diplomacy resisting Reagan's campaign against the (communist) regime, and attracted additional oil companies for capital-intensive exploration and development.[72]

[69]C. McGreal, 'Profiteers' War That Goes on For Ever," *Mail and Guardian*, July 2, 1999.

[70]Reportedly, these companies included Falcon Oil & Gas (10 percent equity partner in Exxon's block 33), involving Franco-Brazilian arms broker Pierre Falcone; Naphta (5 percent, also in block 33) associated with former Israeli General Ze'ev Zahrine, provider of security services to Angolan and Congolese governments; and ProDev (20 percent in Elf's block 32), a Swiss company with Syrian investors. Global Witness, *A Crude Awakening: The Role of the Oil and Banking Industries in Angola's Civil War and Plunder of State Assets* (London: Global Witness, 1999).

[71]Human Rights Watch, *Angola Unravels*; Human Rights Watch, *The International Monetary Fund's Staff Monitoring Program for Angola: The Human Rights Implica-tions* (London: Human Rights Watch, 2000).

[72]Ironically, a large number of Cuban soldiers were deployed to protect U.S. oil in-stallations while the U.S. government sponsored UNITA and the dollar revenues from American companies reimbursed Cuban troops and paid for Soviet weaponry, cf. V. Brit-tain, *Death of Dignity: Angola's Civil War* (London: Pluto Press, 1998). In a similar par-adox, MPLA troops protected the South African diamond company De Beers in its activ-ities with the state-owned company Diamang, while De Beers' corporate taxes in South Africa helped to finance South African support to UNITA, cf. Bridgland, *Jonas Savimbi*. As such, the political economy of Angolan oil and diamonds was fully integrated into the Cold War, with its revenue "cross-subsidizing" both superpowers and their allies.

The clientelist redistribution of oil and state rents involved the presidential entourage, state *nomenklatura*, and privileged sections of the population in mechanisms sustaining a relatively stable internal political order.[73] In continuation with the practice of the former socialist state, civil servants received personal privileges from the state or parastatal companies.[74] High-ranking civil servants, army officers, and politicians accessed profitable privatization schemes and received personalized "annual bonuses" that dwarfed their official earnings.[75] Some foreign oil companies also directly provided goods and services, deducted from the companies' tax bills, to prominent figures or their philanthropic associations, such as the Eduardo dos Santos Foundation, which played, at state expense, a growing role in extending presidential patronage politics and promoting a personal public image.[76] In 1995, 36 percent of the education budget was allocated to overseas scholarships and $400 million was allocated to subsidies on electricity, municipal water, air transport, and housing accessible only to a privileged minority within the population.[77] The subsequent cancellation of subsidies on gas at the demand of the International Monetary Fund and World Bank, conversely, affected the popular economy and household goods prices.

Achieving Peace in a Profitable War Economy

Separating the economic from the political and military dimensions of conflict in the pursuit of a negotiated settlement is a difficult task, given

[73]There is no precise estimate of the value of this redistribution. Oil industry sources suggest $500–800 million per year; World Bank staff estimate that in 1993 about $1 billion was "floating" between the national accounts figures and the government's budget figures' and had been allocated to a parallel military budget and to "transaction commissions"; cf. L. A. Pereira da Silva and A. Solimano, "The Transition and the Political Economy of African Socialist Countries at War (Angola and Mozambique)," in *African Economies in Transition*, ed. J. A. Paulson (Basingstoke, England: Macmillan, 1999), vol. 2, 9–67.

[74]Interview with Sonangol official, Luanda, July 1998.

[75]M. E. Ferreira, "La reconversion économique de la nomenklatura pétrolière," *Politique Africaine* 57 (1995): 11–26; K. Somerville, *Angola: Politics, Economics and Society* (London: Pinter, 1986); Hodges, *Angola*.

[76]C. Messiant, "La Fondation Eduardo dos Santos: À propos de l'investissement de la société civile par le pouvoir politique," *Politique Africaine* 73 (1999): 82–101.

[77]S. Kyle, *Angola: Current Situation and Future Prospects for the Macroeconomy*, CAER Paper 25 (Cambridge, Mass.: Harvard Institute for International Development, 1998); UNICEF, *Un futuro de esperança para as Crianças de Angola. Uma análise da situação da Criança* (Luanda: United Nations, 1999).

the importance of force in the power and security strategies of UNITA and the MPLA. The leaders of both the MPLA and UNITA fought for power and entertained a mutually exclusive notion of power that was only reinforced by the war and the failure of previous negotiated settlements. As both parties progressively lost both local popular and foreign state support, the dependence of their power on resources grew. Though their leaders saw resource control in the 1980s as *part* of power holding, from the early 1990s onward, both sides saw it as an element to *get* power.[78] Control over resource rents was indeed a key mechanism for the sustenance of their power and was dealt with as such by both movements.

Testifying to the importance of diamonds in the second peace process, the position of minister of mines and geology was first on the list of official postings granted to UNITA by the Lusaka Protocol. Yet the protocol failed to provide any details on the management of the sector aside from the obligation to hand over UNITA-held territory to the government. Negotiated solutions failed, and military offensives by the government on UNITA mines in 1997 undermined the peace process. In 1997, Savimbi stated that UN sanctions "would be regarded as an attack on UNITA to which it 'was ready to respond.'"[79] President dos Santos also systematically disregarded reforms requested by the International Monetary Fund when these imposed limitations on military spending or threatened his patronage.

For both belligerents, however, resource commodification and marketing depended on third parties, thereby opening avenues to influence peddling. International businesses were crucial in generating these revenues and sustaining the reluctance of the Angolan ruling elite to abandon violent bids to get or preserve state power and to implement reforms.[80]

Regulating the Oil Sector

Oil corporations developing huge new fields in the context of high oil prices long remained largely impervious to criticisms of their role in the conflict in Angola. The oil industry is also difficult to place under control, because of the size and political leverage of companies, the high capital and strategic stakes involved, and the long-term strategy adopted. However,

---

[78] Author interview with Abel Chivukuvuku, 2001.

[79] Human Rights Watch, *Angola Unravels*.

[80] The case of arms companies is not discussed here; for an analysis, cf. Human Rights Watch, *Angola Unravels*; United Nations, *Report of the Panel of Experts* (New York: United Nations, 2000).

the sector is exposed to some degree of public and international pressure. Beginning in 2000, most oil companies emphasized their shift toward "corporate citizenship," but this was not much translated into practice within Angola beyond often-politicized philanthropy. The provision by oil companies of their tax and royalty payments to the government as part of the "oil diagnostic" requested by the International Monetary Fund within the framework of a Staff Monitored Program of reforms was an important first step that should be followed by full public transparency in this sector—enforced, for example, through stock exchange regulations.[81] A greater degree of democratic participation over oil revenue allocation in the interest of peace and just redistribution remains crucial (see below).

Regulating the Diamond Sector

The alluvial diamond sector and trading in rough diamonds are notoriously difficult to control because of the small size of companies, potential profits, and the short-term strategy of businesspeople. Yet the diamond industry is now confronting its responsibility for Angola's misery, and important progress was achieved in a relatively short time in the early 2000s by international standards.

Given the importance of diamonds in funding the war, it may appear surprising that sanctions against UNITA's diamond trading were imposed only in June 1998. In fact, previous attempts had failed. In 1993, Belgian members of parliament proposed a ban on imports of UNITA diamonds, but the resolution failed.[82] Several reasons have been advanced. Technically, the diamond trade is difficult to control because of the secrecy of trade networks and the difficulty of asserting the origin of diamonds when semipolished or mixed with diamonds of other provenance. Financially, the industry and major importing countries (e.g., Belgium and Israel) have not favored constraining controls. Because of the mobility of the trade and importers, Belgium in particular feared losing out on a lucrative sector. Increased underground trading could also have undermined the De Beers–Central Selling Organization cartel and the stability of high prices. De Beers subsequently changed its strategy and attempted to create an image of "clean" diamonds to strengthen its brand, rather than the whole industry.

[81]Human Rights Watch, *The Oil Diagnostic in Angola: An Update* (London: Human Rights Watch, 2001).

[82]About 80 percent of world rough diamonds pass through Antwerp. Cf. Misser and Vallée, *Gemmocraties*.

To tighten sanctions on UNITA, the UN Sanctions Committee set up an independent Panel of Experts in mid-1999 (UNSC Resolution 1237). As the first of its kind, the panel drew inspiration and expertise from the investigative UN panel on the genocide in Rwanda. Such panels have since been replicated in Sierra Leone and Liberia, as well as in the Democratic Republic of the Congo, and a more permanent Monitoring Mechanism has replaced it in Angola. Though the UN Security Council took no further concrete measures based on the recommendations of the panel, such as so-called secondary sanctions against sanctions busters, the United Nations was able to unusually "name and shame" sanctions busters.[83] Aside from private sanctions busters, the report detailed cases of UN diamond sanction busting by authorities in the Congo (Brazzaville), Côte d'Ivoire, Rwanda, and the Democratic Republic of the Congo. It specifically singled out the heads of state in Togo and Burkina Faso for facilitating, in exchange for payment by UNITA, arms purchases (by providing end-user importation certificates and logistics), diamond and financial dealings, as well as travel facilities and protection to UNITA members and their families.[84]

The first panel's report also criticized Belgium for failing to effectively regulate its rough diamond market, the largest in the world.[85] Even the Angolan government waited until September 1999 to improve a fraudulent diamond certification system used by officials and dealers to launder UNITA diamonds, demonstrating the opportunistic self-interest prevalent in this industry.[86] Though by late 2000, the Angolan government claimed to have routed UNITA from diamond areas, the United Nations reported that UNITA "continues to mine diamonds and move them to the market."[87] Its diamond revenues, however, declined significantly, and though it is difficult to point at the relative importance of the sanctions, panel reports, and military factors, this new regulatory focus on the war

---

[83]See UNSC Resolution 1295. For a critique, including the lack of investigation in two key countries, the Democratic Republic of the Congo and Israel, cf. Human Rights Watch, *The U.N. Sanctions Committee on Angola: Lessons Learned?* (London: Human Rights Watch, 2000); Action for Southern Africa, *Waiting on Empty Promises: The Human Cost of International Inaction on Angolan Sanctions* (London: Action for Southern Africa, 2000).

[84]United Nations, *Report of the Panel of Experts.*

[85]United Nations, *Report of the Panel of Experts.* Belgium was, however, one of the most regulated countries and published official statistics.

[86]*O Pensador*, Newsletter of the Angolan Embassy in the United States, 1999.

[87]"IRIN Focus on Interim Sanctions Report," *IRIN* (Angola), October 31, 2000.

economies is deemed to stay and be extended to other rebel movements and their supporters.

A number of nongovernmental organizations, such as Human Rights Watch and Global Witness, continue to put pressure on the Angolan government and international corporations to bring about transparency and accountability in the resource sectors. Angolan pressure groups have also pursued a similar agenda (e.g., Group for Reflection on Peace). As an example of a qualified success, the Fatal Transactions campaign (associating Global Witness, NiZA, Medico International, and NOVIB) against "conflict diamonds" from Angola, the Democratic Republic of the Congo, and Sierra Leone, triggered along with the UN reports an international process of reform.[88] The Kimberley Process Certification Scheme, which was put in place in 2003—and later joined by an industry convinced of the need to keep a "clean" image of diamonds in front of mounting evidence of complicity with belligerents—created an international system of certification that is helping to prevent conflict diamonds from reaching the legal market.

A Regulatory Framework for War Economies

Directly financing the conflict and aggravating the security dilemma by providing the means for an arms race, oil and diamond revenues also act as strong disincentives for rival groups to reach any sustainable agreement on political and economic reforms. Even if more could be gained at a national level from peace than war, many of the most influential people—at all levels—have a stake in the war economy, its distortions, and corruption opportunities.

A negotiated settlement has to harness the role of the private sector in the conflict and prevent the continuation of "business as usual" that played such a negative role in the course and impact of the conflict.[89] A first step is to ensure that all financial dealings of companies are made fully transparent and accountable. This can be achieved by regulating access to goods and financial markets, such as through stock exchange transparency requirements for listed companies (i.e., the publication of all net payments to govern-

[88]Global Witness, *Campaign Launched to Stop Billion Dollar Diamond Trade from Funding Conflict in Africa* (London: Global Witness, 1999). On Sierra Leone, cf. A. Alio, "Diamonds Are Forever . . . but Also Are Controversies: Diamonds and the Actors in Sierra Leone's Civil War," *Civil Wars* 2, no. 3 (1999): 43–64.

[89]P. Le Billon, *Regulating Transnational Businesses during Armed Conflicts* (London: Overseas Development Institute, 2001).

ments by listed companies and their subsidiaries) or certification schemes for commodity markets such as diamonds or timber.

Second, the investigation and criminalization of sanctions busting should help in ending the bankrolling of belligerents fueling the conflict and impeding peace. Notorious diamond and arms dealers are still not under an international mandate of arrest despite appearing in UN sanctions-busting reports. At an international level, the possibility of legally empowered partnerships between a permanent sanctions-monitoring mechanism under the UN Security Council, an investigation and international warrant capacity under Interpol, and a universal jurisdiction held by the International Criminal Court should be examined.

Third, beyond "naming and shaming" and other rhetorical measures, a regulatory framework should deprive belligerents of revenues allowing them to follow a double agenda of peace transition and rearmament, as has happened twice in Angola. Business dealings with belligerents could come under an internationally supervised mechanism of tax collection over key resource sectors and budgetary allocation, using escrow funds and strict sanctions to ensure compliance (figure 5.1).[90] Populations would benefit from tax transfers to social services, while the respective administrative and military structures of belligerents would receive monitored budgetary support to implement their effective integration into the new government structure. Businesses themselves should be deterred from carrying out activities outside such a mechanism through a system of incentives and sanctions bringing together international legislation with investigation and prosecution agencies. If successful, and in the absence of alternative sources of support, opting out of a peace process should become a costly if not financially impossible alternative for belligerents. With regard to Angola, the military and economic upper hand of the government since the late 1990s meant that such a scheme was not in its interest. Beyond the conflict, it is unlikely to accept any thorough form of economic supervision—at least as long as oil prices remain high.

Although there is now more certainty about a lasting peace in Angola, other major domestic uncertainties and challenges remain, including ban-

---

[90]Such a scheme has been attempted as a measure of conflict prevention and budgetary allocation to priority sectors in Chad in relation to the development of the oil sector and pipeline through Cameroon. The UN panel on Liberia has also recommended a similar scheme for the earnings of the Liberian shipping and corporate registry.

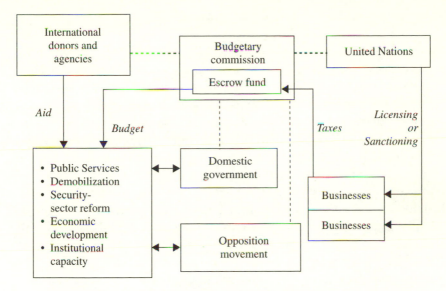

Figure 5.1. Interim Peace Consolidation Tax and Budgetary Regime

ditry by military and UNITA fighters, the resettlement of 3 million displaced people, and the diversification and growth of the economy outside the oil and diamond sectors. Armed opposition in the Cabinda enclave continues to challenge the Angola government, even though the separatist movement is only a minor security threat for it. Most important, the government and political forces also need to reform a pattern of economic and political governance long criticized as corrupt. Repeated failures to bring about transparency in the oil sector in particular have resulted in criticisms and disengagement from nongovernmental organizations, the International Monetary Fund, and some major donors.[91] Though the government long blamed the war for its incapacity to deliver on poverty alleviation and accountable politics, this reason may soon appear as a false pretense if the government fails to rapidly deliver peaceful conditions. To accomplish this, it will need to tackle banditry and rein in army generals and provincial governors, accept and promote genuinely democratic politics, bring about economic reforms, and manage the problem of the succession of President Dos Santos, who scheduled general elections for 2006.

[91]Human Rights Watch, *Some Transparency, No Accountability: The Use of Oil Revenue in Angola and Its Impact on Human Rights* (New York: Human Rights Watch, 2004).

Conclusion

As illustrated by the case of Angola, a resource-rich context can affect the role of need, creed, and greed in armed conflicts. As suggested by I. William Zartman, need can constitute the first paving stone of the road to hostilities, prepared by the greed of the incumbent rulers. The contrast between widespread poverty and resource wealth can exacerbate a feeling of destitution that will help awareness and mobilization, especially among educated and economically or politically frustrated groups. Creed can continue to pave this road, for the sharpness of this contrast will contribute to define confrontational identities between "exploiters" and "dispossessed"—with socialized and territorialized identities matching the pattern of rent redistribution and the sites of resource exploitation. Finally, greed can easily fall into place as a result of vast wealth at stake and the opportunistic context that hostilities provide.

In this light, it is not Angola's natural resources—oil and diamonds—that were the cause of the Angolan conflict. Yet the political economy and spatial distribution of Angolan oil and diamonds affected the course of the conflict. Oil and diamonds provided means for each contender to sustain a hegemonic and militaristic attitude, thereby influencing political institutions and military options. Natural resources did not only prolong war by providing the means and rewards of fighting. Because it is embedded in political ideologies and colonial practices of indivisible power holding and violent resource extraction, the political economy of oil and diamonds also sustained the conflict by exempting contending leaderships from compromise, public legitimacy, and political accountability.

Even if he had not had diamonds, Savimbi would probably have gone back to war in 1992. Yet diamond revenues had a terrible impact upon the Angolan population, because UNITA's military capacity and support network in the 1990s relied on a continued flow of diamond revenues. After 1997, UNITA was increasingly restricted in its access to large diamond revenues and the logistical and political networks to which they were connected. As a result, UNITA came to hold a much weaker political and economic position than the government. Beyond the rebellion issue, the current capture by and incorporation of diamond rents into presidential patronage politics, as well as the local resistance this political economy generates, cast doubts on the ability of Angola to follow Botswana's diamond windfall path to development. Although the oil rent helped to prevent a military takeover by apartheid South Africa and UNITA through a military buildup, the ensuing conflict was devastating and economic management was disastrous. Beyond its military victory over UNITA, the government still needs to build power through political legitimacy, starting with improved economic management.

Oil and diamonds had become major political resources serving the interests of belligerents and justifying their warmongering behavior. On one hand, UNITA was able to sustain a degree of popular support thanks to the idea that it was fighting a foreign elite stealing national wealth. Through this discourse, the rebel movement linked the greed of current rulers to the creed and needs of a "genuinely Angolan" impoverished population. Even if not supporting UNITA or its xenophobic accents, such a discourse was widely confirmed and echoed by independent observers, thereby delegitimating the government. On the other hand, the government argued that UNITA was a group of greed-driven bandits sustaining the needs of poor people and disregarding creed by imposing war upon the country and abusing mostly rural populations. In this regard, the government benefited politically from an international sanctions regime against UNITA that nearly monopolized international initiatives and further marginalized Savimbi.

The significant role of resources in the Angolan conflict demonstrates the importance of addressing economic agendas in wars. Targeted economic sanctions can work and are made more efficient by such regulatory innovations as UN expert panels. Yet they cannot impose peace in the short term and may lead to a radicalization of abuses and predation upon local populations. Sanctions remain the symptoms of failed peace processes, more than tools of constraint to bring about an end to renewed conflict. Peace processes therefore need to include resource exploitation and fiscal reforms in their early stages to both strengthen political commitments and enforce economic constraints against the greed of rulers and the risk of a return to war. Just as important, such reforms have to participate in alleviating both the needs of marginalized people and the discrimination that reinforces creed and the appeal of violence.

Chapter 6

The Democratic Republic of the Congo: Structures of Greed, Networks of Need

Erik Kennes

On May 17, 1997, an alliance of rebel troops, under the leadership of the Rwandan, Ugandan, and Angolan armies, took power in Kinshasa, the capital of the newly renamed Democratic Republic of the Congo (DRC), formerly Zaire. The regime of Mobutu Sese Seko had imploded. The rebels' formal leader, Laurent Kabila, skillfully maneuvered to free himself from his foreign "protectors" by trying to create his own power base. When he finally asked the Rwandan and Ugandan troops to leave, this decision set in motion a plan to oust him from power that had been prepared many months before, with the active support of former Tanzanian president Julius

Erik Kennes is research associate at the Africa Museum, Tervuren, Belgium. He has held research and teaching positions at the University of Antwerp and the Université de Mbuji-Mayi, Zaire, and he has published widely on the politics of central Africa as well as war and mining-sector issues in the Democratic Republic of the Congo. He is also the author, with Munkana N'Ge, of *Essai biographique sur Laurent Désiré Kabila*, Cahier Africains 57–59 (Institut Africain and CEDAF/L'Harmattan, 2003), among other works.

Nyerere. In August 1998, the Rwandan and Ugandan armies invaded the DRC again, supporting a loose Congolese rebel coalition without any legitimacy or support among the Congolese population. Contrary to their expectations, they did not succeed in ousting Kabila, who received assistance from the governments of Angola, Zimbabwe, and Namibia. After a few months, the war resulted in a stalemate; the country was split, and the armies were digging themselves in, trying to organize a war economy to finance their military operations and enrich their respective political and military commanders.

Laurent Kabila was assassinated on January 16, 2001, and was succeeded by his son Joseph. Although the new regime has been more open and politically engaged in an evolving situation, its basic nature remains unchanged. The Congolese rebel movement disintegrated into several factions; the Rwandan and Ugandan governments gave their support to one or more of these factions according to their economic or strategic interests. A year later, in September 1999, an initial agreement was signed in Lusaka. Finally, after heavy international pressure and Southern African peace initiatives, a peace agreement between the implied governments and rebel movements was signed in Pretoria on December 17, 2002. An agreement was reached on a transitional constitution on March 6, 2003. A government of national unity was formed on June 30, 2003, in which nearly all rebel factions, Joseph Kabila's government, the political opposition, and civil society are represented.

How is one to interpret the Congo war in terms of need, greed, and creed? The pioneering research of Paul Collier and his team has demonstrated that public discourse about grievance most often hides a real motivation of greed. As with most comparative statistical analyses, this research provides some direction for further investigation. Quite evidently, the nearer one comes to the empirical realities of a particular case, the more the relevant factors have to be multiplied. Even a sequential approach—explaining the origins and development of a civil war as a sequence of need, creed, and greed—however useful it may be, enables us only to grasp the surface of the conflict. Even if the need–creed–greed sequence develops a general explanation of the logical development of a civil war, the distinction is analytical; in the real world, the three terms are not only sequential but cumulative. In other words: "need" may constitute the basic feature of the preconflict situation, but it is still there at the end and craves for a solution. In this chapter, the relationships between need, creed, and greed are examined for the Congo case.

The Structure of Opportunity

For decades, the Congo has been described in terms of decay; according to Young and Turner, its downturn already had started in 1974.[1] Most of the characteristics put forward by Collier and Hoeffler as proxies for the opportunity model were present in the DRC since the beginning of the 1980s—although some indicators (e.g., mean income per capita, male secondary schooling, growth rate of the economy, and availability of military equipment) deteriorated dramatically during the 1990–97 period.[2] The absence of civil war during the whole Mobutu regime, though the conditions for its outbreak were objectively present, has indeed puzzled most analysts of the DRC.[3] It must be stressed that the only instance of genuine civil war in the DRC has been the rebellion of 1964–65; essentially, all secession attempts have been induced from abroad.[4]

Other aspects of the situation before the outbreak of the war are at least as important. The deinstitutionalization of public life (political as well as economic), the implosion of the formal and informal state structures, the disappearance of internal conflict resolution mechanisms, and most of all the ethical void have created ideal preconditions for the outbreak of (civil) war. This last factor is partly subjective, action-related, and nonmeasurable, but it is fundamental. Decades of economic and political mismanagement

[1]Crawford Young and Thomas Turner, *The Rise and Decline of the Zairian State* (Madison: University of Wisconsin Press, 1985), 399.

[2]See Paul Collier and Anke Hoeffler, *Greed and Grievance in Civil War*, World Bank Research Paper (Washington, D.C.: World Bank, 2001), 3–6. Available at http://econ.worldbank.org/files/12205_greedgrievance_23oct.pdf. Curiously, Collier and Hoeffler consider the period from September 1991 to December 1996 as a period of civil war, while the first Congo war only started in October 1996 (p. 32).

[3]The only real conflicts have been the two Shaba wars in 1977–78; but even here, the conflict was organized from abroad and the attacking Katangese army did not enjoy massive popular support.

[4]Contrary to the expectations from Collier's model, this civil war did not follow a dramatic decline in per capita income, but a radical shift in the economic structure of the country and the creation of new social inequalities; conversely, the proportion of uneducated youth was important in the provinces that went into rebellion. See Jean-Claude Peemans, "Le contexte socio-économique des 'rébellions' congolaises, 1960–1965," in *Rébellions-révolution au Zaïre 1963–1965, vol. I*, ed. Cathérine Coquery-Vidrovitch, Alain Forrest, and Herbert Weiss (Paris: L'Harmattan, 1987), 84–102. It is very probable that the same outcome (civil war) in several cases may be produced by *different combinations* of causal factors. In this sense, an analysis along the method developed by Charles Ragin may yield interesting insights. See Charles Ragin, *Fuzzy-Set Social Science* (Chicago: University of Chicago Press, 2000).

and the banalization of corruption and theft (exemplified by presidential practice) have destroyed the frames of reference for a public ethic. The nomination of incompetent army generals under Mobutu contributed to the delegitimization of social and political hierarchies. This tendency was radicalized under Laurent Kabila, when just about anyone was appointed at any place, independent of education, experience, or competence. This created the impression that any position of power could be occupied by anyone—"Why not me?" The massive recruitment of child-soldiers also contributed decisively to an inversion of the traditional values that had guaranteed social cohesion: the child overruns the parents, the younger commands the older, social life becomes regulated by violence.

There is no doubt that the war in the DRC has been fueled by an accumulation of grievances that ignited an explosive situation that was "prone to conflict." Need creates grievance, and cumulative grievance creates a "proneness" to conflict. It is difficult to distinguish between need and greed, because politics in the Congo has almost always been associated with greed or "the politics of the belly." The whole process of poverty, private accumulation, and violence created need, but it had a direct influence on greed. If traditionally, economics is integrated in a structure of social relations and hierarchies, the breakdown of this structure opens the way for arbitrary management of the economic space: Anything goes. Obviously, this evolution was powerfully boosted by a demographic element: an explosive growth of unemployed and often uneducated youth without any prospects for a decent future.[5] Before 1996, satisfaction of need through violence was a privilege of the Zairean national army. After the army's implosion, violence became a realistic option for the majority of the unemployed youth. In this sense, the absence of any other option makes greed generally acceptable and creates an ideal situation for rebel army recruitment.

Therefore, an important question becomes: *Whose* greed? Need necessarily becomes greed for the majority of the population living in misery. Greed without (objective) need is confined to the leaders and organizers;

---

[5]As Roland Marchal notes, the proportion of youth without employment opportunities is taken by Collier as an indicator for the "opportunity model," whereas it may as well be taken as a condition for grievance. Roland Marchal, "The Economic Analysis of Civil War According to Paul Collier: A Sociologist's View," paper prepared for conference on the economic analysis of conflict: problems and prospects, Social Science Research Council, Washington, April 19–20, 2004, 2. Available at http://www.ssrc.org/programs/gsc/publications/gsc_activities/globalization_conflict/marchal.doc.

the use of the term is usually limited to this set of actors. As is argued by William Zartman in chapter 10 of this volume, the connection between need, opportunity, and civil war is mediated by the actor. Evidently, need creates discontent that may lead to conflict; but it always needs a particular configuration of forces and at least political/military entrepreneurs to organize and mobilize this discontent toward subjectively attainable goals. A lack of organizing force can only lead to massive pillage, as happened in the DRC during the 1991 and 1993 waves of looting. No civil war erupted at that time.

The connection between "need" (and "opportunity") and "civil war" thus becomes much more complex, and both terms must be qualified. We briefly qualified "need" above; but the term "civil war" is, in the case of the DRC, simply inaccurate. When looking at the "entrepreneurs" triggering the armed conflicts of 1996–97 and 1998–2003 in the DRC, it is obvious that the main actors were foreign. It is true that the 1996–97 war enjoyed massive support from the Congolese population, even if not led by it, but this was not the case in 1998. Both wars can only be understood in the context of the new regional configuration of power following the implosion of the Mobutu regime. Even if smaller-scale conflicts were present before 1996 in the DRC, it is highly questionable whether this would have led to a civil war without outside involvement. This takes us back to very classical power politics and, consequently, to creed.

Multiple Layers of Creed

The origins and causes of the DRC war can convincingly be described in terms of creed. It is only when the warring parties got stuck in their respective positions that their greed became the main motivating factor for pursuing the war—and, partly, for the formation of a transitional government. The complexity of the Congo war is due to its inextricable combination of three levels of conflict: regional, national, and international. The beginning of the process leading up to the civil war is to be found in the Congolese Kivu province. The situation in this province led to a war as a consequence of the Rwandan genocide in 1994. The conflict erupted in 1996–97 and had, from the beginning, a national and international dimension. The 1998–2003 war was the cumulative result of layers of crises in all their complexity.

The Regional Level: Kivu Province

From the beginning, the conflict in Kivu province revolved around access to land in this fertile and densely populated area.[6] Land access is regulated by the local customary chiefs and is thus determined by ethnicity. Most ethnic groups have this possibility of access, but immigrant groups without a recognized customary chief do not. The numerically most important immigrant group is constituted by the Kinyarwanda speakers, Hutu as well as Tutsi. This group was formed through successive waves of immigration from Rwanda and Burundi, starting from before Belgian colonization. They almost never were authorized to create an administrative entity for themselves.

As an alternative to submitting to the customary chief of a local ethnic group for access to land, they tried to accede through the modern system of individual property rights, available only to Congolese nationals. Hence the fundamental importance of the Congolese nationality law: It determines access not only to political power but also to economic power through land rights. A liberal nationality law in 1972 granted Congolese nationality to all immigrants from Rwanda and Burundi before January 1, 1950.[7] This law opened up the opportunity for a group of wealthy Rwandophone businessmen to become big landowners in land-scarce North Kivu. They were supported by the powerful Rwandophone director of the cabinet for President Mobutu and constituted a powerful section of the Zairean political and economic elite.[8]

The tension between ethnic Rwandans and the other ethnic groups in Kivu province was thus to an important degree caused by social inequality. The ensuing backlash to exclude ethnic Rwandans from Congolese citizenship was thus fundamentally a struggle for economic power. The 1981 nationality law disenfranchised most ethnic Rwandans from Congolese

---

[6]See Koen Vlassenroot, "Identity and Insecurity: The Building of Ethnic Agendas in South Kivu," in *Politics of Identity and Economics of Conflict in the Great Lakes Region*, ed. Ruddy Doom and Jan Gorus (Brussels: VUB University Press, 2000), 263–88.

[7]See Célestin Nguya-Ndila, *Nationalité et citoyenneté au Congo/Kinshasa: Le cas du Kivu* (Paris: L'Harmattan, 2001).

[8]Mobutu preferred to use members of ethnic minority groups as his close collaborators; their limited constituency made them all the more dependent on the president. This was especially true for ethnic Tutsi in the Congo.

citizenship, but the law was never implemented by the administration.[9] Violent conflicts emerged in North Kivu in 1992–93 among "original" Congolese ethnic groups and Congolese Hutu who, through the years, had become a demographic majority in some areas. It is highly unlikely, however, that these local conflicts would have developed into a full-scale war without the involvement of the neighboring countries. Although the situation calmed down by the end of 1993, the 1994 genocide dramatically changed this situation.[10]

International Involvement

The massive influx of Hutu military personnel—both the former Rwandan Armed Forces regulars (ex–Forces Armées Rwandaises) and the militias (Interahamwe)—transplanted the Hutu/Tutsi conflict to the Kivu region. Not only did it create severe insecurity for the local population, but it also ignited local conflicts and progressively structured them along the Hutu/Tutsi divide.[11] The interpretation of the local antagonism in terms of Hutu/Tutsi and, in a later development, in terms of Congolese "Bantu" versus Tutsi "Nilotics," became dominant among the local population until today.[12]

The antagonism against a Kinyarwanda-speaking group of large landowners (mostly Tutsi) or against a group (mostly Hutu) that had succeeded in marginalizing the local population in some areas is understandable, especially because a foreign Rwandan army had destabilized the whole region. But the grievance against a small ethnic group that had emigrated from Rwanda during the nineteenth century is atypical. This was the situation in South Kivu. The Banyamulenge Tutsi, which were Congolese from a his-

[9]See Vunduawe Te Pemako, *A l'ombre du Léopard: Vérités sur le régime de Mobutu Sese Seko* (Brussels: Editions Zaire Libre, 2000), 339–46.

[10]See Jean-Claude Willame, *Banyarwanda et Banyamulenge: Violences ethniques et gestion de l'identitaire au Kivu*, Cahiers Africains 25 (Tervuren, Belgium, and Paris: Institut Africain and CEDAF/L'Harmattan, 1997), 67–68.

[11]See Cyrus Reed, "Guerrillas in the Midst: The Former Government of Rwanda and the Alliance of Democratic Forces for the Liberation of Congo-Zaire," in *African Guerrillas*, ed. Christopher Clapham (London: James Currey, 1998), 134–54.

[12]See Emmanuel Lubala Mugisho, "La situation politique au Kivu: Vers une dualisation de la société," in *L'Afrique des Grands Lacs: Annuaire 1997–1998*, ed. F. Reyntjens and S. Marysse (Anvers and Paris: CERGLA and L'Harmattan, 1998), 307–33. Available at http://www.gralac.org.

torical point of view, were marginal, lived in relative isolation, and did not represent a social or economic threat to the local population.[13]

The preexisting antagonism between the Banyamulenge and the neighboring ethnic groups, dating from colonial times, was an ordinary and historic one between agriculturalists and pastoralists. There was a slight change when a few Banyamulenge experienced upward social mobility; local politicians targeted the Banyamulenge during the 1980s in a move to create a proper ethnic following among the rivaling groups. This latent antagonism, of a type that is rather common in the DRC, was dramatically enhanced under the influence of the Hutu army in the DRC after the genocide. The association of "Banyamulenge" with "Tutsi" was exacerbated by politicians in Kinshasa, who wanted to exclude the entire Kinyarwanda-speaking population in the DRC from political participation. Because the Banyamulenge are an easily targetable minority group, they asked for help with their much more powerful neighboring regime in Rwanda. For the Rwandan leader Paul Kagame, the Banyamulenge issue was an ideal point of leverage for getting rid of the Hutu army in the Congo and of the supporting regime of President Mobutu. Both objectives could only be realized, however, through a dramatic shift of U.S. policy in the region in favor of the "new generation of African leaders," such as Kagame or Uganda's Yoweri Museveni.[14]

The very real support from the United States and the United Kingdom for the governments of Uganda and Rwanda should not obscure the fact that the fundamental stakes in the 1996–97 as well as the 1998–2003 wars are the struggle for regional hegemony. The Mobutu regime was, in 1996, no more than a paper leopard who had lost control over events: A simple nudge from abroad was enough for it to crumble down. The power vacuum in central Africa was immediately filled by neighboring Rwanda, Uganda, Zimbabwe, and Angola.

[13]The origin of the Banyamulenge is contested. For an account from Banyamulenge sources, see Joseph Mutambo, *Les Banyamulenge* (Kinshasa: Saint Paul, 1997); Manassé Ruhimbika, *Les Banyamulenge (Congo-Zaïre) entre deux guerres* (Paris: L'Harmattan, 2001); and Mgr. Kanyamachumbi, *Les populations du Kivu et la loi sur la nationalité* (Bukavu: Editions Select, undated). For discussion and analysis see Willame, *Banyarwanda et Banyamulenge*; and F. Reyntjens, S. Marysse, C. André, V. Parqué, P. Dupont, Lubanda Lunanga, and Mafikiri Tsongo, *Conflits au Kivu: Antécédents et enjeux* (Anvers: CERGLA, 1996), available at http://129.194.252.80/catfiles/0251.pdf.

[14]See Vunduawe, *A l'ombre du Léopard*, 417–21.

Rwanda has real security concerns, although they are not the only motivation for its involvement, as discussed below. By presenting itself as the protector of all ethnic Rwandans in the DRC, it made its power politics internationally acceptable. The second war, from 1998 to 2003, was not simply an immediate reaction to Tutsi persecution in the DRC but had also been carefully planned many months before, when it had become obvious that Laurent Kabila was not willing to implement the political and economic projects of his godfathers. From many accounts, it seems very plausible that the fundamental strategy of Rwanda was the de facto control over the Kivu region, for military and political as well as economic reasons.

The strategic agenda of Uganda was much less clear, and its security concerns about the activities of some smaller opposition groups in the DRC in the border regions with Uganda are less convincing. Angola and Zimbabwe were drawn into the war upon demand from Kabila, whereas Angola seemed to be primarily motivated by its struggle against the rebel group, UNITA, discussed more fully in chapter 5 of this volume by Philippe Le Billon. Zimbabwe was involved for reasons of rivalry with South Africa over regional hegemony.

The Stakes at the National Level

Contrary to what should be expected from the Collier–Hoeffler approach, the 1996–97 war leading to the implosion of the Mobutu regime was not initiated within the Congo but in Dar es Salaam, Kampala, and Kigali. Congolese participation was initially limited to small groups of combatants, mobilized and armed by Museveni. Laurent Kabila had merely a handful of followers, organized as the Alliance of Democratic Forces for the Liberation of the Congo (AFDL).[15] It is perfectly true that the political struggle against Mobutu during the 1990–96 years liberated the population from its fear and contributed to its massive mobilization in 1996–97. It is also certain that the Congolese "political class" had no interest in a solution for the political crisis, which created the impression that only military force could push through political change. But the military operations were led by the armies from the neighboring countries, and by a Congolese (Katangese) army in exile in Angola since 1967. The grievances against the Mobutu

---

[15]On the trajectory of Laurent Kabila, see Erik Kennes, with Munkana N'Ge, *Essai biographique sur Laurent Désiré Kabila*, Cahier Africains 57–59 (Tervuren, Belgium, and Paris: Institut Africain–CEDAF and L'Harmattan, 2003).

regime were at the same time massive, and there cannot be any doubt about the popular support for the war.

The situation changed dramatically with the 1998 war, which lacked almost any popular support from within the DRC. There were, indeed, grievances, finding their origin in the politics of exclusion of Kabila. He recruited very heterogeneous political personnel from within the Congolese diaspora or from anyone who had a link to his personal history. Competence or merit in the political struggle against Mobutu were of little or no importance. Among the groups that felt unrightfully excluded are leftist intellectuals, who had hoped for the creation of a new political order; former Mobutists or their family members, who had been expropriated by the new regime; and Banyamulenge and ethnic Tutsi, who continued to be excluded under Kabila and, even more so, who were mobilized by Kigali and Kampala to stage a second war against the Congolese president.

These groups formed the Rally for Congolese Democracy (RCD) in August 1998. The RCD "liberation" movement disintegrated into many factions and ultimately was reduced to its Banyamulenge leadership, under the strict control of Kigali. Because of its instrumentalization by Kigali, its greed (see below), and its utter incompetence, the RCD was always hugely unpopular. The situation of the Congolese Liberation Movement (MLC)—led by Jean-Pierre Bemba, the son of one of the core figures of the Mobutu regime—was slightly different. The MLC was formed around a group of young intellectuals, but behind the scenes it regrouped essentially the former Mobutist military and political elite. If there is one grievance animating the MLC, it is the exclusion of inhabitants from the Equateur province (the former power basis of Mobutu) from the exercise of power under the Kabila regime. Many had also been expropriated. The MLC was initially the "Ugandan rebel movement," whose equipment and training were provided by Kampala, but Bemba succeeded in gradually emancipating his movement from his Ugandan protector. In the end, if in addition to neighboring states' involvement, grievances played a role in 1998, it was because of political and economic exclusion—a common cause for political conflict in the DRC.

Stuck in Greed

From the discussion above, it is obvious that the Congo war cannot be simply characterized as grown out of greed. But as with many similar cases, the military operations got stuck in a stable, self-serving stalemate, the different armed groups dug themselves in along the front lines (substantially

unchanged since 1999), and greed took over from creed.[16] A violent economy of war took shape (see below). The majority of the Congolese population united against the "foreign aggressors"; the "rebel movements" and
the foreign armies met stubborn armed and unarmed (civil society) resistance in the Kivu region.[17] The engagement of the Congolese population
fiercely contrasted with the hopeless division and opportunism of the Congolese political and economic elite.

Endless negotiations and decisive South African and European involvement were necessary before a formal peace agreement was reached and a
political formula found that could possibly lead to general elections.[18]
However, the impression that politics took over again may partly be an op-
tical illusion; need, creed, and greed are cumulative rather than consecutive.
It is true that the military structure of the economy of plunder became less
visible, even if it did not disappear altogether; and important international
involvement has kept the process together and has pushed for elections. But
the practice of plunder and the pervasive opportunism from the members of
government and administration have not diminished at all. Neither has
need; with the exception of some improvements in the security situation
and some isolated actions for economic reconstruction, the living conditions of the population have not been improving. Artisanal mining is still responsible for a huge part of the meager household income.

From the analysis above, and for that matter from the analysis of Collier and his team, one should conclude that no lasting solution to a civil
war can be found without taking the road of economic reconstruction—
even if, as in the case of the DRC, heavy political and diplomatic pressure
was necessary to force neighboring governments to withdraw their troops

---

[16]The bulk of the fighting was actually done by the foreign armies; the Congolese
armed groups were mostly occupied with ransoming the civilian population.

[17]Though Collier et al. show that ethnic diversity reduces the risk of conflict, the
Congo displays an enormous ethnic diversity. See Paul Collier et al., *Breaking the
Conflict Trap: Civil War and Development Policy* (New York: Oxford University Press
for World Bank, 2003), 57–60. This diversity was reduced to a conflict between the
"Bantu" against the "nilotic" Tutsi; ethnicity is not a given but is a weapon in a politi-
cal and military struggle, as Collier himself suggests (p. 69).

[18]See Jean-Claude Willame, *L'accord de Lusaka: Chronique d'une négociation
internationale*, Cahiers Africains 51–52 (Tervuren, Belgium, and Paris: Institut
Africain–CEDAF and L'Harmattan, 2002), and Paule Bouvier (with Francesca Bom-
boko), *Le dialogue intercongolais: Anatomie d'une négociation à la lisière du chaos*,
Cahiers Africains 63–64 (Tervuren, Belgium, and Paris: Musée Royal de l'Afrique Centrale and L'Harmattan, 2004).

and give up their territorial ambitions. But how to reconstruct a devastated country with its destroyers still present? The enormous difficulties inherent in this operation have become obvious in the first decade of the 2000s, as international organizations, such as the World Bank and the United Nations (through its Mission in the Congo), are called to work through technocratic administrations that are more or less isolated from the appetites of (many) government members.

The following sections of this chapter constitute an analysis of the Congo war from the perspective of need and greed, abstracting from creed, with the aim of exploring several paths that may help the Congo emerge from its quagmire. A realistic solution implies structural changes: Economic interests must be acknowledged—not negated—and reintegrated and transformed for the profit of the national Congolese economy. A purely moral approach has a very limited bearing in a context of poverty and social structural and ethical implosion. A productive reorientation of economic interests seems to open up a more realistic perspective.

Extreme poverty and the lack of perspective on economic improvement have led, in the DRC, to social dislocation. Here, I explore the thesis that the most central problem in the DRC is one of social and ethical implosion. In the search for areas of social and ethical cohesion, one inevitably runs into the myriad networks of the informal economy, one of the most important foundations for a realistic process of renewal in the DRC. These networks present an aspect of social cohesion, and also of independent economic and political power, more specifically for the mining sector. They can counterbalance an exclusive reliance on the (shaky) state and political power structures on the national level, and they may constitute a degree of protection against foreign interests.

This exploration, of course, complements the more classical institutional analysis. In addition, it does not directly address another tragic development in the DRC, dramatically intensified by the war: the hundreds of thousands of street children in all urban centers. They are the most visible expression of the social dislocation of the DRC and still constitute an explosive reservoir for any entrepreneur of violence.

A Network War

The Congolese war economy is the brutal acceleration of an evolution begun decades ago. In this evolution, the formal economy is only a small part of the whole economy, where the concept of network—imprecise though it may be—is critical. The war in central Africa has aptly been described as a "network war,"[19] but the emergence of networks that have gradually subverted and finally replaced formal institutions in the Congo is an intensified local version of a global process, identified by Mark Duffield:

> The changing competence of the nation-state is reflected in the shift from hierarchical patterns of government to the wider and more polyarchical networks, contracts and partnerships of governance. . . . The expansion of governance networks means that states are now part of much wider and sometimes ill-defined structures of authority.[20]

The evolution from hierarchy to polyarchy is directed by worldwide pressures for the liberalization and intensification of communication and contacts. For the particular case of the Congo, it is imperative to explain in detail to what "local" and "global" specifically refer, and to analyze the important gatekeepers: the national and/or foreign authorities.

On the level of the nation-state (i.e., the Congo/DRC), the logic of the internal evolution (which is self-destructive) governs the nature and evolution of the specific arrangement between political/military elites and the existing economic circuits and explains not only state survival or failure but also the nature of the economic networks that evolve out of the process of state implosion and collapse. The type and degree of organization of these networks will explain the degree of resistance against attempts at outside control.

During the war, the gatekeeper between the local and the global level was not only the national state, as it was replaced by a regional power structure composed of alliances of militarized state structures or, more accurately, by structures of military commercialism. On the regional level, political and strategic motives were determinant at the outset. But these political motives were progressively transformed on the ground into economic considerations ("the richer I am, the more I'll have to say") and, to a lesser extent, by the search for corporate and collective security, as described. The army, as the last and ultimate embodiment of national sov-

---

[19]Tim Raeymaekers, *Network War: An Introduction to Congo's Privatised War Economy* (Antwerp: IPIS, 2002).

[20]Mark Duffield, "Globalization, Transborder Trade and War Economies," in *Greed and Grievance: Economic Agendas in Civil Wars*, ed. Mats Berdal and David M. Malone (Boulder, Colo.: Lynne Rienner, 2000), 71. See also Mark Duffield, "Post-Modern Conflict: Warlords, Post-Adjustment States and Private Protection," *Civil Wars* 1, no. 1 (1998): 65–201.

ereignty, has become privatized and a private commercial actor itself. The
nature of the army and the degree of its influence are crucial for understanding the role played by third countries in controlling the relationship
between the local and the global. Since the installation of the transition government, these structures have coexisted with the official institutions, but
they have not disappeared.

The nature of the link with the "global economy" is determined first of
all by the commodity or resource involved and by its importance and value
for the global markets (and not just for one national market, as was the
case with many closed structures in the previous era between the colony
and its colonizer). The nature of this link will be decisive for the possibilities of control by the regional and even national actors. The nature and
strength of the local or state networks affects the capacity of control by outside actors and more global forces. One must differentiate between networks with a deeper local density and new networks that have developed
during the war. Following an observation by the late Hugues Leclercq (a
professor at the University of Louvain), one should make the distinction between a really "popular" economy, the formal state-related economy, and
the marginalized population that is not participating in either of the two levels. In conclusion, we will have to consider the prospects for a new political and commercial compromise among all the actors involved, and the possibilities for the implementation of a more inclusive political order. The
possibility for this compromise will determine the survival of the Congo as
a unitary state.

The National Level: Construction and Deconstruction of Politico-Economic Networks

The first type of network to be discussed consists of intermediaries between
the global and the local levels. The general evolution is simple: An formal
institutional framework created at independence and modified under the
regime of President Mobutu was gradually emptied of all content and subsumed under local informal politico-commercial clientelist networks. As a
consequence, the capacity for resistance against foreign interests by the
Congolese polity as a whole was seriously weakened. The Mobutu regime
was characterized by a constant interplay between a formal institutional
network that was meaningless or not respected and an informal structure
of power. The same dualism characterized the economy of the country: The
formal economy gradually crumbled, to be subsumed under the steadily

growing power of the informal economy. Under Kabila's regime, the formal structures all but disappeared.

The Mobutu Regime

To say that Mobutu's regime was one of personal rule is almost an understatement. Having been pyramidally structured along lines of clientelism, the radical Zairianization measures of 1973–74 created a group of powerful "big men" patrons, of two types.

The first type had very few links with their communities and were, at first, much more dependent on the president than others. Among those were politicians of Rwandan descent—among whom was Kengo wa Dondo, Mobutu's prime minister from 1982 to 1986, 1988 to 1990, and 1994 to 1997, who since the 1980s had headed a very powerful political network. These "big men" controlled huge chunks of the most profitable sectors of the formal economy, through middlemen in the public enterprises network, the central bank, the customs control offices, and so on. These structures of control were created by the predatory politico-commercial elite at the expense of the ordinary structures of state and administration that they had superseded. A second type of patron had much more legitimacy because of a policy of redistribution; a rather classic example is Jonas Mukamba, who for more than ten years was the patron of the very rich diamond region in the Kasaï.

These different networks steadily gained more autonomy, and they emptied the Zairian and the Congolese state of its substance. As explained by Gauthier de Villers, the relationship to the law (and formal institutions) became purely opportunistic: The law was only to be used when it suited the needs of the patron(s) of the network.[21] The real scope and reach of a state function were thus much less determined by its formal attributions than by the position of the incumbent in the power network. The "shadow state" became a full reality. Nonetheless, these informal networks feed on the different levels of both the formal and informal economies. The politico-economic elite could only maintain its position by siphoning off revenues from the "formal" or "modern" economy as well as by staying

---

[21]Gauthier De Villers and Jean-Claude Willame, *République Démocratique du Congo: Chronique politique d'un entre-deux-guerres, Octobre 1996–Juillet 1998*, Cahiers Africains 35–36 (Tervuren, Belgium, and Paris: Institut Africain and CEDAF/L'Harmattan, 1998), 13–14.

rooted in the informal economy of transport, small trade, craftsmen's trade, diamond and gold digging, and the like. Most politicians were also involved in economic activities, going from the management of huge plantations to the employment of a driver and a truck to transport goods from the hinterland to the capital.

Much more than the influence of corruption on lower levels of government, the problem within the system was first and foremost the ruthless plundering of state resources by the key figures in the politico-economic elite. The economic substance of the country was thus eaten away—not only the leaves, but also the trunk and the roots. Because such a system thrives on the constant provision of economic and financial resources, and because outside financial support was diminishing, the system inevitably had to collapse. The country underwent an impressive series of structural adjustment and standby programs since 1976, but the core ruling elite always succeeded in diverting the cost of these programs away from their own shoulders to the population. The budget cuts in the social sectors never affected their own lifestyles.

Mobutu, who was well aware of the danger inherent in the autonomization of networks outside his direct control, tried to integrate as many people as possible by constantly creating new organs for co-optation. The *Official Gazette* of Zaire during the 1980s displays an impressive series of nominations to new institutions of the government, the administration, and the army.

The Privatization of Political Space

The "liberalization" of political activity, declared by President Mobutu on April 24, 1990, and the subsequent creation of myriad political parties meant the reconfiguration of the politico-commercial networks, whereby Mobutu's network lost control over many branches that gained a considerable degree of autonomy.[22] These branches, constituted by the new political parties, were quickly confronted with the problem of financial resources:

> It is then (during the eighties) we have witnessed the creation of a new mode of political governance: no longer through a system of public administration and formal institutions (as in 1972–73) but through

[22]On the creation of political parties, see Gauthier De Villers and Jean Omasombo Tshonda, *Zaire: La transition manquée 1990–1997* (Tervuren, Belgium, and Paris: Institut Africain and CEDAF/L'Harmattan, 1997).

politico-commercial elites where dominant groups exclusively work through networks. Thus, power was in the hands of a series of institutions but supported and controlled by elites: the national bank, [the Katangan mining company] Gecamines, the security apparatus.[23]

In July 1994, Kengo wa Dondo again became prime minister. He succeeded in gaining some international acceptance for his government, but his network had taken power again, especially through the control of key lucrative public enterprises. He embarked on a program of economic privatization (see below), but he in fact continued to privatize the state.[24] This privatization progressively emptied the public sector of its content. In a series of penetrating analyses of the economic policy of the country since the 1980s, Mabi Mulumba demonstrates that even the monetary emission was privatized. The monetary reform of October 1993 and the introduction of new banknotes only served to print money for the ruling elite, but it created a disaster for the population. Some series of banknotes were even printed twice—by a nonlicensed private company—and immediately privatized by members of the concerned politico-commercial network.[25] Officials of or linked to the National Bank went into speculative operations.[26] Tom de Herdt demonstrates that all moral boundaries concerning the use of monetary policy were sacrificed for the sake of factional struggles among the different politico-commercial networks.[27] Even the army had become an instrument for the organization of lucrative operations on behalf of the leading generals. The two most central institutions of a state were thus both privatized. When the AFDL liberation movement toppled Mobutu,

---

[23]Hugues Leclercq, cited in Belgian Senate, *Final Report of the Parliamentary Commission of Inquiry into the Exploitation and the Legal and Illegal Trade in Natural Resources of the Great Lakes Region, with Regard to the Present Situation of Conflict and the Implication of Belgium*, Session 2002–3, February 20, 2003, 29.

[24]It must be admitted that Kengo and his cronies were not the only ones responsible for the breakdown of the Congo; some very powerful generals had totally privatized the army; i.e., they only used it for their personal profit and to put the Kengo government under pressure.

[25]See Mabi Mulumba, *Les dérives d'une gestion prédatrice: Le cas du Zaïre devenu République Démocratique du Congo* (Kinshasa: Centre de Recherches Pédagogiques, 1998), 154–74.

[26]See Ndiang Kabul, *La banque centrale du Congo: Tome I—La guerre pour la gestion du compte du Trésor* (Kinshasa: CEDI, 1999).

[27]Tom de Herdt, "Democracy and the Money Machine in Zaire," *Review of African Political Economy* 29, no. 93 (2002): 459.

his regime crumbled because it itself had destroyed formal legitimate institution and because its own networks destroyed themselves in internal factional conflict.

The formal economy had also collapsed, and an informal economy was widely developed. In the midst of the monetary chaos, the value of the national currency (the zaire) had become purely fictional; but the myriad small traders and artisanal workers in the network of the informal economy de facto determined the local value of the banknote.[28] The informal economy, which functions on the basis of trust and core ethical values, is necessary for survival for the large majority of the population; it is the economic component of the shadow state. But it is not a default category for anything outside itself; it is a monetized segment, and its actors are poor, but an important part of the population still is outside even this network. Parts of the population live in absolute poverty in totally isolated regions or are part of the refugee population or the child-soldiers.[29] The section of the population outside the informal economy does not participate in this moral network either. Its position outside both the formal and informal economies means that it lives in a total social and ethical void, posing an enormous problem for the reconstruction of Congolese society.

The Laurent Kabila regime

As a result, the Zairian/Congolese state structures (or the illusion left) simply needed a nudge to crumble, like a consumed termite hill. The new regime failed to undertake reconstruction in depth. The somewhat naive hope for a new, nonpatrimonial political order in the Congo underestimated the enormous difficulty of institutionalization in a situation of complete informalization. Total disregard for the law by the new regime made it clear that institutionalization was not really on its agenda. All initiatives taken by the Kabila regime for the creation of new institutions were improvised, random, purposeless, and reacting to the needs of the moment.

Still more important, the new regime did not succeed (or did not want) to create its own new networks in Congolese society. The new government

---

[28]Hugues Leclercq, *Le nouvel ordre politique et les enjeux économiques du conflit en République Démocratique du Congo: Mise en perspective du dialogue intercongolais* (Tervuren, Belgium: Congolese Expert Group of Belgium/Le groupe d'expertise congolaise de Belgique, 2001), 39–41. Available at http://129.194.252.80/catfiles/2295.pdf.

[29]Leclercq, *Le nouvel ordre politique*, 46.

officials were not recruited from the former networks but were former participants in the 1960s rebellion or their family members, members from the diaspora in Europe and the United States, or simply friends or relatives of the president. The only link among the members of the "new elite" was their relationship to Laurent Kabila's personal history. The system of clientelism under Mobutu had at least in some instances a degree of legitimacy, if a patron respected the implicit ethic of redistribution within the network. This was not the case with patrons-without-roots such as Kengo wa Dondo, or with the new elite under Kabila. The lack of sociological density of the new regime helps to explain their lack of legitimacy: Their core members siphoned away what little money there was left but did not reinvest in their country. Their lack of knowledge of the unwritten moral codes and the very delicate equilibriums among population groups and networks proved, in the end, to be fatal for the acceptance of the new regime. Although it does not give a full explanation for the war that broke out in 1998, the absence of new network structures helps explain the participation of a number of formerly important network patrons in the rebellion. Even the legitimacy that the rebellion gave to Kabila for his defense of the country against the invaders had virtually disappeared by 2000.

The Mining Sector in the Congo:
Opening Up and Crumbling Down

As with all formal structures in the Congo, the formal mining sector also was overtaken by informal networks.[30] But this is a long-term trend, caused by factors on the international and the national levels and not merely by the war. The networks in the informal mining economy started developing decades ago.[31] Another observation of Duffield is crucial in this respect: the similarity between the peace and the war economy. The "war economy" as it has developed since the beginning of the war in 1998 is to a large extent a radical version of the peace economy existing before. It is somehow the

---

[30]A more detailed discussion of this section appears in Erik Kennes, "Le secteur minier au Congo: 'déconnexion' et descente aux enfers," in *Annuaire des Grands Lacs 1999–2000*, ed. Filip Reyntjens and Stefaan Marysse (Anvers and Paris: CERGLA–Université d'Anvers and L'Harmattan, 2000), 299–342, available at http://www.gralac.org.

[31]Mark Duffield, "Globalization, Transborder Trade and War Economies," 79–82.

worst possible conclusion of a long history of "extraversion," whereby the country and its elites were directly linked to the "global" economy and took advantage of it to construct their own political order and power base.[32] I have sketched above how the political structures faded away. What was left, and which new structures replaced the old? Because the present war economy in the Congo concentrates mainly on mineral resources, I give a broad outline of evolution in the mining and minerals sector.

The Evolution of the Mining and Minerals Sector

Few sectors have attained the degree of globalization of the mining and minerals sector, ever since the very beginning of its operations. Metals and minerals were among the very first commodities whose prices were fixed at a global level. In the colonial period, the market had a limited number of buyers and sellers, and supply and demand were predictable, as were prices and investment decisions. The situation changed at independence with the emergence of an important third actor: the nation-state. The new entity depended heavily on revenue from the mining sector to establish its legitimacy. During the 1970s, a fourth actor was added: the big development banks, which were able to add finance and guarantees for mining projects.

The 1980s and 1990s, however, saw a constant decline in real terms of prices for base metals, making the mining sector less attractive for investors. The more risky sections of large mining companies such as prospecting were shed, and new smaller companies run by highly competent personnel dismissed by the larger companies took on the risky operations. Though the risk associated with prospecting is very high and the chances for success very low, potential earnings can be enormous. Once a discovery is made, it can be sold to a major company for huge profits. In 1996, the speculators Robert Friedland and Jean-Raymond Boulle sold the jackpot discovery of an enormous nickel deposit at Voisey's Bay, Canada, to Inco, a major company. The huge profits made by Boulle enabled the company to engage in speculative prospecting in the Congo.

Speculation reflects a fundamental change in the world economy. With the pressure of growing liberalization of commercial and financial markets, the mining industry had to raise part of its capital on the stock market. The

---

[32]See Jean-François Bayart, "Africa in the World: A History of Extraversion," *African Affairs* 99, no. 395 (2000): 217–67.

imperative of rapid profitability for stakeholders forced the mining companies to look for rapid and secure profits, where competitive advantage is conferred by flexibility and ability to operate globally—in a word, delocalization.

The opening up of the mining sector in a context of institutional decay
had other important consequences.[33] Because of the underexploitation of
many concessions and deposits, many prospecting results became available
at little or no cost. Together with the availability of new technologies for exploitation, many deposits became profitable again. Then, with the end of
apartheid, the mining sector in South Africa was opened. This meant that
the traditional closed structure of the mining houses (characterized by close
integration among finance, production structures, and management contracts with subsidiaries) was gradually abandoned in favor of a global liberalization. The apex of this development was the move by Anglo American
(still the biggest mining company in the world) from South Africa to London,
to become a global player. The company juxtaposes African opportunities
with the broader picture at a world level. Anglo can thus associate with junior companies to exploit promising deposits (as happened with the huge
gold deposit Sadiola Hill, Mali, with the junior Iamgold) or invest directly
in a country (as happened with its decision to engage in Konkola Deep
Mining in Zambia).

Globalization in the mining sector contributed to the final breakdown
of the previous integration of mining interests into the nation-state structure. This model was one of long-term engagement of major companies
with the government of a country, whereby a de facto monopoly is granted
to the company. The company bought security and was not really forced to
keep up with international developments. It was easy for a company to link
up with the country's informal elite networks.

The Belgian Congo was a prime example of a closed system where mining companies and administrative structures exercised hegemony in close
collaboration, making considerable investments in the economic and social
sectors possible after World War II.[34] After independence, the Congolese

---

[33]Magnus Ericsson and Andreas Tegen, *African Mining in the Late 1990s: A Silver
Lining?* CDR Working Paper 99.2 (Copenhagen: Centre for Development Research,
1999), available at http://www.cdr.dk/working_papers.

[34]Cf. the seminal study of Jean-Luc Vellut, "Les bassins miniers de l'ancien Congo
Belge: Essai d'histoire économique et sociale (1900–1960)," *Les Cahiers du CEDAF*
7 (November 1981).

state tried to control this structure by nationalizing the mining sector in 1967. The Congolese and Zairean state, however, never developed the necessary management capacity and merely used the mining sector (especially the Gecamines in Shaba/Katanga) as its main source of revenue.

This changed radically during the 1990s. Having been reduced to a purely formal construction and struggling for survival, the state became a partner dominated by an elite faction willing to sign any agreement—even though it had become incapable of fulfilling its obligations. The mining companies had to look beyond their traditional footholds and become players on a global level, thereby cutting their long-term links to former partners.

In the period 1995–96, the government embarked on a program of limited privatization of parts of the mining sector. Several major and junior companies tried to bid for the most interesting concessions. In some instances, junior companies succeeded in outbidding larger actors. Most of the contracts that would shape the mining sector in the Congo for the two years to come were signed in August 1996 in the last year of the Mobutu regime. When the AFDL army swept over the country, it did so in an exceptionally favorable international environment for mining investment. The large international availability of risk capital, the prospects for a Congolese political renewal, and the active promotion and support of Canadian companies by the Canadian government resulted in a massive arrival of mining company representatives in Kinshasa and Lubumbashi.

The new mining administration appointed by Kabila in 1997–98 was not able to control the sector and direct it toward more productive objectives. In the name of a "fight against monopolies," smaller concessions were awarded—but often to companies that were not very trustworthy. The result was that the major mining companies withdrew and waited for better times to come. Junior companies were often unable to find funding for their projects. In 1998–99, many projects collapsed. The wave of globalization had withdrawn from the country. Companies like Anglo preferred to invest in stable countries such as Mali or Tanzania. Barrick Gold had a huge concession in the Northeast of the Congo (Kilo Moto) but choose to not yet develop it. This evolution was proof that a free market does not develop as a force of nature but is the product of an institutional structure. What should have been a paradise for free marketers with a virtual absence of state structure turned into a nightmare. Regional interests became predominant, and the dark side of globalization forcefully emerged with the war that started in 1998 through the irruption of the international criminal economy.

The Burgeoning of the Informal Mining Economy

The informalization of the mining economy started in 1982, when the liberalization of trade and exploitation of gold, diamonds, and precious materials was decreed.[35] This put an end to the state monopoly for the trade in diamonds and to the very restrictive regulations for artisanal diamond and gold exploitation. The state no longer regulated access to the exploitation of artisanal mining (only Congolese nationals had been admitted) and to the trade in precious substances (only officially licensed trading posts, or *comptoirs*, had been allowed to buy and export artisanal diamonds or gold).[36] A state agency, the National Expertise Centre (Centre National d'Expertise) controlled the value and price of exported diamonds, gold, and the like for fiscal reasons.

Since the mid-1990s, the informal economy has become dominant in the DRC. According to (necessarily very rough) estimates, it represented two-thirds of the gross domestic product in 1998, when the DRC war started.[37] Within this economy, artisanal mining is very important; revenue from diamond mining alone was estimated at about $800 million in 1998.[38] Indeed, artisanal diamonds represented an average 53.1 percent of the value of total exports in 1997–99, against 12.9 percent for 1985–89.[39]

At the bottom of the network, artisanal diggers try to find diamonds and gold (in rivers and hard rock) in territories outside the mining concessions. They sell their produce to a "negotiator," who sells it to the *comptoirs*. The *comptoirs*, which are located in the capital as well as in the urban centers near an area of exploitation, are the connecting link with the world market. A huge network for trade in diamonds and gold was thus created; the

[35]By the Ordinance-Law 82-039 of November 5, 1982, *Journal Officiel* (Kinshasa), no. 22, November 15, 1982, 9–11.

[36]The official MIBA diamond mine concluded an agreement in 1985 with De Beers for the sale of the total diamond production with a guaranteed minimum price. This agreement was canceled in 1997 when Kabila took power. The higher prices for MIBA diamonds obtained in 1997 are probably an indication that the prices fixed by De Beers were undervalued. See Hugues Leclercq, "Le rôle économique du diamant dans le conflit congolais," in *Chasse au diamant au Congo/Zaire*, ed. Laurent Monnier, Bogumil Jewsiewicki, and Gauthier de Villers, Cahiers Africains 45–46 (Tervuren, Belgium, and Paris: Institut Africain–CEDAF and L'Harmattan, 2001), 49–50.

[37]Belgian Senate, *Final Report of the Parliamentary Commission of Inquiry*, 23. The gross domestic product for 1998 was estimated at no more than $11 billion.

[38]Belgian Senate, *Final Report of the Parliamentary Commission of Inquiry*, 23.

[39]Leclercq, "Le rôle économique du diamant dans le conflit congolais," 60.

state only controlled the entry and exit points. This retreat of the state and its normative order was replaced by a sophisticated system of internal economic, social, and even moral regulation:[40]

> An impressive apparatus of unwritten rules and traditional customs, diffusely elaborated by the whole of the artisanal mining network, is sanctioned by a plurality of informal and more or less hierarchical civil authorities. These authorities rely on policing militias. The entire system gives to this very harsh and violent living world a degree of stability and a minimal order and security without which no exploitation of precious substances is possible. Within this informal framework, all transactions are concluded and finalized on a purely commercial basis. They are subject to a very real competition where all parties have a remarkable knowledge of the gem quality of the stones and of their market value in dollars or in local money; they know the price of the day and the current exchange rates, and they refer constantly to the dollar price at the diamond market in Antwerp.[41]

The artisanal diamond and gold mining has a clientelistic structure, mirroring the organization of Congolese society as a whole. Local patrons control one or more local areas of exploitation. In a very interesting case study, Jean Omasombo analyzes the local fiefdom of Henri Monewiya Malanga, known as "Pikoro," the president of the Association of Mineworkers of the Oriental Province, a microsociety with its own economic circuits, social hierarchies, and even rules of justice. Pikoro's practice of power was a copy of the Mobutist state. When the new Kabila regime took power, Pikoro was arrested and his concession declared state property. There are rumors, however, that he restarted his activities during the most recent war, under rebel authority.[42]

The local patrons and the *comptoirs* inevitably need protection and security, and they are forced to find terms of agreement with the local and

---

[40]The normative order of the state and the normative order of the informal economy grew steadily closer over the years, together with the crumbling of the formal political and economic order.

[41]Leclercq, "Le rôle économique du diamant dans le conflit congolais," 47–78.

[42]Jean Omasombo Tshonda, "Les diamants de Kisangani: De nouveaux seigneurs se taillent des fiefs sur le modèle de l'état zaïrois de Mobutu," in *Chasse au diamant au Congo/Zaire*, ed. Monnier, Jewsiewicki, and de Villers, 79–126.

national authorities. Many levels of administration levy formal and informal taxes on the income of the *comptoirs*; on a higher level, ministers, army
generals, and traders participate actively in exploiting and trading in diamonds, gold, and precious substances. During the last years of the Mobutu
regime, many army generals and close collaborators controlled their own
networks of exploitation and trade. The operators of the *comptoirs*—who
are integrated into the same circuit of foreign, mostly Lebanese, traders—
continuously adapt their strategies to the incumbents in power by changing the official structures of their enterprises.

A description of artisanal gold digging around the concession of the
private mining company Sominki in South Kivu is given by Ambroise
Butambo.[43] When the owners of the company had lost interest in the exploitation of local gold and tin and cuts were made in expenditures for social and community activities, a network of artisanal gold diggers, calling
themselves Nindjas, developed at the margin of the concession. Gold diggers went to live inside the gold mine, digging when the regular diggers did
not. Thanks to the revenue generated by their activities, their standard of
living improved and some economic activities could develop in this very
isolated area. The network of Nindjas was dependent on the network of
local traders and gold merchants in the area and had to cooperate with the
mining police.

These two examples at least indicate that some networks have a proper
sociological density and some leverage over their own economic situation.
They have a degree of social power and a capacity for resistance against
outside influence and domination. Several conflicts occurred between the
Congolese government and the diamond traders, in which the latter gained
the upper hand (see below). In purely economic terms, the percentage of
added value siphoned off by outside actors is considerably lower for the
diamond and gold trade than for other types of mineral exploitation; that
is, the network succeeds in controlling a bigger part of the revenue.

This had important consequences for the economy of war that emerged
after August 1998 in the DRC. When the armies of the Congo's neighbors
invaded the country, they found an already existing formal and informal
structure of exploitation of mineral resources. Their capacity for controlling
these existing structure depended, among other factors, on the degree of

[43] Ambroise Butambo Katambu, *Capitalisme minier et droits de l'homme en
RDCongo: La croisade des Nindja contre la Sominki* (Huy, Belgium: Les Editions du
Trottoir, 2002).

resistance they experienced from the artisanal networks. The Zimbabweans did not interfere directly but tried to control this exploitation by signing official agreements with the Congolese government for the control of parts of the official economy (e.g., with the state-owned diamond-mining company MIBA or the copper/cobalt-mining company Gecamines). The Rwandans and Ugandans sometimes engaged in direct exploitation of the mining sites, but they often replaced the patrons at the top of the existing networks. In this way, control of the entry and exit points passed into foreign hands.

In a context of domination by foreign armies and by rebel forces without the slightest interest in the well-being of the population, and in the absence of serious foreign investors, the self-organization of the population is an important element in the struggle against the plundering of the country.[44] Seemingly important factors in the construction of this autonomy are the duration of the network, the characteristics of the resource, the type of exploitation, and the importance of the resource for the world market. In the next section, I illustrate this with a brief summary of resource looting in the DRC.

Looting and the Militarization of Networks

Stefaan Marysse, a professor at the University of Antwerp, has suggested a useful economic definition of looting: the proportion of added value leaving the country without compensation, be it as a similar value of imports in goods or money.[45] From this perspective, the plundering of the country during the war is, in a sense, a continuation of former practices by other actors. However, the replacement of national economic or political elites by foreign army commanders led to a significant increase of noncompensated added value leaving the country.[46] The militarization of the existing networks of artisanal miners has indeed intensified the plundering of the

[44]The local networks are not an idyllic situation of "people's power" at all; however, they represent a possible starting point for community-centered development.

[45]Belgian Senate, *Final Report of the Parliamentary Commission of Inquiry*. It is not very productive to define "looting" as "illegal exploitation" in a country such as the DRC where the law has not been applied for decades.

[46]Looting is not new and was, of course, also practiced under the Mobutu regime. But the system of clientelism and redistribution conferred a degree of legitimacy to some segments of the clientelist systems.

country. In the territories occupied by the Ugandan or Rwandan forces, the intermediary between the local and the international levels became a group of army officers engaged in practices of "military commercialism."[47] Because it had become impossible for ordinary mining companies to set up a structured activity in the war-ridden DRC, the "military merchants" cooperated with operators from a shadowy international criminal economy. The links were not only made with criminal buyers of precious substances but most of all with the mafia of the international arms trade.

The relationship of these "national actors" (because they are officers of a national army, directed by the president of the neighboring country) with the local networks was diverse. Very generally speaking, the Rwandan occupation (with the help of the RCD/Goma rebel movement) was much more systematic, and the revenue that was generated made more profit for the Rwandan state as such. The Ugandan occupation relied much more on local commanders, was less directed from the presidency, and made more profit for individual army officers.[48]

Still, the degree of control that could be exerted by the invading army structures was very much differentiated. It was presumably the least intensive for the diamond trade. Research done in the early stages of the war indicated already that the Rwandan and Ugandan army officers controlled the payment of taxes by the *comptoirs* and the patrons of local business networks. Interestingly, these patrons were also active during the last decade of the Mobutu regime.[49] This business network cooperated with Ugandan officers but was also, through intermediaries, active in the government-controlled part of the country. It could thus speculate on the different value of the Congolese franc in government-controlled and in rebel-controlled territory. This was totally in line with operations executed during the last years of the Mobutu regime. Indeed, in an effort officially designed to control the exchange rate of the Congolese franc, Prime Minister Kengo concluded an agreement in July 1995 with a private "exchange office," Qualitoles, to buy

---

[47]Christian Dietrich, "Commercialisme militaire sans éthique et sans frontières," in *Annuaire des Grands Lacs 2000–2001*, ed. Reyntjens and Marysse, 333–64. Also see Belgian Senate, *Final Report of the Parliamentary Commission of Inquiry*, 54.

[48]These individual army officers may themselves control a clientelistic network in their own countries and redistribute parts of the stolen wealth, as is the case with Salim Saleh. See Madelaine Drohan, *Making a Killing: How and Why Corporations Use Armed Force to Do Business* (Toronto: Random House of Canada, 2003), 292.

[49]Pierre Lumbi, *Guerre en RDC: Enjeux économiques: intérêts et acteurs* (Kinshasa: Observatoire Gouvernance Transparence, 2000).

local currency every month for a value of $20 million. If Qualitoles could succeed in stabilizing the exchange rate of the Congolese franc, it could privatize a function of the Central Bank.[50] In fact, the network behind Qualitoles speculated on the varying value of the franc in different regions of the country. The real aim of the operation, however, was to establish control over the diamond trade in the Congo: The $20 million was to be generated by a *comptoir* being made part of the operation, which would be granted a diamond purchase monopoly.[51] The whole operation failed, mainly because it is impossible to control the artisanal diamond mining economy.

Indeed, all efforts to do so have failed. The Kabila regime tried several times to install some type of monopoly, without success.[52] Indeed, the diamond economy in the Kasai region represents a significant independent economic power. This was illustrated by the power struggle between the Kabila government and the local diamond traders over the discovery of a 265.85-carat diamond outside the official MIBA concession. Kabila's security services captured the diamond, to be sold to finance the war effort. In his confrontation with the network of diamond traders, both locally and on the international market, he had to give in and restore the diamond to its owner; the whole Kasai region threatened to rebel, and no one wanted to buy the diamond from the Congolese president.[53]

When the Kabila government granted a diamond concession to the Zimbabwean military-commercial complex, the Zimbabweans quickly got stuck in the complex network of the artisanal diamond trade. They could only maintain their presence by establishing total military control over a kimberlite concession.[54] It should be added that the MIBA state-owned

[50]During the war, a faction of the RCD concluded an agreement with the speculator Van A. Brink to set up a privatized central bank, with the right to issue money. The counter value of the money was to be guaranteed by diamond reserves.

[51]See Mabi Mulumba, *Les dérives d'une gestion prédatrice: Le cas du Zaïre devenu République Démocratique du Congo* (Kinshasa: Centre de Recherches Pédagogiques, 1998), 175–91.

[52]This applies only to the artisanal diamond mining. In 1985, a purchasing monopoly was introduced for the diamonds produced by the official MIBA mining company. In 2003, the same operation was mounted in favor of the Israeli company IDI diamonds. See Gauthier de Villers, with Jean Omasombo and Erik Kennes, *Guerre et politique: Les trente derniers mois de L. D. Kabila*, Cahiers Africains 47–48 (Tervuren, Belgium, and Paris: Institut Africain–CEDAF and L'Harmattan, 2002), 281–87.

[53]Gauthier de Villers, "L'affaire 'Ngokas,'" in *Chasse au diamant au Congo/Zaire*, ed. Monnier, Jewsiewicki, and de Villers, 233–40.

[54]See Kennes, "Le secteur minier au Congo," 319.

diamond company has been the object of ruthless plundering by its director, Jean-Charles Okoto, a member of a network linked to circles around President Kabila. Another member of this network, a close aide to Kabila, tried for four months to violently loot the diamond region around Tshikapa, until the president was forced to call him back.

The situation is slightly different for the region occupied by rebel forces. The rich diamond concessions around Kisangani were discovered during the 1980s; their operation is purely artisanal and is not linked to formal diamond mining exploitation. The network is also ethnically more diverse and had to organize in much more unstable circumstances than the network in the Kasai region. Still, if it has a lesser capacity of resistance, the added value controlled by the network itself is high, estimated between 75 and 80 percent of the diamond revenues, while 20 to 25 percent go abroad.[55] Prices paid for diamonds in Kisangani amount to about 65 to 70 percent of the price paid in Antwerp. According to Leclercq, the profit from diamond trading in this region is realized indirectly; the foreign currency generated by the sale of diamonds is used not only for the trade in household goods but also for the trade in arms, which generates much more important benefits.[56]

This means that the network of artisanal diamond traders is relatively powerful in comparison with networks concerned with other types of commodities. The reasons are linked to the history of the artisanal diamond trade; it could operate, during the 1980s, in a relatively stable environment regulated by the law on artisanal trade. The diamond trade itself has an internal ethical code, which is widely respected. Diamonds are easily transportable, can be hidden anywhere, and are found over a huge part of Congolese territory that no army can control. Most important, the expertise about diamonds is available at many levels of the network. Diamond diggers are often able to make a rough assessment of the quality and value of their find; information is widely available about the prices on the world market.

The situation is also different for the gold trade.[57] Huge gold reserves are present in the eastern and northeastern parts of the DRC, and gold was always

---

[55]Belgian Senate, *Final Report of the Parliamentary Commission of Inquiry*, 34.

[56]Often the same businessmen, at a higher level in the chain, are active in diamonds as well as in the arms trade. See Belgian Senate, *Final Report of the Parliamentary Commission of Inquiry*, 39.

[57]Much less research has been done about the gold trade in the DRC.

traded through networks directed toward Uganda and Burundi (partly because of close links of Nande traders with Uganda; partly because of the creation of free trade zones in Uganda and Burundi). When the 1998 war broke out, Uganda and Rwanda apparently could exert a much more intensive influence on the structure of the trade. Gold trade was partly redirected toward Rwanda; already in 1998, Rwandan army commanders forced local artisanal gold diggers to work for their profit.[58] Half a decade later, Uganda still played several armed militias against each other in the Ituri region and "imported" a huge amount of gold from the DRC.[59] Militias sell gold to buy arms. The added value kept in the country seems lower than for the diamond trade, at least in a militarized setting; gold diggers in the Kilo Moto concession, when controlled by Ugandan military, keep only 50 percent.[60]

The gold network is seemingly less powerful than the diamond network, even if the characteristics of the commodity are very similar. More research is needed, but it seems that militarization of the gold-trading networks is much easier because they overlap with trade routes from before the war.[61] The bulk of the gold concessions is also to be found inside the territory controlled by foreign armies; and the international cohesion of the gold trade seems much less than for diamonds.[62]

The situation is much more different for the coltan trade. Coltan, or colombite-tantalite ore, is a relatively new commodity.[63] Exploitation started during the war. The coltan diggers at a local level were organized in camps where a proper social life developed around digging, women, and beer. Some coltan networks linked up with local traders in the region. Others were rapidly militarized by Rwandan troops, which controlled some sites of

---

[58]Katambu, *Capitalisme minier et droits de l'homme en RD Congo*, 156–59.

[59]Gabriel Kahn, "Le pillage se poursuit en RDCongo," *Marchés Tropicaux*, no. 3034, January 2, 2004, 2770–771.

[60]Belgian Senate, *Final Report of the Parliamentary Commission of Inquiry*, 119.

[61]Stefaan Marysse and Cathérine Andre, "Guerre et pillage en République Démocratique du Congo," in *L'Afrique des Grands Lacs: Annuaire 2000–2001*, ed. Marysse and Reyntjens, 321–323. One of the few studies on this topic is a very good one by Jeroen Cuvelier, *The Political Economy of Resource Trafficking in the Democratic Republic of the Congo*, IPIS Report (Antwerp, IPIS, 2003), 12–30.

[62]The degree of national and international control over the gold trade may possibly be influenced in the future by international developments. The absorption of Ashanti by Anglogold makes the latter the undisputed leader in gold trade on the African continent.

[63]Tantalite was exploited as a by-product of cassiterite (it was, e.g., secretly exported from the tin mine of Manono in 1963) but was never highly valued before the war. Niobium (or columbium) was exploited in Luheshe by the company Somikivu.

exploitation and purchasing *comptoirs*.[64] According to estimates, 60 percent of the added value of the coltan exploitation and trade remains in the
DRC. However, the distribution of this value inside the network is highly
uneven. The coltan digger gets between 10 and 20 percent of this value;
the trader and intermediaries get 50 percent, and the exporter the remaining
part.[65] As is the case for the gold trade, revenue is generated for rebel forces
and foreign armies by levying taxes. In the case of coltan, it seems that the
local digger, much more than the gold or diamond digger, is powerless. This
is linked to the nature of the product, the structure of international trade,
and the war origin of the coltan exploitation.

The extraction of colombo-tantalite from the coltan ore requires sophisticated technology, only available in high-technology enterprises. The value
of the ore is determined by the (variable) concentration of tantalite. This
means that the price of the ore can only be determined by a limited number of
laboratories present in the urban centers. A local digger can thus easily be manipulated by the intermediate buyers, as happened during the period of the
"coltan boom" toward the end of 2000, when the prices for coltan soared to
unprecedented heights. The local digger did not profit proportionally, to the
benefit of the intermediaries. Prices for coltan are often not publicly known,
because an important proportion of the trade in tantalite is done through long-
term contracts between producers and buyers. Information about the prices
for tantalite on the international market are thus often not available.

Finally, the origin of the coltan trade during the war created an immediate
militarization of the trade. Still, it partly used existing trade networks with
a certain degree of independence. When the RCD/Goma rebel movement
tried to introduce a monopoly on the purchase and sale of coltan, it had to
back down after a few months under pressure of local traders but also from
the Rwandan army, which preferred not to have the trade controlled by its
rebel movement.

Despite the technology needed for the extraction of tantalite from the
ore, coltan is "lootable" because its volume is relatively reduced. Commodities such as cobalt or copper are not so easily "lootable" because of
their volume and the industrial process needed for their extraction before

---

[64]See the following excellent studies: Didier de Failly, "Coltan: Pour compren-
dre . . .," in *L'Afrique des Grands Lacs: Annuaire 2000–2001*, ed. Marysse and Reyntjens, 279–306; and Patrick Martineau, *La route commerciale du coltan congolais:
Une enquête* (Montreal: GRAMA-UQAM, 2003).

[65]Belgian Senate, *Final Report of the Parliamentary Commission of Inquiry*, 70–71.

they can be transported abroad. The Gecamines copper mine produced very important volumes of copper and cobalt before 1990. A combination of a long-term fall in copper prices, very bad management of the company, and the destruction of its technical apparatus led to its total breakdown.[66] Because of the relative profitability of cobalt, the more interesting parts of the company were conceded by the Kabila government to its Zimbabwean allies. Because the company was under constant pressure to generate money, this could not lead to its revival.[67] Gécamines officials and unscrupulous local businessmen and traders participated substantively in looting what is left of the company.

The population, driven by poverty, invented its own form of artisanal mining economy: the exploitation of more easily accessible low-grade copper/cobalt ore or *heterogenite*. All over South Katanga, myriad exploitation sites of heterogenite emerged. The network is not headed by foreign army officers but by Congolese government officials and foreign traders. The trade has become a means of living for a huge chain of officials, all of whom levy their taxes; for a truckload of 20 tons, no fewer than twelve officials have to be paid.[68] At the bottom of the network, the local population (with women and children, estimated at about 70,000) is digging for this relatively low-paid ore.[69] The conditions of exploitation are often terrible; a recent report gives details about the exploitation of heterogenite in the former uranium mine of Shinkolobwe, where high levels of radioactivity have been registered.[70]

[66]Especially since the outbreak of the 1998 war, the Gecamines and their installations have been the object of ruthless plundering by Gecamines officials and networks of unscrupulous traders.

[67]The same process occurred with the state-owned diamond mining company MIBA. Pressure from the government led to the virtual destruction of the production apparatus, the plundering of the company by its officials (mining police, management), and the use of unacceptable violence toward diamond diggers in the region. See *Rapport sur des violations des droits de l'homme liées à l'exploitation du diamant du Kasai Oriental* (Mbuji Mayi, D.R. Congo: CEFOP–Kasai Oriental, 2001).

[68]ASADHO/KATANGA, *Rapport circonstanciel de l'ASADHO sur la situation des Droits socio-économiques dans la province du Katanga: Mines du Katanga—Contamination radioactive organisée par l'Etat—Cas de la mine de Shinkolobwe* (Lubumbashi, Congo: ASADHO/KATANGA, 2003), 16.

[69]See Cuvelier, *Political Economy of Resource Trafficking*, 61.

[70]ASADHO/KATANGA, *Rapport circonstanciel de l'ASADHO*. The local gold exploitation in Kimpese is also done in unacceptable conditions. See *CDH-BRIEFS* (Centre des droits de l'homme et du droit humanitaire, Lubumbashi), no. 1 (March 2000): 2–3.

The price of heterogenite, again, depends on the concentration of cobalt in the ore. This can only be measured by specialized laboratories in the urban centers. Again, the opacity of the process leaves much room for price manipulation. The heterogenite diggers are represented in the Association des Exploitants Miniers Artisanaux du Katanga, but this organization, through agreements on price control, protects the buyers more than the diggers.[71] Some trading networks are relatively new and operate in the formerly government-controlled as well as in the formerly rebel-controlled territory.[72] A heterogenite digger in Shinkolobwe sums up their situation:

> In our country, nobody cares about us; the political, administrative and military authorities only care about their own families and their many mistresses, abandoning us to the mercy of [foreign] traders and entrepreneurs who only think about their own interests regardless of the human or ecological damage they cause. If we try to go and live in their countries, they do not hesitate to chase us as animals, handcuffed in "charter flights of shame." And as death watches us everywhere, we are only free to choose from which death we will die . . . some die of malaria, others by bullets at the front of one or another rebellion. . . . I have chosen to die by radioactive contamination. We are all doomed.[73]

Artisanal Mining Networks and Prospects for Peace and Reconstruction

When the "African World War" started in the DRC in August 1998, the situation was very fragile at all levels. The mining boom of 1995–97 had considerably slowed down, much less risk capital was available, and the mining sector preferred to consolidate in safer areas than the DRC. On the national level, the regime of Laurent Kabila was diplomatically more isolated than the regimes in Kigali and Kampala. Most of all, the governing political elite was composed of many returnees from abroad who had lost contact with the very complex realities in Congolese society. Moreover, the Kabila regime had evinced most of the former political and military elite

---

[71]The trade in heterogenite is linked to the Zambian mining sector and trade to South Africa. The ore is partly refined in Zambia.

[72]Cuvelier, *Political Economy of Resource Trafficking*, 59–64.

[73]ASADHO/KATANGA, *Rapport circonstanciel de l'ASADHO*, 28.

under the Mobutu regime. The former clientelistic structure had been abolished and not replaced by a new one. As a consequence, the Kabila regime in Kinshasa had few reliable links between the national government and Congolese society at a local level. In the formal mining sector, the regime created a total imbroglio and legal insecurity; just like its predecessor government, it authorized speculative and unreliable companies to enter the game.[74]

On June 30, 2003, a Government of National Union was installed as a result of the 1999 Lusaka and 2003 Pretoria agreements to end the war. What is the resulting situation on the international, national, and local levels, and what are the perspectives for peace and reconstruction—for the attenuation of a rebellion based on need and the elimination of a government based on greed?

The global mining industry has gone through difficult times during the war, not only because of the low metal prices but also because of its bad public image as a "war-monger industry." Yet the mining industry as a whole is on the verge of an upturn; the sector is being stabilized after a series of takeovers, mergers, and cost-cutting restructurings, and demand for metals and minerals is high because of China's economic growth.[75] The investment of Anglo American in the important Konkola Deep Mining copper/cobalt project in Zambia in 2001 and its sudden withdrawal in January 2002 probably indicates that huge mining companies will follow a very cautious policy.[76] Their horizon is no longer Africa but the world. The extremely bad state of all infrastructure in the DRC makes other countries more attractive. During the last months of 2003, several junior companies returned to the DRC and tried to secure new or formerly attributed concessions. A junior company such as the Canadian Banro has gone through all

[74]E.g., the important gold concessions of Tele, Panga, and West Ngayu were granted to Starpoint Goldfields, a previously unknown company without much experience. In May 2002, they still claimed ownership of the concessions, even though they had redirected their activities to the sale of medical equipment. See Guy Franceschi, *Basisbegrippen en Kort Overzicht m.b.t. de Goudindustrie in de D.R. Congo*, Report for the Commission of Inquiry of the Belgian Senate (Brussels: Belgian Senate, 2002), 11.

[75]Raw Materials Group, *Mining Journal's State of the Industry Report* (London: Mining Communications, January 2004).

[76]Anglo American, "Zambia Copper Investments Limited ('ZCI') Concludes Strategic Review of its Investment in the Konkola Copper Mine ('KCM') Operations in Zambia," press release, January 24, 2002. Available at http://www.angloamerican.co.uk/press/2002/24012002.asp.

the stages of the turmoil in the country since 1995 and considers its stake in gold exploration in South Kivu too important to let go. The problem for the DRC in the global mining environment will be twofold: how to attract serious and nonspeculative investors, and how to have them operate in a legal framework that is profitable for the country.

A new mining code for the DRC was adopted in 2002, under pressure from the World Bank, which wanted to adapt the country's legislation to a new global investment climate and the rules of international competition. Although it is too early for a firm evaluation, recent studies on the effect of new legislation on the development of African countries, however, warrant some skepticism. Very liberal tax and profit repatriation rules and the important reduction of state regulation of the private sector reportedly only produced a limited contribution of the mining sector to the development of the national economy.[77]

The "international community" (first of all South Africa) put heavy pressure on the belligerents to conclude a peace agreement. Since the installation of the new union government, important amounts of development financing and debt reduction have been pledged. One positive development is undoubtedly the important interest of South Africa in the DRC; a visit of President Thabo Mbeki to the DRC in 2004 resulted in cooperation agreements and a pledge of massive investment, especially in the mining sector.[78]

The international community also finances the newly formed transitional institutions, with their 5 presidents and deputy presidents, 36 ministers, 25 deputy ministers, 150 senators, and 500 representatives in parliament. The participation of as many politically and militarily important groups as possible in a government of national union was the price to be paid for peace, even if their expenses are paid by foreign funding. But this group lacks internal cohesion. It is made up of former Mobutist officials, of the new political elite recruited by Laurent Kabila and Joseph Kabila, of opportunists who took up arms to take power in Kinshasa, of rebel leaders controlled by Kigali or Kampala, of political opposition politicians, and of civil society leaders. Most wait for the next elections that they hope to win and form a more cohesive political elite.

---

[77]Bonnie Campbell, ed., *The Challenges of Development, Mining Codes in Africa and Corporate Responsibility* (Montreal: GRAMA-UQAM, 2003). See the summary in "African Mining Codes Questioned," *Mining Journal*, February 14, 2003, 106–9.
[78]*Le Soir* (Brussels), January 16, 2004.

In this period of muted rivalry and need for financial resources (in view of the coming elections), each political "big man" tries to keep his hold on his own network of exploitation and even his own military. The cohesion created by the Mobutu regime is lacking, as is the clientelist but centralized structure of his system. Moreover, the Congo's neighbors, even if formally withdrawn from the country, have not necessarily given up their ambitions. This cautious assessment is supported by the unpublished part of the final report of the UN Panel of Experts on the Illegal Exploitation of Natural Resources and Other Forms of Wealth of the Democratic Republic of the Congo, which warns about the continuing looting of the country's natural resources.[79]

It is thus not at all certain that the national state, in its formal and informal structures, will be able to defend the interests of the population against foreign pressure, in this particular case from the global mining industry and from the international criminal economy. During the war, the intermediate agencies were made up of the rootless and noninstitutionalized Congolese regime and structures of military commercialism. Since the peace agreements, they have been replaced by an uncohesive, temporary coalition of internationally legitimated political actors, several of which have serious criminal records and do not wish to modify their identification of politics with looting.

How, then, to empower a population whose need resurges as a product of total exhaustion after years of a terribly cruel and lethal war? Is it possible to use the myriad networks of the informal mining economy as the basis for "people-centered" development? Do they offer a minimal foundation for a social ethic absent at the international and national levels? The answers are not simple.

A number of penetrating studies by the anthropologist Filip De Boeck have clearly shown the difficulties of constructing a productive and redistributive economic network from the networks of diamond diggers. Indeed, the informal diamond economy reaffirms but also inverts traditional moral values in an unproductive manner. Finding a diamond is a matter of luck; it may give the lucky diamond digger sudden and unexpected monetary

---

[79]United Nations Security Council, "Letter Dated 15 October 2003 from the Chairman of the Panel of Experts on the Illegal Exploitation of Natural Resources and Other Forms of Wealth of the Democratic Republic of the Congo Addressed to the Secretary General," UNSC S/2003/1027, October 23, 2003. See the detailed text of section 5 of the Panel of Experts' final report.

wealth. The analogy between digging a diamond and hunting an animal leads De Boeck to interpret the whole process of diamond digging as a trial to affirm one's male identity, in the same manner as the social ethos of hunting. The money earned from diamond digging serves not for accumulation but for conspicuous consumption (beer, women, etc.); the ability to spend money reinforces, again, one's male social identity and makes it visible. A purely "modern" phenomenon thus reaffirms "traditional" values. At the same time, the protectors of the moral tradition of the village condemn this type of consumption as it is not redistributive and does not make a profit for other members of the social network. In fact, the money earned from diamonds is part of a world of the whites, of modern capitalism, and as a consequence, of sorcery. Because finding a diamond is matter of luck, someone who fails to find a diamond is under a spell. To control the parameters of luck, one has to use sorcery, that is, invert the traditional cycle of the flow of life (as, e.g., to kill a child or a parent, to give up a vital part of the body, to commit incest). This money is dangerous; it is possessed by the diamond hunter but can also take possession of him:

> Diamonds totally isolate people and turn upside down the ordinary bonds of solidarity and reciprocity to replace them with destructive mechanisms of redistribution typical for sorcery.[80]

The negative effect of the diamond economy on a local level is thus the restructuring of traditional social relations. The young (who have the money) will become socially more important than the elders. This phenomenon is generalized all over the country, be it under the form of diamond or gold diggers or child-soldiers who invert traditional social and moral hierarchies through the social power of the gun.

Although current practices link money to sorcery, the criticism of aimless consumption nevertheless offers a moral basis for reinvesting the money in a productive family, commercial, or ethnic network. De Boeck advances the thesis that the economy of diamond diggers permits the reinvention and internalization of the demands of the world of modern capitalism. The challenge thus becomes to build an "internalized" bridge between this informal economy and the formal mining economy, so that the mining

---

[80]Filip De Boeck, "Comment dompter diamants et dollars: Defense, partage et identité au Sud-Ouest du Zaïre (1980–1997)," in *Chasse au diamant au Congo/Zaire*, ed. Monnier, Jewsiewicki, and de Villers, 171–208.

companies will no longer function as a force for the destruction of the informal networks but will establish productive relations with the networks and thus acquire a form of legitimacy.

The informal networks of artisanal mining therefore potentially offer a possible stepping-stone for reconstruction. As often the only means of living for the population, they should not (and cannot) be abolished: They represent a foundation for a development-oriented economy, to meet local need. Internal regulation of the informal mining sector (for which the diamond sector may provide some inspiration), the creation of centers for technical information about exploitation and evolution on the world market, the promotion of humane working conditions, the development of independent artisanal miners' associations with trade union status—all can contribute to a reorientation of the sector. Such measures may create a basis for dikes against greed, for resistance against looting by national or foreign elites, and for negotiation with mining companies that care less about the social and environmental conditions of exploitation. Indeed, it would create the conditions for legitimate mining exploitation, based on an agreement with local communities and leaving room for artisanal mining:

> A powerful informal popular economy supported by civil society may, in the DRC, resist with great efficiency against the spoliation efforts of a politico-commercial elite in power.[81]

Obviously, this can only work in a stable legal and institutional environment, one capable of stimulating the positive aspects of the informal mining economy. The new mining code provides for such a framework. The problem in the DRC, however, has never been the law but its lack of application. Implementation could be brought about by a cohesive national elite, but most of all through local empowerment based on knowledge dissemination, transparent procedures for the election of legitimate leaders of artisanal miners, and a higher degree of control over the miners' own revenues. This is one of the more realistic options to be taken for reconstruction and pacification "from the bottom" to curb greed and meet need. At the same time, one cannot avoid the problem of a minimal reconstruction of stable state institution, if only to avoid the danger that empowered artisanal miners would be mobilized by entrepreneurs of violence.

---

[81]Leclercq, "Le rôle économique du diamant dans le conflit congolais," 68.

7

Economic Resources and Internal Armed Conflicts: Lessons from the Colombian Case

Marc Chernick

Colombia has experienced more than fifty-seven years of war, making it the longest-running twentieth-century internal armed conflict that has endured into the twenty-first century. The first decade of the conflict, from 1948 to 1958—a period known simply as La Violencia—was the bloodiest phase, with an estimated 200,000 dead. However, by the 1990s, the violence had escalated again to levels not seen since the 1950s. This unexpected expansion of the war coincided with the insertion of the Andean region into the

Marc Chernick is research associate professor in the Department of Government and the Center for Latin American Studies at Georgetown University. He has worked as an adviser to the World Bank, the United Nations Development Program, the Swiss Peace Foundation, and the Norwegian Foreign Ministry on issues of political violence, peace, and rural development in Colombia, and for the U.S. Agency for International Development in other countries in Latin America and Africa. He is the author of *Repensando el proceso de paz en Colombia* (Ediciones Aurora, 2005) and the editor and coauthor of *Conflict Prevention and Early Warning in Latin America: The Case of Colombia* (United Nations Development Program, Georgetown University, and Universidad de los Andes, 2005).

world economy as an exporter of illicit narcotics, principally coca paste and cocaine.[1]

The drug export boom radically transformed Colombia's deep-rooted and long-standing armed conflict: It provided resources to the Colombian guerrillas that led to a steady increase in recruitment, armed actions, geographic mobility, military capacity, and technological prowess. The burgeoning drug trade also created a new class of economic elites and rural landowners as drug money was laundered through investments in large estates in the countryside, particularly the cattle lands in the northern part of the country. Finally, it drew in the major regional power, the United States, which was eager to provide military assistance to repress the northward flow of drugs.

The transformation of the Colombian conflict in the 1980s and 1990s raises important questions on the relationship between resources and armed conflict. In the Colombian case, there appears to be a clear and direct correlation between the advent of new and abundant sources of financing and the territorial expansion and increased intensity of the war. The critical question for scholars and policymakers studying the economic underpinnings of internal wars, however, is: How much weight should be assigned to the variable of economic resources, both in the Colombian case as well as in others? In Colombia, does the altered economic landscape and the access to financial resources following the boom in illegal commodity exports alone explain the expansion of this conflict? Does the introduction of these resources into the conflict overshadow other explanatory variables, minimizing the importance previously placed on historical grievances and other factors normally associated with civil wars and domestic insurgencies, such as social exclusion, economic inequality and political repression? Or—stated differently, and using the language employed by the economist Paul Collier—does greed trump grievance as the primary causal factor in explaining this seemingly intractable armed conflict?[2]

The answers to these questions will have far-reaching consequences for strategies for war making and possible peace settlements. Stated generally, if economic resources are the critical variable, then a counterinsurgency strategy of choking them off could seriously weaken an insurgent group's

---

[1]Coca is the plant from which cocaine is derived following a two-step refining process to isolate the coca leaf's alkaloids. The two steps are from coca to coca paste, and from coca paste to cocaine hydrochloride. The plant is native to the Andean region, particularly the foothills extending into the Amazon basin.

[2]See Paul Collier, *Economic Causes of Civil Conflict and Their Implications for Policy* (Washington, D.C.: World Bank, 2000).

ability to wage war and thus could help force a resolution at the negotiating table. Concomitantly, if greed is the primary motivating factor for insurgency, then negotiated political arrangements may hold little appeal to the insurgent groups if they do not include issues of access to and control of key economic and financial resources.

Because its internal armed conflict has spanned more than half a century of modernization and a succession of commodity export booms—and busts—Colombia presents a good case to explore these issues. Moreover, it provides an opportunity to sort out the relationships among causal and facilitating variables on the origins and duration of armed conflicts. During distinct phases of the conflict, resources have played a critical role. As the violence stretched out over decades, the financing and resource base altered as Colombia's position in the global economy—and indeed the global economy itself—was transformed. In the early decades, coffee production was at the center of the violence. In the 1960s and 1970s, the war became a low-intensity conflict assisted by outside financing from international state actors—primarily the United States, the Soviet Union, and Cuba. In the final phase, beginning in the 1980s, only the United States remained as a significant international state actor involved in the Colombian conflict, providing direct support for government forces. International state support for guerrilla forces disappeared following the collapse of the Cold War in the late 1980s, while at the same time, U.S. assistance dramatically expanded with the war on drugs and, after September 11, 2001, with the war on terrorism.

Yet in this final, post–Cold War phase of the conflict, the other actors—guerrillas and paramilitaries—began to raise revenues directly from illegal activities related to the drug trade and the petroleum sector, employing such practices as extortion and illegal protection payments. These groups also turned to lucrative criminal activities such as kidnapping and widespread shakedowns and blackmail of multinational, national, and local commercial activities of all stripes—cattle, bananas, coal, retail interests, and a broad range of productive and commercial enterprises—following a more generalized pattern of post–Cold War conflict seen elsewhere in the world.[3] It is

[3]See Mary Kaldor, *New and Old Wars: Organized Violence in the Global Era* (Cambridge: Policy Press, 1999). Also see Tamara Makarenko, "Terrorism and Transnational Organized Crime: The Emerging Nexus," available at http://www .st-andrews. ac.uk/academic/intrel/research/cstpv/pages/pub_other.html. Both Kaldor and Makarenko argue that globalization has provided new opportunities for insurgent and terrorist groups to link with international criminal networks, often bringing together multiple criminal enterprises such as the illegal arms and narcotics trade and the blurring of lines between organized criminal syndicates and terrorist and insurgent movements.

this newer dimension of the conflict that has raised so many questions as to the very nature of the insurgencies. Are criminal pursuits a means to finance a war that is essentially political? Or have the criminal activities become the principal end in themselves, exercised behind a facade of political justification? How can we tell? This chapter attempts to answer these questions by reviewing the relationship between resources and war in each phase of the Colombian conflict.

It will argue, *first*, that despite the conflict's evolution over a fifty-year period, there is great continuity between its early and later phases. Continuity exists in political actors, regions affected by the violence, and expressed grievances and political positions of the groups, even as the resource base has been transformed in the conflict's different phases.

Second, in the final phase of the conflict beginning in the mid-1980s, the drug trade played a major role in reshaping the nature and scope of the conflict, and it came to influence the activities of individual groups. In the case of the Colombian guerrillas, particularly the Fuerzas Armadas Revolucionarias de Colombia (Revolutionary Armed Forces of Colombia, or FARC), the emergence of the illicit coca/cocaine economy in territory already under their control helped it to evolve from a relatively small, rural, long-term peasant insurgency into a sizable army of more than 18,000 armed soldiers with military projection and political influence throughout the national territory. At the same time, a sizable percentage of the FARC's fighting force was increasingly dedicated not to military strategy or politics but to criminal pursuits, including kidnapping, extortion, and controlling elements of the illegal drug markets.

The other major guerrilla group, the Ejército de Liberación Nacional (National Liberation Army, or ELN), which was founded in 1966 as a small group of pro-Cuban revolutionary students, also expanded its presence beginning in the mid-1980s. It also gained access to new resources as a result of a commodity export boom that facilitated the group's expansion and transformation from an armed organization nearly defeated militarily by the Colombian Armed Forces in the early 1970s into a formidable military force of about 5,000 fighters. For the ELN, the economic resource that facilitated its resurrection was not illicit narcotics but petroleum. In the 1980s, significant oil fields were discovered in the department (or state) of Arauca, a sparsely populated area on the Venezuelan border. Colombia became a net exporter of petroleum in 1986. Oil was subsequently found and exploited in Casanare on the eastern plains (*llanos orientales*) and Putumayo in the south in the 1990s, triggering an oil boom that recast the foundations of the Colombian economy.

The ELN staged its resurrection by demanding "revolutionary taxes" of the large multinational oil firms and construction companies that had been hired to construct a network of pipelines from the drilling sites to the petroleum terminals on the Atlantic coast. The ELN also relied heavily on kidnapping to raise revenues.

An analysis of the FARC's or the ELN's collective military, political, and criminal activities leads to the conclusion that these organizations do resemble a sort of "post–Cold War" hybrid of criminal and insurgent groups, in somewhat the terms described by Mary Kaldor. Nevertheless, this chapter argues—as did a succession of Colombian presidents from 1982 to 2002 during periods of peace talks—that the FARC and the ELN are still predominantly political/military movements with deep roots in the political and social conditions of the country.

Third, this chapter examines the relationship between the accumulation of economic resources and political-military strategy. The available evidence indicates that the expanded resource base of the FARC and the ELN have been used to pursue their military and political objectives: (1) to build an army capable of confronting the armed forces and the right-wing paramilitary forces with the goal of taking state power, or forcing a political settlement; (2) to protect and expand their financial resource bases to sustain their insurrectionary strategies; (3) to destabilize and challenge the state at the local and regional levels; (4) to establish alternative power structures in selected regions to compete with the state for territorial control, or to influence state spending in certain areas by indirectly controlling municipal politics. These are the actions of insurgent groups with a political agenda, not organized criminal syndicates dedicated primarily to the accumulation of capital for individual gain.

Fourth and finally, the chapter concludes that resources *are always* a decisive factor in any sustained armed struggle or protest movement. Movements cannot endure without a resource base. However, resources are one element, together with grievance, ideology, strategy, and often international conditions. Resources are *a* factor; they are not *the* factor.

Phases of Conflict in a Fifty-Year War:
Coffee and Violence in the 1940s and 1950s

War first broke out in the mid-1940s between the Liberals and Conservatives, the two historic, elite-dominated, multiclass parties (table 7.1). Conservatives and their paramilitary allies controlled and had access to state

Table 7.1. *Phases of Conflict in Colombia, 1946–2003*

Phase	Principal Armed Actors	Political Deaths	All Homicides	International Context	Economic Context
Phase 1: La Violencia, 1946–64	Liberals/Liberal guerrillas Conservatives/Conservative paramilitaries (*pájaros*) Communist self-defense groups Armed forces (at service of Conservative government)	200,000	200,000	Post–World War II— Korean War—beginning of Cold War in Western Hemisphere	Coffee boom, 1948–58
Phase 2: Guerrillas— state— low- intensity conflict, 1964–84	Guerrillas: FARC, ELN, EPL, M-19 National Front government/ armed forces	21,000	126,000	Cold War	International support for insurgent groups
Phase 3: Multipolar violence, 1982–2002	Guerrillas: FARC, ELN. EPL Paramilitaries (after 1997 formed AUC) Armed Forces	60,000	418,000	Final phase of Cold War, Post–Cold War, war on drugs, war on terrorism	Coca/cocaine boom, 1982–present; Petroleum boom, 1986–present; Coffee bust, 1998–2004

Note: FARC = Fuerzas Armadas Revolucionarias de Colombia; ELN = Ejército de Liberación Nacional; EPL = Ejército Popular de Liberación; M-19 = April Nineteenth Movement; AUC = United Self-Defense Forces.

Sources: Author's research. Homicide sources: Phase 1: Doctor Carlos Lemoine, Compañía Colombianá de Datos; cited in Paul Oquist, *Violencia, conflicto y política en Colombia* (Bogotá: Instituto de Estudios Colombianos, 1978). Phase 2: Policía Nacional Dijin, data from Consejería para los Derechos Humanos, 1991; and Policía. Nacional, data from Departamento Nacional de Planeación, 1998. Phase 3: Policía Nacional, data from Echandía Castilla, 1999; and Observatorio del Programa Presidencial para los Derechos Humanos y DIH, Vicepresidencia de la República, 2002. Political Violence since 1975: Data bank of Justicia y Paz.

resources. They deployed elements of the police and army against individuals and property belonging to the enemy party, the Liberals, without institutional constraints or fear of punishment. For their part, Liberal partisans and guerrillas were forced to rely on local support and the local economy to conduct the war. The economic base for war making in this period was facilitated by the boom in coffee prices that, in part, was stimulated by the Korean War that increased state coffers and enriched local coffee farmers. The coffee boom helped sustain this first phase of the conflict—again, known as La Violencia—which represents one of the bloodiest episodes in Latin American history and caused approximately 200,000 deaths.

Several historians have studied the connection between coffee and conflict.[4] The three most violent departments, Viejo Caldas, Antioquia, and Tolima, were also the three largest coffee producers. They accounted for 60 percent of all deaths in this period and for about two-thirds of all coffee production.[5] The historian Charles Bergquist, in his analysis La Violencia, skillfully links the national-level partisan hatreds and competition to a more microsociological analysis centered on a web of economic, social, and political relations in the coffee regions. Bergquist writes:

> From the beginning, political contention at the local level was deeply enmeshed with the struggle for land and other forms of property, for access to jobs and credit, and for protection from police and the law. The stakes in this struggle in the rural areas (where most Colombians still lived in the 1940's and 1950's) forced local rank and file to support the most sectarian and opportunistic leaders of the parties at the national level, those willing to use their power and talents for exclusively partisan ends.[6]

Coffee in Colombia by midcentury was mostly produced on small and medium-sized estates selling to a monopsonistic public–private enterprise, the National Federation of Coffee Growers. The purchase and export of

---

[4]See Charles Bergquist, *Labor in Latin America: Comparative Essays on Chile, Argentina, Venezuela and Colombia* (Stanford, Calif.: Stanford University Press, 1986); Bergquist, *Coffee and Conflict in Colombia, 1886–1910* (Durham, N.C.: Duke University Press, 1986); Marco Palacios, *El café en Colombia 1850–1970*, 2nd ed. (Mexico City and Bogotá:. El Colegio de México and El Ancora Editores, 1983).

[5]Bergquist, *Labor in Latin America*, using data provided by Paul Oquist, *Violencia, conflicto y política en Colombia* (Bogotá: Instituto de Estudios Colombianos, 1978).

[6]Bergquist, *Labor in Latin America*, 301.

coffee beans through networks linked to a few North American and European food conglomerates that controlled roasting, sales, and distribution were the original source of the wealth and economic power of the nation's oligarchic elites.

However, by the 1940s, the social stability of the small coffee-estate economy was beginning to break down, even as global demand and prices soared. The incentives were to consolidate holdings and streamline production:

> By the late 1940s, the struggle [for land] had become both more desperate and less collective than it had been in the early 1930s. More desperate because land suitable for coffee cultivation had largely been appropriated and put to use by that time. . . . More desperate as well perhaps because subdivision of family owned farms through inheritance rendered many farms unviable, at a time when growing competition for land appropriate to coffee cultivation intensified and made reconsolidation of viable family farms more difficult.[7]

Beneath the partisan-directed warfare, the coffee economy was transformed:

> Many farmers tried to take advantage [of the violence] in one way or the other. They encroached on lands abandoned by victims or tried to purchase them at a low price. Landowners paid armed groups for protection and bought out frightened *arrendatarios* (renters) and sharecroppers and neighboring smallholders at ridiculous prices.[8]

All violence cannot be reduced to coffee. Violence permeated through non-coffee-producing areas such as Boyacá and the eastern plains, though hereto, the violence was supported through an economic base of large-scale cattle-raising in areas where the Liberal Party was dominant and could resist the Conservative-directed violence.

The studies of this earlier period of internal warfare in Colombia provide some provocative data on the relationship between resource mobilization and war that bear on the central questions addressed in this chapter. The most intense period of La Violencia—indeed the most violent period of all the phases of the fifty-seven-year conflict from 1946 to the present—

[7]Bergquist, *Labor in Latin America*, 303.
[8]Ibid., 302.

coincides with the height of the coffee boom of the 1950s. Despite the mass bloodletting, the coffee crop was harvested, bought by the National Federation of Coffee Growers, and exported abroad. Coffee production, world price per pound, and homicide rates all soared and peaked between 1948 and 1953 before falling precipitously in the period afterward. Between 1948 and 1953, almost 150,000 people were killed. In 1951 alone, more than 50,000 persons (or 404 per 100,000) perished, marking the single most violent year in Colombian history. At the same time, coffee prices, after fluctuating between 10 and 15 cents per pound during the Great Depression, began a steady rise in the late 1940s, cresting at almost 80 cents in 1951, before falling back to about 45 cents in the early 1960s (figures 7.1 and 7.2).

Yet few would argue that coffee was the primary source of the conflict. The overarching cleavage between Liberals and Conservatives and the bloody competition over access and control of state power at the national, regional, and local levels spurred and perpetuated this war, which resembled a nineteenth-century Latin American civil war in the mid–twentieth century. However, conflict over coffee production helped fuel the war. Moreover, coffee provided the resources to sustain organized armies of Liberal guerrillas and communist self-defense groups.[9] It also represented up to 80 percent of the foreign exchange revenues of the authoritarian state dominated by the Conservative Party.[10] In this phase of the war, coffee

[9]Although the violence of the 1940s and 1950s reveals a dynamic where a commodity export boom helped sustain armed conflict, it is also true that commodity busts can also generate war. The analyses of the Colombian "War of a Thousand Days" (1899–1902), during which an estimated 100,000 people perished, indicate that war was generated mostly as a result of the crash of the coffee market after a decade of expanded exports. See Palacios, *El café en Colombia*; and Bergquist, *Labor in Latin America*. However, the midcentury dynamic of export boom and warfare is the pattern that will reappear at the end of the twentieth century with the drug and petroleum export booms. Curiously, as we shall see later in this chapter, the early years of the twenty-first century feature elements of boom *and* bust, including a major depression in the coffee-growing regions as the world price crashed in 2001 and 2002 below 65 cents per pound after reaching a high of $2.40 in 1977 and hovering at about $1.50 in the mid-1990s (see figure 7.3). The coffee regions continue to be among the most violent areas of the country.

[10]In 1949, the Conservative president Laureano Gómez won almost 100 percent of the vote in a hastily scheduled election, while followers of the Liberal Party boycotted the voting and Liberal guerrilla armies expanded their scope and base of operations. See Alex Wilde, in his "Conversations among Gentlemen: Oligarchical Democracy in Colombia," in *The Breakdown of Democratic Regimes: Latin America*, ed. Juan Linz and Alfred Stepan (Baltimore: Johns Hopkins University Press, 1979).

Cents

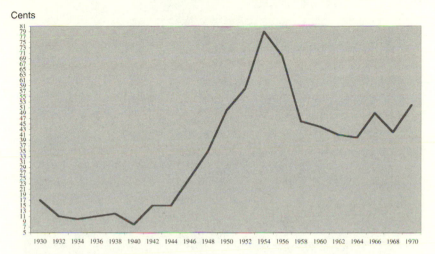

Figure 7.1. Price per Pound of Colombian Coffee, 1930–70.
Source: Federación Nacional de Cafeteros de Colombia, unpublished data
supplied to the author.

Homicides

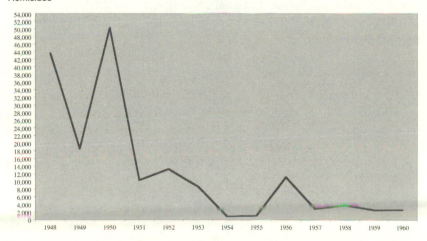

Figure 7.2. Deaths Caused by La Violencia in Colombia, 1948–60.
Source: For 1948–57: Carlos Lemoine, Compañía Colombiana de Datos, cited
in Paul Oquist, *Violencia, conflicto y política en Colombia* (Bogotá: Instituto
de Estudios Colombianos, 1978), 16, 59. For 1957–61: Policía Nacional, cited
in Departamento Nacional de Planeación, "Los costos económicos de la crim-
inalidad y la violencia en Colombia," *Archivos de Macroeconomía*, March 10,
1998.

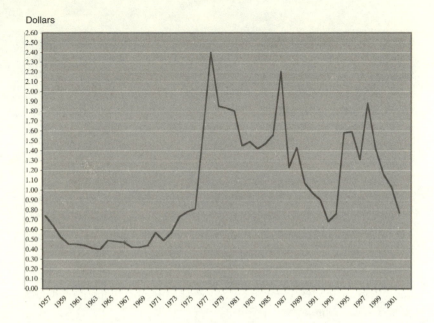

Figure 7.3. Price per Pound of Colombian Coffee, 1957–2001.
Source: Federación Nacional de Cafeteros de Colombia, unpublished data supplied to the author.

provided resources but did not shape the duration of the fighting or the political issues at stake. It diminished in intensity only when both parties agreed to share power, first through bipartisan support of a bloodless military coup in 1953 and then through a power-sharing agreement signed in 1957 and implemented one year later, which was known as the National Front.

Low-Intensity Conflict and External Intervention in the 1960s and 1970s

The violence did not end with the National Front's power-sharing agreement between the Liberals and Conservatives. In the next phase of the violence, the conflict was transformed from a civil war led by the leaders of the two oligarchically dominated parties that manipulated local conflicts for partisan ends into a guerrilla-based insurgency led by dissident liberal guerrillas, communists, and a new generation of revolutionary groups that opposed the elite party agreement. The war was a classic low-intensity conflict. Deaths in combat and political violence in most years did not pass the threshold of 1,000 deaths that some have posited as a minimal definition of civil war.[11]

However, even in the years of relatively low levels of violence, the political regime was strongly shaped by the persistent insurgent conflict. Although nominally democratic, the political system was characterized by a continuous application of the state of siege, the use of military mayors and governors, the curtailment of civil liberties, and armed confrontations between insurgents groups and the state.[12] During the National Front, all participation outside the two recognized parties was constitutionally banned for sixteen years while social protest from groups outside the regime was criminalized, repressed, or co-opted. The National Front came to rely increasingly on the armed forces to maintain public order. By the late 1970s, human rights violations, political prisoners, torture, and extrajudicial actions to confront perceived enemies had become standard practices and had begun to undermine the credibility and the legitimacy of the regime.[13]

The FARC was formed in 1964 by a group of dissident Liberal guerrillas that had refused the National Front's offers of amnesty and by leaders of the communist self-defense groups that had been first organized in the late 1940s. The ELN was founded by Colombian students in Havana, many of whom came of age in the youth wings of a dissident Liberal faction, the Revolutionary Liberal Movement, which rejected the National Front but did not advocate armed struggle.[14] By then, the coffee boom had subsided,

[11]For a discussion of what constitutes a civil war, see Roy Licklider, "How Civil War Ends: Questions and Methods," in *Stopping the Killing: How Civil War Ends*, ed. Roy Licklider (New York: New York University Press, 1993).

[12]Marc Chernick, "Insurgency and Negotiations: Defining the Boundaries of the Political Regime in Colombia," Ph.D. dissertation, Columbia University, 1991.

[13]See Gustavo Gallón Giraldo, "La república de las armas: Relaciones entre Fuerzas Armadas y Estado en Colombia, 1960–1980," *Serie Controversia* (Bogotá), no. 109–10; and Gustavo Gallón Giraldo, *Quince años de estado de sitio en Colombia: 1958–1978* (Bogotá: Editorial América Latina, 1979).

[14]For narratives of the early years of the FARC and the ELN as recounted by their leaders, see Jacobo Arenas, *Cese el fuego: Una historia política de las FARC* (Bogotá: Editorial Oveja Negra, 1985); and Carlos Medina Gallego, *ELN: Una historia contada a dos veces* (Bogotá: Rodríguez Quito Editores, 1996).

though coffee production would steadily expand throughout the 1960s and boom again in the mid-1970s, mid-1980s, and mid-1990s.

The second stage of the conflict, the period 1958–82, coincided with the direct spread of the Cold War into the Western Hemisphere following the United States–backed overthrow of a reformist government in Guatemala in 1954 and, decisively, following the Cuban revolution of 1959. In this second phase of the conflict, guerrilla partisans relied somewhat on the local economy but also were given assistance by external state actors—particularly from the Soviet Union in the case of the FARC, and from Cuba in the case of the ELN. At the same time, the government and armed forces entered into new military cooperation and financial assistance arrangements with the United States.[15]

The United States worked closely with the Colombian armed forces throughout the 1950s and early 1960s. Colombia was the only Latin American nation to contribute troops to the UN "police action" in Korea. By the mid-1950s, U.S. military advisers were in Colombia, assisting the armed forces in the later phases of La Violencia and gaining early experience with irregular warfare on the eve of the Vietnam War. Following the Cuban revolution and the inauguration of the Alliance for Progress in 1961, U.S. advisers played a major role in shaping the counterinsurgency policies of the National Front. They were instrumental in a series of bombing campaigns against the self-defense communities of Liberal and Communist guerrillas that refused to accept the National Front in 1964 and 1965. These campaigns led directly to the transformation of armed self-defense communities into mobile guerrilla units and the founding of the FARC. After this period, however, the interest of the United States was hijacked by the war in Vietnam. The conflict moved into its low-intensity phase, and direct U.S. military assistance and involvement diminished.

Still, the relationship between the Colombian and U.S. military forces remained close throughout the 1960s and 1970s, and the two countries were successful in containing the low-intensity war. In 1973, the ELN was surrounded in Anorí (Antioquia) and was virtually annihilated. For its part, the FARC in this period was little more than a remote force of peasant fighters operating in areas where the state's presence was weak or nonexistent, such as the inaccessible colonization zones in the intermontane regions or along

---

[15]For an overview of U.S. military assistance to Latin America during the Cold War, see Brian Loveman, *For la Patria: Politics and the Armed Forces in Latin America* (Wilmington, Del.: Scholarly Resources, 1999).

the agricultural frontier where agricultural land gives way to rainforest. Its actions were generally far from the major urban centers of political and economic power.

Yet as guerrilla support appeared to ebb in the countryside, newer urban movements began operations. The most notable group was the M-19, or April 19th Movement, which was founded by dissident FARC guerrillas together with supporters of the former military leader turned populist politician, General Gustavo Rojas Pinilla.[16] Yet the M-19, despite initially garnering some support among the urban poor, middle-class university students, artists, and intellectuals and conducting some spectacular "armed propaganda actions" that embarrassed the regime, did not represent a military threat to the National Front. By the early 1980s it was mostly pushed out of the country's principal cities and was forced to operate like other Colombian guerrilla movements in the advantageous terrain of the Colombian countryside.

Multipolar War and the Drug and Petroleum Export Boom at the End of the Twentieth Century

With the implosion of the Cold War in 1989 and the collapse of the Soviet Union in 1992, the external funding and logistical support for the insurgent groups disappeared. Ironically, just as the guerrillas lost access to external resources in the post–Cold War world, the United States reengaged directly in Colombia's armed conflict, this time at the head of a major antinarcotics effort implemented throughout the Andean region.

---

[16]Rojas Pinilla founded a political movement in the 1960s called the National Popular Alliance (ANAPO). Despite the National Front's restrictions on third-party participation in elections, Rojas managed to get on the ballot for the 1970 presidential elections, listed as a faction of the Conservative Party. Many of his followers believed he won that election but was denied victory through electoral fraud. The name of the new guerrilla movement was taken from the day of the presidential elections, April 19, 1970. The M-19 was a leading protagonist in the peace processes of the 1980s and early 1990s. After signing a ceasefire agreement with the government in 1984, it later accused the government of betrayal and seized the Palace of Justice in downtown Bogotá, holding members of the Supreme Court and others in the building hostage. The action provoked the armed forces to retake the building, killing more than 100 people inside, including all the guerrillas and 11 members of the Supreme Court and Council of State. In 1990, the M-19 again entered into talks with the government, this time leading to its disarmament and demobilization and its conversion into a political party. For a good history of the M-19, see Darío Villamizar, *Aquel 19 será* (Bogotá: Editorial Planeta, 1996).

Even before the demise of the bipolar world, however, new currents of financing had already emerged for the guerrillas, re-creating some of the dynamics and tendencies found in the first phase of the conflict with the coffee boom. The boom in coca production and cocaine exports created new inflows of capital into the country—though this time they were illegal and most of the direct export profits remained outside the control of the state. As it had in the 1950s, a commodity export boom spurred by soaring international demand facilitated a dramatic expansion of the war.

The drug export boom reshaped the conflict and the armed actors in multiple ways. The scope and intensity of the war widened and increased. Moreover, it no longer remained a class-based insurgency of leftist guerrillas in arms against the state. It was now transformed into a multipolar conflict with the emergence of a new actor: right-wing paramilitary groups. The paramilitary organizations represented a pro-state, counterguerrilla force founded by the armed forces, local landowners, and nouveau riche drug entrepreneurs who by the mid-1980s were heavily investing their profits in landholdings in the countryside. One study reveals that drug traffickers bought land in 399 municipalities in 27 of the country's 32 departments, totaling more than 5 million hectares of land.[17] According to the most extensive study of the phenomenon, paramilitary activity correlates most strongly with the regions where drug traffickers have invested in land, not for narcotics production but for investment purposes.[18] The social base of the paramilitaries can be found in the traditional landowning elites and political bosses of rural Colombia, bolstered by the massive influx of narco-investments.[19]

[17]See Alejandro Reyes, "Compra de tierra por narcotraficantes," in *Drogas ilícitas en Colombia*, ed. Francisco Thoumi et al. (Bogotá: Ariel, Naciones Unidas–PNUD, Ministerio de Justicia, and Dirección Nacional de Estupefacantes, 1997).

[18]Reyes, "Compra de tierra por narcotraficantes." See also maps prepared by Alejandro Reyes for United Nations Development Program, *Informe Nacional de Desarollo Humano de Colombia 2003: El conflicto, callejón con salida* (Bogotá: United Nations Development Program–Colombia, 2003); and *Prevención de conflictos y alerta temprana: El caso de Colombia*, ed. Marc Chernick (Washington, D.C., and Bogotá: United Nations Development Program, Georgetown University, and Universidad de los Andes, 2005).

[19]See Mauricio Romero, *Paramilitares y autodefensas 1982–2003* (Bogotá: Editorial Planeta, 2003); and Germán Palacio y Fernando Rojas, "Empresarios de la cocaína, parainstitucionalidad y flexibilidad del regimen político colombiano: Narcotráfico y contrainsurgencia," in *La Irrupción del Para-Estado*, ed. Germán Palacio (Bogotá: ILSA, CEREC, 1990).

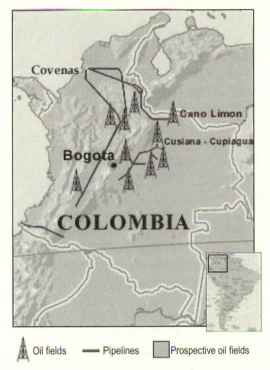

Figure 7.4. Colombia's Oil Fields and Gas Pipelines.
Source: Ecopetrol.

The petroleum boom beginning in the mid-1980s also fundamentally reshaped the nature of the war. It brought multinational oil companies and construction companies into the center of the conflict and provided funding to all sides (figure 7.4). Oil revenues were tapped by the state for security concerns, and the major multinational oil companies paid the Colombian armed forces directly to protect their investments. Conversely, the multinational companies became targets of extortion by the guerrillas and greatly contributed to guerrilla coffers, particularly those of the ELN. A German multinational construction company, Mannesmann Anlagenbau AG, the firm that won the contract to build the pipeline leading from the Caño Limón oil field in the eastern plains to the Caribbean petroleum port of Coveñas, has publicly admitted that it paid more than $2 million in 1985 for the release of three of its construction workers. The ELN claimed that the German construction company paid out more than $20 million during the

Barrels

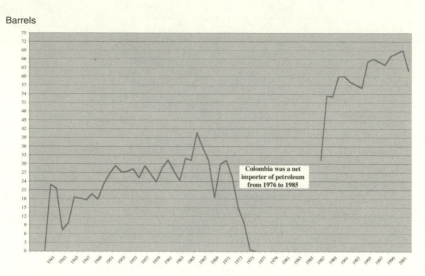

Figure 7.5. Colombia's Petroleum Exports, 1941–75 and 1986–2001 (millions of barrels).
Source: Ecopetrol, unpublished data supplied to the author.

grueling one-year time frame stipulated in the contract to complete construction of the pipeline.

On the third side of this triangle of violence, paramilitary groups also received funding from the petroleum companies (figure 7.5). Additionally, they became heavily involved in contraband oil and gas sales. Finally, in 2002, the United States became directly involved when Congress authorized more than $98 million to create a special battalion of the Colombian army charged with protecting the Mannessmann-constructed Caño–Limón–Coveñas pipeline. This pipeline is operated by Los Angeles–based Occidental Petroleum Company.

Beyond commodity exports, the paramilitary and guerrillas resorted to widespread criminal activities to fund their wars. For the guerrillas, kidnapping became one of their most lucrative sources of income. The Colombian Army and the National Planning Department, the state planning agency, estimate that the FARC and the ELN received $1.2 billion in ransom between 1991 and 1998.[20]

---

[20]Pax Christi Netherlands, *The Kidnapping Industry in Colombia* (Utrecht, Netherlands: Pax Christi Netherlands, 2001), 35; also see http://www.paxchristi.nl.

In 1990, annual kidnappings surpassed the 1,000-victim mark. In 1998, this figure more than doubled. In 2002, according to the nongovernmental organization País Libre, a group dedicated to combating kidnapping, there were 3,706 recorded cases. A total of 50 to 70 percent of all kidnappings are committed by the FARC and the ELN, with approximately 28 percent of these attributed to the former and 24 percent to the latter. About a third of these are motivated for political reasons; the rest are primarily an exercise in extorting money.[21] This accelerated escalation of criminal activity—and clear violation of International Humanitarian Law[22]—has also radically altered the face of the conflict.

Resources have been important in this war, from coffee to coca, but have also led to erroneous speculation about the causal factors of violence, particularly during the most recent phase of the conflict. The remainder of this section more closely examines the relationship between one actor and one commodity: the FARC and the cocaine export boom.

The FARC and the Drug Trade

Beginning in the late 1970s and early 1980s, the Andean region emerged as the center of an illegal commodity export boom based on the cultivation of the coca leaf and its subsequent refinement into cocaine hydrochloride (HCl). In the 1980s, the coca plant was principally grown in the Chapare region of Bolivia and the Alto Huallaga River Valley of Peru. In this initial period, Colombia was only a minor producer of coca. Yet the finished product, cocaine HCl, was produced, controlled, transported, and marketed by large-scale Colombian organizations, the Medellín and Cali cartels. The United States–led drug war succeeded in reducing coca production in Peru and Bolivia; according to the U.S. Drug Enforcement Administration, coca cultivation in Bolivia declined by approximately 75 percent and in Peru about 70 percent from 1995 to 2000 (figure 7.6). It also achieved success in dismantling the large-scale Colombian cartels through the killing, imprisonment, or extradition to the United States of its leaders.

---

[21]See the Web site of Fundación País Libre, http://www.paislibre.org.co.

[22]For a discussion of International Humanitarian Law and conventions against kidnapping, see Human Rights Watch, *Colombia beyond Negotiation: International Humanitarian Law and Its Application to the Conduct of the FARC-EP* (New York, Human Rights Watch, 2001).

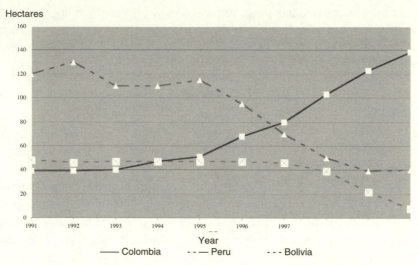

Figure 7.6. Andean Net Coca Cultivation, 1991–2000 (thousands of hectares). *Source:* U.S. State Department, *International Narcotics Control Strategy Report* (Washington, D.C.: U.S. Government Printing Office, 2001).

However, the net effect of the drug war was to concentrate production of *both* coca and cocaine in Colombia, converting southern Colombia into the principal producer of coca. Further, in place of one or two large cartels, hundreds of smaller Colombian organizations were drawn into the drug trade.

The coca boom was to have a direct impact on the FARC. Coca production climbed steadily in FARC-controlled areas, mostly in the southern parts of the country in the departments of Guaviare, Caquetá, and Putumayo throughout the 1980s. It boomed in the 1990s as coca cultivation migrated from Bolivia and Peru into Colombia as a result of the U.S. war on drugs.

The FARC, though founded well before the coca/cocaine export boom, now had access to unprecedented levels of financial resources as well as new social bases of support centered on the coca peasant farmers and the large community of itinerant laborers who, by definition, were outside the jurisdiction of the state. The coca/cocaine boom was soon supplemented by an opium poppy boom on microestates at higher elevations (above 9,000 feet) in guerrilla-controlled territories. The overwhelming majority of these activities were concentrated in areas where the state's presence was minimal or nonexistent and where the FARC had long exercised authority in the vacuum left by the state.

The guerrillas initially raised revenues by charging "revolutionary taxes" to the coca farmers and the traffickers who entered the zones to purchase coca paste for later refinement into cocaine HCl. The FARC charged "revolutionary taxes" on all productive and commercial activities in areas where they asserted some influence. In the coca zones, they charged 10 to 15 percent on the sale of the coca paste, as well as fees for the traffickers' use of clandestine airstrips. Over time, the guerrillas became more involved in the drug trade, as will be described below.

The illicit coca trade became one of the FARC's largest sources of funding; by the 1990s, it was providing anywhere from $100 to $200 million annually, about 50 to 60 percent of the guerrilla's revenues. The other 40 to 50 percent came from kidnapping, legal investments, and extortion of a wide range of other productive, extractive, and commercial activities.[23]

Studies of the early periods of the coca/cocaine boom reveal that the FARC was initially caught off balance by the rise in coca production when it appeared in its zones of influence in the distant colonization zones in the northern Amazon basin. They were uncertain how they should respond to this economic windfall, both for themselves and for the peasant farmers who barely lived above a subsistence level. The settlers in these zones, who had previously produced few agricultural products, had limited access to markets and no state support. The majority were refugees from the violence in the interior of the country.[24]

Interviews with residents in Caquetá reveal that the FARC, as the dominant authority in the zone, initially attempted to prohibit coca production among the peasant farmers. The peasants resisted. The FARC had to choose between alienating the population and changing its politics.[25] The FARC understood the potential economic benefits from the emerging economic

[23]See Nazih Richani, "The Political Economy of Violence: The War System in Colombia," *Journal of Interamerican Studies and World Affairs* 39, no. 2 (summer 1997): 37–81. There is great debate about these figures. Some place the FARC's total earnings as high as $900 million, or a billion dollars a year, though this seems highly improbable given the size of the Colombian economy, the total illegal export earnings, and the position of the FARC in the overall illegal economy.

[24]Jaime Eduardo Jaramillo, Leónidas Mora, and Fernando Cubides, *Colonización, coca y guerrilla* (Bogotá: Universidad Nacional de Colombia, 1986); William Ramírez Tabón, "La guerrilla rural en Colombia: Una vía hacia la colonización armada," in *Estado, violencia y democracia*, ed. W. Ramirez Tabón (Bogotá: Tercer Mundo, 1990).

[25]Juan Guillermo Ferro, "Las FARC y su relación con la economía de la coca en el sur de Colombia: Testimonios de Colonos y Guerrilleros," *L'ordinaire Latino-americain* (IPEALT, Université de Toulouse-Le Mirail) 179 (January–March 2000).

boom that was making "the agriculture frontier" bloom with coca plants. But politically, the decision to accept the drug trade represented both benefits and costs. On one hand, the FARC saw an opportunity to consolidate its social bases among the population and gain legitimacy in a strategic part of the country. Yet on the other hand, as the FARC became more deeply involved in the cultivation of illicit crops, its relationship with other national actors deteriorated. Intellectuals, labor, students, and left-leaning parties increasingly condemned the FARC's involvement with the drug trade.[26] Support in urban areas and throughout the country declined.

The FARC's relationships with the narcotics trade, as well as with the populations that depend on the coca/cocaine industry for their livelihood, have changed over time and have varied from region to region. In one region that has been closely studied, Caguán in the department of Caquetá, the guerrillas began by charging a *gramaje*, or 10 percent of the price per gram of coca paste.

Fearing an influx of drug traffickers and outside criminal elements, the FARC formed "self-defense" groups among the population to maintain order. As with the self-defense groups in other areas, these also soon began to abuse the population and provoke great resistance. The booming drug trade did indeed lead to a massive internal migration of fortune seekers, refugees, criminals, and drug traffickers and sparked a rise in delinquency, drug abuse, burglary, homicides, prostitution, and other social ills. The "self-defense" groups exhibited little interest in maintaining order and were preoccupied with the drug trade. According to one inhabitant interviewed in Caguán, by the late 1980s, the community petitioned the FARC to assert greater control over the area.[27]

---

[26]Ferro, "Las FARC." See also "Colombian Intellectuals and the Guerrillas," including a letter signed by Colombia's Nobel laureate Gabriel García Márquez and many of the nation's leading intellectuals denouncing the FARC's involvement in the drug trade, in *Violencia in Colombia 1990–2000: Waging War and Negotiating Peace*, ed. Charles Bergquist, Ricardo Peñaranda, and Gonzalo Sánchez Gómez (Wilmington, Del.: Scholarly Resources, 2000), 214–24.

[27]Ferro, "Las FARC," 10. I did extensive research in Caguán in 1986–1987. At that time, the FARC was cooperating with the government in promoting alternative development measures, substituting coca for rubber. This was done in the context of the cease-fire agreement signed in 1984. My research and observations reveal a similar phenomenon described by Ferro: a strong political presence but little social control over the negative effects of the burgeoning drug trade. See Chernick, "Insurgency and Negotiations," 266–67.

From 1984 to 1987, the FARC entered into a cease-fire agreement with the government, and in Caguán there was an interesting coexistence among guerrillas, drug traffickers, and a few representative state agencies that had entered the area with the cease-fire accords. The cease-fire broke down in June 1987 following the outbreak of combat between the Army and the FARC in Caquetá. With the return to war, the FARC asserted greater control of the zone. The FARC guerrillas became directly involved in policing and dispensing justice. They moved to organize the coca market, imposing price controls and quotas on the amount of land that could be cultivated. They centralized purchases and established direct relations with the traffickers who bought the coca paste. They placed controls on those who came into the zone.[28] In short, the FARC provided a degree of economic and social order for a lawless activity in an area only minimally penetrated by the state. The guerrillas were able to exercise control over a major source of revenue. They also claimed that they were defending the interests of the peasants and negotiating the best price possible for their crops at a time of severe economic crisis in the Colombian countryside.[29]

What has the FARC done with the hundreds of millions of dollars it has gained from the illicit drug economy? It has mostly invested in augmenting the size of its military force and expanding its territorial presence. From 1984 to 2002, the FARC grew from a force of about 4,000 men and women under arms to an army of more than 18,000 fighters. By the late 1990s, the FARC had more than 70 fronts, or *frentes*—its standard military unit consisting of between 50 and 500 guerrilla fighters—as well as a network of unarmed supporters and sympathizers in each of the country's thirty-two departments or states. By 2002, it also had built a sizable "urban militia" force in the country's principal cities, Bogotá, Medellín, and Cali, and other second-tier cities; some estimate the FARC's urban militias comprise an additional 12,000 men and women with access to explosives and arms.[30]

[28]Ferro, "Las FARC."

[29]Alfonso Cano, "La cuestión agraria y la paz: Eradicar el latifundio única alternativa," in *Resistencia* (Revista de las FARC), no. 116 (August–September 1999); also see "Mama Coca: Conversaciones de Paz—Cultivos ilícitos, narcotráfico y agenda de paz," *Ed. Indepaz—Mandato Ciudadano por la paz*, June 2000; and FARC-EP, *Taller: Narcotráfico en América Latina y el Caribe*, http://www.six.swix.ch/farcep/Documentos/taller_Narcotrafico.html.

[30]See Alejandro Reyes, "La violencia política," in *Prevención de conflictos y alerta temprana*, ed. Chernick.

The FARC has purchased sophisticated arms and has built homemade munitions factories. It has systematically constructed an army with an agenda to take power. Many of their territorial movements and choices of regional military activity follow strategic plans related to corridors for arms trafficking and contraband, access to lucrative financial resources, exploitation of state and regime weaknesses, and consolidating sites of military advantage. After four decades of military activity, a national guerrilla movement can no longer be viewed exclusively through the prism of regional grievances and local sources of rebellion; it must also be viewed through the lens of strategic and military decisions.

However, the military dimension is but one factor. The FARC guerrillas have also deployed their resources to implement successive political strategies, many of which revolved around the ups and downs of a series of peace processes that were attempted between 1982 and 2002.[31] In 1985, within the context of a cease-fire agreement, the FARC founded a political movement, the Patriotic Union party (UP), which was legally constituted and which ran candidates for office. After the breakdown of the cease-fire accords in 1987 and the massive assassinations of UP leaders, including the murder of several elected officials and two presidential candidates, the FARC's leaders moved to strengthen their military capacity but also founded a clandestine political movement, the Bolivarian Movement.[32] During the 1990s, the FARC twice resumed negotiations with the government, in 1990–91 and 1998–2002.

Moreover, the FARC leadership moved to increase its influence and control over local municipal governments in the areas where it has a strong military presence. This strategy was implemented after 1988, when Colombians began to directly elect their mayors, and later, in 1991, when the central budget was decentralized and municipalities for the first time had substantial resources. Following the breakdown of peace talks in February 2002, the FARC began a strategy of threatening elected mayors, giving all the country's 1,091 mayors a choice of resigning or facing death. More than

---

[31]Marc Chernick, "Negotiating Peace amid Multiple Forms of Violence: The Protracted Search for a Settlement to the Armed Conflicts in Colombia," in *Comparative Peace Processes in Latin America*, ed. Cynthia Arnson (Stanford, Calif., and Washington, D.C.: Stanford University Press and Woodrow Wilson Center Press, 1999).

[32]FARC-EP, *Manifiesto del movimiento bolivariano por la Nueva Colombia*, http://www.movimientobolivariano.org/manifiesto.htm; FARC-EP, *Discurso del lanzamiento del Movimiento Bolivariano por la Nueva Colombia*, http://www. movimientobolivariano.org/lanzamiento.htm.

200 resigned; most of the rest continued to govern from secure areas in distant regional capitals under great protection. The FARC's strategy was to make the country ungovernable. It is waging a war to take power or, short of that, to force negotiations that will address issues of political, social, and economic reform—particularly related to agrarian reform, rural development, and social participation free of repression and human rights violations. During twenty years of negotiations, these themes recur repeatedly at the negotiating table. The FARC also wants to negotiate institutional guarantees for political participation that ensures their role in local, regional, and national governance.[33]

Some have asserted that the FARC has nevertheless become so involved in the narcotics trade that the line between war and crime has become sufficiently blurred as to become meaningless.[34] In November 2002, the U.S. government formally indicted the FARC's second-in-command, Jorge Briceño, better known as "Mono Jojoy," for drug trafficking and terrorism, though it has not filed charges against the FARC's supreme commander, Manuel Marulanda Vélez. The United States has also requested the extradition of several mid-level FARC commanders to stand trial for drug trafficking. These include Fabián Ramírez, the commander of the FARC's Fourteenth Front, which operates in the prime coca-producing department of Caquetá; Tomás Molina, also known as the "Negro Acacio," the commander of the FARC's Sixteenth Front, which operates in the isolated department of Vichada bordering Venezuela; and Henry Castellanos, also known as "Romaña," a member of the Central Command of the FARC's

[33]Gustavo García Arenas and Mónica Roesel, eds., *Las verdaderas intenciones de las FARC* (Bogotá: Corporación Observatorio Para La Paz, 1999); FARC-EP, *38 Años de FARC-EP*, http://six.swix.ch/faracep/Nuestra_historia/38_aniversario_de las_FARC-EP.htm; FARC-EP, *Plataforma para un gobierno de reconstrucción y reconciliación nacional*, http://www.movimientobolivariano.org/plataforma.htm. For official documents of the peace process from 1998 to 2002 including government and guerrilla negotiating positions, see Oficina del Alto Comisionado para a Paz, Presidencia de la República, *Hechos de paz, Vols. I–VIII* (Bogotá: Presidencia de la República, 1998–2002). For an earlier record of FARC positions during negotiations in the 1980s, see Jacobo Arenas, *Correspondencia secreta del proceso de paz* (Bogotá: Editoral La Abeja Negra, 1989).

[34]A former Colombian army colonel wrote a widely circulated book titled *The FARC Cartel* that helped solidify this perspective among many military personnel and policymakers in Washington and Bogotá. See Coronel Luís Alberto Villamarín Pulido, *El cartel de las FARC* (Bogotá: Ediciones Luis Alberto Villamarín Pulido, 1996).

"Eastern Bloc," which oversees twenty-two fronts in the eastern part of the country. Fabián Ramírez has been accused of being the FARC's liaison with the Brazilian mafia led by Fernando da Costa, also known as Fernandinho Beira Mar. Fernandinho is accused of being a major arms supplier for the FARC as well as a trafficker in FARC cocaine. Another FARC member, Carlos Bolas, was captured in Suriname and then extradited to the United States on charges of drug trafficking.[35] The escalating levels of indictments and extraditions belie the image of the FARC as a peasant insurgency that simply taxes the local coca trade.

The line is blurring. Yet the FARC cannot be solely reduced to these activities. Its military and political operations across all areas of the national territory—in coca- and non-coca-producing regions—reveal an organization that is far more complex, with deep historical roots in the politics of twentieth-century Colombia. Its political strategies during periods of both open hostilities and formal peace negotiations reveal a movement that is, for better or worse, a central political actor in Colombia's politics.

Indeed, the U.S. Drug Enforcement Administration—the U.S. government agency that most closely analyzes the structure of the drug trade in Colombia—has characterized the FARC's involvement in the drug trade quite accurately, neither minimizing nor exaggerating its role. In a March 2002 report, the administration's intelligence unit wrote:

> Since the 1970s, drug traffickers have made temporary alliances of convenience with leftist guerrillas, in some instances with right-wing paramilitary groups, in other cases, to protect their drug interests. While individual members of the FARC, such as 16th Front Commander Tomás Molina, are involved in some aspects of the Colombian drug trade, there is no credible intelligence that the FARC as an institution has evolved into a drug-trafficking organization. In any case, neither insurgents nor paramilitaries are the glue that holds the drug trade together.[36]

---

[35]The public record of FARC indictments can be found on Web sites operated by the U.S. Department of State, the U.S. Drug Enforcement Administration, and the Colombian Ministry of Defense. See http://usembassy.state.gov/colombia/wwwsaf002.shtm, http://www.usdoj.gov/dea/fugitives/internl/, and http://www.cgfm.mil.co/ingles/noticijs488i.ht.

[36]DEA Intelligence Division, "The Drug Trade in Colombia: A Threat Assessment," http://www/usdoj.gov/dea/pubs/intel/02006/index.htm.

The Relationship between Resources and Conflict

Paul Collier states:

> The economic theory of conflict argues that the motivation of conflict is unimportant; what matters is whether the organization can sustain itself financially. It is this, rather than any objective grounds for grievance which determine whether a country will experience a civil war. . . . Economic theory of conflict assumes that perceived grievances and the lust for power are found equally in all societies. Groups are capable of perceiving that they have grievances more or less regardless of objective circumstances. . . . Whether conflict is motivated by predation, or simply made possible by it, these two accounts come to the same conclusion: rebellion is unrelated to objective circumstances of grievance while being caused by the feasibility of predation.[37]

This is a provocative argument. However, it ignores—or at best is overly dismissive of—a large body of social science research on the causes and factors that contribute to rebellion. The literature is multidisciplinary and incorporates historical, psychological, sociological, political, and economic dimensions of violent conflict across a broad range of cases. Some of the early studies of violent conflict, conducted by Ted Robert Gurr and others, emphasized aggregate psychological conditions that lead people to rebel.[38] Others, such as Eric Wolf in his classic comparative study of peasant revolutions and Jeffrey Paige in his work on Vietnam, focused on types of exploitative conditions found in rural social relationships as triggers for war.[39] Jeffrey Race and Joel Migdal examined the role of political and military organizations and ideology in the creation and sustenance of guerrilla insurgencies.[40] Samuel Huntington focused on the mobilization and social dislocation inherent in the process of modernization. He also noticed the combustible alliance that can emerge between intellectuals and peasants.[41]

[37]Collier, *Economic Causes of Civil Conflict*, 4.

[38]Ted Robert Gurr, *Why Men Rebel* (Princeton, N.J.: Princeton University Press, 1970).

[39]Eric Wolf, *Peasant Wars of the Twentieth Century* (New York: Harper & Row, 1969); Jeffery Paige, *Agrarian Revolution* (New York: Free Press, 1975).

[40]Jeffrey Race, *War Comes to Long An: Revolutionary Conflict in a Vietnamese Province* (Berkeley: University of California Press, 1972); Joel S. Migdal, *Peasants, Politics and Revolution: Pressures toward Political and Social Change in the Third World* (Princeton, N.J.: Princeton University Press, 1974).

[41]Samuel P. Huntington, *Political Order in Changing Societies* (New Haven, Conn.: Yale University Press, 1968).

James Scott and Samuel Popkin outlined, respectively, what have become known as the "moral economy" and "political economy" approaches, emphasizing in the first a defensive reaction against the atomizing influences of market forces and capitalism, and in the second, the rational choice of individual peasants to maximize benefits.[42] There is also a well-developed body of literature pioneered initially by Theda Skocpol that focuses on regime and state structures and international linkages.[43]

Further, Charles Tilly and others have written about the role of resource mobilization in sustaining rebellion and revolution.[44] Here, resources are broadly defined to encompass both material resources as well as nonmaterial resources such as authority, commitment, friendship, and trust, and are viewed within an integrated analysis of the dynamics of social mobilization, insurrection, and revolution.

The question is: Why has Collier privileged one element—resources (here recharacterized as greed)—and simply dismissed the rest of the literature on the subject? The Colombian case does not support this effort. Resources have played a role in sustaining and expanding the conflict. However, the origins of conflict are not in a struggle over resources, nor can its longevity be reduced to the boom-and-bust cycles of legal and illegal commodity exports.

Collier asserts that the articulation of grievances is primarily a public relations gesture or propaganda exercise. Those who accept it are, borrowing Lenin's famous phrase, "useful idiots." Yet it is hard to believe that supporters of these of groups could have endured for decades if the expression of grievance by both the left and the right was simply a facade for predatory practices. The country is characterized by extreme injustice, the worst human rights violations in the Western Hemisphere, killings of political and social activists, assassinations of public officials, rampant political and economic kidnappings, commercial extortion, and large processes

[42]James C. Scott, *The Moral Economy of the Peasant: Rebellion and Subsistence in Southeast Asia* (New Haven, Conn.: Yale University Press, 1979); Samuel L. Popkin, *The Rational Peasant: The Political Economy of Rural Society in Vietnam* (Berkeley: University of California Press, 1979).

[43]Theda Skocpol, *States and Social Revolutions* (Cambridge: Cambridge University Press, 1979).

[44]Charles Tilly, *From Mobilization to Revolution* (New York: Random House, 1978); Doug McAdam, *Political Process and the Development of Black Insurgency, 1930–1970* (Chicago: University of Chicago Press, 1982).

of structural exclusion related to land, political power, and economic opportunity.

Any theory of civil war, then, needs to build on the large body of research and cases. The Colombian experience suggests that resource mobilization (greed) alone does not explain the origins or the duration of the war. Other factors—such as grievances, ideology, leadership, military strategy, and international factors—are also key.

There is abundant evidence that in the post–Cold War, post–September 11 world, many insurgent groups have turned to criminal enterprises to sustain their actions and that the line between armed insurgency and organized crime is blurring. It is precisely for these reasons that the other factors are so central to the analysis. Only an understanding of grievance, ideology, political objectives, and international linkages can provide an accurate analysis of the conflict.

In Colombia, the roots of conflict are social and political. However, the Colombian guerrillas now strategize over resource acquisition; they have asserted control over much of the lower ends of the coca/cocaine trade and have become deeply involved in kidnapping and in extortion of the petroleum and other industries, both domestic and foreign. The paramilitaries and the state also strategize over resources. They do this within the context of a war that has become increasingly territorial and where the state presence is limited in much of the national territory. Choking off the existing resource base of one of the armed actors would likely alter their actions as they look for a new resource base. In Colombia, the long history of this protracted conflict suggests that other sources of financing are readily available and that the armed actors would adjust. A settlement, then, must be based on addressing the other dimensions of the conflict.

Such a solution is possible, though twenty years of failed negotiations underscore the great difficulty in reaching final agreements. However, the search for peace will be facilitated when the state and elements of the international community—particularly the United States—recognize the complexity and multiple causes of the conflict and do not hide behind a tempting but misleading analysis of greed.

8

Surviving State Failure: Internal War and Regional Conflict in Afghanistan's Neighborhood

Paula R. Newberg

There is a palpable risk that Afghanistan will again turn into a failed state, this time in the hands of drug cartels and narco-terrorists.

—Antonio Maria Costa, executive director, UN Office on Drugs and Crime,
Afghanistan Opium Survey 2003

You ask what we're going to do and the answer is: "I don't really know."

—Donald Rumsfeld, U.S. secretary of defense, press conference, Kabul,
quoted in *Far Eastern Economic Review*, October 16, 2003

Paula Newberg is a guest scholar at the Brookings Institution and special adviser to the United Nations. She is an international consultant focusing on the political economy of states in transition and conflict who has worked with the United Nations in central Europe, central Asia, south Asia, and Africa; she was an adviser to the United Nations in Afghanistan between 1996 and 1998, and again between 2002 and 2004. Among her publications are *Politics at the Heart: The Architecture of International Assistance to Afghanistan* (Carnegie Endowment for International Peace, 1999) and *Judging the State: Courts and Constitutional Politics in Pakistan* (Cambridge University Press, 1995).

In their *Opium Survey 2003*, the United Nations and the Government of Afghanistan reported that Afghanistan produces 75 percent of the world's opium, 7 percent of the country's population of 24 million profited from the $2.3 billion trade, and all but four of the country's thirty-two provinces were now engaged in poppy cultivation and opium production. The executive director of the UN Office on Drugs and Crime observed soberly, "Out of this drug chest, some provincial administrators and military commanders take a considerable share: the more they get used to this, the less likely it becomes that they will respect the law, be loyal to Kabul and support the legal economy. Terrorists take a cut as well: the longer this happens, the greater the threat to security within the country and on its borders."[1] The minister of finance was blunter, warning that without a major shift in policy and resources, Afghanistan risked becoming a "narco-state where all legitimate institutions become penetrated by the power and wealth of drug traffickers."[2] Cross-border trafficking in arms and drugs has put the entire country at risk, and by the autumn of 2003, the UN Security Council identified almost every border district as "high risk," and the UN had suspended relief operations in four provinces.[3] Even as NATO expands its domain in Afghanistan (its first non-European exercise) and as international security forces take tentative steps to move beyond their base in Kabul, the transborder trade in weapons and drugs threatens Afghanistan's recovery from war.

Two years after a United States–led international Coalition attacked Afghanistan to remove the Taliban movement from power and destroy the al Qaeda network, Afghanistan appeared, once again, to be perched on the brink of conflict and state failure. And once again, but even more perniciously, trafficking in drugs and arms is a major factor shaping continuing war and the decline of the Afghan state. And once again, Afghanistan's internal conflicts cannot be distinguished from the security of south and central Asia.

This trend was predictable, but not necessary. When the international Coalition attacked Afghanistan on October 7, 2001, it radically changed the face of central Asia. One month earlier, the Taliban was poised to take

[1] UN Office on Drugs and Crime, *Afghanistan Opium Survey* (Vienna: UN Office on Drugs and Crime, 2003).

[2] Reported in the *Economist*, September 27, 2003.

[3] Jean-Marie Guejhenno, UN undersecretary general for peacekeeping, communication to the UN Security Council, press release, UN Office on Drugs and Crime, October 24, 2003.

control of the country, but shortly after the attack, it lost Kabul. After the assassination of the Northern Alliance leader, Ahmad Shah Massoud, just days before the terrorist attacks on the World Trade Center and Pentagon, the Alliance might well have imploded, but as a proxy for Coalition forces, it emerged triumphant and quickly dominated forces that took control of Kabul and the transitional government established by the Bonn Accords of December 2001. Uzbekistan and Pakistan, previously exiled to the far edge of the West's diplomatic screen, turned into important allies in the war, as the international Coalition scurried to find footing in a region that it had so recently shunned. For a three-month moment, Afghanistan seemed like the most important place on Earth. And for the first time in three decades, many Afghans believed they might finally escape the curse of war.

In the years that have passed since this incursion, the previously obscure details of Afghanistan's conflicts have been front-page news. Because the presumed reach of international terrorist organizations, and particularly al Qaeda, was built in part on critical relationships between Afghanistan's Taliban movement and a variety of international partners (including extralegal, nonstate actors) that ranged well beyond the vast landscape of south and central Asia, the political economy of Afghanistan's wars looms large as we reconsider the pathology of internal and regional conflicts across the globe. But Afghanistan's problems predate the rise of the Taliban movement and the infections of global terrorism. In the two decades before the Taliban took power, the flow of men, money, and materiel across Afghanistan's porous borders set the terms under which local fighters and tribal leaders waged war with the help of foreign powers against their own leaders and the Soviet army. Two years after the fall of the Taliban movement, Afghanistan remained a state enveloped by an internal war that derived its sustenance from complex global economic relationships, including a renewed and burgeoning trade in narcotics that threatens the future stability of the state. In addition, because terrorist organizations of global reach were facilitated by international financial relationships that spanned the distance from Afghanistan's deserts to international urban centers worlds away, dismantling Afghanistan's war economy is now assumed to be a crucial step in ending international terrorism.

The multiple factors that have sustained war in and around Afghanistan—including the ways that the financing of war has empowered a changing array of individuals, groups, and states; the deep influences of Afghanistan's neighbors on its internal politics; and the complex relationships between power and ideology—have set a context for Afghanistan's recovery from war, and the investment of its neighbors in future peace. Afghanistan's recovery from its many twentieth-century struggles depends as much, or more, on disentangling the external relationships that allowed war to commence and continue.

Some outside commentators argue that Afghanistan has always been and will continue to be perilously divided, and the best that can be imagined for Afghans is a state that manages its affairs in a climate of perpetual, domestic strife. Others believe that Afghanistan has always been a proxy for more powerful military and ideological forces, and that its warring parties, which once used Western capital to finance fighting against the Soviet Union, simply substituted narcotics monies to prolong their power struggles at the end of the twentieth century. Still others assume that Afghanistan is by nature the source of regional and global threats that include terrorism and narcotics, joining expansive international agendas to the insular character of Afghan politics in ways that risk the stability and security of the surrounding region. And many observers assume that the motivations for factional fighting have been primarily ideological—anticommunist, antimodernist, Islamist, pro-Western—rather than built into the structure of the Afghan state and its role in the regional and international economies.

These journalistic observations are partly true, but they rely on speculation more than analysis and are incomplete and occasionally misguided. War in, around, and with Afghanistan has evolved during the past thirty years as an intricate web of political, economic, and strategic problems that are difficult to untangle and equally difficult to escape. And like many other prolonged complex political emergencies that involve multiple actors and a multitude of clashing interests, Afghanistan's internal conflicts have taken on habits that are hard to break. Over the course of almost three decades, they have transformed the political geography of south, southwest, and central Asia, setting the stage for political change across the globe.

By outlining the political economy of Afghanistan's wars, this chapter provides a context for understanding the political and economic challenges that Afghanistan and its neighbors face as they attempt not only to reconstruct the Afghan state but also to remove incentives for future war and terrorism in south and central Asia. This analysis is based on two primary observations. First, today's wars in Afghanistan can only be understood as part of a three-decade span of internal and regional conflicts. The critical elements of this period include deep-seated problems of governance and development that predated the anti-Soviet war of the 1980s and remain, in familiar but nonetheless changing forms, to this day. They are symbolized

by ongoing struggles between the weak transitional administration based
in Kabul and the still-powerful tribal leaders and warlords who dominate
the peripheries, and by struggles for domestic control in contrast to the
military and financial power vested in an international Coalition that remains embedded in Afghanistan's countryside and strongly influences
its government. Even more, they encompass the antiterrorism campaign
against al Qaeda and remnants of the Taliban in Afghanistan and its
neighbors.

Second, Afghanistan's wars have all been multidimensional and all em-
bracing. The same factors that promoted and prolonged war led to state
failure; the failed state, in turn, fostered more war. As much as Afghanistan's
wars have been regional and global phenomena, their first victims have always been the Afghan people. War left them impoverished, diseased, hungry, unemployed, and displaced, and it alienated them from their state and
economy. In the end, war created a governance crisis of proportions far
more profound than those that provoked the crises of government thirty
years ago. Even as Afghanistan prepares new instruments of governance—
a constitution, the mechanics of a formal economy, and elections—it is
clear that the country will take years to recover, no matter how conserva-
tively that recovery is defined and managed. The challenges to recovery, including violent contests to the idea of a central state enabled by an ever-
continuing trade in arms and narcotics, remain lethal indeed.

Since the decline of the Taliban, voluminous information about Afghanistan's economy of conflict has been uncovered during the course of the
antiterrorist campaign against al Qaeda in Afghanistan and elsewhere. But
this information is neither complete nor fully analyzed, and official intelligence is still inaccessible to the public. Data on Afghanistan's economy
during the war years is unreliable and incomplete, and reporting on the
country's politics has always been limited by war conditions. The following
analysis is therefore by necessity illustrative rather than comprehensive. Investigations into the causes and consequences of global terrorism suggest
that international financing networks—from Asian narcotics to African
diamonds to complex banking practices at once primitive and highly sophisticated[4]—have supported Afghanistan's wars, and that these wars have

[4]On informal practices used to support trade in Afghanistan in the absence of a
formal banking system and unified currency, see M. El Qorchi, S. M. Maimbo, and J. F.
Wilson, *Informal Funds Transfer Systems: An Analysis of the Informal Hawala System*
(Washington, D.C.: International Monetary Fund, 2003).

facilitated the further growth of terrorism. Who rules Afghanistan, and who profits from its wars, is not a question that can be answered within the country's often imposing isolation; indeed, new information raises as many questions as it answers. Links among al Qaeda, the Taliban movement in Afghanistan and Pakistan, and militant Islamist political groups in south and central Asia offer one small window into the intricate financial and political relationships that now characterize our increasingly globalized economies.

Afghanistan's Neighborhood

Civil conflicts and prolonged war have been almost permanent features of Afghanistan's political and economic landscapes for more than thirty years. Virtually every aspect of the country's successive wars—civil clashes (1973–79), anti-Soviet insurgency (1979–89), post-Soviet anticommunist internal conflict (1989–92), pre-Taliban and Taliban conflict (1992–2001) and the current war against al Qaeda specifically and global terrorism generally that is centered in Afghanistan—has involved cross-border and global transfers of personnel, capital, and military equipment.

Although it is possible to trace the roots of Afghanistan's present discord to the state's formative days, the direct antecedents of today's conflicts arose in the early 1970s. Since the years when members of the nascent Islamist opposition movement took refuge in Pakistan at the invitation of Prime Minister Zulfiqar Ali Bhutto, when Pakistan's insurgency and counterinsurgency actions in Baluchistan spilled over its own borders to include Afghanistan and the shah's Iran—a time when India's and Pakistan's nuclear aspirations tinged the entire region's political ambitions with deeply hued risk—the politics of south and southwest Asia have been tightly entwined in Afghanistan. Afghanistan has also been integrally involved in shaping the way that central Asian states have coped with their post-Soviet burdens and responsibilities, at home and in their relations with the international community.

Afghanistan's wars have been, and continue to be, intrinsically regional and, by extension, international. No matter how trenchant the local disputes that ignited and nurtured them, none could be sustained without active political and economic involvement from neighboring states, foreign donors, and nonstate actors in the region and beyond. Afghanistan's wars have represented complex challenges for the Afghan state, its neighbors, and the international community for more than a quarter-century. These challenges exist today not only because the nexus of national and international events and actors has often made the idea of peace so difficult to entertain but also because decisions made in the 1980s still resonate in Afghanistan's neighborhood and more distantly across the globe.

The Afghanistan war of the 1980s was prosecuted with the help of global financing that not only helped bring down the Soviet Union but also set the stage for future regional insecurity. Permeable borders offered passage for people, funds, and the instruments of fighting—all through explicit policies initiated in Moscow, Washington, Beijing, Riyadh, and Islamabad.[5] Continuing formal assistance to fighting factions that were proxies for superpowers but intensely local for their purveyor made it impossible to contain violence within Afghanistan's borders. The strategic choices that helped lead to the defeat of the Soviet Union in 1988–89 also weakened Afghanistan and its neighbors economically and politically, and these choices provoked increasingly tense relationships within the region. Regional insecurity is paramount among these factors: The anti-Soviet war spawned organizations that evolved into global actors that still participate in other conflicts (Chechnya, Indonesia, central Asia) and are implicated in a wide range of global threats.[6] Moreover, Afghanistan lives in proximity to several praetorian states whose preoccupation with asserting control often overrides their concern for political participation and equity.[7]

Just as its neighbors have influenced Afghanistan during the past several decades, so Afghanistan's wars have played major roles—intimately, intricately, and inexorably—in the development of south, west, and central Asia. Pakistan's military and the authoritarian states of central Asia have

[5]Riaz M. Khan, *Untying the Afghan Knot: Negotiating the Soviet Withdrawal* (Durham, N.C.: Duke University Press, 1991); George Crile, *Charlie Wilson's War: The Extraordinary Story of the Largest Covert Operation in History* (Boston: Atlantic Monthly Press, 2003).

[6]See, e.g., United Nations, "Letter from the Chairman of the Security Council Committee Established Pursuant to Resolution 1267 (1999) Concerning Afghanistan Addressed to the President of the Security Council," S/2002/65, January 15, 2002, sections 10 and 11, and similarly S/2002/541, May 13, 2002, sections 26, 27, 43, 44; and Human Rights Watch, *Afghanistan: Crisis of Impunity: The Role of Pakistan, Russia and Iran in Fueling the Civil War* (New York: Human Rights Watch, 2001).

[7]See, e.g., International Crisis Group, *Central Asia: Crisis Conditions in Three States*, Asia Report 7 (Washington, D.C.: International Crisis Group, 2000); Martha Brill Olcott, *Revisiting the Twelve Myths of Central Asia* (Washington, D.C.: Carnegie Endowment for International Peace, 2001); Paula R. Newberg, "Praetorian Passages: Central Asia at the Edge of War," in *The Maze of Fear: Security and Migration after September 11th*, ed. John Tirman (New York: Social Science Research Council, 2004).

been indirectly sustained by Afghanistan's cautionary instability. Long, permeable borders; relatively easy access across the mountains for guerrilla group and drug dealers; frail and inaccessible economies further isolated by Afghanistan's wars; opposition movements and local conflicts influenced by Afghanistan's ideological warfare—all these factors, plus the renewed patronage of the global antiterrorism campaign, have helped to deepen central Asia's praetorianism.

Local Interests, Foreign Influence

Afghanistan's conflicts in the 1970s and 1980s pitted urban, Persian-speaking elites against rural, Pukhto-speaking peasants, questioned the role of monarchy and its successors, and frayed the fragile ties that bound the state.[8] In this sense, competition for state resources was bound tightly to choices about the kind of state that Afghanistan could and should become. Although this was essentially an intra-Afghan ideological debate, foreign influence was always close at hand. During the 1950s and 1960s, Afghanistan demarcated the line between Soviet and Western power; and as a result, it received assistance from donors across the international aid spectrum. Plentiful aid meant bountiful diplomatic engagement as well; when the Cold War turned into a hot conflict that engulfed Afghanistan, every donor felt that it had a historical link to Afghanistan, a foothold in Afghan civil society, and a right to help determine the country's future.

The Afghan monarchy liberalized during this period; at the same time, disputes crystallized between and within the political left and right, and a nascent Islamist opposition was formed with help from neighboring Pakistan. (Pakistan's socialist prime minister was not Islamist, but by patronizing the most conservative of Afghanistan's political critics, Bhutto helped set in train a sequence of ideological clashes that later turned violent and bitter in both Afghanistan and Pakistan.) The weakened monarchy fell prey to interfamilial conflict, Afghanistan became increasingly unstable, the Afghan-Soviet border appeared increasingly disruptive, and quite quickly, foreign influence and support turned local disputes into foreign-backed war. Diplomatically, local interests were subsumed and then overshadowed by a multinational effort to undercut, and then dissolve, the Soviet Union.

[8]Paula R. Newberg, *Politics at the Heart: The Architecture of International Assistance to Afghanistan* (Washington, D.C.: Carnegie Endowment for International Peace, 1999).

Concretely, prosecuting war became a supply-side as much as a demand-driven engagement.

The anti-Soviet Afghan war of the 1980s turned a large portion of south and southwest Asia into an extended battlefield. Alliances were established and supported to recruit and move guns and fighters across the region's many borders, establishing patterns of cross-border cooperation and competition that continued throughout the Taliban period and are echoed today in the West's patronage of the Northern Alliance and in tendentious post-2001 relationships among Pukhtuns across the Pakistan–Afghanistan border. Since the moment that Soviet troops entered Afghanistan in December 1979, the topography of war, statehood, and alliance politics in the region has been transformed from an Afghan-specific problem to one captured by international interests.

Beginning in 1981, the United States led an international campaign to provide weapons, training, and cash to the Afghan mujahideen as they battled Soviet forces for almost a decade. Throughout this period, Western assistance leveraged the rise and occasional fall of the seven Sunni-majority mujahideen groups based in Pakistan, and to a much lesser extent, the Shia-majority exile groups based in Iran. At the same time, although much less reported, Afghan tribes affiliated with these groups were engaged in profit taking from trade in poppies and opium. The practice was widespread: at one time or another, reports surfaced about narcotics trading among almost all mujahideen groups and their leaders, regardless of political sensibility or tribal origin. The same foreign interlocutors that coordinated formal assistance easily facilitated the narcotics trade: Pakistan's Inter-Service Intelligence and National Logistics Cell; its army and police; and, by extension, it was often assumed, U.S. intelligence agencies. At the same time—perpetuating a climate of contradiction that has so often colored Afghanistan's war economy—the U.S. Drug Enforcement Administration was busy trying to stem cultivation and refinement on Pakistan's side of the Afghanistan-Pakistan border. The line demarcating the two countries was conveniently blurred—due variously to the incapacity of the Pakistan government to patrol the border, the disinclination of the West to block supply routes for Afghan fighters and escape routes for refugees, and confusions within the U.S. government about how much to sanction Pakistan while it was so important to the mujahideen cause—and small refining factories moved across the border to avoid closure and maximize profits. This was war: Money bought guns, need generally overrode creed, and creed was to some extent indistinguishable from greed.

By the time the 1988 Geneva Accords made it possible for Soviet troops to withdraw completely in February 1989, billions of dollars had been spent on all sides to prosecute a war that refused to end. The problems that caused the original civil conflict remained—who would run the state, why, how, and on behalf of whom? Fighting continued with stockpiled armaments (although this was prohibited in the accords) and additional capital from a wide range of suppliers. In the period from 1989 to 1992, mujahideen were pitted against the Communist government in Kabul; after the fall of the government, they were pitted against one another. These hard years renewed intra-Afghan rivalries and fighting that would continue for another decade.

Local and international rationales for continued conflict were almost impossible to unravel. Chaos in postcommunist Afghanistan led to the rise of the Taliban movement, a group initially described as peacekeepers among agitating forces within Afghanistan. The Taliban—nurtured in Pakistan and viewed with sympathy by outsiders keen to quell disturbance— quickly took on the ambitions of power holders within Afghanistan.[9] During its early period, from late 1994 until it reached Kabul in the autumn of 1996, the Taliban consolidated its reach across southern Afghanistan. Later, when battlefield obstacles slowed its progress toward the north, it built on its agrarian, Pukhto-speaking base to expand and refine its ideological precepts and practices and, with time, to draw even closer to like-minded, militant supporters outside Afghanistan. Local rationales for pursuing war were reasserted during the middle Taliban period, but only by expanding its cross-border, regionwide ideological and financial support structure.

Men and money, however, came at a high price. Foreign-recruited Taliban—now known as al Qaeda, but then simply known as "Afghan Arabs" who would stand in for Afghans who were increasingly disinclined to fight—helped to radicalize a movement already inclined toward militancy and to deepen links between some elements of the Taliban and like-minded groups in Pakistan, central Asia, and beyond. By the summer of 2001, the seeds of contradiction were clearly visible. On the one hand, the Taliban seemed poised to gain control of the remainder of Afghanistan, and for the few days between the assassination of its major rival, Ahmed Shah Massoud, and September 11, 2001, its future military dominance

---

[9]See Ahmed Rashid, *Taliban: Militant Islam, Oil and Fundamentalism in Central Asia* (New Haven, Conn.: Yale University Press, 2001).

was assumed by many observers to be secured. After several shaky years of recriminatory relationships with the international community, it had also gained a tentative foothold in multilateral diplomacy by banning poppy cultivation and thus appearing to be a maturing player in regional politics.

On the other hand, the Taliban was undercut by its alliances, attitudes, and actions. The Taliban made little effort to govern the country and appeared to rely on financial support from Saudi Arabia, the United Arab Emirates, and Pakistan. Retrospectively, it became clear that it was able to profit from its manner of nongovernance. "Unofficial economic activities," according to the World Bank, were the dominant form of profit taking, and Afghanistan became the world's leading opium producer.[10] Narcotics trading increased exponentially in its early years, for example, as a way for farmers to gain credit to cultivate their lands; according to the U.S. government, the Taliban provided fertilizer and then taxed production (perhaps as high as 20–25 percent) to support fighting, even though the farmers generally had little interaction with the Taliban themselves.[11]

Afghanistan's increasing weaknesses reinforced its social, economic, and political divisions and left the country open to external influences that found this power vacuum convenient and potentially profitable. Every potential benefactor—whether Iran, Pakistan, central Asia, Osama bin Laden, or multinational Islamist organizations—came with independent interests. And each collaborator—narcotics traders and financiers, arms dealers, and militants based in neighboring states—brought a confusing mix of ideologues, allies, and enemies. The Taliban never fully dominated war-riddled Afghanistan, but the effects of war made it impossible for Afghanistan to rise above the Taliban.

[10]John Wall and William Byrd, "Brief Overview of Afghanistan's Economy," World Bank, Washington, October 2001; World Bank, *Afghanistan: World Bank Approach Paper* (Washington, D.C.: World Bank, 2001).
    [11]UN Security Council, *The Situation in Afghanistan and Its Implications for International Peace and Security: Report of the Secretary-General* (New York: United Nations, 2001), section 79; Office of National Drug Control Policy, White House, *Drug Policy Perspectives: Central and Southwest Asia* (Washington, D.C: White House, 2001); Raphael F. Perl, *Taliban and the Drug Trade* (Washington, D.C: Congressional Research Service, 2001); Barnett R. Rubin, "The Political Economy of War and Peace in Afghanistan," *World Development* 28, no. 10 (2000): 1789–1803; Konstantin Parshin, "Anti–Drug Trafficking Effort Could Help Fight Terrorism," Eurasianet, http://www.eurasianet.org.

State Failure

During the long period in which competing groups tried to assert and re-assert political sovereignty through linked civil and cross-border wars, Afghanistan's state failed: War failed the Afghan state, and that failure produced more war. When the Geneva Accords were signed in 1988 and took effect in 1989, Afghanistan had already fragmented—in part along familiar tribal, ethnic, and regional lines that predated war; in part along ideological lines; and in part along lines that reflected the nature, breadth, and depth of the country's deeply international conflict. The whole took on the character of its parts: Afghanistan's fractured state was reinforced by conflicts that became impracticable, insecure, and a threat to its international interlocutors.

State failure became an essential characteristic of war. Its most graphic example came about in the wake of the Geneva Accords: first, when the sitting Communist government was overthrown—after having survived the anti-Soviet war intact—by the remnants of the mujahideen movements; second, when the ragtag, consociationalist, post-Geneva rulers descended into anarchy, giving an opening to the Taliban movement; and third, in the Taliban period, when even the muted echoes of state structure diminished to silence. Since war was renewed in the autumn of 2001 and an interim government was established under the auspices of the United Nations, the threat of continuing state failure has accompanied every action taken by both competitors to Afghan power and the international community.

For almost thirty years, the country's borders were easily penetrable, governance was defined by repression, and the effects of war economy dominated the tattered national and local economies. Foreign policy became an extension of internal war. Cumulatively, the state ceased to function, for itself or on behalf of its citizens; in consequence, local power relations evolved through a mix of traditional and war-related authority—not by dint of popular vote or explicit consensus, but as a result of competing forms of patronage surviving in a political economy of scarcity. These circumstances encouraged economic behavior that challenged rather than supported either recovery or, more broadly, a developmentally rational state. The longer failure continued, the more deeply antistate behavior became anchored.

These characteristics were amply clear when the global war on terrorism began its operations in Afghanistan in October 2001. By reviving old ties from former mujahideen days—paying little heed to the behavior of these leaders during their heyday or after—the global antiterrorism Coalition renewed war in two familiar forms: local conflict to usurp power from the Taliban; and an international effort to rebalance global politics around an antiterrorist fulcrum that was, at least initially, located in Afghanistan. As before, Afghanistan's internal battles became proxies for multinational interests, each considered legitimate in their own ways and by their own followers, but also contradictory and self-defeating. The international effort, called Operation Enduring Freedom, helped its local proxies, the Northern Alliance, to ascend to a partial victory that was then validated in the December 2001 Bonn Accords.

In the period following the installation of Afghanistan's transitional authority, however, the government's efforts to centralize its authority and focus national attention on the difficult demands of reconstruction took place alongside the Western-led Coalition's continued fighting in Afghanistan and across the Pakistan border. Persistent insecurity within Afghanistan hindered reconstruction even more. Afghanistan's fighting went from overdrive to hiatus and then to intermittent, localized fighting; the focus on solving the problem of "terrorisms with global reach" meant, for Afghanistan, continuing proxy fighting through local warlords even after the main air war diminished in intensity. Within a year, Taliban sympathizers in Afghanistan and Pakistan were able to marshal enough resources to challenge the Kabul government and, in some instances, link their efforts to those of warlords who were already in conflict with the weak central government.

The most problematic elements of the failed state continued to plague Afghanistan and its neighbors. Afghanistan had long nurtured a culture of permeability: Its borders could be traversed by anyone with ambition, resources, or pressing need. Although outsiders view the country's high mountain passes as barriers, in fact, they facilitated the provision of resources suited to the terrain. To fight the Soviet Union, Western supporters provided both high and low technology: mules and bullock carts, Stinger missiles and land mines were all made available through sophisticated capital transfers or ancient money-changing practices. Gun and narcotics trades took advantage of the power vacuum at the center and the natural greed of competing aspirants to local political power. Illicit trafficking in illicit substances—already a part of south Asia's economy and increasingly potent in the newly independent states of central Asia—thrived on conditions of state failure, and in so doing, ensured the weaknesses of the Afghan state. The world's largest refugee population made its way across the Iranian and Pakistani borders, living in exile while attempting to maintain ties to land and occupations at home.

The failure of Afghanistan's state was an internal and external phenomenon, with far-reaching, economically relentless consequences for both Afghanistan's politics and those of its neighbors. Fighting Afghanistan's wars meant financing them in ways that could be controlled through local proxies. Poppy cultivation, refinement, and trade were counterparts to the authority structure inherited from the mujahideen. Just as tribal leaders could be affiliated with national parties or transnational religious movements but still control their own geographic areas, so narcotics (and, similarly, arms) trades could be financed and cultivated locally, refined at close distance, and then shipped off with a small measure of profit garnered to power holders through duties on transshipment. This was the traditional way of doing business on the Pakistan-Afghanistan frontier. War upped the ante, the risk, the volume, and the potential profit; with time, however, risk declined and profit increased.

It is often argued that the narcotics trade thrives in conditions of state failure. It is equally true that narcotics traffic creates conditions in which states fail or are incapable of repairing failure. As long as borders are insecure and national authority is weak or nonexistent, traffic in illicit substances can continue relatively unhindered. Local profits are relatively small—the inflation in price is astronomical as opium reaches its distant markets—and can fill some of the gap left by a failed economy.[12] In Afghanistan, where war ravaged the environment and left a starving population, narcotics cultivation provided seed money for small-plot farmers, the equivalent of microenterprise credit for a country without a banking system. On a small scale, the toehold that such economics provides to refiners and producers is threatening enough; writ large across the whole country over a long period, however, such excursions into illegality put the entire state at risk.

Economic fragmentation in the service of war and state failure in the service of political fragmentation are menaces that are easy to replicate. Even while south and central Asia were participating in the continuing breakdown of the Afghan state by patronizing competing power seekers who themselves were involved in illicit trading, their leaders feared the model that Afghanistan offered for internal conflict; in turn, they justified their own autocracies as prophylactics for the viruses of anarchy and im-

[12]Pakistan Regional Office, UN Office for Drug Control and Crime Prevention, *The Role of Opium as a Source of Informal Credit*, Strategic Study 3, Preliminary Report (Islamabad: UN Office for Drug Control and Crime Prevention, 1999).

plosion. The narcotics trade offered a parable in miniature for the entire
region. Because Afghanistan's ruined economy could be described at best
as small and open, every ripple on the economic landscape of its neighbors would turn into a financial tidal wave across the border: If the Pakistani rupee was devalued, the cost of wheat in Afghanistan rose exponentially. The same phenomenon operated in reverse. When the Taliban banned
poppy cultivation in 2001, the price of opium in Iran rose by 300 percent
(although the price in Europe remained the same), but the small economies
of cross-border transit routes were relatively unaffected.[13]

When the 2001 Bonn Accords came into effect, the transitional administration faced the daunting task of bringing postconflict order to a barely
functioning state still enmeshed in war. Some tribal leaders, long accus-
tomed to economic autonomy, gave their localities the character of min-
istates in at least three ways: They levied their own duties; they established
budgets based on local production, bribery that maintains a warlord culture
backed by foreign forces, and cross-border trade in licit and illicit substances; and they engaged in active armed insurgency that risks the minimal security of the state. Although the Government of Afghanistan and
its foreign supporters opposed narcotics cultivation and trading, the structure of competition between the warlords and government made continuing narcotics production very attractive to those challenging the writ of the
newly enfranchised state, and insufficient funding was made available to
offset the lure of narcotics profits for warlords as they challenged the government. Farmers and aid officials alike believed that "warlords have a
strong interest in seeing that the eradication program remains a job only
partly done."[14]

However, farmers continue to be caught in a downward spiral of debt to
cash-rich warlords, and they cannot afford to choose the destruction of
poppy fields over continuing investment in poppy cultivation. Moreover,
to the degree that narcotics have been "taxed" by warlords, this is a local
transaction—local leaders refer to this as a choice between development
dollars and drugs—and these monies are still not shared with the central
government, a policy that at once insulates Kabul from the virus of illicit

---

[13]Hamideh Taheri, interview with Antonio Mazitelli, UN Office for Drug Control
and Crime Prevention, *Nowruz* (Teheran), October 7, 2001; Charles Rechnagel,
"Afghanistan: Taliban Poppy Ban Good News for Pakistan": http://www.rferl.org/
nca/features/2001.

[14]John F. Burns, "Afghan Warlords Squeeze Profits from the War on Drugs, Critics
Say," *New York Times,* May 5, 2002, 14.

production and limits its sources of revenue.[15] As a result, criminality has become a part of the definition of the Afghan state, even while it seeks to change its profile in the international community. This time, however, the contagion has spread even within the country's borders. Traditional poppy-growing areas were once limited to fourteen of Afghanistan's thirty-two provinces, but by 2003 cultivation was spread among twenty-eight provinces and by 2004 to all thirty-four provinces, including paradoxically those northern areas that are within the control of progovernment forces.

Each of these attributes does not simply challenge the capacity of the state to reorganize, reconstruct, and recover but also harbors within it a profound antistate strategy in several ways: by using illegal activities to finance power competition, compromising the state's capacity to engender the rule of law and regulate economic activity, and risking the Coalition effort to combat terrorism by linking local fighting to money laundering and organized crime. In combination with the cross-border patronage of tribal leaders that originated in the wars of the 1980s and 1990s and established relationships that gave the global antiterrorism Coalition a foothold in October 2001, these behaviors underscore the enduring consequences of state failure and the profound difficulties of recovery.[16]

The Region and War

The conduct of the anti-Soviet war was premised on the weakness of the Afghan state and the interconnected informality of neighboring economies. The movement of populations, goods, and services was an essential element of wartime relations among Iran, Pakistan, and Afghanistan. Pakistan's support for the mujahideen was made possible in part by the ease with which people and goods could travel across a border that had never been fully tamed; to a degree, Iran's role was similar. Both countries provided safe haven for millions of refugees; hosted a plethora of political movements and exiled politicians; and, over time, found their own economies and societies drawn into regionwide war.

The movement into Afghanistan of wartime goods, and of fighters and money from the far-flung communities served by transborder Islamic parties and charities, drew Afghanistan into the larger brew of regional dishar-

---

[15]*Far Eastern Economic Review*, October 16, 2003.

[16]David Brunnstrom, "Afghans Seek to Kick Unwanted Top Drug Exporter Tag," Reuters, October 17, 2002.

mony. These wars challenged the political complexion of Iran and Pakistan, influenced the structure of the newly independent states in central Asia, and forced preexisting alliances—within the Muslim world, between Pakistan and China, and between East and West—to change and broaden.

Despite profits from transit duties, skimming off relief funds, donor subsidies, and the complicated transactions that encircled the region's political economy, neither Pakistan nor Iran flourished during Afghanistan's wars. Over the course of two decades, each country encountered its own political instabilities: Iran suffered the devastating consequences of its war with Iraq in the 1980s, and the grueling economic consequences of the 1991 war against Iraq affected the entire region. Iran's global posture, influenced by its own revolution and ideological agendas that influenced its foreign and domestic policies, profoundly affected its relationships with Afghanistan, Turkey, and Pakistan. The changing contours of interstate relations in the Caucasus, the Gulf, and central Asia were caught up in the swift shifts of the Soviet Union's dissolution, as well as Afghanistan's continuing conflicts.

The negative economic effects of Afghanistan's fighting on Iran and Pakistan were particularly hard to absorb. In Pakistan, the anti-Soviet war concentrated power in the hands of conservative political and military leaders whose praetorian inclinations and policies were enduringly divisive at home. At the same time, the evolving agendas of exiles and refugees from Afghanistan and their colleagues and patrons in Pakistan fueled an Islamist opposition whose militantly antistate agendas ultimately risked stability in Afghanistan, Pakistan, and beyond.

The long, intricate relationship between Afghanistan and Pakistan offers a fascinating case study of alliance politics in the late and post–Cold War period. Pakistanis think of Afghanistan as a contagion, and their country as the first victim of the Afghan disease. But Pakistan's explicit policies fueled its own political contradictions. It weakened its own borders by sending and receiving fighters, refugees, and supplies for decades, and it perpetuated an economically imbalanced state, by offering the military supremacy at home as it gained strength from its Afghanistan forays and its close relationship with aid suppliers during the anti-Soviet war. It also sidelined civil society, which became at once politicized and alienated from the state. For the better part of three decades, Afghanistan has therefore been a centerpiece of Pakistan's foreign, military, economic, and domestic policy, and each element has been further exacerbated by untamed parallel economies closely tied to Afghanistan's.

Central Asia has been Afghanistan's second regional casualty.[17] The independence of the central Asian states in 1991 was an indirect consequence of the anti-Soviet war; the dissolution of the Soviet empire was assured by the downfall of its army, leaving small, relatively weak, and very inexperienced states to encounter not only their own independence but also the complex transitional economics of a region that spanned from China to Turkey. During the first years of independence, central and south Asia were effectively blocked from each other's markets by the Afghan conflict—only the drug trade flourished, precisely because it is premised on eluding state regulation.[18] The two regions were joined, however, by the problems that emerged from conflict: massive population movements, an ever-expanding traffic in armaments to and through both regions, narcotics traffic that easily expanded to fill the markets of Western Europe, and attendant illegalities that filled the space that weak states could not control.

The fragile economies in transition of central Asia, the erratic poverty-laced economy of Pakistan, and the ever-evolving economic ambitions of Iran and Turkey were thus joined to a fragmented Afghan economy. Cross-border economic relationships—legal and illegal—became essential to the functioning of war-torn Afghanistan. Axes between Peshawar and Jalalabad, Quetta and Kandahar, Mashad and Herat, and Termez and Mazar-it-Sharif functioned as increasingly integrated labor markets for refugees, migrants, and internally displaced persons, albeit with shifting currencies and commodities values.[19] This pattern of economic relations is common in regional conflicts, but central Asia's weaknesses—in which power is concentrated, authority and responsibility are unequally distributed between state and society and among levels of government, and national economies are neither strong nor dynamic—magnified the effects of illicit economies in Afghanistan's small open economy. During the period of Taliban rule in Afghanistan, it was difficult to tell whether central Asia was responding to the economic-security problematic of Afghanistan, or whether Afghanistan was simply a ready excuse for their own failings. It is clear that Afghanistan remained a focus for south, southwest, and central Asia's foreign and economic policies; that these policies assumed a continuing, pervasive economic

[17]United Nations Development Program, *Reform and International Cooperation for Central Asia* (New York: United Nations, 2002).

[18]See Martha Brill Olcott, *Drug Trafficking on the Great Silk Road: The Security Environment in Central Asia* (Washington, D.C.: Carnegie Endowment for International Peace, 2001).

[19]See Newberg, *Politics at the Heart*.

weakness across the broad region; and that the introduction of foreign assistance to mitigate the effects of humanitarian and political emergencies did not erase the underlying conditions for instability.

Just as Afghanistan's failed state made its economy essentially porous, so central Asia's weak states were caught in a vise of war's extended making. Keen to assert central control, its governments found themselves combating antistate activities from within and protecting themselves from the effects of a new war that emerged from the embers of the Soviet Union. Some of these influences were directly attributable to Afghanistan. Guerrilla forces trained in northern Afghanistan made their way north to the Fergana Valley and were thus positioned to challenge elements of the Kyrgyz and Uzbek states; the Uzbek government responded to this threat by reinforcing its own authoritarianism, and disturbances in southern Kyrgyzstan led the state to respond similarly. Others effects were related indirectly: Tajikistan's civil war had roots independent of Afghanistan's wars, but the response of the Tajik state to violent conflict, and the bargains it was willing to strike to end that war, were colored by fear that uncontrolled violence would turn into another Afghanistan.

In the post-Soviet period, Russian guards continued to protect the easily traversable Tajik border against both drugs and refugees. In all three countries, the volume of drug traffic increased dramatically during the Taliban period, further encumbering their already uneven development and leading to suspicions that narcotics were fueling their own insurgency. Turkmenistan—saddled with a long border with Afghanistan and volumes of natural gas that could not be exported—tried endlessly to pursue a diplomacy based on mediating the Afghan war so that it could release its natural resources to a global market. Both central and south Asia flirted with almost all power holders and aspirants in Afghanistan, as well as foreign companies and financiers, to design and finance a gas pipeline from Turkmenistan to Pakistan (and perhaps onward to India). Dreaming of potential wealth, the region and its few international energy investors gave these efforts more credence than the eccentric Turkmen leadership would otherwise have deserved.

In each instance, neighboring powers were joined awkwardly in several concurrent and inconsistent efforts: to stop narcotics from undermining the economic foundations of all states in the region; to stem other illicit trading in order to capture income for their states; to foster trade and development despite the obstacle of Afghanistan; and to experiment with economic incentives for Afghan stakeholders in order to induce peace. Throughout the 1990s, however, the same actors also reinforced war in Afghanistan: Cross-border arms transfers to all Afghan warring parties continued through the autumn of 2001, even while the same border states continued to vote sanctions against Afghanistan in the United Nations.

In the period since 2001, south and central Asia have again been implicated in the politics of reconstruction for Afghanistan and the broader region. The Government of Afghanistan has attempted to negotiate trade and aid agreements with its neighbors in an effort to secure funding and, even more, secure its own borders. More than three years after the Taliban was removed from power, however, key questions for the region remain unanswered by regional powers and international donors and the Afghan administration itself: Can regional engagement in Afghanistan's reconstruction help to defuse tensions, prevent the resurgence of violence, and halt the destructive effects of underground economies and weak economic regulation? If Afghanistan's wars damaged the region, can the region now help ensure Afghanistan's peace?[20] And more specifically, will the runaway narcotics trade emanating from Afghanistan damage not only regional relationships but also prospects for peace within Afghanistan itself?

Conflict and Competition

The anti-Soviet war was intended to overturn Moscow's sway in the region and overthrow the communist regimes in Kabul and in the Soviet Union. This effort included activities that skirted the boundaries of old-fashioned diplomacy and employed a wide range of economic tools and trades to support fighting. Financing networks expanded across national boundaries, and military assistance included trading in goods, services, and personnel. Barter and countertrade, trafficking in illicit substances, supporting and expanding trade in large and small arms in Afghanistan and among its neighbors—all these activities were undertaken by both direct

[20]See Paula R. Newberg, "The Political Economy of Reconstruction in Afghanistan's Neighborhood," background note for conference on the political economy of displacement in the context of reconstruction, Migration Policy Institute and Center on International Cooperation, Washington, September 17, 2002; United Nations Development Program, *Afghanistan's International Trade Relations with Neighboring Countries* (New York: United Nations, 2001); World Bank, *Afghanistan Border States Development Framework: Approach Paper* (Washington, D.C.: World Bank, 2001); and United Nations Development Program, *Integrated Preventive Development Strategy to Support Human Security in Western and Central Asia* (New York: United Nations, 2002).

and indirect parties to the conflict, including the governments of the United States, China, Saudi Arabia, all Afghanistan's neighbors, and a good many others. The Soviet Union procured weaponry and support from within the Warsaw Pact and outside it, and its evolving relationship with central Asia's socialist republics mimicked the West's efforts to tumble the Soviet state.

Mujahideen groups competed for external support from the beginning of the anti-Soviet war, and the same groups bargained among themselves for arms supplies during the war and fought for power and primacy from 1989 onward. The internecine war among mujahideen after the Geneva Accords came into effect combined greed and powerlessness, and the result was social chaos, economic failure, and the loss of political legitimacy among many mujahideen groups. As long as weapons stocks remained available (and the belief that additional arms would be available persisted, despite prohibitions in the Geneva Accords), the incentive to pursue peace was limited. Although Afghans almost universally supported the anti-Soviet war, despite the devastating deprivation that it imposed, post-Geneva infighting quickly alienated the Afghan population.

Subsequent support for the Taliban was based in part on the universal, if theoretical, appeal of peace, and the Taliban's first efforts to stem the tide of anarchy seemed to many Afghans and some foreign governments to argue in its favor. As the Taliban adopted the characteristics of the discredited mujahideen groups from which its members were recruited, competed for resources of war, and pursued control of the Afghan state, its public appeal waned. The longer factional fighting continued—and it did until September 2001—the less popularity the Taliban was able to maintain among Afghans, and when it engaged in widespread repression to secure its will, it understandably lost popular support.

Similar contests continued until the Coalition antiterrorism campaign in late 2001, and vestiges of such behavior arose again by mid-2002. Between 1997 and late 2001, fighting in Afghanistan was often viewed as competition between one major group, the Taliban movement, and a desperately weakening opposition. But the Taliban period can also be understood as extended local conflicts among competing commanders; as struggles for primacy within the Taliban movement itself; and as competition for external resources and political support from a wide range of foreign patrons, including neighboring states and transnational Islamist groups. The Taliban's military strategy was based on the availability of resources; funds and fighters from extremist Islamist groups pushed the Taliban toward an Islamist militancy to which some, but not all, of its members were initially drawn.

This is the terrain that the antiterrorism Coalition entered in 2001: highly fragmented; riven by armed political competition among small numbers of fighters, many without solid public support; subject to the will of outside powers and the predations of a wide range of antistate actors, including ideological opponents and drug and arms traffickers; and devastated by poverty, disease, and the absence of government.[21] Once the major portion of the air war against al Qaeda was finished, however, the slow process of reconstruction placed the Coalition in the same position that external powers have found themselves in Afghanistan for decades. Thus, the Coalition's forces do not have a mandate to destroy poppy or opium factories, because the same warlords backed the Coalition in its anti–al Quaeda efforts (to the degree that the Coalition left them alone); those warlords remained in the central government until the 2004 elections, and their relative economic power gave them sway over the center. Poverty continues unabated while warlords profit from poppy cultivation, and small-plot farmers are unable to choose alternative agriculture in the face of debt and forced political allegiance to these warlords. "Now we are not happy," reported one farmer, "because the governments that control [President] Karzai . . . are cruel. They freed us from one evil, and now they have delivered us into another one."[22]

Poverty, War, and Aid

The supply of arms and finances to the mujahideen during the anti-Soviet war involved complicated relationships among foreign powers, ideologically sympathetic groups, and a complex network of suppliers across Asia and beyond. In the 1980s, financing the war and financing Afghanistan were seen in the West as almost the same pursuit. The provision of humanitarian assistance was part of the war effort, and many official cross-border relief programs were designed as much to finance fighters as to assist their desperate families. During that period, there was little public discussion about using illicit means to support the war, although the considerable attention paid to narcotics trades originating across the border in Pakistan was assumed to be part of a broader Afghanistan–Pakistan economic conversation. Primarily, however, Afghanistan was seen as a state at war, and the niceties of private profit were not discussed.

[21]S. Lautze, E. Stites, N. Nojiumi, and F. Najimi, *Qaht-e-Pool, "A Cash Famine": Food Insecurity in Afghanistan 1999–2002* (Medford, Ore.: Feinstein International Famine Center, 2003).
[22]Burns, "Afghan Warlords," 14.

Following the Geneva Accords, however, the question of the domestic economy resurfaced. One of the factors that contributed to the downfall of the 1992–94 consociational government was its incapacity to handle the imploding economy. Transshipment and trade in local foodstuffs offered two durable forms of profit taking; since the late 1980s, the economy of the Pakistan–Afghanistan border regions were organized to accommodate war and relief. For this reason, when traders and cultivators were unable to use roadways and the security of economic transactions became critical a public issue in the early 1990s, the Taliban movement could justify its first incursions into Afghanistan by highlighting the rapacity of commanders who tithed economic transaction and further impoverished those who were already too poor to survive more war.

The economy of Afghanistan became increasingly fragmented and localized after 1990. By the mid-1990s, both Afghans and external observers were questioning whether a national economy existed at all. Relief became the primary mechanism for sustaining basic needs in many parts of the country. The delivery of relief, however, was very localized; neither a national government nor a national infrastructure could facilitate distribution, but local commanders could substitute for national leaders. The highly problematic practice of cooperating with local commanders was hardly a practice unique to Afghanistan, but it provoked ethical questions among Afghans as much as it did within the international relief community, and it was later cited by the Taliban as evidence of the moral failings of the West. After the Taliban gained control of major portions of the country, the provision of assistance was more localized—a decision justified publicly by the need to reestablish governance at the local level, and privately by the need to support alternatives to the Taliban.

Relief slowed to a trickle by 2000. International donors—stumped by the Taliban's intransigence and frustrated by ongoing war and the insecurity it reinforced throughout the region—turned their attentions away from Afghanistan. In the short period of its primacy, however, the Taliban movement showed little sign of resurrecting a national economy: Its primary goal was winning the war, not the peace. Its early requests to the international community were to rebuild transport, including airports, and a national telecommunications system—all to further its war aims rather than to rebuild the country. Because it had been rejected by the international community but was championed by militant transnational groups, the Taliban occupied an uncomfortable space defined by the ambitions of others as much as by its own agenda of concerns.

By the late 1990s, fragmentation deepened and unregulated activities flourished. Cash was in short supply—few outside contributors offered as much as Osama bin Laden had just a few years before—and the Taliban collected customs duties along roadways to support its war effort. International aid, however meager it might have seemed, provided just enough relief to stave off starvation, and it appeared to relieve the Taliban of its responsibility to care for the citizenry. The absence of regulation, credit, and justice systems meant that the pursuit of black market activities became an elaborate mechanism to translate trafficking into procurement for war.

Here, again, the interplay of local and international factors contributed to complicated and occasionally contrary diplomacy. Although the international community began to focus more attention on the regional dangers of the narcotics trade—including the threats it posed for profound economic failure—within Afghanistan poppy seeds were a seasonal substitute for otherwise absent credit. To many Afghans, the profit from duties levied on opium was not large enough to merit the kind of attention that outsiders devoted to narcotics trafficking. Just as doing business with commanders was a devil's bargain, so doing business with drug dealers was seen as a necessary evil to stave off starvation in some rural areas. But the geography and demography of war in Afghanistan are primarily about leavings rather than takings: Rampant poverty, the world's largest refugee population, and an economy captured by war made the drug debate seem almost frivolous to many Afghan farmers.

For the region and selected members of the international community, the problem of Afghanistan remained a problem about its criminality and its contagions. Western Europe (along with the United States) worried continually about the availability of poppies from southwest Asia and pursued a narcotics diplomacy based on ending supply rather than reducing demand. Although central Asian members of United Nations–sponsored regional peace talks in the late 1990s complained bitterly that the United States and Europe cared more about drugs than people, the dangerous effects of the poppy trade on their economies and polities kept the issue a salient one for all Afghanistan's neighbors.

In response, the Taliban imposed a ban on poppy cultivation in 2000 and briefly appeared to have achieved remarkable results.[23] Its success

---

[23]The ban lowered the area under production to 185 hectares in 2001 (down from 3,276); in contrast, the area under cultivation in 2003 was estimated to be 80,000 hectares. UN Office on Drugs and Crime, *Afghanistan Opium Survey 2003*.

might suggest that it is easy to turn off the narcotics spigot—but for the coincidence of a devastating drought in poppy-producing areas, the threat of considerable repression to enforce the ban, and complaints from farmers who were left with no credit, seeds, or crops. Equally important, it soon became clear that holding back production would inflate future profits— and thus that banning cultivation was of a piece with the Taliban's plans for continuing war while ignoring the needs of the Afghan population. When the transitional administration in Kabul attempted a similar ban in 2002, it met similar resentment for similar, circular reasons: Banning poppy cultivation can work when the economy functions, but it fails in the absence of jobs, credit, investment, food, and security.[24] The narcotics trade became a metaphor for central Asia's uneven development.

After the Fall, Toward the Future: Surviving State Failure

Despite Afghanistan's stunning reversals in early 2002, it remains a troubled and insecure place. Two million refugees returned within its first post-Taliban year, and a government has been optimistically empowered to lead the country's recovery, but almost every social, economic, and political fissure of the preceding decades resurfaced within the first uneasy days after Bonn. Ethnic tensions ran high; the majority Pukhtuns, the backbone of the Taliban, were ousted from power and were replaced by the Tajik and Panjshiris that had once ruled Kabul, and were backed by Uzbek forces with which they had a long if anxious relationship. Hamid Karzai, a Pukhtun tribal leader, was chosen in Bonn—and later elected by a tribal council and, finally, in national elections in 2004—to lead Afghanistan from war to peace. But the Bonn Accords were not a peace treaty; its authors were the not-quite-unwitting inheritors of the global antiterrorism campaign, not the architects of peace. It was left to the impoverished transitional administration, backed by the United Nations but only marginally financed by the international community, to use reconstruction and development as vehicles to establish peace, and in so doing to correct decades of political and humanitarian catastrophe.

[24]This problem—which pits development against security in places where initiatives to support both should be mutually supporting—has led to sharp conflicts between the relief community and major Coalition actors. Paula R. Newberg, "A Drug-Free Afghanistan Not So Easy," March 7, 2005, http://yaleglobal.yale.edu; and United Nations Development Program, *Afghanistan National Human Development Report: Security with a Human Face* (Kabul: United Nations Development Program, 2005).

Recovering from war takes more than goodwill, and creating the conditions for peace is an even harder task. The Karzai government's first year was plagued by conflict, and in its second year (and later, in the run-up to elections in 2004) political division appeared to increase even as the state began to function more smoothly.[25] The global antiterrorism Coalition pursued a bombing campaign intensely through the first half of 2002, using as allies some of the same commanders and warlords who were challenging the writ of the newly enfranchised Afghan state. Many commanders—some now cabinet members or provincial governors—had violated the rights of Afghan citizens under past regimes; the weak central government has yet to be able to redress past grievances, prevent further abuses, and overcome this bitter history.[26] At the same time, the government struggled with the political legacy of unfinished conflict: Having not actually won the war, it did not officially represent civil society as much as symbolize its circumstances, and initially it could only guess public reaction as new programs were initiated.

The international donor community crafted requirements for the new Afghan government—infrastructure repair, transparent financial management, social development, decentralization, rights protections, and a host of other demands—but these were not wholly or formally endorsed by Afghan society, which remained torn by class, region, tribe, and social agenda.[27] Promised aid was slow to come; donor pledges of $4.5 billion in January 2002 were more an emblem of support for Karzai than a concrete contribution to Afghanistan's redevelopment, and the disinclination of major

[25] A new currency was introduced, financial controls were incorporated into the government's assistance program, infrastructure repairs began haltingly, and political mobilization toward elections was started. See Government of Afghanistan, *National Development Framework*, Draft (Kabul: Government of Afghanistan, 2002). Given the depth of development and political problems, the timing and validity of elections therefore generated considerable debate. See Andrew Reynolds and Andrew Wilder, *Free, Fair or Flawed: Challenges to Legitimate Elections in Afghanistan* (Kabul: AREU, 2003), Christina Bennett and Shawna Wakefield, *Afghan Elections: The Great Gamble* (Kabul: AREU, 2003); National Democratic Institute, Statement of the NDI Pre-Election Delegation to Afghanistan, Washington, D.C., August 18, 2004; Paula R. Newberg, "Afghan Elections: Even If It's Not Perfect, a Ballot Beats a Bullet," *Los Angeles Times*, August 29, 2004.

[26] See Afghanistan International Human Rights Commission, *A Call for Justice: National Consultation on Transitional Justice in Afghanistan* (Kabul: Afghanistan International Human Rights Commission, 2005); and Rama Mani, *Ending Impunity and Building Justice in Afghanistan* (Kabul: AREU, 2003).

[27] Paula R. Newberg, "What Does It Take to Rebuild a State?" *Forced Migration Review* 13 (June 2002): 38–40.

powers like the United States to rebuild war-torn countries added to post-Bonn tensions. With time and rigorous planning, however, funds began to trickle into Kabul, and the contentious issues of development gradually began to take their place in the formal political arena.

If Afghanistan's only challenge were to recover from state failure, its future would be worrisome and undoubtedly unsettled. Among the legacies of state failure, however, are divisive problems that link old-fashioned tribalism to the state's new regional needs.[28] Afghanistan's neighbors find themselves at once encircled by the global antiterrorism campaign and enmeshed in cross-border narcotics and armaments trafficking that their relatively weak states find hard to stop.[29] Afghanistan's eastern border with Pakistan—home to former Taliban fighters who seek to recast not only Afghanistan but also Pakistan in new ideological lights—has become the breeding ground for instability within Pakistan and potentially across the region. The United Nations reported in October 2003 that al Qaeda was securing funding through drugs, and the resurgent Taliban was once again cashing in drug monies for weapons.[30] The economic pressures that pushed Afghanistan's neighbors into difficult and often unsought collaboration in Afghanistan's wars still exist.[31] It will take time to determine whether central and south Asia's states can withstand them without succumbing to the continuing lures of authoritarianism and repression for themselves, or forcing them on their neighbors. There is little doubt that Afghanistan's stability is at least one anchor for central and south Asian peace.

Ensuring that the anchor holds, however, remains everyone's unfinished business. The antiterrorism Coalition was formed to worry about international terrorism, not Afghanistan, and seeds of global unrest have been planted far beyond the Hindu Kush. Al Qaeda's easiest targets and supporters, however, are found in the world's failed states and war-torn societies, in places that are easy to bypass on the way to doing the world's business.

[28]Institute for War and Peace Reporting, "Farmers Enraged by Poppy Crackdown," http://www.iwpr.net/index.pl?archive/rca/rca_200204_114_5_eng.txt.

[29]See Kairat Osmonaliev, *Developing Counter-Narcotics Policy in Central Asia: Legal and Political Dimensions*, Silk Road Studies Paper (Uppsala and Washington, D.C.: Program for Contemporary Silk Road Studies, University of Uppsala, 2005).

[30]Heraldo Muñoz, chairman of the UN sanctions oversight committee, as reported by Paul Haven for the Associated Press, October 14, 2003; Robert McMahon, "UN: Experts Say Al-Qaeda Diverting Assets via Internet, Commodities," http://www.rferl.org/nca/features; Loretta Napoleoni, "Money, Not Religion, Behind Terrorism," Guardian/Dawn Group, November 4, 2003.

[31]Newberg, "Praetorian Passages."

Afghanistan is a telling example of how political instability and a proxy war can easily turn into economic disaster, how illegal trading can topple legitimate state finances in many countries, how local conflicts can quickly turn into regional maelstroms, and how such multilayered conflicts can compromise an entire state system.[32] The test of Afghanistan's potential recovery—and the success of the global antiterrorism campaign—will therefore be seen among its neighbors as much as at home. This is the international community's most profound challenge as well: to pay attention to states like Afghanistan, whose failure mimics the inattention of others, and thus risks whole worlds.

[32]Three years after the interim government took office—and several months after Hamid Karzai won an open election for president—the nexus between conflict, development, and narcotics remained a discomfiting one. In March 2005, after the International Narcotics Control Board reported near-record levels of poppy cultivation in 2004 (http://www.state.gov/g/inl/rls/nrcrpt/2005), the World Bank cited the "vicious cycle associated with the opium economy warlords" as a great threat to Afghanistan's recovery that contributed markedly to increasing economic imbalance (with 15 percent of the population receiving 80 percent of the benefits of growth). "World Bank Says Drugs Now Afghanistan's Economic Lynchpin," Agence France-Presse, March 2, 2005; press release, "The Fight against Narcotics Is On and Will Continue Unabated until a Narcotics-Free Afghanistan," Presidential Palace (Kabul), March 3, 2005; United Nations Development Program, *Afghanistan National Human Development Report.*

9

Economic Factors in Civil Wars: Policy Considerations

David M. Malone and Jake Sherman

The economic aspects of contemporary internal conflicts have acquired new relevance in policy circles. In the past decade, globalization has enabled rival factions, through licit and illicit commercial networks, to better access international markets and thus finance civil wars. Few would ques-

David M. Malone returned to the Canadian Foreign Service in 2004 as assistant deputy minister for global issues. From 1998 to 2004, he was the president of the International Peace Academy, an independent research and policy development institution in New York. Previously, he served as Canada's deputy permanent representative at the United Nations and as director general of the Policy, International Organizations, and Global Issues Bureaus in the Canadian Foreign and Trade Ministry. He is coeditor, with Mats Berdal, of *Greed and Grievance: Economic Agendas in Civil Wars* (Lynne Rienner, 2000) and has written extensively on international security issues. Jake Sherman is a former political affairs officer for the United Nations Assistance Mission in Afghanistan. From 2001 to 2003, he was senior program officer for the International Peace Academy's Economic Agendas in Civil Wars program. He is coeditor, with Karen Ballentine, of *The Political Economy of Armed Conflict: Beyond Greed and Grievance* (Lynne Rienner, 2003).

tion the existence of economic motives throughout the history of warfare, but until recently there has been relatively little systematic research on the exact role of economically motivated actions and processes in generating and sustaining internal armed conflicts. This attention has emerged in the context of research and policy development work both on conflict prevention and on peacebuilding.

The Canadian Foreign Ministry developed a relatively early interest in the role of economic factors in civil wars. This attention coincided with the creation of a new Global Issues Bureau in 1995, which inter alia sought to interlink various policy areas believed relevant to contemporary conflict, including human rights, humanitarian policy, combating international crime and terrorism, and postconflict peacebuilding. Also, during the mid-1990s, Canadian foreign minister Lloyd Axworthy was deeply engaged in developing a "human security" agenda focused on the protection of individuals rather than states. Thus, conditions could not have been more favorable to undertake exploration of how private and group economic gain may have influenced such conflicts as those of Bosnia, Angola, Liberia, Sri Lanka, and Central America.

At the time, much of the academic and policy literature illuminating the economic "drivers" of contemporary civil wars was originating in the United Kingdom in the fields of international relations and economics, sociology, and anthropology. Interested scholars in the United Kingdom had not undergone the drift toward policy-irrelevant modeling and theorizing of their American counterparts in some fields.[1] United Kingdom–based nongovernmental organizations (NGOs) were also beginning to contribute important findings, notably Global Witness's 1998 report calling attention to

---

[1] Some of the most interesting insights emerged from the Adelphi Papers, the series of policy-oriented occasional papers published by the International Institute for Strategic Studies (IISS) in London, whereas several scholars at Oxford University proved to be in the vanguard of reflection on the political economy of contemporary wars. E.g., Mats Berdal, *Disarmament and Demobilisation after Civil Wars: Arms, Soldiers, and the Termination of Armed Conflict*, Adelphi Paper 303 (London: IISS, 1996), and David Keen, *The Economic Functions of Violence in Civil Wars*, Adelphi Paper 320 (London: IISS, 1998). Groundbreaking research in this field was either then or soon thereafter under way within the World Bank's Development Research Group, and the UN University's World Institute for Development Economics Research, in partnership with Queen Elizabeth House at Oxford University. This work drew to some extent on earlier studies by Peter Wallensteen and Ted Gurr. Will Reno and David Keen were bringing to bear on the study of several conflicts in Africa important empirical findings and insights that were to prove vastly influential in ensuing years.

the complicity of the diamond industry and key states in undermining UN sanctions regimes against the National Union for the Total Independence of Angola (UNITA) and the wider links between diamonds and the perpetuation of the Angola conflict.[2]

In 1999, the International Peace Academy; the Center for International Studies at Oxford University; the World Bank; and the governments of Canada and the United Kingdom organized a conference in London focusing on economic agendas in civil wars, and featuring Paul Collier, David Keen, Mark Duffield, and many other leading academics and practitioners. The overall aims in convening these researchers were, first, to improve the understanding of the political economy of armed conflict by examining the economic motivations and commercial agendas of elites from competing factions; second, to assess how globalization creates new opportunities for these elites to pursue their economic agendas through trade, investment, and migration ties, both legal and illegal, to neighboring states and to more distant industrial economies; and third, to examine the possible policy responses available to external actors, including governments, international organizations, NGOs, and the private sector, to shift the economic agendas of elites in civil wars from war toward peace.

In particular, the conference's organizers were keen to examine the kinds of trade-offs that would have to occur among elites, their internal supporters, and their external economic clients for a fundamental shift in incentives and disincentives to take place. It was thought that a proper understanding of these would be critical to the wider question of how best to ensure that the international community can effectively assist transitions from protracted war to lasting peace. There was no sense at the time of how ambitious— indeed, overreaching—these objectives were for one short conference. However, the conference proved instrumental in highlighting this important vector of policy research.[3] It yielded an enthusiastic response from the U.K. government, and word of its tentative conclusions soon spread to other players.[4]

---

[2] Global Witness, *A Rough Trade: The Role of Companies and Governments in the Angolan Conflict* (London: Global Witness, 1998.)

[3] The findings and views from the conference were eventually published in an edited volume: Mats Berdal and David Malone, eds., *Greed and Grievance: Economic Agendas in Civil Wars* (Boulder, Colo.: Lynne Rienner, 2000), which stressed policy relevance in its analysis and prescriptions.

[4] That all of this proved increasingly of interest to policymakers is beyond doubt. Very soon, work in this area was passed on from the U.K. and Canadian governments to the International Peace Academy. The British and Canadian governments were joined in funding this work by Switzerland, Sweden, Norway, and the United Nations Foundation and Rockefeller Foundation.

A convergence of political factors, academic interests, and policy concerns helped to establish this research agenda. Its history is recounted here to underscore how policy-relevant research often gets started: A few interested individuals intrigued by scholarly findings apparently relevant to their professional portfolios, but often without any real knowledge of their own, are able to mobilize funding for further research and are eager to proselytize.

The Political Economy Perspective

Most scholars writing about civil conflict since the Cold War have tended to concentrate on the *costs* of conflict and to treat civil war as a disruption of "normal" social, economic, and political interaction within a society.[5] "Peace" and "war" had been understood as separate and distinct categories, the latter being viewed as inherently "irrational" and dysfunctional.[6] In fact, this dichotomy between peace and war has a long tradition in Western thinking about war and has influenced the way international organizations, most notably the United Nations, approach contemporary civil wars. Yet combatants often have a vested interest in perpetuating conflict—violence often serves a range of political and economic goals, especially within weak or fragmented states.

These dynamics challenge many of the core assumptions that have informed thinking and guided policy with respect to civil wars in the 1990s and the 2000s. Indeed, the very notion of a "comprehensive political settlement," used to describe many of the peace agreements brokered by the United Nations during the past decade, suggests that the formal end of armed hostilities marks a definitive break with past patterns of conflict and violence. This has rarely been the case.

Contemporary conflicts in parts of Africa, Central America, the Balkans, and Southeast Asia have all shown that an end to fighting does not mean that the underlying causes of conflict have been addressed. Grievances and conflicts of interest persist beyond the formal end of hostilities, and they continue to exert a strong influence on the politics and the process of "postconflict"

---

[5]E.g., Michael E. Brown and Richard N. Rosecrane, eds., *The Costs of Conflict: Prevention and Cure in the Global Arena*, Report of Carnegie Commission on Preventing Deadly Conflict, Carnegie Corporation of New York (Lanham, Md.: Rowman & Littlefield, 1999).

[6]Cf. David Keen, "War and Peace: What's the Difference?" in *Managing Armed Conflicts in the 21st Century*, ed. Adekeye Adebajo and Chandra Lekha Sriram (Portland, Ore.: Frank Cass, 2001).

peacebuilding.[7] Transitions from war to peace, as the experiences of the 1990s show, are more usefully seen as involving "a realignment of political interests and a readjustment of economic strategies rather than a clean break from violence to consent, from theft to production, or from repression to democracy."[8]

Economically motivated violence and the economic activities of belligerents may be powerful barriers to war termination. The cases of Sierra Leone, Somalia, Cambodia, and El Salvador all demonstrate that war—even when triggered by legitimate social, economic, and political grievances—over time may be transformed into an alternative system of profit and power that overwhelmingly favors certain groups at the expense of others. In many conflicts, violence is a means to control trade, appropriate land, exploit labor, extract benefits from humanitarian aid, and ensure continued control of economic privileges and assets. Thus, groups benefiting from violence—both during conflict and within war-torn societies emerging from conflict—may have substantial economic interests in preventing the advent of peace, democracy, and accountability for human rights abuses. Furthermore, the criminalization of economic relations in wartime frequently leaves lasting developmental distortions which, if left unattended, can fatally undermine subsequent efforts at postconflict reconstruction.

A further dimension of this issue is the effect of economic "globalization" on the ability of combatants, war profiteers, and other entrepreneurs to sustain and benefit from conflict. Increasingly, these actors have been able to tap into global networks of production and exchange, both licit and illicit, establishing ties to corporations, diaspora organizations, arms brokers, international organized crime, and corrupt governments reaching well beyond war zones to the world's capitals and major financial centers. For

----

[7]The challenges of peace implementation was the subject of a joint research project undertaken by the International Peace Academy and the Stanford University Center for International Security and Cooperation between 1997 and 2000. The project examined the sixteen peace agreements between 1980 and 1997 in which international actors were prominently involved. Its full findings were published in *Ending Civil Wars*, ed. S. Stedman, D. Rothchild, and E. Cousens (Boulder, Colo.: Lynne Rienner, 2002). See also Stephen J. Stedman, *Implementing Peace Agreements in Civil Wars: Lessons and Recommendations for Policy Makers*, IPA Policy Paper Series on Peace Implementation (New York: International Peace Academy, 2001).

[8]Mats Berdal and David Keen, "Violence and Economic Agendas in Civil Wars: Some Policy Implications," *Millennium: Journal of International Studies* 26, no. 3 (1997): 798.

example, in Cambodia, the government and the Khmer Rouge (with the complicity of the Thai military) had few difficulties selling rubies and high-grade tropical timber on the world market; in Liberia, Charles Taylor was able to export large quantities of rubber and timber to Europe; and in Sierra Leone, warlords financed their military operations and accumulated personal wealth through the sale of diamonds on the world market.[9] The result has been to adversely influence the balance of incentives in favor of peace. Perhaps nowhere is this more evident than in Angola, where oil revenue- and illicit diamond-financed conflict resulted in the failure of two United Nations–brokered peace accords, atrocious loss of life, and crippling poverty for Angola's people—yet millions in profit for Angola's rival elites.[10] The corollary question for policymakers is therefore how to make peace more profitable than war.

Existing and Emerging Policy Responses

The types of economic activities and resource flows that fuel civil wars are diverse. Some are licit; others are clearly criminal. Some are necessary to civilian welfare (which may predate conflict, or be exacerbated by it); others are manifestly predatory. Although a number of these activities directly feed armed hostilities, most economic behavior contributes to conflict in more diffuse and indirect ways, with some also playing a vital role in the livelihoods of civilian populations. This complicated reality presents policymakers with the twofold challenge of accurately assessing the impact of discrete economic behaviors on conflict dynamics and of designing effective policy responses.

A range of policy instruments exist at the national, regional, and international levels to influence economic agendas in civil wars. Many of these were applied, with varying degrees of effectiveness, to a number of intrastate conflicts in the 1990s. These fall into several categories: the coercive (e.g.,

[9] There is little to differentiate the behavior of the legitimate government of President Eduardo dos Santos in Luanda from that of the late Jonas Savimbi of UNITA in terms of their "warlordism," including in its predatory economic dimensions.

[10] The death—in combat—of Jonas Savimbi opened up the possibility of a lasting cease-fire between the government and UNITA, but, as a Global Witness report indicated, the system of highly profitable and deliberate political and economic disorder that the war created remains the principal obstacle to reversing decades of destruction (Global Witness, "All the President's Men," March 2002).

UN Security Council–mandated sanctions; intergovernmental agreements on money laundering); the exemplary (often focusing on basic human needs of civilian populations such as food and health, e.g., corridors of peace negotiated for specific purposes); the financial (multilateral and bilateral assistance and potentially funding from certain key private-sector actors); and the rhetorical. At the time the London conference on economic agendas in civil wars was convened, little comprehensive work had been done to critically evaluate the role and possible limitations of these instruments. Recent work by the International Peace Academy (IPA), Fafo, the Overseas Development Institute, and other organizations is beginning to address this lacuna.[11]

Fortunately, policy development in this field need not be from scratch but is able to draw upon (at times) well-developed and successful initiatives in other areas. Economic sanctions and arms embargoes—increasingly in their "smart" or targeted version—remain the most widely used regulatory instrument wielded in conflict zones, but they are but one mechanism in a growing framework of possible responses. This framework has evolved rapidly during the past five years, though not necessarily in response to civil wars. These new initiatives include the suppression of money laundering, regulating the export of weapons, combating narcotics trafficking, targeting international organized crime, and minimizing the negative impact of private-sector activities. Much of this progress has been in response to advocacy campaigns by international NGOs, as well as the threat posed by transnational organized crime and international terrorism. Several key developments are highlighted below.

The certification of natural resource sectors implicated in financing armed conflict is an issue that has largely emerged out of attention to sanctions violations, particularly in the case of diamonds. Of great concern was how to avoid an outright boycott of diamonds, which would have devastated the economies of "clean" producers while effectively denying "conflict diamonds" access to international markets. The Kimberley Process—

---

[11]P. Le Billon, J. Sherman, and M. Hartwell, "Policies and Practices for Regulating Resource Flows to Armed Conflicts," background paper prepared for the International Peace Academy conference on "Policies and Practices for Regulating Resource Flows to Armed Conflicts," Bellagio, Italy, May 21–23, 2002; Fafo, *Economies of Conflict: Private Sector Activity in Armed Conflict* project; the Overseas Development Institute is also undertaking research examining potential regulation of transnational corporations in situations of armed conflict.

a regulatory initiative of diamond-producing and -selling states, NGOs, and industry that was introduced by South Africa following Security Council and General Assembly Resolutions—seeks to establish minimum common rules for rough diamond certification. The Kimberley Process relies on a "chain of warranties" intended to provide an audit trail linking each diamond to its mine of origin. An effective global certification regime will require implementation and compliance by relevant governments and industry actors alike, and it will have to simultaneously contend with corruption that would enable new laws to be circumvented. The lack of industry transparency—for example, the lack of consistent trade statistics—and the absence of guidelines for self-assessment and monitoring remain significant challenges to the Kimberley Process.

Moreover, it is far from certain that a regime such as the Kimberley Process can eliminate the illicit trade in diamonds, much of which occurs outside official channels, let alone the patronage and criminal networks it feeds, and thus prevent state failure. The "chain of warranties" idea is being applied on a more limited basis for the timber industry, identifying wood harvested from sustainable sources. Similar certification and warranty systems are used or are being considered to address other "conflict" commodities—notably timber.

A potentially more far-reaching issue is how to track the proceeds of criminal activity by leaderships in civil wars through thickets created internationally to conceal tax evasion and money laundering. Targeting the finances of combatants may be a cost-effective means of influencing the behavior of recalcitrant factions in civil conflicts. The required technology and expertise are already highly developed in the context of drug traffickers and terrorists and could be applied to belligerents.

The Organization for Economic Cooperation and Development's (OECD's) Financial Action Task Force on Money Laundering (FATF) is among the most effective instruments available in this arena. It comprises twenty-nine countries and has issued forty recommendations on accounting standards, mandatory reporting of suspicious or large financial transactions, elimination of anonymous accounts, and other measures. The FATF was initially a regional body, but its influence is increasingly global. The FATF was long faulted for failing to censure countries that routinely permitted—if not encouraged—the laundering of illicit profits through their domestic financial institutions. In 2000, the FATF issued a "blacklist" of fifteen "noncooperative" countries that were inadequately combating money laundering. In 2001, the FATF took the unprecedented step of demanding that Russia, the Philippines, and Nauru pass money-laundering legislation or face sanctions, including delaying the processing of international financial transactions, and withholding loans from the International Monetary Fund and World Bank. This leverage creates a powerful incentive for compliance by nonmember countries.

The FATF's member states monitor and rank each others' efforts to combat financial crimes, but there is no similar system in place—at least at the international level—to rank or certify financial institutions. In response, Jonathan Winer, a former U.S. State Department official, recently proposed the creation of a global "white list" under which international commercial financial institutions would agree to principles of transparency, anti–money laundering, and external compliance monitoring. In exchange, such an institution would be added to the list, and pending a transition period, would be rewarded with preferential selection in the deposit and processing of financing from the World Bank, United Nations, and other public and multilateral agencies. Such an initiative not only creates a financial incentive for compliance but also supplements national regulatory efforts, particularly where governments have little direct means to enforce these standards.[12]

The cooperative relationship between international organized crime networks and local armed groups in all areas of illicit crime and the related increase in official corruption has been of growing concern to the international community as a whole. The United Nations has studied the subject at a number of important meetings, ultimately leading to the 2000 UN Convention against Transnational Organized Crime, the first legally binding UN treaty on the subject. The convention is a comprehensive and coordinated attempt to address the links between corruption and crime. By requiring member states to add four criminal offenses to their domestic laws—participation in an organized criminal group, money laundering, corruption, and obstruction of justice—it should strengthen national institutions in combating such crime. Nonetheless, regulatory approaches to organized crime have a history of failure—and a global approach faces enforcement on a global level.

Measures to combat international terrorism offer yet another potential legal and policy framework through which to control the finances sustaining civil war. The UN International Convention for the Suppression of the Financing of Terrorism, for example, requires states to criminalize the pro-

---

[12]Jonathan Winer, "How to Clean Up Dirty Money," *Financial Times Weekend*, March 23–24, 2002, 1.

vision or collection of funds for acts defined as offenses by previous UN antiterrorism conventions, to provide legal assistance with investigations and extradition regardless of bank secrecy laws, and to cooperate with one another in investigations and extraditions when these offenses are committed.[13] The convention may have applications for the control of financing for civil wars, especially from diasporas located in OECD countries. Because of its broad definition of "terrorism," this convention applies to murders or physical violence perpetrated against noncombatants during war, though arguably only by nonstate actors and not acts of "state terror." The utility of these instruments as a means of conflict resolution and prevention has been less tested, though targeted financial sanctions and asset seizure have been applied against several rebel groups and governments with mixed results. The United Nations' Counter-Terrorism Committee, tasked with monitoring implementation of Security Council Resolution 1373 on combating international terrorism, likewise has important implications for policy work on illicit economic behavior in armed conflict, though admittedly it may be premature to consider any expansion of its mandate.

Finally, the international private sector—most obviously extractive industries (petroleum, mining, timber) but also the finance and insurance industries—play a critical, if mostly unintended, role in many conflict zones. Until recently, most firms have adopted a studiously "neutral" stance on civil strife, disclaiming any political agenda at all. Now, firms are increasingly aware—due in part to NGO advocacy—not only that their operations on the ground and in global markets may inevitably exacerbate conflicts but also that their profits and reputation may suffer as a result. Consequently, there are a growing number of voluntary, statutory, and (less frequently) legally binding "corporate social responsibility" initiatives that seek to minimize these negative aspects of private-sector behavior.

Under Secretary General Kofi Annan, the United Nations has begun to address the role of private-sector actors in armed conflict, as well as their potential contribution to conflict prevention. The UN Global Compact— a voluntary initiative requiring participating companies to commit themselves to nine principles related to human rights, labor, and the environment— selected business and armed conflict as the theme of its first roundtable discussions. Nonetheless, as a voluntary initiative, the compact lacks any monitoring of compliance or enforcement. Apart from their desire to be good

---

[13]UN International Convention for the Suppression of the Financing of Terrorism, December 1999, http://untreaty.un.org/English/Terrorism/Conv12.pdf.

corporate citizens, private-sector actors are unlikely to become good corporate citizens if it is not in their economic interest to do so. They are not inclined to modify their business practices if it will place them at a disadvantage vis-à-vis their competitors, particularly less reputable firms motivated solely by profits rather than broad social benefits.

A different approach, albeit one on a specific issue, is that of the United States' and United Kingdom's Voluntary Principles on Security and Human Rights, which are both a set of principles concerning use of private and public security forces and a tripartite dialogue on security and human rights with (an initial eight) companies in the extractive and energy sectors and several NGOs. The ongoing dialogue provides participants with the opportunity to review the principles and ensure their continuing relevance and efficacy. Through the participation of additional companies with similar concerns in other operating environments and their home governments, it is hoped the principles will set an emerging global standard on the use of private security. Ironically, the requirements for participation in the dialogue may exclude some non-U.S. or non-U.K. firms seeking to participate due to their questionable behavior in areas of armed conflict—the very environment in which firms are most in need of accountable security with clearly delineated responsibilities.

Challenges for Government Policy Development

Different governments have had different reasons for coming to grips with issues concerning economic activities in conflict. Though some have done so reluctantly, others have done so more willingly. Yet even the best of intentions often fall victim to the types of trade-offs that policymakers must, as a practical matter, make to accommodate diverse, and often highly influential, constituencies. A case in point is Canada, a country deeply involved in mining activities, not only domestically—Canada is a diamond-mining and oil-producing country—but also abroad. Canadian companies are deeply engaged in mineral extraction in the Democratic Republic of the Congo, for example. For these reasons, individuals in the Canadian government are sensitive to natural resource issues. Several years ago, it became known that the Canadian oil company Talisman was involved in exploiting an oil field in central Sudan in partnership with companies from Malaysia and China. It was clear that the revenue derived from this drilling activity was contributing significantly to funding the Sudanese government's military campaign against rebels in the country's south, albeit unintentionally.

The Canadian foreign minister, Lloyd Axworthy, was deeply troubled by this relationship. As an initiator and energetic advocate of a "human security" agenda, he believed that the Canadian government could not permit the relationship between a Canadian oil company and a government engaged in war against its own people to continue unchallenged. He sought to convince the Canadian government that a halt should be put to Talisman's activities in Sudan. However, he was essentially stopped cold in his tracks. Talisman was a major employer in Calgary, and most political circles held that the Canadian government should be promoting job creation within the country rather than undermining it. Perhaps partly as a result of this experience, Axworthy was extremely supportive of research and policy development work on the issue of linkages between resources and internal armed conflict, hoping that such research might, in the future, inspire a different policy response from the government.

A second example involves the response of the British government to (previously tolerated) secrecy by its financial sector. Several individuals within the British Cabinet have been keen to tackle corporate misbehavior in conflict countries as well as the role of the U.K. financial sector in serving as a haven for ill-gotten gains deriving from such conflicts. It was a source of deep embarrassment to some in the British government when, following the death of the Nigerian dictator Sani Abacha, some of his expropriated wealth turned up in U.K. banks.[14] That governments and major international banks only turned their attention to tracking down the fruits of Abacha's corruption once he was safely dead (and some of his family safely in jail) was shocking to those advocating an "ethical" foreign policy. Others in the British government took the view that, while it was a worthy goal to try to "clean up" London's financial institutions, this should not be achieved at the risk of destroying it as a financial center to the benefit of rivals like Switzerland.

These opposing positions highlight the trade-offs that industry and, by extension, government face when deciding whether to adopt socially responsible policies. On one hand, firms—in this case, British banks—face a reputational risk should they get caught on the wrong side of a politically sensitive issue, though many have survived what should have been crippling scandals (e.g., the Bank of New York). On the other hand, greater

---

[14]The Abacha family agreed to restitute $1 billion to Nigeria from the late dictator's estate, nevertheless being allowed to keep at least $100 million, the source of which has not been fully elucidated.

transparency, including disclosure of private trusts and shell accounts, risks a likely loss of market share to London's Swiss rivals. (British policy circles had long been worried that while the United Kingdom respects the decisions of the UN Security Council, including sanctions, Switzerland—which would not join the United Nations until September 2002—was not formally obligated to do so.) The protection of London's comparative advantage as the world's leading financial center was of real concern to many policymakers of all political stripes, and it influences British policy in a variety of fields.

These are but two examples of the types of quandaries that those in government, particularly at the cabinet level, actually face when attempting to undertake more ethical policies. These are not abstract issues for them; real interests—and real money—are at stake. Policymakers naturally feel a responsibility to watch over the interests of a variety of constituencies within their countries, while simultaneously wanting to pursue policies abroad as virtuous as possible.

Economic Factors and the United Nations' Work on Conflict

The UN Secretariat and the Security Council became engaged in issues of illicit economic behavior during armed conflict in part serendipitously, largely through the Council's tendency during the 1990s to frequently invoke economic sanctions.[15] Early sanctions regimes, far from being successful, often achieved the opposite of their intended effect—humanitarian crises deepened, while dictatorial regimes became more entrenched and combatants continued their ability to wage war. Sanctions often lacked effective implementation and enforcement on the ground, enabling open circumvention by smugglers of arms, fuel, natural resources, and other commodities. Thus, the instrument was seen in Ottawa and other capitals as increasingly dysfunctional.

With its election to the Security Council for a term in 1999–2000, the Canadian government focused part of its efforts within the Council on sanctions reform. In January 1999, Canada took over the chairmanship of the Council's Angola Sanctions Committee. Canada's ambassador to the United Nations, Robert Fowler—knowing that sanctions against UNITA, the rebel group led by Jonas Savimbi, were widely flaunted within Africa and beyond—commissioned an in-depth independent study by a panel of

[15]From 1990 to 2000, the United Nations imposed sanctions six times more frequently than during the prior forty-five years of its history.

experts on the taxonomy of sanctions busting in Angola. The panel sought to improve the effectiveness of sanctions—both minimizing their unintended consequences and improving their enforcement. The resulting report, which was quite earth shaking by UN standards, named a number of African countries that were deeply engaged in sanctions busting. It also named Belgium, Ukraine, Israel, and some other countries in the industrial North that were in deep collusion with African partners in processing the proceeds of sanctions busting, arguably making most of the money out of the transactions. The United Nations subsequently established independent Panels of Experts on Sierra Leone and Liberian sanctions, and, in 2001, on the exploitation of natural resources in the Democratic Republic of the Congo (DRC).

The DRC report, initiated by France (which found the Angola report incomplete and objectionable, perhaps in part because most of the countries mentioned in connection with sanctions-busting Africa happened to be Francophone-African ones), was problematic because it contained many assertions, most of which rang true to those knowledgeable on the Great Lakes region, but very little hard proof. This is illustrative of the problems such an investigation faces. Indeed, the absence of hard data may not be surprising; individuals involved in the looting and their corresponding institutions in the North have a great deal to lose in both financial terms and in standing. Quite simply, lives are at stake—people are assassinated for much less than talking to Security Council investigators.

Consequently, the Security Council study group had tremendous difficulty getting their interlocutors to agree to be quoted in the DRC report, or to allow specifics to be quoted. Thus, the study proved highly atmospheric—and probably in its main lines absolutely true—but was also extremely difficult to act upon in the absence of more specific information. Furthermore, the study was mandated to focus on Uganda and Rwanda, which are involved in the conflict in the DRC, but to ignore the depredations within the Congo by Zimbabwe, Angola, and Namibia, which are involved in the conflict, at the request of the Congolese government. The report also ignored the looting by forces loyal to the Kabila government in Kinshasa, thus obscuring an important part of the overall picture. Therefore, the report was rightly criticized as unbalanced, and the study group was asked to report on the activities of these other actors as well.

By late 2001, there was discussion within the Security Council on the establishment of a Permanent Monitoring Mechanism to take over the functions of the independent ad hoc panels, though the exact form of the mechanism and under whose authority it will rest continued to be matters of considerable debate. Because the previous reports have challenged some of the Permanent Five Members of the Security Council's often vested interests within the continent, there has been an effort by some members of the Council to rein in the independence of any eventual mechanism, while still others were trying to broker an arrangement whereby independent investigations would be supported by a permanent institutional capacity within the Secretariat and thus would remain free from interference by the Council.

In the mid-1990s, none of the close observers of the Council would have predicted this evolution. The attention that the Council now places on sanctions busting, on natural resource exploitation, and increasingly on private-sector activity in conflict zones marks a recognition of the relevance of these issues to the maintenance of international peace and security. This attention will be the norm in the future, rather than the exception. Yet this progress also highlights a difficult question—when the international community actually possesses enough knowledge to take effective action to prevent such behavior, will the Security Council—particularly the Permanent Five Members—find a form of action that is helpful and that leads to positive results? Or, as often in sanctions cases, will it make decisions that are politically convenient in the short term but are counterproductive over time? This remains to be seen.

Future Priorities

Several final points of interest to policymakers are related to the future of policy development in this area—Paul Collier, Frances Stewart, Peter Wallensteen, and many other scholars having now been successful in capturing their attention. The first concerns the relationship between policymakers and academic research, which provides an important means of evaluating and refining—if not challenging—the practices and underlying assumptions of policymakers. The international policy community responsible for conflict prevention, conflict resolution, and peacebuilding is largely responsive to academic research. Sometimes, however, this research is both too complicated and abstract to be of ready use to the policy community. Econometric data in particular, as Andrew Mack has recently pointed out, is "largely incomprehensible to most policy makers."[16]

---

[16]Andrew Mack, "Civil War," *Journal of Peace Research* 39, no. 5 (2002): 515–26.

As a result, academic findings may inadvertently fall on a deaf audience, while policies continue to be formulated and prioritized without the benefit of important insights. Furthermore, contradictory findings—often with radically different policy implications—not only complicate the formulation of effective policies but also deepen the skepticism with which many within the United Nations regard the research community.[17] High-quality research findings may intrigue policymakers such that they begin thinking through the issues themselves. Generally, however, research must be made more accessible and its contradictions reconciled if it is to be of practical use.

Second, more thought needs to be given to designing incentives and disincentives for leaders to end conflict, or for preventing its outbreak. Civil wars often are triggered by power-hungry elites unconcerned about the tactics through which they seek and maintain power. Some time ago, IPA sponsored a retreat on conflict prevention involving UN Security Council members and some others. At one point, Nigeria's ambassador intervened, noting, with reference to a particular African country embroiled in conflict, in essence, that academic factors—by which he meant structural causes—"are all very nice, but where I sit, bad people are tremendously important." Not only in Africa, "bad people" have wreaked havoc in their own countries and in neighboring ones. In each of these cases, it would be difficult to assert that in the absence of those individuals the situation would be exactly the same. Policymakers are more sensitive to this factor than are academics, but research on how the agendas of such individuals can be favored or inhibited obviously remains important in policy terms. International actors involved in resolving armed conflict must reach a consensus on the types of behavior to proscribe, for this will influence whether to accommodate or co-opt rebel leaders through power sharing, or to pursue more coercive measures to isolate them.[18]

A third, related area for further research draws on the experience of policy actors in the 1990s in creating new instruments to prosecute crimes against humanity, war crimes, and genocide in order to establish if there

---

[17]E.g., Mack notes that with respect to the relationship between primary commodity dependence and the risk of armed conflict, Paul Collier and Anke Hoeffler have found a positive correlation, whereas Jim Fearon and David Laitin have found "slight or no evidence."

[18]Michael Brown, ed., *The International Dimensions of Internal Conflict* (Cambridge, Mass.: MIT Press, 1996), 613–14.

are any "lessons learned" here for the international white-collar crime field. The 1990s saw tremendous progress on legal instruments to punish war criminals, but there was no parallel effort to address large-scale international white-collar crime. There was interest in international legal mechanisms to address economic crimes such as gross embezzlement and extortion by political and military actors, but not yet much energy behind this issue.

A related area requiring further systematic investigation involves defining what a regulatory system that actually worked in the OECD world would look like. In the industrial world, the OECD has been able to agree on measures to combat corruption as it affects companies headquartered in OECD countries. But OECD countries continue to do very poorly in combating white-collar crime related to these various conflicts and taking place within OECD countries. Existing regulatory frameworks are very fragile and suffer huge gaps, overlapping in conceptual terms, but are often not mutually reinforcing for purposes of enforcement. In theory, they cover a great number of situations and contingencies, but as anyone who follows this policy field closely knows, the regulatory frameworks have essentially failed at every level. It is now possible to wonder whether an international legal regime could be constructed to address economic crimes by heads of state and other elites, including grand corruption and embezzlement. Any practical planning seems far off, and it may appear utopian to even think today of such a regime, but the International Criminal Court seemed totally utopian in 1990, and it entered into force in 2002, only twelve years later. IPA has initiated work along these lines.

Fourth, there is a strong consensus that the terms "civil war" and "internal conflict" do not sufficiently capture the key regional and global dimensions of most contemporary conflicts. In many cases, such as the former Yugoslavia, the Great Lakes region of Africa, and south central Asia, regional factors are crucial, not only to the onset of warfare but also to the character of the ensuing conflict and the challenges of peace implementation.[19] These regional dynamics range from direct efforts by regional actors, both official and private, to influence the political economy of armed conflicts (e.g., through explicit military alliances with one or another warring party

---

[19]The Center on International Cooperation at New York University is currently undertaking a study on regional conflict formations and strategies for conflict management and resolution; see http://www.nyu.edu/pages/cic/projects/projects.html.

or the provision of safe haven and supplies), to the spillover effects of states seeking to stem the flow of refugees and combatants across borders, to regional trade flows and other economic interactions. Better understanding is needed on the particular regional dimensions of war economies: how they affected the character and duration of conflict; and the challenges that these activities and their legacies pose for those seeking to promote peace through the control of economic behavior. Likewise, greater attention to the regulatory efforts undertaken by regional actors to stem the illicit extraction and trade in natural resources is needed, because these efforts may hold important lessons for international actors, including how to best coordinate with regional efforts; and how regional interests, either official or private, may be complicit in and profit from this illicit activity, thereby rendering regulatory initiatives ineffective.

Fifth and finally, there is the question of addressing corporate roles in conflict situations. This is not a matter of codes of conduct—which may or may not work, and may, as many NGOs claim, be mainly window dressing for shabby corporate practices—or of external regulation per se. Rather, it is about refining existing knowledge of the way licit businesses' operations, regardless of their intentions, may contribute to the outbreak and duration of violent conflict. This includes, first, developing a better understanding of companies' strategies and motivations in situations of conflict; second, acknowledging the legitimate concerns of corporations in conflict zones; and third, soliciting their views in developing more effective responses, both voluntary and binding, available to them and to other stakeholders, including international policymakers, to minimize the former's direct or indirect contributory role in violent conflict.[20] Overcoming the possible loss of competitive advantage to less scrupulous rivals and the prospect of privately bearing the costs of supplying the public good of conflict prevention remain principal barriers to collective action. Likewise, the financial and insurance sectors must be given greater attention—both for their contributory role in illicit transactions, and as a potential source of leveraging corporate compliance.

---

[20]Under the auspices of its Economic Agendas in Civil Wars project, IPA has begun a dialogue involving private sector actors. Though it will probably not lead to any published work, these discussions may help elucidate firms' strategies in conflict countries and thus lead to mutually beneficial and more effective initiatives for promoting peace and reconciliation in the countries involved.

Conclusions: Some Early Findings

At the outset of the IPA project on the political economy of conflict, a number of broad propositions ran through research on economic factors in civil wars. This included an assumption that global economic flows (trade, aid, and investment) affect the incidence, duration, intensity, and character of armed conflict; that economic factors are consequential to warring elites decisions to pursue war and peace; that greed and not grievances is the chief driver of armed conflict; that countries with a high dependence on natural resources have a higher risk of conflict, and that resource wars have their own dynamics; and these that linkages are amenable to policy intervention. Five important findings emerged in the early stages of IPA's research, since completed. Some of these findings have necessitated refining or revising earlier propositions, and others have had policy implications unforeseen at the project's outset.

First, it is often difficult to separate "economic" factors from "political" factors (let alone those that are social or cultural). Both are sources of conflict, but the interplay and relative importance of these factors varies not only between conflicts but also among different actors within a specific conflict and over its duration. Thus, conflict may not be about greed *or* grievances but a combination of greed *and* grievances.[21] In some cases, the control of economic activities may be the principal motivation for the initiation or perpetuation of conflict, but this is not to say that wars are solely about greed. In fact, the existence of grievances, whether economic, political, or social, appears to be the most persuasive motivation for conflict. Poverty, social inequality, rapid economic decline, large numbers of young unemployed males, and radicalized identity politics may all, under the right conditions, provide the necessary catalyst for conflict, particularly when accompanied by repressive, illegal, or extralegal behavior on the part of governments. However, primarily political motivations for conflicts can

[21]On the basis of statistical models by Paul Collier, conflicts were thought more likely to be caused by "greed" than by "grievance." Proxies for greed were seen as good predictors for civil conflict; proxies for grievance less so. The former included an economy largely dependent on primary commodities (oil, minerals, timber, agricultural products), large numbers of (unemployed) young men, and low levels of education. Proxies for grievance included economic inequality, a lack of political rights, and government incompetence. Paul Collier and Anke Hoeffler, *Greed & Grievance in Civil War*, Policy Research Working Paper 2355 (Washington, D.C.: World Bank, 2000); updated 2001, and available at http://www.worldbank.org/research/conflict/papers/greedgrievance_23oct.pdf.

then "mutate" into economic agendas: pillaging, seizing land, exploiting labor, and controlling trade. These economic motivations, however, appear more significant in sustaining, prolonging, and transforming conflict rather than in causing it.[22]

Second, it is important not to confuse what makes armed conflict feasible with what motivates it. Valuable natural resources are not in and of themselves a reliable indicator of where conflict is likely to occur. The presence of natural resources, particularly those that are easily lootable, do appear to make conflict more feasible when underlying grievances already exist, for they offer a ready means of financing rebellion.[23] This explains in part why, for example, not all diamond-producing countries experience conflict. Resources may also become a source of genuine grievances being mobilized on behalf of political agendas, as when state institutions responsible for their equitable management instead engage in private, criminal accumulation, or when there is a real or perceived maldistribution of revenues between regions of production and national capitals. Thus, formerly stable diamond-producing countries may become conflict prone if poor management and corruption gain the upper hand, as in Sierra Leone.

Third, as the civil wars of the 1990s demonstrated, exploitation of civilians to enrich powerful individuals and groups is carried out by both governments and rebel groups. Dichotomies between what constitutes "licit/legal" versus "illicit/criminal" behavior in civil wars (and, indeed, elsewhere) are more usefully seen as normative categories deriving from a notion of the state having a monopoly over interaction with global markets and over the legitimate use of force. Viewed as such, sovereignty does not legitimate corruption, predation, or repression on the part of the state, just as rebellion is

---

[22]Indeed, fairly early on, Paul Collier and others accepted that factors of "greed" better explain the duration of conflict than its outbreak. One of the most rewarding aspects of IPA's work in this area has been the flexibility of Collier and some of his colleagues, notably Nicholas Sambanis, in taking on board perspectives initially at least in apparent conflict with their own findings. Consequently, and due also to progress in their own methodology, these have evolved considerably. Challenges remaining to be addressed are how statistical models drawing on national accounts can deal with the phenomenon of largely regional conflicts and how political factors can be integrated into statistical models—the proxies so far have been too rough to be of real use.

[23] Related, different types of natural resources appear to have different affects on the intensity, duration, and incidence of conflict. Michael Ross, "Oil, Drugs and Diamonds: The Varying Roles of Natural Resources Vary in Civil War," in *The Political Economy of Armed Conflict: Beyond Greed and Grievance,* ed. Karen Ballentine and Jake Sherman (Boulder, Colo.: Lynne Rienner, 2003).

not a priori a criminal endeavor, as when conducted in self-defense. Effective policy intervention requires a case-by-case examination of the link between opportunity and motive not only of armed groups but also of states, as well as of the wider socioeconomic and political context in which they both operate. This has important implications not only for international decisions on when and how to intervene in ongoing conflicts but also for how to mitigate unintended negative humanitarian consequences.

Fourth, the policies of donor states, the United Nations, International Monetary Fund, World Bank, and multinational corporations should not be examined solely from the point of view of their role in conflict areas. A broader examination should be made of the impact of, for example, international economic policies (neoliberalism, structural adjustment, etc.) on state capacity and of patterns of consumption in the industrial North on the security and development of the developing South. Without more far-sighted policies to address the underlying causes of conflict—such as those that support legitimate and inclusive governance and poverty reduction, resource management and market diversification, and legal and financial reform—the conflicts of the present will prove difficult to resolve, and the peace settlements of the future will be even more difficult to sustain.

Fifth, the changing nature of resource flows in war economies in the context of globalization, including the growing importance of private actors, has led to a need for a new generation of legal instruments and policies, including partnerships among donors, private companies, multilateral organizations, NGOs, and governments. Existing international and regional conventions, national legislation and bilateral agreements, codes of conduct, and market pressures already provide a well-developed legal and policy framework for addressing many of the resource flows that sustain armed conflict—including the suppression of money laundering, regulating the export of weapons, and targeting international organized crime. Generally, these initiatives are well developed and have the compliance of states and nonstate actors. Individually some states, including Canada, have both the will and capacity to limit resource flows originating in or destined for conflict zones. But many countries, particularly those in the global South, lack adequate financial means or the enforcement capacity necessary for effective implementation. Likewise, multilateral organizations in Europe, Latin America, and parts of Africa have developed robust initiatives.

Yet even the most effective policy responses are ultimately likely to have diminishing returns, as both new illicit activities and networks fill the void and new means develop to evade detection. Where existing regulatory efforts have proven successful in particular areas—combating money laundering from narcotics, for example—this success has often not been translated into strategies for combating related activities—such as tracing proceeds from ill-gotten gains from looting or grand corruption.

Moreover, the existing regulatory framework is neither uniform in its application nor comprehensive in its reach, facilitating the ability of criminals to stay ahead of the law and confusing the efforts of legitimate actors to comply with it. The United Nations has an important role to play, not only in supporting national and regional efforts to control illicit economic behavior in civil wars—many of which efforts hold particular promise—but also in establishing norms for such behavior and in addressing the issues of structural prevention noted above. The United Nations is clearly moving in these directions, but more work remains to be done.

10

Need, Creed, and Greed
in Intrastate Conflict

I. William Zartman

One does not have to be a Marxist or an economist to recognize that all conflicts are about resources. But one does not have to be a pastor or a psy-
chologist to also recognize that all conflicts are about identity. Nor does
one have to be a humanist or a political scientist to see that all conflicts are
about basic needs. Thus to claim that conflicts are matters of greed, or rights,

I. William Zartman is the Jacob Blaustein Professor of International Organization and
Conflict Resolution and director of the Conflict Management Program at the Paul H.
Nitze School of Advanced International Studies, Johns Hopkins University. He is a
pioneer in the field of negotiation analysis, is the author of numerous works on North
Africa, and has written or edited more than a dozen books on conflict resolution and
negotiation issues, including, most recently, *Preventive Negotiation: Avoiding Conflict
Escalation* (Rowman & Littlefield, 2000), *Power and Negotiation* (with Jeffrey Rubin;
University of Michigan Press, 2003), and *Cowardly Lions: Missed Opportunities to
Prevent Deadly Conflict and State Collapse* (Lynne Rienner, 2005). He is most grate-
ful for the assistance of Andreas Hipple and Akiko Onken in the research for this chap-
ter, for the good comments of Cynthia Arnson and Peter Davis, and also to the Foreign
Policy Research Institute for starting him on this project's path.

or grievances is profoundly uninteresting. If the claim is exclusionary, it is simply wrong; if the claim is contributory, it is banal. The interesting questions are how these factors relate to each other in causing and sustaining conflict, and how, not whether, conflict is related to these three factors. Are they sequential or phasal, or always concomitant, and under what conditions? These questions are important not only for the analytical understanding of the nature of conflict but also for devising appropriate policies to reduce conflict. This inquiry, then, seeks to balance the table of analysis toward a better reflection of reality in the understanding of the etiology of violent intrastate conflict. Beyond its substantive findings are some deeper questions of social science methodology, epistemology, and ontology.

Sources of Conflict

Social science inquiry hangs on a pendulum. Putative explanations emerge and draw the momentum of scholarship to them, lining up true believers and drawing the fire of true doubters, until a counterproposition appears in turn and the pendulum swings in a new direction. The movement encourages exclusivist and exaggerated claims in order to draw attention to a new explanatory angle, and so it fuels the work of debunkers. Much value is lost in the process, and the pendulum only comes to rest on one side or in the middle much later, often unnoticed as the debate moves elsewhere.[1]

Of course, the movement is not as sharply defined as the pendulum image may suggest, as the study of internal conflict shows. The new thrust of explanation that was launched immediately after World War II, which focused primarily on interstate conflict, was that wars begin in people's minds, with less attention to the material conditions that made their minds turn to war.[2] As the Cold War took over the postwar peace, people's minds viewed internal conflict as the work of international forces, notably communist interference in internal affairs, providing a reverse mirror for Marxist materialist explanations of conflict. With the rise of anticolonial nationalism, the

---

[1]Thomas Kuhn, *The Structure of Scientific Revolutions* (Chicago: University of Chicago Press, 1962, 1970). This effect is the subject of many presentations in *Science* magazine. For an illustrative discussion, see Michael Balter, "Search for the Indo-Europeans," *Science* 303 (February 27, 2004): 1323–26, which ends: "'There is no need to set up the Kurgan and farming hypotheses at variance with one another,' says April McMahon, a linguist at the University of Sheffield, United Kingdom. 'But sadly, this is something that [people] have a tendency to do.'"

[2]Jessie Bernard, T. H. Pear, Raymond Aron, and Robert Angell, *The Nature of Conflict* (New York: UNESCO, 1957).

focus turned to ascriptive rights and their denial as the cause of conflict.[3] Why external interference was able to take hold was dealt with only by a minority of scholars.[4] Later, in reaction, it was proposed that internal conflict was the consequence of poverty, a putative direct link that is hard to kill. It has only been much later that research has turned to seeking to identify the conditions under which poverty does indeed lead to conflict. In turn, this search produced the more focused work on relative deprivation.[5]

However, as the Cold War waned, new events introduced new conditions to be explained, drawing attention to ethnicity and religion, or concerns of identity, and leading in turn to debates about the role of identity—eternal or primordial versus the conditional.[6] Yet the pendulum had swung too far, leaving a large unoccupied area for material explanations, and the latest wave of scholarship has churned up economic explanations of conflict.[7]

---

[3]Rudolph Emerson, *Empire to Nation* (Cambridge, Mass.: Harvard University Press, 1960); Emmanuel Wallerstein, ed., *Social Change* (New York: Wiley, 1966).

[4]James Rosenau, ed., *International Aspects of Civil Strife* (Princeton, N.J.: Princeton University Press, 1964), a rare book ahead of its times.

[5]James C. Davies, "Towards a Theory of Revolution," *American Sociological Review* 27 (1962): 5–18. James C. Davies, "The J-Curve of Rising and Declining Satisfactions as a Cause of Some Great Revolutions and a Contained Rebellion," in *Violence in America*, ed. Hugh Davis Graham and Ted Robert Gurr (New York: Bantam Books, 1969); Ted Gurr, *Why Men Rebel* (Princeton, N.J.: Princeton University Press, 1970).

[6]Benedict Anderson, *Imagined Communities* (New York: Verso, 1991); Francis Deng et al., *Sovereignty as Responsibility* (Washington, D.C.: Brookings Institution Press, 1996), esp. chap. 3, "Identity."

[7]Michael Intriligator and D. Brito, "A Predatory–Prey Model of Guerrilla Warfare," *Synthesis* 76, no. 2 (1988): 235–49; Jack Hirschleifer, "The Analysis of Continuing Conflict," *Synthesis* 76, no. 2 (1988): 201–33; M. Lichbach, "An Evaluation of 'Does Economic Inequality Breed Political Conflict?' Studies," *World Politics* 41, no. 4 (1989): 431–71; D. Brito and Michael Intriligator, "An Economic Model of Guerrilla Warfare," *International Transaction* 15, no. 3 (1989): 319–29; M. R. Garfinkel and S. Skaperdas, *The Political Economy of Conflict and Appropriation* (Cambridge: Cambridge University Press, 1996); David Keen, "War: What Is It Good For?" *Contemporary Politics* 2, no. 1 (1996): 23–36; David Keen, *The Economic Functions of Violence in Civil Wars*, Adelphi Paper 320 (London: International Institute for Strategic Studies, 1998); Paul Collier and Anke Hoeffler, "On Economic Causes of Civil War," *Oxford Economic Papers* 50 (1999): 563–73; F. Jean and Jean-François Rufin, eds., *L'économie des guerres civiles* (Paris: Hachette, 1996). Note that this strain of scholarship is quite different (even if not entirely unrelated) from the longer-standing work on the economic consequences of conflict, for which economics is the dependent—not independent—variable; see Paul Collier, "On the Economic Consequences of Civil War," *Oxford Economic Papers* 51 (1999): 168–83; F. Stewart and V. Fitzgerald, eds., *War and Underdevelopment*, vols. 1 and 2 (Oxford: Oxford University Press, 2000); J. C. Murdoch and Tod Sandler, "Economic Growth, Civil Wars and Spatial Spillovers," *Journal of Conflict Resolution* 46, no. 1 (2002): 91–110.

Each of these explanations has enriched understanding, yet each has tended to claim that it has *the* key, to the exclusion of the others.

Previous claims to exclusive explanations have been tempered in the ensuing debates and inserted into a bundle of causes, but the new wave of economic claims is still fresh. Of course, economic explanations—and indeed, exclusively economic explanations—of conflict are not new. The latest previous round was composed of the whole body of Marxist scholarship, according to which conditions of economic exploitation produced alienation and rebellion, both in and between nations. The causal mechanism for conflict was not a direct result of poverty but rather a more sophisticated relationship mediated by sociopolitical structures. However, little of this analysis has proven to be relevant for current intrastate conflicts, if indeed for any conflicts. The current return to a search for an economic key to conflict responds to a new wave of evidence, corresponding to a post–Cold War decline in ideology as a driving force and a rise in seemingly purposeless rampages animated by personal gain. The new phenomenon has attracted a new body of scholarship, as is appropriate, including attention from the World Bank, which, in the absence of an ability to recognize political causes, has sought an economic explanation for the debilitating conflicts that hamper its reconstruction and development efforts.[8]

In this situation, it is not yet clear exactly what the economic claim to causality is. If the argument is that resources sustain rebellions, or that rebellions need resources, or that political entrepreneurs use resources to pursue conflicts, it is unexceptionable and perhaps unexceptional. But if it is that the maldistribution of resources has no relation to conflict, or that the drive for personal (as distinguished from group) gain in resources is the cause of conflict, or that ideological or identity grievances are a hoax without operative effect on the course of conflict, it is empirically wrong and ideologically perverse.

Paul Collier and Anke Hoeffler, for example, "find little evidence for grievances as a determinant of conflict. Neither inequality nor political oppression increase the risk of conflict."[9] But economists, as well as other social scientists, are far from united behind the Collier–Hoeffler thesis on the causes of conflict; Ola Olsson and Heather Congdon Fors apply a game

---

[8]Indeed, it can be said that the World Bank's Development Research Group has done a great service in getting the bank to recognize political causes to conflict by calling them economic. See Paul Collier et al., *Breaking the Conflict Trap: Civil War and Development Policy* (New York: Oxford University Press for the World Bank, 2003).

[9]Paul Collier and Anke Hoeffler, *Greed and Grievance in Civil War*, Working Paper 2002-01 (Oxford: Centre for the Study of African Economies, Oxford University, 2002), 2; available at http://www.csae.ox.ac.uk/workingpapers/pdfs/2002-01text.pdf.

theoretical approach to find that the Congolese wars against both Mobutu and Laurent Kabila were "triggered by institutional grievance."[10] Ballentine identifies "effective governance" as "the critical variable mediating the relationship that Collier has posited between natural resource dependence and the opportunity for rebellion."[11] In analyzing recurrent civil wars, Barbara Walter argues that "civil wars will have little chance to get off the ground unless individual farmers, shopkeepers, and potential workers choose to enlist in the rebel armies that are necessary to pursue a war, and enlistment is only likely to be attractive when two conditions hold. The first is a situation of individual hardship or severe dissatisfaction with one's current situation. The second is the absence of any nonviolent means for change . . . a higher quality of life and greater access to political participation have a significant negative effect on the likelihood of renewed war."[12]

But there is a deeper dimension to the current debate, which is related not just to a new twist in events but also to new epistemologies.[13] It stems from the use of different research methods using different types of data. Most research on internal conflict in the postwar period has focused on in-depth case studies used to test explanatory propositions, with increasing formality.[14] The data tend to be longitudinal or sequential, because

[10]Ola Olsson and Heather Congdon Fors, "Congo: The Prize of Predation," *Journal of Peace Research* 41, no. 3 (2004): 321–36. The "institutional grievance" variable used in this article is modeled as deliberate institutional differences between formal- and informal-sector production. This is intended to reflect factors including the strength of property rights and the rule of law that the ruler can control directly.

[11]Karen Ballentine, "Beyond Greed and Grievance: Reconsidering the Economic Dynamics of Armed Conflict," in *The Political Economy of Armed Conflict: Beyond Greed and Grievance*, ed. Karen Ballentine and Jake Sherman (Boulder, Colo.: Lynne Rienner, 2003), 259–83; the quotation here is on 265.

[12]Barbara F. Walter, "Does Conflict Beget Conflict? Explaining Recurring Civil War," *Journal of Peace Research* 41, no. 3 (2004): 371–88; the quotation here is on 371.

[13]Charles C. Ragin, "Turning the Tables: How Case-Oriented Research Challenges Variable-Oriented Research," *Comparative Social Research* 16, no. 1 (1997):27–42; Scott Gates, "Empirically Assessing the Causes of Civil War," paper presented at an International Studies Association meeting, New Orleans, 2002; Nicholas Sambanis, "Using Case Studies to Expand Economic Models of Civil War," *Perspectives on Politics* 2, no. 2 (2004): 259–70.

[14]Alexander George, "Case Studies for Theory Development," paper presented to the Symposium on Information Processing in Organizations, Carnegie-Mellon University, Pittsburgh, 1982; Alexander George & Thomas McKeown, "Case Studies and Theories of Organizational Decision-Making," *Advances in Information Processing* 2 (1985): 21–58; I. William Zartman, ed., *Elusive Peace: Negotiations to End Civil War* (Washington, D.C.: Brookings Institution Press, 1995); Ballentine and Sherman, *Political Economy of Armed Conflict*.

this approach grew out of historical studies and so is generally process oriented. Propositions may be inductively or deductively derived, but they are used to guide the evaluation of individual cases analyzed in some detail, with causal relationships explicitly posited. This description is obviously an ideal type, more or less rigorously followed in individual scholarship. The previous case study chapters place this work in this tradition. Such studies are more interested in arguing and illustrating how resources, identity, or needs operate in known instances of conflict than in when they operate, and they spend little time on absent effects, noninstances, or control cases.

It is doubtless the loose formalization of this approach, its small numbers of cases, and its deference to case idiosyncrasy that gave rise to a newer methodology now in vogue.[15] This newer research uses aggregate data on the largest number of cases possible either to test or generate deductive propositions through correlation or factoring. Despite careful coding, it needs to group large numbers of diverse cases together into types, and it is more interested in showing statistically significant correlations than in finding causality or in explaining the category of exceptional cases. Indeed it is more interested in "proneness" than in causality, focusing on the opportunity for conflict rather than the motivation of those who seize that opportunity (yet using seized opportunity as the proxy variable for opportunity per se). Yet opportunities are only half the explanation (and arguably the smaller half) if no one is motivated to seize them. In the words of Willie Sutton, banks are robbed because that's where the money is (or, in the words of the new methodologists, banks have a proneness for being robbed for that reason), but it takes an entrepreneur to take advantage of that opportunity (or proneness) and be a bank robber. The methodology aims to show whether resources, identity, or penury correlate with conflict rather than to explain and test why or how, and it spends little time on apparently deviant instances. It therefore often ignores some basic research questions: What is it in the correlation that provides causality? And, given several effects of the same cause, which, when, and why?

Furthermore, the methodology can only handle comparable, quantifiable data, and so, because it has no "feel" for its subject, has to rely on indicators

[15]See I. William Zartman, "Comparative Case Studies," in *Methodologies of Negotiation Research*, special issue of *International Negotiation* (ed. Peter Carnevale) 10, no. 1 (2005):3–15.

or "proxies"; subjective elements must be objectified to become data.[16] This means that it can only handle data that are quantitatively, objectively measurable and explain only that for which it has data, and in the interest of precision it must make inflexibly quantitative definitions. Such studies do not explain civil conflict; they explain conflict with more than 1,000 deaths, which is a bit like explaining human growth by starting at the age of twelve years. Its indicators, such as per capita income or economic growth, are often far away from the effect they are proxying, such as proneness. Thus, the resource school of analysis shows that poverty does not correlate with conflict, which has been known for sometime, but deduces from that fact that grievances have no role in causing conflict, using poverty as a proxy for grievances, as if all poor people were equally rebellious about their condition. Unexplored is the question why poverty leads to (correlates with) conflict in some instances and not others, and which instances those may be— again, the which–when–why question.

Meanings and Models

To get beyond single factor explanations of internal conflict and place the various factors in proper perspective, one has to first explore the meanings of the key elements and the relationships that exist among them. These elements have been posited at the beginning as basic needs, identity, and resources, as the stakes of conflict, or as grievances, rights, and greed as the motivations of conflict. But so identified, they stand on different sides of causality, not just apples and oranges but pits and peels, different parts of apples and oranges. To group them on the same causative level of theories in relation to conflict, however, in the sense used here, grievances occur over a deprivation of basic needs of some sort, claims of rights based on identity react to discrimination, and greed over resources relates to opportunity, termed in the titular shorthand of this work as "need," "creed," and "greed." Each bears some examination, beginning with need.

---

[16]"Thus, objective grievance is not a powerful primary cause of conflict, conflict may generate [objective? subjective?] grievances which become powerful additional risk factors"; Collier and Hoeffler, *Greed and Grievance in Civil War*, where "objective grievances" were indicated by ethnic polarization, political rights, political openness, and ethnic group size, but not how people felt about these situations, with the apparent assumption that all people feel the same about the same situations.

Even if poverty and conflict do not always coincide, it takes little imagination to see that grievances over deprivation of basic needs have a motor role in conflict. Needs are general qualities required by people for their existence. Satisfied people (which is not the same as rich people) do not revolt, by definition. Satisfaction and dissatisfaction can relate to many values, not just welfare or well-being. Grievances come from unmet needs, unwarranted deprivation, felt hurts, and resentment against the withholding of just deserts, and thus they relate to other dimensions such as distribution and justice. The operative terms—satisfaction, unmet, unwarranted, felt, hurts, resentment, even needs—are all subjective and are felt differently by different people at different times. Distribution concerns the "what" or subject of grievances, which is ultimately related to the basic material elements that people feel they need, whether directly or indirectly as repression, exclusion, and nonparticipation in the control over allocation through positions and values. (In)justice concerns the "why" or reason for grievances. Various theories have sought explanations of when distributions or deprivations are viewed as unjust. The most powerful are the Syllogism of Aristotle: "Inferiors become revolutionaries in order to be equals, and equals in order to be superior;"[17] and the Davies-Gurr theory of relative deprivation of falling satisfactions measured against rising expectations. For all its insight, the first does not deal with the question of when, and the second still leaves much room for interpreting the answer.

One answer comes in terms of the second factor, claims based on identity or creed. Some types of conflict begin when people feel discriminated against for ascriptive reasons, for what they are. Ascriptive identity is a quality specific to groups and can derive from race or ethnicity, but also from other fixed but less genetic attachments such as religion or nationality. Like need, creed itself does not provide conflict. It is only when two identities are in a zero-sum relationship to each other—that is, when one cannot be oneself except at the expense of the other's being itself—or when need is restricted or targeted to an identity group that conflict arises. Similarly, not all identities are sources of conflict, and the notion of primordial conflicts lingers only in the minds of journalists. Justice often joins identity, when aroused, to provide the bridge for Aristotle's Syllogism—why were we unjustly deprived and why should we be justly favored? But, again, the fact that only some identities are sources of conflict does not mean that no

---

[17] Aristotle, *Politics* (Oxford: Oxford University Press, 1960), 242.

identities are, posing again the which-when-why question. Targeted discrimination offers a hypothetical answer, and one that provides a bridge between poverty and resources.

Like needs and identity, resources are stakes over which conflict takes place. Though some explanations emphasize the demand side of resources, as a target of competing and conflicting demands, a current strain of economic explanations focuses on the supply or availability of resources as a source and explanation of conflict.[18] Resources may be seen as a subject of conflict over general deprivation or over specific discrimination against one or more identity groups, but they can also be seen positively, as opportunity and an invitation to acquisition. Yet, without falling into the trap of over-rationality, there must be some motivational element of dissatisfaction with the current state of affairs, either to make individuals (and especially followers) take the risks of conflict or to seek the financial benefit that outweighs that risk. Which takes the causal search back to grievances again.

What is needed is a model or models of the process of violent conflict generation and sustenance that is or are supported by enough significant cases to be testworthy, and that can then be the subject of more refined aggregate data analysis to find frequencies and then of detailed case analysis to test applicability and explain the difference between apples and oranges rather than staying on the level of fruit.

The initial question in building such a model is, Where to begin? In reaction to claims of superficially proximate beginnings, some have argued for going back to a distant determinate condition, such as independence, colonization, or precolonial society. Both the proximate and the distant approaches adopt a predetermined point, the first too near to the event to provide a full sense of causality, the second too deep in a regress often ideologically established to handle significant events. It would be more faithful to notions of cause to start with the outbreak of violence and push back behind the reasons for that outbreak to the reasons for awareness of a problem that eventually would cause the outbreak. From then, the study can move forward to analyze the violence and its persistence. If the inquiry is to answer the which–when question, it needs to focus on process. Thus, the model needs to begin with the identification of a context made of conditions that caused awareness of a problem and a conflictual reaction.

---

[18]See I. William Zartman, ed., *Governance as Conflict Management* (Washington, D.C.: Brookings Institution Press, 1995); and Deng et al., *Sovereignty as Responsibility*, esp. chap. 2.

In the cases studied here, these conditions were characterized by a deprivation of some sort. In conditions of penury, some parts of the population felt neglected. However, this broad fact raises several questions in order to be the beginning of a satisfying explanation. How much do the theories of deprivation explain? Why were the populations neglected? Why, among lots of neglected people, did they specifically feel neglected? Though there is no doubt that poverty alone does not explain the rise of rebellion, because many poor peoples are not in revolt, poverty was nonetheless the common characteristic in the cases studied, and more specifically poverty expressed as material deprivation relative to heightened expectations.[19]

The source of the rise in expectations can be varied. In some cases, it was independence that did not provide the expected dividends. In other similar cases, it was a peace agreement to end a civil war that brought benefit inadequately or unequally. In still other cases, it was a promised modernization effort that produced the same generally or unequally disappointing results. The relevance of an explanation based on deprivation relative to heightened expectations appears to be generally present.[20] But that explanation is still almost as coarse as the poverty explanation itself. Without any contrivance, one can always, or often, find some source of falling satisfactions that lie at the bottom of aggressions born of frustration. Again, the only problem is that, as is known, not all frustrations lead to aggression.

Another contributor to the conflict context is the absence of effective state authority and governance, often expressed as a failed or collapsed state.[21] In some cases, it was a weak state incapable of providing the supplies due to the population, often unable to get back on its feet after a previous round of internal conflict or independence war. At other times, it was a state that had completely collapsed, emptied of its resources and capabilities, often by a rapacious leader who privatized the public domain into his own pocket, alienated the population, and even on occasion destroyed

---

[19]For an excellent discussion of the complex role of poverty in causing and maintaining conflict, see Collier et al., *Breaking the Conflict Trap.*

[20]The Davies J-curve and Gurr relative deprivation theories (see footnote 5 above) were an early expression of prospect theory.

[21]"Collapsed state" is used here to refer to "a situation in which the structure, authority (legitimate power), law, and political order have fallen apart" (Zartman, *Elusive Peace*, 1). "Failed states" are those that have fallen decisively short in performing one or more of their functions but that still exist as a structure of governance. Robert I. Rotberg, ed., *State Failure and State Weakness in a Time of Terror* (Washington, D.C.: Brookings Institution Press, 2003); Robert I. Rotberg, ed., *When States Fail: Causes and Consequences* (Princeton, N.J.: Princeton University Press, 2004).

civil society. Worse than general incapacity is concentrated capacity and prebendal corruption, in which poverty is caused by (and causes) the rapacious leaders to corner the major resources of the state, repressing those who would protest their exclusion. Thus, the cause behind the conditions of generalized or localized deprivation was sectoral or comprehensive incapacity on the part of the state and greed on the part of its rulers. Yet again, if a state's collapse almost inevitably brings out the dogs to fight over its corpse, state failure or lesser types of state weakness are only steps in the collapsing process and do not always lead to conflict.

But perhaps the problem is being looked at from the wrong end. Poverty, specifically as sensitized by relative deprivation, creates the conditions out of which conflict can grow; state incapacity, from weakness through failure to outright collapse, creates the conditions out of which poverty and deprivation can grow. The causal chain can apply to the entire state or to neglected regions, producing different types of conflict.[22] Together, these elements create a condition that can be referred to under the label of need, to be described and explained by appropriate terms of analysis and constituting the subjective and objective contributions to a sense of grievance. Both of these elements are necessary but insufficient components in the emergence of internal conflict. What is needed is some additional element that pulls conflict cases out of preconflict conditions, a trigger that sets off the reaction or a catalyst that crystallizes the supersaturated solution. Frequently the search for such an element has turned to aspects of the existing conditions, such as depth of poverty, or critical mass, or population concentration. But these are merely dimensions of the basic conditions, often to be created once the conflict has started or in the act of triggering it. What is needed is an exogenous variable, and one that takes into account the vagaries of the human or social phenomena that are being examined.

One such element is the political entrepreneur. It would be the beginning of infinite regress into the soul and psyche to push the inquiry back further into a search for what makes an entrepreneur. It is sufficient to note that it takes a leadership agent to crystallize the subjective reactions to objective conditions into conflict.[23] It takes a pyromaniac to throw a match into the

---

[22]Zartman, *Elusive Peace.*

[23]Michael Brown, "The Causes and Regional Dimensions of Internal Conflict," in *The International Dimensions of Internal Conflict*, ed. Michael Brown (Cambridge, Mass.: MIT Press, 1996), 575 et seq.; Tui de Figueiredo and Barry Weingast, "The Rationality of Fear," in *Civil Wars, Insecurity and Intervention*, ed. Barbara Walter and Jack Snyder (New York: Columbia University Press, 1999); Jane Holl [Lute] et al., *Preventing Deadly Conflict* (New York: Carnegie Corporation, 1997), 29–30.

social tinder heap. The state weakness creates an open space for those who would fill the vacuum; the deprivation gives them a cause to do so.

However, the political entrepreneurs can rarely—indeed never—mobilize an entire population. Not only may the need or deprivation be selective as a result of targeting or discrimination by the government (or by natural or accidental condition), but even more important, the effectiveness of the entrepreneur depends on his (or her) ability to make a selective appeal to a part of the population. Mobilization in his—and their—cause depends on his ability to seize on their sense of identity as a positive source of consolidation and on their sense of discrimination as a negative source. Again, whether they are objectively worse off than others in the population is only of secondary importance; as in many things in social politics, the subjective sense of targeted deprivation is made more credible by objective evidence but is not dependent on it. Identity becomes the major resource in the generation of conflict, and so the process passes from need to creed.

Identity is involved in all conflicts, albeit in many different forms. In the current era, it frequently takes the form of ethnic identity, in part because the ethnic group is the most easily mobilizable social grouping, and in part—and as a consequence of that fact—because discrimination frequently is conducted by one ethnic group against another. In a previous era, identity was often based on a nationalist appeal in an anticolonial situation. In both eras, religion has contributed to reinforce both forms of identity, or on occasion to replace them. But in a previous era, class also provided a dominant form of identity appeals, furnishing an easy identification of both the target and agent of discrimination. In all cases, creed forms a potent base for justice and a rallying appeal for support and redress.[24]

Because identity becomes an element in the generation of conflict, it has its own dynamic of mobilization. In an initial political stage of petition, the aggrieved group's spokespeople request redress from discrimination by the authorities backed by the symbolic mobilization of the referent group; if not satisfied, the conflict moves to a consolidation phase, where political entrepreneurs compete for exclusive leadership of the referent group and work to unite it behind them in their internal political rivalry, seeking to eliminate each other. Once consolidation has taken place, the emergent leader can then turn back to the conflict with the authorities and use the consolidated support group as an arm against the government. The identity group covers the spectrum of the sources of power; it supplies troops,

[24]Georg Simmel, *Conflict* (Glencoe, Ill.: Free Press, 1955); Lewis Coser, *The Functions of Social Conflict* (Glencoe, Ill.: Free Press, 1956).

legitimacy, money, subsistence, cover, and other elements needed for the struggle. With these supports, the identity group and its leadership can turn to confrontation.[25] At this point, the course of the conflict can be affected by many things but essentially is determined by the relation of forces between the two sides.

The course of the conflict, in its turn, has feedback effects on its own evolution. Though resolution is unlikely during the consolidation phase, where intraparty and not interparty politics are predominant and resolution is a distraction to consolidation, continuing progression in the confrontation phase toward some form of resolution follows what may be termed an even course, in which energies and attentions shift their focus from the conflict to the terms of resolution. If attempts at resolution then collapse, a return to conflict is required, leading to new attempts at resolution. Resolution can take the form of asymmetrical victory, or a stalemate that impels the opening of asymmetrical or symmetrical negotiations, depending on the relation of forces between the two sides.

However, if the conflict becomes stuck in its confrontation stage, other directions open up. The more prolonged the struggle, the more the resources become strained and the more the search for resources becomes important, even dominant. At the same time, the more prolonged the struggle, the more the tactical question—that is, the debate over how to conduct the struggle, and principally over whether to adjust the ends and seek a compromise solution, or adjust the means and turn to more violent tactics— becomes important and hence divisive.[26] Factionalism throws the conflict back into the consolidation phase and opens the rebellion to divisive tactics on the part of the government. Return to consolidation in turn moves the conflict back into a phase where resolution is not on the agenda and away from the confrontation phase where resolution is the natural evolution. Because resources then become more and more difficult to obtain, the conflict leadership is drawn into an ever-intensifying search for the means to keep the conflict going, to the neglect of the ends themselves. The more prolonged the struggle, the greater the pressure and temptation to move into a time of greed. Privatized means become the only way to keep the followers, because the original ends of need and creed show little

---

[25]Zartman, *Elusive Peace*; I. William Zartman, "Toward a Theory of Elite Circulation," in *Elites in the Middle East*, ed. I. William Zartman (New York: Praeger, 1980).

[26]Richard Gibson, *African Liberation Movements* (Oxford: Oxford University Press for the Institute of Race Relations, 1972).

chance of being attained, and tactics become oriented toward the attainment of means, to the neglect of ends. The conflict enters the stage of the soft, self-serving, stable stalemate (an "S[5]" situation), a comfortable resting place for the rebellion and an acceptable division of territories for the government.[27] At best, the conflict falls prey to the curse of Robin Hood, where life in the Greenwood becomes sustainable and enjoyable, and victory, if it ever comes, sounds the death of the Merry Men and their leader.

Meanwhile, back in the capital (a place where conflict studies often forget to look), the prolonged conflict has a series of negative consequences. Although, by providing an external enemy, the conflict in some cases seems to work to the reinforcement of the state whose corruption and weakness was at the origin of the conflict and its progression, its contribution is a false coherence that adds nothing to the strength and purpose of the state and drains its resources. If there is any strengthening of the state, it is in its repressive capabilities as it tries to keep the allegiance of its own people but that may further alienate them if it does not provide effective security and protection. Less frequently, the conflict may strengthen the legitimacy of the state among those who are fed up with the ability of armed groups to create mayhem.

In other cases, pursuit of the conflict directly contributes to further state collapse. Not only does the state lose territory, resources, and capabilities to the rebellion, but the conflict weakens the state's ability to carry out its functions toward its own people in its own territory, tending toward further alienation of its own people, resources, and security, and reducing its own rulership to a narrow group focusing on its own resources. In a word, in the worst-case scenario, too often reproduced, there is a race to greed on both sides of the conflict. Although the result is often the same in both types of cases, the two paths are different, a difference that calls for further analysis and explanation.

In sum, the model of internal conflict begins with state neglect at a time of rising expectations, producing a fact and a sense of deprivation, or grievance, in the first act termed need. This feeling is mobilized into conflict by political entrepreneurs who cultivate and build on the fact and perception of the targeted deprivation of an identity group, moving the conflict into the second act, termed creed. Identity is not only the basis of conflict; it is also

---

[27]Zartman, *Elusive Peace*; I. William Zartman, "Analyzing Intractability," in *Grasping the Nettle: Analyzing Cases of Intractability*, ed. Chester Crocker, Fen Hampson, and Pamela Aall (Washington, D.C.: United States Institute of Peace Press, 2004).

a means and the source of other means necessary to sustain the conflict. In the course of confrontation, the conflict may move to victory for one side or another, or to resolution. But if it bogs down, falling short of resolution and outrunning its resources, it can lead to a search for means that replaces the original search for ends, moving both parties into the third act, termed greed. Greed, in the third stage, deforms and obscures the original bases in need and creed, and it hijacks the conflict from social (group) to personal (individual) benefits.

Models and Reality

A social science model is not a toymaker's model, a scale replication of reality, faithful in every detail. It is closer to a fashion model—a stylized, idealized version that can be used to measure or evaluate the ordinary that necessarily diverges from it. The need–creed–greed model may not find an absolute coincidence with the reality of all the cases studied here, but the cases do illustrate both the general lines of the models and some important variations.

The model begins with conditions of poverty and deprivation deriving from a weakened or collapsed state, often caused by state greed. Three cases illustrate outright collapse, imposing need on all but a select few of the entire population. Sierra Leone provides the strongest example, as shown by Jimmy Kandeh in chapter 4, where the governments of Siaka Stevens and then Joseph Momoh emptied the state of its substance and carried it away in their pockets. When the popular sectors outside the All Peoples Congress made their protest known, repression was added to deprivation. Sierra Leone was a small-class imitation of Zaire under Mobutu Sese Seko, who privatized a rich state, deprived its population of its riches, and bought off any potential counterelites who might seek to represent the alienated population, as analyzed in chapter 6 by Erik Kennes. In Angola, too, as Philippe Le Billon points out in chapter 5, state collapse was caused by the intempestive withdrawal of the colonial regime that had done nothing to prepare for its succession, as occurred in the first wave of state collapse in a number of African countries (including earlier in the pre-Zaire Congo).[28] Those of the Popular Movement for the Liberation of Angola (MPLA) who came to power ran a corrupt machine as selective in its ben-

---

[28]I. William Zartman, ed., *Collapsed States: The Disintegration and Restoration of Legitimate Authority* (Boulder, Colo.: Lynne Rienner, 1995).

efits as the colonial elite it replaced. Anticolonialism itself is a redistributive conflict in that the marginalized native population seeks to obtain the benefits—indeed the increased benefits after the Korean War raw material boom of the 1950s—of which it was deprived under a colonialism that preached modernization, civilization, and development; the population is then once again deprived of the independence dividends when the nationalist state is unable to get on its feet. In a reinforcing reversal of the model in all three cases, state greed was piled on popular (and banned opposition elite) need to create the conditions for revolt. In all these cases and the many others that they represent, deprivation was felt relative to the expectations raised by the political success of the nationalist anticolonial movement, which provided no generalized benefits on taking over power.

Other cases began with a lesser level of state failure, and collapse only came after the conflict. Afghanistan was a case of need generated by state failure, as Paula R. Newberg shows in chapter 8, but from a different source. A search for the contextual roots of the conflict goes back to the 1960s and 1970s, when the monarchy weakened the state in the process of liberalizing itself and fell prey to interfamily conflict, and the individual warring factions then further weakened the state by turning to foreign countries for outsourcing to meet their own need. Elizabeth Picard's analysis in chapter 2 shows Lebanon as another case in which new social forces felt a need born of deprivation relative to the established *zu'ama*, who controlled the political power of the state and the economic resources of the land rents. Colombia and Peru were cases only of selective or partial failure, as respectively demonstrated by Marc Chernick in chapter 7 and by Cynthia McClintock in chapter 3, not through any generalized weakening of the institution but through its ability to fulfill its supply functions toward the disinherited populations of the interior, particularly in terms of security and distribution of resources. Indeed, in the areas they controlled, these states were actually strengthened by their role in the conflict.

The Colombian case is special in its source of feelings of need. The end of La Violencia in 1958, like the end of the anticolonial struggle in Africa and elsewhere, brought heightened expectations for peace dividends. But the settlement was only among the warring factions of the bourgeoisie and specifically excluded new social forces in the population, creating need feelings of relative deprivation that could be used for mobilization at the hands of the M-19 movement, the National Liberation Army (ELN) and the Revolutionary Armed Forces of Colombia (FARC). In Peru, ethnic indigenous isolation and neglect sharpened need, which was heightened by targeted creed discrimination. An important lesson of these latter cases is that state's collapse is not the necessary if insufficient condition for violent conflict; short of actual collapse, even a state's failure to fulfill important supply and control functions toward important segments of the population can create the necessary conditions.[29]

But weakened and even collapsed states that can neither supply nor control their populations only offer the opportunity; it takes political entrepreneurs to seize it. They came from student leaders and former noncommissioned officers in Sierra Leone, such as Abu Kabba and Foday Sankoh, who were trained in Libya, supported by fellow Libyan trainees in Liberia, and joined by banned opposition leaders from the Sierra Leone Peoples Party (SLPP).[30] In Zaire, they also came from opposition leaders inside the country and in exile, such as Etienne Tshisekedi and Laurent Kabila. In Angola, they came from rival nationalist leaders, such as Agostinho Neto, Eduardo dos Santos, and Jonas Savimbi, possessing various quantities of organization, ideology, and charisma. In Afghanistan and Lebanon, they were *zu'ama* of various ethnic factions excluded from power and its benefits, such as Gulbuddin Hekmatyar and Ahmed Shah Massoud, and as Walid Junblatt and Nabih Berri, respectively. In Colombia and Peru, they were ideological spokesmen for disinherited or marginalized parts of the population, such as Manuel Marulanda and Abimael Guzmán, respectively.

Analysis needs to go further to give generalized, conceptual explanations of why political entrepreneurs arose and succeeded in these cases and not in others, or what it was that enabled these sociopolitical groups to provide a supply of entrepreneurs and these individuals to emerge successful out of this supply. Perhaps that challenge may be too great for social science analysis and is best left to the luck of the draw, the chance of the moment, the work of free will, the right person in the right place at the right time. But one element is clear, and that is that the political entrepreneur seized on some identity factor to mobilize support within the opportunity offered by felt need. The nature of the identity factor that turned need into

[29]In systemic terms, the functions of a polity can be divided into inputs, comprising supports and demands from the population to the state, and outputs, comprising supply and control from the state to the population; for a properly functioning political system, the four functions should be in balance. David Easton, *A Systems Analysis of Political Life* (New York: Wiley, 1965); Zartman, *Governance as Conflict Management.*

[30]Ibrahim Abdullah, "Bush Path to Destruction: The Origin and Character of the Revolutionary United Front/Sierra Leone," *Journal of Modern African Studies* 36, no. 2 (1998): 203–35; Abdul Koroma, *Sierra Leone: The Agony of a Nation* (Freetown, Sierra Leone: Andromeda, 1996).

creed was determined by the nature of the society in which the deprivation occurred.

In some cases, the most readily available identity source was ethnic, but even ethnic identity was mixed with and expressed in other identity terms such as religion and ideology. In Angola, the dominance of the *mestiços* and Mbundus within the MPLA and the marginalization of the Ovimbundu and Bakongo to the south and northeast provided a ready base for mobilization behind the National Union for the Total Independence of Angola (UNITA) of Savimbi (himself a *mestiço*) and the National Liberation Front of Angola of Holden Roberto (also *mestiço*), respectively. The violent conflict in Zaire began with the Banyamulenge, explicitly targeted by Mobutu's regime, but then spread to all neglected groups outside the capital. The marginalization and deepening impoverishment of the Peruvian Indians made them the ready targets of Shining Path (Sendero Luminoso), although its message was in ideological rather than ethnic terms. In Colombia, too, the mobilizing appeal was made in geographic and class terms within a heavy ideological message, with class and geography reinforcing each other. In Afghanistan, while the original forces were the supporters of tribal warlords, that very nature of identity mobilization opened the way for the Taliban's ostensibly nontribal or antitribal religious identity as a greater unifying force. Even in Lebanon, where ethnicity or religion is usually invoked as an explanation, the following of the leaders was almost exclusively ethnoreligious but the conflict was intraethnic, within and over—not between—identity groups, and the mobilizing message particularly among the Druze was ideological. Finally, in Sierra Leone, where ethnicity is also usually cited as the source of the conflict, the conflict was one of class cutting across ethnic lines and the mobilizing message reflected its nature; the youth in Sierra Leone discovered their identity as disinherited lumpens.

Sharp conclusions can be drawn about the role of creed. Identity was prominent and crucial in all these conflicts, and there is no reason to suspect that they are not typically representative of internal conflicts in general. It is necessary to appeal to a followership in some terms, and preexisting identities provide a convenient handle if it fits. Political entrepreneurs recruit and mobilize their followers by identifying them as targeted and disinherited parts of the national population, and when their identification fits the situation it contributes to their success. If the appeal is made in ethnic terms to people who do not feel need in terms of that form of creed or in class (ideological) terms to people who feel discrimination as fierce ethnicists, it will fall on deaf ears. Such was the limitation on the Taliban's appeal in

Afghanistan. The cases have shown that ethnic identity tends to need reinforcing in other terms if it is to gain sufficient supporters. Ethnic identity
may be more intense because of its narrowness, but religious and ideological identity provides a broader and more unifying appeal. The relative
strengths of ideological vs. national identities are very situational, as Joseph
Stalin found out despite his attempts to define the national question,[31] but
ethnicity is not always the trump. It has to be based on experience and often
has to be reinforced by other coincident cleavages. Finally and curiously,
leaders need not come from the identity group to which they appeal. Both
in class and ethnic cases, political entrepreneurs may well come from a
different group than their followers, although this is less likely to occur in
cases of religious identity. It should be noted that "leaders" and "political
entrepreneurs" are used here conceptually and functionally, not necessarily referring to unchanging individuals. Individuals may fall prey to rivals,
often over the tactical question, and may seize their opportunities and fill
their functions well or badly, beyond the reach of any conceptual analysis.

Once the violent conflict is engaged, it can move to asymmetrical victory, to hard symmetrical or mutually hurting stalemate (MHS) and resolution, or to soft, stable, self-serving stalemate (S^5) and entrenched conflict. In the first, one side has the resources to overcome the other; in the
second, both find the resources to check each other; in the third, both tend
to become absorbed in a competitive search for resources. The evolution of
the conflict in not likely to be linear but rather may bounce from one path
to another. After some times on the all three paths, the conflicts in Angola
and Sierra Leone finally ended in a government victory, despite some ap-
pearances of soft stalemates, hard stalemates, and negotiated agreements.
In the process, however, the UNITA rebels and the Revolutionary United
Front (RUF), respectively, assuaged their grievances and neglect by exploiting the diamond resources of their countries, turning need and creed
into greed. The Congo and Lebanon have presented a similar evolution,
with an MHS ending in a negotiated agreement slowly turned to government advantage, in the Congo in 1999 through clever government politics
and in Lebanon in 1987 through external (Syrian) protection. In the
process, however, parties on both sides in the Congo left their need and
creed grievances behind and turned to greed for lootable resources—diamonds, coltan, and copper, among others; while in Lebanon it was drugs,

[31]Joseph Stalin, *Marxism and the National Question* (New York: International Publishers, 1942).

land, and remittances that became the privatizable resources for the new militia entrepreneurs.

In two other cases, the struggle continues, leading to a resurgence of greed. In Colombia, the original demands of the rebellion have been all but forgotten as the Merry Men of the FARC and the ELN have learned to enjoy living in Sherwood Forest and benefiting from the drug trade and oil trade extortion, while the militias born of the state or parts of it, or in which the state has acquiesced, such as the United Self-Defense Forces of Colombia (AUC), rival them in the same pursuit. The victim is the civilian population, while the state benefits and concentrates on enhancing its security. In Afghanistan, the struggle in its latest form has reverted to a reinforcement of religious motivations and also to profiteering from the drug trade, as creed and greed vie for the allegiance of the troops on both sides. Finally, although Peru is an instance of asymmetric victory (if indeed the conflict is over), greed is appearing to emerge as Sendero Luminoso attempts to reinvent itself in the country's coca-growing regions.

Again, the cases are eloquent in their lessons. Greed does come in, but only in the course of a prolonged, bogged-down conflict stuck in an S^5 situation. Greed is a mark of the evolution of a conflict that has left its "normal" course toward either victory or stalemate and settlement. It is not possible to give a term to that "normalcy," in the sense of an even approximate period of time, but it is clear that when both outcomes begin to appear elusive, the temptation to turn the means into ends begins to arise. Though that temptation is easy to succumb to when privatizable resources are readily available, greed is the mother of great inventiveness, building roadblocks, billing bribes, requisitions, protection schemes, and other ways of turning a good cause into a money-making scheme. Besides greed, the tactical question—whether to fight or to compromise—is the other source of divisions and distraction from the main goal; it was the source of difference between Kabila and Tshisekedi and then between Jean-Pierre Bemba and Tshisekedi in the Congo, between Carlos Castaño and other AUC leaders in Colombia, and between the SLPP and the RUF in Sierra Leone. Ironically, debates and divisions over the tactical question only weaken the rebellion and promote the S^5 stalemate.

Greed in the state promotes rebellion, prolonged failure in the rebellion's struggle for rights and grievances promotes greed among the rebels, and greed within the rebellion promotes greed within the state. States on the road to failure—the initial precondition of the conflict—fall into the clutches of a ruling elite increasingly devoted to making money out of their position, at the expense of state functions. The state treasury is the primary lootable resource, and greed and grievance are two sides of the same coin, the one practiced by privatizing rulers and the other the reaction to that occurrence. If the weakened state retains enough responsive capability to push the rebellion into a prolonged, intractable conflict, the rebel leaders face the temptation to turn to private gain because the social cause of the conflict is blocked. Locked in a conflict that it is not winning, state leaders might be expected to launch a major reform program and overtake the original causes of the conflict; unfortunately, such examples are practically nonexistent: The state leaders no longer have the capacity to do so, and so they sink deeper into repression and kleptocracy. Mobutu's Zaire, Aristide's Haiti, Siad Barre's Somalia, Doe's and then Taylor's Liberia, and many others, are examples. Thus, greed occurs initially within the state, later (after a soft stalemate) within the rebellion, and then again within the state. Or, in other words, state collapse or failure gives rise to rebellion, but prolonged rebellion leads to state collapse, not so much at the hands of the rebellion as by self-destruction on the part of the state itself. It is this vicious cycle that brings about prolonged and intractable conflict in the poorer areas of the world.[32] State collapse and failure as a precursor to conflict has already been noted, but state collapse occurred in Lebanon and Afghanistan in the course of the conflict.

Greed, when it sets in, destroys the solidarity and motivation of creed. Or is it that greed sets in when the solidarity and motivation of creed have proved inadequate? There is little in the evidence to support the latter, although if there were, it would strengthen greed as a normal evolution or motivation rather than an aberration. Yet the reverse appears to be true from the empirical record; the rebellion's troops and followers are mobilized and motivated by a sense of deprivation and discrimination, expressed through appeals to identity as targeted populations, not by get-rich-quick schemes based on lootable resources. In most cases, it is only once the troops were mobilized that kleptomania sets in. Picard, writing of Lebanon, expresses well the phenomenon there but also in Sierra Leone, Colombia, Afghanistan, and Angola (but also Algeria, Sri Lanka, Liberia, and elsewhere): "In the beginning, moved by religious [or other identity] conviction and drawn by personal loyalty, they had seen no alternative to their enrollment in the war. However, they soon became able to impose themselves on the traditional

---

[32]Crocker, Hampson, and Aall, *Grasping the Nettle*; Mary Kaldor, *New and Old Wars* (Stanford, Calif.: Stanford University Press, 1999), 92.

elite and the leaders in the contest, for they had mastered an additional source: armed violence organized on a large scale and at a high level. These new militia entrepreneurs seized opportunities to use public means to private ends." In addition, in many cases, greed has a tendency to be greedy: UNITA in Angola shows that loot floats to the top, using a lack of alternatives plus repression to keep its followers following.

Finally, in another vicious circle, entrance into the greed phase weakens the ability to come to a resolving settlement of the conflict, just as it has arisen because of that same inability. The lesson of both ends of the problem is clear: It is important to reach an outcome—victorious or negotiated—early because the later evolution of the conflict makes it extremely difficult to resolve. Thus the largest lessons fit together well: It is important to strengthen the state and its ability to perform its supply and control functions, so that debilitating conflicts of need and the creed do not arise and further weaken the state and sap its functions. But if violent conflict arises, it is important to assure either one side's victory or a stalemate leading to settlement, lest the unresolved conflict become intractable and unresolvable. And victory or settlement is possible only by recognizing and tending the need and creed bases of the conflict.

Whether victory or settlement is better is still open to debate, in the current controversy over agreement durability.[33] Some studies assert that one-sided victory is more stable, although longer-term analysis underscores that grievances and rights unattended merely go underground, to arise again as the source of more violent conflict at a later, readier date. Rebel victory may be longer lasting than government victory if a new political system is created as a result, bringing the rebels into power but leaving place for the vanquished as well; no study has as yet made this distinction or agreed on a satisfactory period over which to measure it. Other studies indicate that

---

[33]Fen Osler Hampson, *Nurturing Peace* (Washington, D.C.: United States Institute of Peace Press, 1996); Barbara Walter, *Committing to Peace* (Princeton, N.J.: Princeton University Press, 2001); Stephen John Stedman, Donald Rothchild, Elizabeth Cousens, eds., *Ending Civil Wars* (Boulder, Colo.: Lynne Rienner, 2002); Bruce Bueno de Mesquita and D. Lalman, *War and Reason* (New Haven, Conn.: Yale University Press, 1992); Suzanne Werner, "The Precarious Nature of Peace: Resolving the Issues, Enforcing Settlement, and Renegotiating," *American Journal of Political Science* 43, no. 3 (1999): 912–34; Collier et al., *Breaking the Poverty Trap*; Virginia Page Fortna, "Inside and Out: Peacekeeping and the Duration of Peace after Civil and Interstate Wars," *International Studies Review* 5, no. 4 (2003): 97–115; Barbara Walter, "Explaining the Intractability of Territorial Conflict," *International Studies Review* 5, no. 4 (2003): 137–53.

settlements last longer, especially when they address the deeper causes of the conflict and when they provide for forward-looking mechanisms to handle future outbreaks;[34] certainly an agreement involving both sides of the conflict and providing for future institutions of cooperation, resolution, and reconciliation should form the basis of a longer-lasting and more stable outcome than merely effective repression.

Prevention and Management

This analysis indicates three moments of intervention when something can be done to reverse the conflict process—literally, at the beginning, the middle, and the end. Each requires some basic remedies but of a different sort.

The possibilities of prevention in times of need depend above all on the strengthening of the state so that it can perform its functions of supply, and secondarily of control. Governance is conflict management, conducted through these two output functions, which must be kept in balance to meet the input functions of support and demand from the population.[35] Weak states unable to meet the demands of their citizens in general or in groups with appropriately balanced provisions and with judicious controls when necessary are both inviting conflict and ill prepared to handle it. There is often the feeling that weak or even failing states are best left alone because they are not making headlines, but weak states are conflicts waiting to happen. The analysis, backed by the cases, has shown that weak states saddled with rising expectations are ready opportunities for political entrepreneurs in conflict, whose appearance is merely a matter of chance. That is too much of a risk for the states, their populations, and ultimately the world community to take.

Even more serious, the preceding analysis indicates that state weakness and state greed feed on each other in a vicious cycle. Shrinking resources and supplies incite leaders to corner the remaining small quantities of available benefits for themselves, thus further reducing state capacity and heightening popular restiveness over unfulfilled expectations and unfilled

---

[34]Christian Thuderoz, *Negotiations* (Paris: Presse Universitaire de France, 2003); I. William Zartman and Victor Kremenyuk, eds., *Peace vs. Justice: Negotiating Forward- and Backward-Looking Outcomes* (Lanham, Md.: Rowman & Littlefield, 2005).

[35]Zartman, *Governance as Conflict Management.*

need. The outcome is either a "time at the trough" mentality, in which a succession of military leaders take power for brief, enriching periods, as in Sierra Leone, or a more stable because more repressive term of office that only makes the final conflict more intractable, as in Zaire/Congo. Dealing with the need base of conflict often requires first dealing with the state greed base of need.

State weakness and collapse are the result of many causes, at all levels. External forces, such as drought or terms of trade for primary exports, take their toll, beyond the capabilities of the state to handle the challenge. Internal incapacity or self-destructiveness is involved, for government leaders embarked on a wrong path are not eager to admit mistakes and change course; when taking the wrong path becomes profitable and profit becomes its motive, appeals to civic spirit and future conflict avoidance lack persuasiveness. As in the case of political entrepreneurs of conflict, the occurrence of state leaders capable of facing their challenges is also a matter of chance. The international community, working through interested states or international institutions, can also let its concerns with global politics override local needs for help and can thus contribute to state weakness and conflict, as well as to state strengthening and responsiveness.[36] The wide range and interlocking nature of state failure's cause makes it difficult to forestall the creeping onset of need.

The focus on overcoming state failure is a swing of the contemporary pendulum. In the previous century, the focus of concern was rather on limiting the excess powers of the state.[37] Prevention rose as a subject of analysis in the 1990s, but it is difficult to practice, because the causes of state weakness and collapse are notoriously inhospitable to efforts to remedy the situation, and so it has fallen away as a subject too difficult to handle.[38] Avoiding state collapse and failure obviously does not mean swinging the pendulum so far in the opposite direction that it revives the concerns of the previous era, but that danger is far away. In the post–Cold War era,

---

[36]Robert Rotberg, ed., *Preventing Failure* (Princeton, N.J.: Princeton University Press, 2004); I. William Zartman, "Early and 'Early Late' Prevention," in *Making States Work*, ed. Simon Chesterman, Michael Ignatieff, and Ramesh Thakur (Tokyo: United Nations University Press, 2005).

[37]Theda Skocpol, "Bringing the State Back In," *Items* 36, nos. 1–2 (June 1982): 1–8.

[38]The preventive—mislabeled "preemptive"—action in Iraq has also illustrated in reality all the problems of support and consequences that the prevention debate brought out in discussion, and probably helped to squash the earlier focus on prevention.

where international political rivalries are not strong enough to justify the effort and expense of propping up weak allies, state building needs to be restored to importance because of the threat of the quicksand of failure and collapse that will impose domestic casualties and draw in the external world when remedies become much more difficult and costly.[39]

The cases illustrate various reasons for the neglect of prevention or for its deflection when attempted. Notoriously rapacious governance lay at the heart of state weakness and collapse in Stevens' Sierra Leone and in Mobutu's Zaire; Cold War disinterest protected the kleptocratic regime in Sierra Leone; and Cold War interests protected incompetent regimes in Zaire and Afghanistan and even supported debilitating conflict in Afghanistan and Angola. Internal pacts that had outrun their usefulness provided the basis for state weakness and marginalized populations in Lebanon and Colombia.

The sad fact is that, given these causes and the international norms of the times, preventive intervention would have been extremely difficult to accomplish. It was attempted in 1979 in Zaire, and the regime completely undid Western efforts to reform the government; *fin de régime* opportunities in the first half of the 1990s were let slide by the interested Troika of Belgium, France, and the United States with studied inattention.[40] Syrian mediation was attempted at the outset of the Lebanese civil war in 1975 and, lacking sufficient international backing, was rebuffed by the parties intent on pursuing their conflict, until the Arab states finally handed the collapsed state back to Syria ten years later.

Changing norms in the twenty-first century may strengthen the possibilities for constructive intervention in such cases and remove the reasons of global politics to protect incompetent regimes, but they also remove the interest in costly and delicate interventions in poor, weak, "unimportant" states. Prevention is admittedly hard to practice and to justify.[41] The threat of widespread conflict as a result of state weakness and discrimination

[39]Bruce Jentleson, ed., *Opportunities Missed, Opportunities Seized: Preventive Diplomacy in the Post–Cold War Period* (Lanham, Md.: Rowman & Littlefield, 2000); I. William Zartman, *Cowardly Lions: Missed Opportunities to Prevent State Collapse and Deadly Conflict* (Boulder, Colo.: Lynne Rienner, 2005).

[40]Zartman, *Cowardly Lions.*

[41]Gareth Evans and Mohamed Sahnoun, ed., *The Responsibility to Protect: Report of the International Commission on Intervention and State Sovereignty* (Ottawa: International Development Center, 2001); Chesterman, Ignatieff, and Thakur, *Making States Work.*

may improve the justification for intervention by the international community, but appropriate and effective practices remain elusive.[42]

State strengthening involves building the institutional capacity for handling demands and sharpening appropriate policy responses. Institutional capacity comes from trusted, accountable, and representative bodies and routines for processing needs and responding to them equitably; appropriate policies come from clear analysis and informed responses. If these are not provided domestically, as a result of the weaknesses of the state they are needed to remedy, it remains for the international community to advise, urge, and impel reforms. "Compellence"—the opposite of deterrence—is still beyond international norms and capabilities.[43]

Dealing with conflict in its middle period, while still in the creed phases, may be more promising, if only because the conflict provides its own urgency and justification for some remedial action. At this period, control of conflict requires first an end or at least suspension of its violence and then the crafting of a new political system capable of responding to the grievances that caused the conflict in the first place. Managing a conflict already in course has the advantage of dealing with more or less clear sides and grievances, which may not have been clarified in the earlier period. It also has the advantage of operating with a ripening context, where a mutually hurting stalemate can either be seized or, if absent or unperceived, produced by the intervener to push the parties into consideration of measures for managing the conflict. But it has the disadvantage of taking place in the midst of fresh wounds as well as grievances, when it is no longer possible to end the conflict by addressing the original substantive complaints. Thus the invention of a new political system to bring in the marginalized is likely to be an additional, procedural requirement for the restoration of harmony.

It is rare to find the capacity for such measures among the parties to the conflict themselves, which tend to be too busy and engrossed in the conflict to think of and be attentive to measures to end it. Mediators from the outside are needed: The parties to a conflict need help. Such mediators may be required to act as communicators, to get the parties to hear each other; or as formulators, to get them to focus on new ideas for a solution; or even as manipulators, to expand their options and provide better outcomes to draw

[42]Collier et al., *Breaking the Conflict Trap.*
[43]Thomas Schelling, *The Strategy of Conflict* (Cambridge, Mass.: Harvard University Press, 1960), 195.

them away from conflict.[44] Problems abound in such mediation: The conflict may not be ripe enough to turn the parties' attention to resolution, a solution may require legitimizing unappetizing parties, needs for justice can trouble the search for peace and rebuilding, reconstructing may require heavy outlays from external sources with only indirect interest in the area, and heavy-handed intervention may be necessary to bring unwilling combatants to conciliation.

Such measures were tried in many of the cases. Interested neighbors and states further abroad made attempts at mediation and reform in Lebanon in the late 1970s and early 1980s, in Afghanistan in the late 1980s and early 1990s, and in Sierra Leone, Angola, and Zaire in the early and middle 1990s. For the most part, these failed because a good effort was pursued halfheartedly, addressing only some of the sources of grievance, without the necessary perseverance and pressure required to overcome the conflict. The Colombians themselves undertook a major constitutional reform toward a new political system in the early 1990s; the reform efforts were compromised by assassination campaigns of right-wing militias allied to the army, the burgeoning drug trade, and the continued neglect of rural areas. The cases indicate the way to control conflict but also underline the deep investment in political engagement required to make the mediation and reform work.

Beyond the mediations themselves lay the reforms required: Procedural demands for inclusion, not just redress of past substantive grievances, were the subject of reforms in the political systems of Lebanon, Colombia, Zaire, Afghanistan, Angola, and Sierra Leone. Because they were not satisfied with promises of new supplies and distributions, marginalized groups and populations demanded to be among the suppliers and distributors. It is important to note that at this stage, it was not a struggle for material resources that motivated the groups and underlay the settlement but a demand for political resources through the sharing of power to decide the distribution of resources. Variously styled identity groups in Lebanon, Sierra Leone, Zaire, and Angola "wanted in" and would not be satisfied by a mere redistribution of resources by a government they no longer saw as legitimate.

---

[44]Saadia Touval and I. William Zartman, eds., *International Mediation in Theory and Practice* (Westport, Conn.: Westview Press, 1985); Saadia Touval and I. William Zartman, "International Mediation after the Cold War," in *Turbulent Peace*, ed. Chester Crocker, Fen Hampson, and Pamela Aall (Washington, D.C.: United States Institute of Peace Press, 2001).

The process of bringing them in to some degree or other brought an end to the conflicts at the creed stage.

If obstacles to conflict reduction in the previous periods were not enough, it is at the "end" of the conflict, when the race to greed has denatured the rebellion and further weakened the state, that the task of ending the conflict becomes the most daunting. Rebels need to be bought out of their lairs, but eviscerated states need to have their dry bones reassembled to get the business of governance started. For some reason (which may have to do with matters of legitimacy, curiously), it has seemed easier to buy off rapacious rulers than thieving thugs, as is shown by the cases of Jean-Bedel Bokassa of the Central African "Empire," Charles Taylor of Liberia, François Duvalier and Raoul Cedras of Haiti, the late Idi Amin of Uganda, and Fernando Marcos of the Philippines, among others.

In the end, it is doubtful if conflicts that have passed into the greed period can be brought under control without military force. Greedy leaders—both rulers and rebels—are not just money-greedy; they are power-greedy at the same time. The only way to bring them under control is to threaten, or eventually eliminate, the supply of power and money. Experiences in Peru, Afghanistan, Angola, and Sierra Leone show that rebel movements tend to fall apart when their charismatic and usually greedy leader is removed, especially if the state also begins to respond to the underlying popular grievances born of need at the same time. Experiences in the Congo, Sierra Leone, and Lebanon show that the state, or what is left of it, is up for grabs when the greedy and usually charismatic leader is removed, either to be further looted or to be reconstructed, depending on the leaders available for succession. Removal seems to be the key to change in both cases. It took more or less fifteen years and the direct military intervention of an external force to bring the conflicts under control in Lebanon, Sierra Leone, and Zaire/Congo,[45] much longer if one goes back to the roots of the conflict. In Colombia, their drug habit has made both the FARC and AUC fully unmanageable, with no prospects for control, and remnants of Sendero Luminoso in Peru have also begun to take up the habit. Furthermore, it takes an extremely well-disciplined military not to fall prey to the same temptations of greed as the ones they were sent to bring under control, as experiences in the same four conflicts show.

---

[45]This is also the case for Angola, if the stories about the covert external assistance in Savimbi's assassination are accurate.

At the end of this process comes state collapse, if it did not come earlier, with the enormous cost and effort that reinstatement involves.[46] At the beginning of the twenty-first century, Afghanistan and Sierra Leone are international wards, painfully emerging from their collapse, and Lebanon and the Congo were occupied by their neighbors. Climbing back up the hill to the reinstatement of legitimate and responsive authority has been an exhausting challenge for all four. If Lebanon is ahead of the others in that climb, it is because its peace agreement came a decade and more earlier and because the strong arms of Syria were used to install the state, legitimate or not. In Colombia, Peru, and Angola, the state has actually been strengthened to varying degrees by its response to its conflict. Yet the writ of the state in Afghanistan, the Congo, Colombia, and Angola still remains ineffective in large parts of its own territory, and the rebellions in many of these countries have become so indomitable because they have been incurably hooked on drug money. All these cases are the strongest argument for dealing with conflict early, before poverty becomes discrimination and both governance and protest become privatized. As for need, creed, and greed, the ills that conflicts breed: It is best to stop them early, lest the need feed creed and creed feed greed.

[46]Zartman, *Collapsed States*.

Index

Note: Notations of *n*, *t*, or *f* after page numbers indicate notes, tables, or figures.

Abacha, Sani, 245
Abidjan accord, 102
academic research, policymakers and, 248–49
accumulation strategies, 110
aerial interdiction program, 76–77, 80
Afghanistan: anti-Soviet war, 212, 214–15, 221, 225–26, 227; conflict and competition, 225–27, 275; as failed state, 206; identity mobilization, 273; journalistic notions, 209; as narco-state, 207; Northern Alliance, 214, 218; Operation Enduring Freedom, 218; overview, 19–21; political entrepreneurs, 272; regional conflicts, 211–13, 221–25; state failure, 206, 217–21, 271; transitional administration, 210, 218, 220, 225, 230, 233*n*
African World War, 172
agrarian reform, 56
agriculture: drugs in Lebanon, 33, 34; Lebanon, 31, 31*n*; Peru, 55–56
air bridge denial program, 76–77, 80
Alipio, 79
Alliance for Progress, 190
All People's Congress (APC) party, 87, 92–93
alluvial diamonds, 111, 133
al Qaeda: Afghan Arabs, 215; effort to eradicate, 21; funding through drugs, 232; Taliban link, 19, 207, 208, 211; targets and supporters, 232
alternative development, 198*n*
Alvor Accords, 113
Amal, 25, 32, 33, 35, 37, 47

Amal Shiite militia forces, 25
amnesties, Angola, 122, 123
Anglo American, 160, 161, 173
Anglogold, 169*n*
Angola: Cold War, 16, 108; as collapsed state, 270–71; diamond sector, 116, 120, 128, 132; DRC invaded, 140–41; elites, 131, 239; independence wars, 16, 107–8, 112–14; nationalist movements, 112; natural resources, 107; oil, 6*n*, 116, 121–22, 129–33, 134, 138–39; overview, 16–17; political entrepreneurs, 272; second war, 147, 148. *See also* MPLA (Popular Movement for the Liberation of Angola); UNITA (Popular Movement for the Total Independence of Angola)
Angolanization, 114
Angola Sanctions Committee (UN), 246–47
Annan, Kofi, 243
anticolonialism, 270–71
anticolonial nationalism, 257–58
antidrug police, 62
antiterrorism legislation, 69, 70, 72–74, 78
antiterrorist police, 73
Aoun, Michel, 25, 45, 45*n*
Apurímac, Peru, 55
Arafat, Nasser, 32
Arana Franco, Luis, 70, 74
Aristotle's Syllogism, 263
armed conflict: designing prevention, 249; natural resources, 96–97
armed strike, 68

Armenian ASALA, 31
arms trade: Afghanistan, 205, 215, 218; Africa, 134, 135; Colombia, 200; diamond sales, 168, 168*n*; gold mining, 169; military merchants, 166
artisanal diamond mining, 163, 167, 168; redistribution effects, 175–77
artisanal gold mining, 163–64, 168–69
artisanal mining: DRC, 150, 162, 163; militarization of, 165–77; networks and peace prospects, 172–77; reconstruction of networks, 177
ASCORP, 118, 128, 129
ascriptive identity, 263
Ashanti, 169*n*
assimilados, 112, 113, 119
Association des Exploitants Artisanaux du Katanga, 172
Axworthy, Lloyd, 235, 245
Ayacucho, Peru, 55, 56, 81, 82

Bah, Ibrahim Baldeh, 101
Bakongo population, 112, 114
banditry, 137
banking: DRC, 156, 157; exchange rate speculation, 166–67; Lebanon, 28*n*, 43, 44; secrecy laws, 245–46; UK, 245–46
Banyamulenge Tutsi, 146–47, 149, 273
Barrick Gold, 161
Bedie, Henri Konan, 102
Beirut, 46
Belaúnde Terry administration, 71, 82
Belgian Congo, 160–61
Belgium, 118, 133, 134, 247
belligerents, reforms to curb, 136
Bemba, Jean-Pierre, 149
Berdal, Mats, 4
Berri, Nabih, 40*n*
Bhutto, Zulfiqar Ali, 211, 213
Bicesse Peace Accords (1991), 115, 126
big-men patrons, 154, 175
Bio, Stephen, 102
black market activities, 229
Bockarie, Sam (Maskita), 100
Bolas, Carlos, 201
Bolivarian Movement, 200

Bolivia, 195
Bonn Accords (2001), 208, 218, 220, 230
border regions: Afghanistan, 219, 228; illicit trade, 219; Syria-Lebanon, 30, 30*n*
Botswana, 96, 96*n*, 138
Boulle, Jean-Raymond, 159
Briceño, Jorge (Mono Jojoy), 201
building construction regularization, 40
Bundu, Abass, 93
Burkina Faso, 102, 127
Burundi, 145, 169
Bush, George W., 80

Cabinda Enclave Liberation Front, 113*n*, 137
Caisse des Carburants (State Fuel Fund), 34–35
Cambodia, 238, 239
Cameroon, 136*n*
Canada, 159, 161; in DRC, 244; mining and minerals sector, 244; sanctions reform, 246, 254
Canadian Banro, 173–74
Canadian Foreign Ministry, 235
capital flight, 42
capitalism, Lebanon, 48–49
Carter, Jimmy, 124
case studies, 261–62
Castellanos, Henry, 201
causality, 261
cease-fire agreements: Colombia, 199; Lebanon, 47, 49
central Africa, resource research, 3
central Asia: Afghan regional conflict, 222, 223–25, 232; anti-Soviet war in Afghanistan, 212; drug trade, 223, 224; praetorianism, 212
Central Intelligence Agency (CIA), 69
central state: Afghanistan, 21; notion rejected, 20
certification of natural resource sectors, 240–41
Chad, 136*n*
chain of warranties, 241
Chamoun, Camille, 35
Chechnya, 212

Chekka racket, 37*n*

child soldiers: DRC, 143, 157, 176; Sierra Leone, 87, 97–98, 99

China, 59, 173, 222, 226, 244. *See also* Maoist ideology

Christians in Lebanon, 24–25, 45*n*; drug income, 31; ethnic cleansing, 36; internal history, 25; militia defeat, 35; Palestinian refugees, 38

civic action projects, 72

civil servants, 39

civil society: Pakistan, 222; role of NGOs, 105

civil wars: Afghanistan's history of, 211; basic assumptions, 237; designing prevention, 249; economic agendas, 3, 239; after end of Cold War, 2; momentum, 8–9; per Collier, 4; preconditions for, 143–44; prevention and management, 278–84; primary commodity exports, 6; variables and risk, 4, 6; warlords and economics, 8. *See also* conflicts

Clark amendment, 124

clientelism: big-men patrons, 154; clientelist presidency, 118; Lebanon, 48–49, 50; networks in DRC, 18, 153–58, 175; oil revenues, 130; oil and state rents, 130–31, 131*n*

Coalition forces: attack on Afghanistan, 19, 207–8, 231; international terrorism, 232; renewing war, 217–18

cobalt, 124, 170–71

coca eradication programs: Peru, 14, 61–62, 80

coca-growing areas: grower unrest, 80–81; Peru, 53, 54, 60–62, 76, 77, 78–79, 81

cocaine trade: Colombia, 179; decline in Peru, 76–77, 83; Sendero Luminoso revenues, 69, 79

coca production: coca prices, 76, 80; Colombia, 179, 179*n*, 192, 195; income decline in Peru, 15; Peru, 13, 76, 80

coffee prices, 186, 187*f*

coffee production, 180, 184–88, 190

Cold War: Afghanistan, 213; Angolan independence, 108; conflict prevention neglected, 280; effect of logic, 1; internal conflict frameworks, 257; in Latin America, 190; oil and diamonds, 130*n*; "old" and "new" wars, 2; strategic actors in Angola, 16

collapsed states, 2. *See also* state collapse

collective identity, 25

collective memory, 24

Collier, Paul: argument summarized, 96; causes of conflict, 259–60; critiques of, 7; economic theory of conflict, 203; on greed factors, 253*n*; greed vs. grievance summarized, 4–6; influence of, 4; primary commodity importance, 109

Colombia: coca production, 77; conflict continuing, 275; constitutional reform, 282; drug cartels, 196; multipolar violence, 183*t*, 191–95; oil rents, 6*n*; Peru coca growing, 61, 76, 77; phases of conflict, 183*t*; political entrepreneurs, 272; relative deprivation, 271; selective or partial state failure, 271; La Violencia, 178, 181, 183*t*, 184–88. *See also* drug trade; ELN; FARC

coltan (columbite tantalite) trade, 169–70; defined, 18*n*; foreign armies in Congo, 18

commodity exports. *See* primary commodity exports

Communist Party of Peru, Patria Roja, 81, 82

Communist Party of Peru—Pukallacta, 82

Communist Party of Peru. *See* Sendero Luminoso (Shining Path)

communist self-defense groups, 188, 189, 190

Compaoré, Blaise, 86, 101–2

comparative case studies, 261–62

compellence, 281

comptoirs, 162, 163–64, 170

conflict actors, 9

conflict diamonds, 120, 126, 135, 240

conflict prevention/resolution, policies per Collier, 6–7

conflicts: confrontation phase, 268; consolidation phase, 267–68; mobilization dynamic, 267–68; nature of, 256–57; preconflict conditions and triggers, 266; prevention and management, 278–84; prolonged, 269; resolution phase, 268; sources of, 257–62; stages, 274; stalemates, 274; task of ending, 283. *See also* civil wars

confrontational identities, 138

Congolese Liberation Movement (ML)C, 149

Congo. *See* Democratic Republic of the Congo (DRC, formerly Zaire)

consensus democracy, 24

Conservative party of Colombia, 184, 186, 188

conservatives, Lebanon, 46

constitutional reform, 282

consumption, traditional vs. modern, 176–77

Conteh, Hassan, 103

co-optation, 122, 155

copper, 170–71

copper/cobalt ore, 171, 172n

corporate codes of conduct, 243, 251

corruption: Angola, 118, 129–30; DRC, 143; grand corruption, 250; Lebanon, 13, 27, 50; OECD measures, 250; oil and diamond revenues, 13; policy instruments, 21; prebendal, 266; reforms, 137; Senderista appeal, 65–66; tracing proceeds, 255

Côte d'Ivoire, 102–3, 127

Council of the South, 40n

coups d'état, Sierra Leone, 86–87, 88

creed. *See* need, creed, and greed argument

Cuango Mining Corporation, 127

Cuba: in Angola, 112, 114, 124; oil interests, 130, 130n

Cuban revolution, 190

cultural antagonisms, Lebanon, 24

currency issues, 157

da Costa, Fernando, 202

data issues, 261–62

death squads. *See* paramilitary groups

De Beers, 130n, 133, 162n

Defensoría del Pueblo (Peru), 74

Degregori, Carlos Iván, 58

Dembo, Antonio, 123

demobilization processes, 115

Democratic Allied Front for the Liberation of the Congo (AFDL), 148

Democratic Republic of the Congo (DRC, formerly Zaire): institutional grievances, 259; international involvement, 146–48, 244; interventions, 116; Kivu province, 144–46, 150; network war, 151–53; origins and causes of war, 144; overview, 17; Panel of Experts report, 247; sanctions, 247; UNITA support, 129

deprivation, theories of, 265

deregulation, benefits to conflict entrepreneurs, 10

developers, Lebanon, 39

development banks, mining and minerals, 159

Diamang, 130n

diamond certification system, fraudulent, 134

diamond digging, male identity and, 175–76

diamonds, alluvial, 111

diamond sector: Angola, 116, 120, 128, 132; big-men patrons, 154; certification systems, 134, 135, 240–41; conflict diamonds, 120, 126, 135; DRC, 167; explanatory significance, 85–86; feasibility of conflict, 253; foreign armies in Congo, 18; functions of, 138; informal sector, 158, 162–65; invading army patrons, 166; Kabila monopoly, 167; Kamajors, 104; Kasai region, 167; Kisangani region, 168; liberalized, 162; looting in Sierra Leone, 15, 85, 96–97; military officers, 103; Nigerian officers, 104; purchasing monopoly, 167n; regulating, 133–35; sanctions campaign, 134–35; Sankoh role, 99–100; Savimbi's rule, 122; Tshikapa region, 168; UNITA,

108, 116, 124, 125–29; UN peace-keepers, 105

diamond smuggling: Sierra Leone, 100, 102

diaspora: political divisions, 45; role of, 51; sectarian support, 44–45, 49

diaspora complex, 44

diaspora remittances: benefits of conflict, 5; Lebanon, 13, 29, 42–43, 42*n*, 44, 51; policies to control financing, 243

discrimination: identity and, 262, 263, 267

displaced populations: Afghanistan, 218, 223; Angola, 116, 137; DRC, 157

dollarization, 43, 44

domestic rents, 46

Dondo, Kengo wa, 154, 156, 156*n*, 158, 166

donors. *See* foreign donors

dos Santos, Eduardo, 112, 115, 118, 131, 132, 137, 239*n*

DRC. *See* Democratic Republic of the Congo (DRC, formerly Zaire)

drought, 57, 57*n*

drug cartels, 196

drug eradication programs: Afghanistan, 220; Peru, 14, 61–62, 80

drug trade: Afghanistan, 20–21, 207, 208, 216, 218, 219–21, 229, 232; capital accumulation, 32; central Asia, 223, 224; intensification of conflict, 7; Lebanon, 13, 28, 29–34, 51; overview of Colombia, 18–19; profitability in Lebanon, 32, 32*n*

drug trade in Colombia: FARC link, 181, 195–203; major groups, 179

Druze Parti Socialiste Progressiste, 32, 33, 36, 47

econometric data, 248

economic agendas, 139; in civil wars, 239; notion of, 8

Economic Agendas in Civil Wars project, 251*n*

Economic Community of West Africa Monitoring Group (ECOMOG), 104–5

economic conditions: Afghanistan, 210, 228–29; Angola, 117, 130; Colombia, 199; DRC, 142, 143, 162; effects of breakdown, 143; informal mining economy, 162; Lebanon, 12*n*, 46; Peru, 14, 56–57, 63, 69, 74, 82; Sierra Leone, 95, 95*t*

economic crimes, 22, 250

economic crisis, Lebanon, 34

economic decline, Peru, 63

economic development: Afghanistan, 20; Peru, 71; role in causing conflict, 7*n*

economic dimensions: of civil wars, 4, 238; of conflict, explaining, 258; Lebanese conflict, 26–28, 46; means and ends, 2; political agendas vs., 2; poverty and, 143–44; as primary motivation, 109; Sierra Leone, 85; system of profit and power, 238

economic exploitation, effects of, 259

economic growth, Lebanon, 26

economic inequality, 5

economic policies, effect on South, 254

economic resources: armed conflict and, 179; availability and rebel groups, 9; Lebanon, 28; role in war, 8–9; strategizing over, 205

economic sanctions. *See* sanctions

Eduardo dos Santos Foundation (FESA), 131

education: Angolan budget, 131; employment opportunities related, 98; levels and opportunity, 16; Peru, 14, 58, 64; as proxy for need, 96; risk of conflict, 98; Sierra Leone, 94; teachers focus of guerrillas, 58, 64

elites: Angola, 131, 239; DRC, 172, 174, 177; greed and, 275–76; individual behaviors, 249; Lebanon, 24, 25; role of economic factors, 252; Sierra Leone, 85–86, 92, 94; tracking finances of, 241; trade-offs necessary for peace, 236

El Murr, Michel, 40*n*

El-Ndine, Talal, 101

ELN (Ejército de Liberación Nacional), oil rents, 6*n*, 19, 181–82, 190, 191, 193–94, 195

El Salvador, 238
emigration: Lebanon, 27, 28, 42, 42n; reasons for financial support, 44
end of Cold War: civil wars after, 2
Essy, Amara, 102
ethical void, 142–43, 157
ethnic cleansing, 36
ethnic conflicts, 2; Afghanistan, 230, 273–74; Angola, 115, 273; Congolese diversity, 150n; discrimination in Peru, 14, 58, 273; identity and, 267; land related, 41; Lebanon, 12, 24, 41; polarization among groups vs., 4; Sierra Leone, 95
ethnic identity, and political entrepreneurs, 273–74
ethnicity and Shining Path ideology, 59
exclusion, politics of, 149
expertise gap in Middle East, 42
external rents, 46
extortion: Colombia, 180, 182, 193, 197, 205; Peru, 79–80
extraversion process, 159

Fadika, Kemoh, 88
failed states. *See* state failure
Falcon Oil & Gas, 130n
FARC (Fuerzas Armadas Revolucionarias de Colombia, Revolutionary Armed Forces of Colombia): financing, 196; influence of drug trade, 19, 181; military dimension, 200; origins, 189–90; peasant farmers, 197–98; Peruvian link alleged, 79–80; ransoms, 195; self-defense groups, 198; size and influence, 181, 191, 199
Fatal Transactions campaign, 135
FATF. *See* Financial Task Force on Money Laundering
financial sectors: Lebanon, 28n; London, 245–46; monitoring, 242, 251; secrecy for conflict beneficiaries, 245–46; white list, 242
Financial Task Force on Money Laundering (FATF), 241–42
Fondo Nacional de Compensación y Desarrollo Social (National Compensation and Social Development Fund, or FONCODES), 75
food aid, 75, 228–29
forced displacement campaigns, 38–39, 38n
Forces Armées Rwandaises, 146
foreign actors: Afghanistan, 20, 213; Angola, 16; DRC, 17, 144; policy responses studied, 236; Sierra Leone, 16
foreign aid: Afghanistan, 213, 231–32; central Asia, 224; dependence, 110
foreign donors: in Afghanistan, 20, 211, 228–29, 231–32; policies and larger impact, 254
foreign investment, 74
formal economy, 151, 153, 157, 176–77
formal sector, mining, 158
Forrest, George, 127
Fourah Bay College, 87, 88, 90, 93
Fowler, Robert, 246
France, 247
Frangieh, Sleiman, 29–30, 37, 37n
Franque, Ranque, 113n
free market, institutional structures and, 161
Friedland, Robert, 159
Fujimori, Alberto, 67, 68, 69, 70, 72, 73, 77; rural support, 75
fundamentalist movements, Lebanon, 37–38

Gadhafi, Mu'ammar, 90, 91
Gambia, 90, 103
game theoretical approach, 259–60
García, Alan, 71–72, 75
García Márquez, Gabriel, 198n
garimpeiro generals, 129
garimpeiros (freelance diamond diggers), 125, 126
Gecamines mining company, 127, 156, 161, 165, 171, 171n
Gemayel, Amine, 40n
Gemayel, Bachir, 35
Geneva Accords (1988), 215, 226
genocidal oil, 121–22
Glasol trading company, 127
global economic flows, 252

global economy, link with, 152–53, 159
Global Issues Bureau, Canada, 235
globalization: benefits from conflict, 238–39; crime networks, 180*n*; dark side of, 10; elite opportunities, 236; impact on civil wars, 234; mining and minerals, 159–60; monopolies, 160; role in civil wars, 9–10
Global Witness, 235–36
gold concessions, 173*n*
gold mining: artisanal, 163–64
gold trade, 171*n*; foreign armies in Congo, 18
gold-trading networks, 168–69
Gómez, Laureano, 186*n*
Gordon, Olu, 90
governance: Afghanistan, 20; as conflict management, 278; failures and grievance, 10; policies supporting, 21–22; Sierra Leone overview, 16
governance crisis, Afghanistan, 210
governance networks, 152
Government of National Union, DRC, 173
gramaje, 198
greed: as cause or motive, 15; Colombian case, 204; elites and, 275–76; governance issues, 10; inventiveness of, 275; Lebanon, 27, 47; militia leaders, 47
greed versus grievance debate, 4–6
grievances: against Mobutu, 148–49; Colombia, 204–5; cumulative in DRC, 143; deprivation of basic needs, 262–63; economic vulnerability, 110; failures of governance, 10; feasible or durable, 7; institutional grievances, 259–60, 260*n*; manipulation of, 111; narrative of grievance, 5; objective, 7; objective grievance, 262*n*; operative terms, 263; public discourse as mask, 141; Savimbi's historical, 121–22; threats to subsistence, 65–66; types in Sierra Leone, 92
Grupo Especial de Inteligencia (Special Intelligence Group, or GEIN, Peru), 69–70
Guei, Robert, 102

guerrillas: alternative power structures, 182; criminal enterprises, 205; criminalization, 86; reasons for insurgency, 203–4; salaries, 62–63. *See also by individual group*
Gulf Oil (now Chevron), 130
Guzmán, Abimael, 52–53; capture of, 14, 15, 53, 68; as caudillo-teacher, 60; image, 69, 70; imprisoned, 77; jail conditions, 78; left opposition to, 82; legal maneuvers, 78; lifestyle, 63; negotiations, 70–71; political solution, 78, 79; teachers targeted, 58, 64; views of, 66–67

Hanciles, Cleo, 90
hashish, 29–30
heroin poppy production, 81
heterogenite, 171–72, 172*n*
Hizbollah, 25, 31, 32, 33, 37, 43
Hoeffler, Anke, 4
Holden, Roberto, 112
Houphouët-Boigny, Félix, 102
Huancavelica, Peru, 55, 57
Huaynalaya, Robert, 82
humanitarian assistance, 227
human rights: Afghanistan, 231; Colombia, 189, 205; Peru, 71–72, 73, 83; policy responses, 244
human rights organizations: Peru, 74
human security agenda, 235, 245
Hutu groups, 145, 146
Hutu/Tutsi conflict, 146

Iamgold, 160
ideal types, 261
identity: ascriptive, 263; discrimination and, 262, 263, 267; ethnic conflicts, 267; explaining conflict, 258; political entrepreneurs and, 267, 272–73; social class, 267; as source of conflict, 262, 263–64
identity-based grievances, Angola overview, 17
identity mobilization, 37
ideology, decline in, 259
immigrant groups, Congo, 145

income levels, Peru, 55–56
independence movements: Angola, 16, 107–8, 112–14; Congo mining sector, 160–61
Indonesia, 212
industrial workers, Lebanon, 27n
inflation, Lebanon, 43
influence peddling, 132
informal economy, DRC, 151, 157, 176–77
informal mining economy, 158, 162–65
informal networks, 154–55
institutional grievances, 259–60, 260n
Instituto de Defensa Legal, 74
insurance sectors, 251
insurgents. *See* guerrillas
intellectuals, guerrillas and, 198, 198n, 204
internal frontiers, 36–37
internal refugees. *See* displaced populations
international community response, 21, 236
International Criminal Court, 250
international criminal economy, DRC, 175
international diamond industry, 126
international drug networks: Lebanon, 34; Peru, 61
International Monetary Fund, 131, 132, 133
International Peace Academy, 8, 236
international policy community, 248–49
international terrorism, policy approaches, 242–43
Iparaguirre, Elena, 71
Iran, 220, 221, 222
Iraq, 279n
Israel: diamonds, 118, 133; Golani Brigade, 33; Lebanese factions, 25; sanctions busting, 247
Italy, 40n

Jackson, Jesse, 101
Jetley, Kumar, 104
jihâd, 24
Jiménez Baca, Benedicto, 69, 70

judges, 73–74
judicial system, Peru, 72–74

Kabba, Ahmed Tajan, 86
Kabba, Ali, 89
Kabila, Joseph, 141
Kabila, Laurent: appointments, 143, 158; cobalt, 171; death of, 141; De Beers agreement, 162n; diamond monopoly, 167; exclusion, politics of, 149; foreign protectors, 140–41; isolation, 172–73; mining administration, 161; networks, 157–58; overthrown, 148; party, 148; regime, 157–58; takeover, 18
Kagame, Paul, 147
Kamajors (local militias), 94, 104
Kanga, Max, 103
Kanu, Abu, 91
Karzai, Hamid, 227, 230–31
Keen, David, 3, 4
Khmer Rouge, 239
kidnapping, Colombia, 180, 182, 194–95, 197, 205
Kimberley Process Certification Scheme, 135, 240–41
Kinyarwanda speakers, 145, 146, 147
kleptocracies, 9n, 276
Konkola Deep Mining copper/cobalt project, 173
Kouwenhoven, Gus Van, 101–2
Kuhn, Thomas, 257
Kurdish PKK, 31
Kurdish tribes, 30
Kyrgyzstan, 224

labor movement: Sierra Leone, 88
labor power: Lebanon, 41–42
Lagos, Edith, 55
land: Colombia, 184, 185, 192; displacement in Lebanon, 38–39, 38n, 40–41; DRC, 145; ethnic divisions related, 41; Palestinian refugee camps, 38; significance in Lebanon, 41, 51; symbolic stake, 51; taxes on transactions, 39
land speculation: Lebanon, 28, 29
law, lack of application, 177

Lebanese businessmen in Sierra Leone, 103

Lebanese diamond traders, 164

Lebanese Forces, 25, 30, 33, 35, 36, 37, 40n, 43–44, 47

Lebanese miracle, 42

Lebanization, 27

Lebanon: border regions, 30, 30n; civil war effects on drug trade, 30; civil war functions, 50; conflict prevention, 280; debate over nature of civil war, 23–24; drug consumption, 30–31; external rents, 32; intraethnic conflict, 273; middle classes, 27; oil, 13, 28, 29, 32, 34–35, 50; overview, 12–13; political entrepreneurs, 272; relative deprivation, 271; resource debate, 12; Second Republic, 50; unique features, 24. *See also* Christians in Lebanon; diaspora remittances, Lebanon; drug trade, Lebanon; militia groups, in Lebanon

Liberal guerrillas, 188, 189, 190

liberalization: benefits to conflict entrepreneurs, 10; mining and minerals sector, 160; peace or war as outcomes, 22

Liberal Party of Colombia, 184, 186

Liberia: diamonds from Sierra Leone, 16; Libyan policy, 90; profits for elites, 239; refugees from Sierra Leone, 94; UN panel on Liberia, 136n. *See also* Taylor, Charles

Libya: Africa policy, 90; Kabba as student organizer, 89; political training, 90, 91

living standards, Peru, 14

Lomé peace agreement, 101, 102

lootability: commodity exports as principal source, 5; concept questioned, 19; lootable vs. unlootable resources, 6n; resource looting, 165–72; resource rents, 111

looting: Congo, 175; data on, 247; defined, 165; postconflict concerns, 100; tracing proceeds, 255

low-intensity conflicts, Colombia, 180, 183t, 190–91

Lukamba, Paulo (Gato), 123

Lusaka agreement (1999), 173

Lusaka Protocol (1994), 115, 116, 126, 127, 128

M-19 (April 19th Movement), 191, 191n

Malanga, Henri Monewiya (Pikoro), 163

Malaysia, 244

Mali, 160, 161

Mannesmann Anlagenbau AG, 193–94

Mansaray, Rashid, 91

Maoist ideology: Peru, 55, 59, 81, 82; Savimbi's use, 120

Marulanda Vélez, Manuel, 201

Marxism, on conflict, 257, 259

Marxist ideologies, 83

massacres: Lebanon, 24; Peru, 60, 71

Massoud, Ahmad Shah, 208, 215

Mbeki, Thabo, 174

Mbaye, Fatou, 100

mediators, outside, 281–82

mestiços, 108, 112, 113

military: Angolan diamonds, 128–29; clientelism in Angola, 118; Colombia, 182, 198; DRC implosion, 143; DRC privatization, 156, 156n; Peru, 62, 71–72; privatized and commercial, 152–53; Sierra Leone, 102

military commercialism, 152, 166

military coups: Colombia, 188; Sierra Leone, 86–87

military governments, Peru, 56, 60

military governors, 189

military spending, Angola, 129–30

militia entrepreneurs, 47, 48

militia groups, in Lebanon, 46–47; cooperation among, 33; demobilization, 43–44; diaspora, 43; drug activities, 30, 31–32; drug proceeds, 32; as entrepreneurs, 47, 48; financing logic, 35; fiscal domains, 36–37; income and control, 13; land issues, 39, leadership, 36–37, 47; oil smuggling, 34–35; outside financing, 29; religious conflicts, 35; territorial illusions, 36

Mingo, Dennis (Superman), 100

minimum wages: Lebanon, 42n; Peru, 64

Minin, Leonid, 101–2

mining codes, 174, 177

mining and minerals sector: Canada, 244; Congo, 18, 159–61; liberalization, 160; privatization, 161; South Africa, 160; working conditions, 171; world prices, 1

Mobutu Sese Seko, 17–18, 127; appointments, 143; dualism, 153–54; fragility, 147; governance changes, 155–56; lack of civil war, 142; mining, 161; networks, 154–55; regime ending, 140; struggle against, 148–49

models, 264

modernization without revolution, 48–49

Molina, Tomás, 201–2

Momoh, Joseph, 92, 93, 94

monetary system, DRC, 156, 157

money laundering, 43, 241–42, 254, 255

monopolies, 160

Montesinos, Vladimiro, 69

moral economy, 204

Movement for Progress in Africa (MOPA), 90–91

Movimiento Revolucionario Túpac Amaru (Túpac Amaru Revolutionary Movement, or MRTA), 61

MPLA (Popular Movement for the Liberation of Angola), 16, 112; accommodation and co-optation, 122; antitribalist policy, 121; criticism of, 119; diamond clientelism, 129; diamond sector control, 127; ideology and presidential politics, 117–19; notion of power, 132; oil revenues, 129–31; on UNITA, 139

mujahideen: Afghanistan, 217, 219, 221, 226, 227; Pakistan, 214–15

Mukamba, Jonas, 154

multilateral institutions, Lebanese recovery, 12

multinational corporations, regulation of, 240*n*, 243–44

Museveni, 148

Namibia, 116, 129

naming and shaming sanctions, 134, 135

Naphta, 130*n*

National Expertise Centre (DRC), 162

National Federation of Coffee Growers,185k, 186

National Forum for the Restoration of Democracy, 92

National Front (Colombia), 188, 189, 191

National Intelligence Service (SIN, Peru), 69

nationality law, DRC, 145–46

National Liberation Front for Angola, 16

National Liberation Front of Angola (FNLA), 112, 120, 273

National Patriotic Forces of Liberia (NPFL), 100, 101

National Popular Alliance (ANAPO), 191*n*

National Provisional Ruling Council (NPRC), 92, 103

nation-state framework: DRC, 152, 159; Lebanon, 48–49

natural gas, 224

natural resource rents, 6

natural resources: armed conflict, 96–97; dependence on, 252, 260; early Angolan conflict, 123–25; feasibility of conflicts, 253; functions of, 138; Lebanon, 40, 40*n*; as motive for war, 109; role of, 139

Nauru, 242

Ndorgbowusui uprising (1983), 94

need, creed, and greed argument: Angola, 107–8, 138; conflict-related, 256–57; contextualizing the debate, 12–22; greed controlling, 276–77; Lebanon, 51; as model, 270; natural resources, 138; refocusing the debate, 22; Shining Path (Peru), 54, 55, 61; Sierra Leone, 84–86, 96; summarized, 11–12

need factor: combination with grievances, 252–53, 252*n*; Lebanon, 26

negotiated settlements: Angola, 131–37; assumptions behind, 237; Cold War conflicts, 1; Colombia, 199; durability, 277–78; foreign aid tied, 174; greed weakening, 277; Lebanon, 47; mining

in DRC, 173–74; private sector role, 135–36; role of "spoilers," 3n; stages and outcomes, 274–75. *See also* peace processes
negotiations: Angola, 115, 123; Colombia, 200, 201; Shining Path (Peru), 70–71; UNITA diamond control, 127
Neto, Agostinho, 112, 117
networks in mining sector (DRC), 158–65
network war, 151–53
New York Accords, 114
Nigeria, 104, 105, 245
Nindjas, 164
Njala University College, 87
nongovernmental organizations (NGOs): Angola, 135; Sierra Leone, 105
nonstate actors: Afghanistan, 20; economic resources, 9
Norman, Hinga, 104, 104n
nutritional consumption, 57, 64, 65–66
Nyerere, Julius, 140–41

objective grievance, 262n
Occidental Petroleum Company, 194
OECD (Organization for Economic Cooperation and Development), 241, 250
oil: Angola, 116, 121–22, 124, 132–33; Colombian boom, 181–82, 186n, 193–94, 193f, 194f; functions of, 138; genocidal oil, 121–22; military spending in Angola, 129–31; regulating, 132–33; Talisman in Sudan, 244–45
oil companies, foreign, 130, 131, 132–33
oil prices, 123–24, 130; militias in Lebanon, 32
oil rents, 130; Angola, 138–39
oil resources: Angola, 16–17; boom in Colombia, 19; Lebanon, 13
oil smuggling, Lebanon, 28, 29, 34–35, 50
Okoto, Jean-Charles, 168
open markets, war profiteering, 22
opium poppy production: Afghanistan, 20, 207, 214, 216, 219, 221, 233n; Colombia, 196–97; Taliban ban, 220, 229–30, 229n

opportunity: causality and, 261; greed over resources, 262; lack of, 16; motive and, 254
opportunity model, 142–44
oppressed identity, 144
organized crime, policy instruments, 21, 242
Osores Ocampo, Rodolfo, 54n
Ottoman holdovers: fiscal domains, 37; patrimonial domination, 48; sectarianism, 38; sources of wealth, 48; tax collection, 41
Ovimbundu population, 113, 117, 119, 121, 122

País Libre, 195
Pakistan: Afghan disease, 222; Afghanistan regional issues, 211, 213, 215; anti-Soviet war, 221, 222; Coalition ally, 208; intelligence, 214
Palestinian refugee camps, 38
Palestinian Salvation Front, 31
Palomino, Nelson, 80
Pan-African Union (PANAFU), 90–91
paramilitary groups, Colombia, 19, 180, 182, 192–93, 194, 202, 205, 275
patrimonial domination, 48
Patriotic Union party (UP), 200
patronage: Afghanistan, 217; Angola, 129, 138; economic resources and personalist rule, 9
Payne, Donald, 101
peacebuilding, postconflict, 237–38
peacekeeping missions: Angola, 116; beneficiaries in Sierra Leone, 104–5; diamond trade profits, 15
peace processes: assumptions, 237; Colombia, 200–201, 205; Democratic Republic of Congo, 141, 150; economic resources and, 179–80; recommendations, 139; reforms to process, 136. *See also* negotiated settlements
peasant farmers: Afghanistan, 219, 220, 227; coca growers in Colombia, 197–98; coca growers in Peru, 61; FARC and, 197–98; Lebanon, 34; Peru, 55–58; Sierra Leone, 94

peasant self-defense patrols, 15, 68, 71, 72
Pena, Arlindo (Ben Ben), 125
pendulum image, 257, 258
People's Progressive Party, 93
personalist rulers, 9; Angola, 117–19
Peru: asymmetric victory, 275; Maoist ideology, 55, 59, 81, 82; political entrepreneurs, 272; selective or partial state failure, 271. *See also* coca-growing areas; drug trade; economic conditions; Sendero Luminoso; university students
petro-regime, 119
Philippines, 242
pillage: DRC, 144; Sierra Leone, 85
PLO (Palestine Liberation Organization), 25, 32
plundering: DRC mining networks, 165; DRC state resources, 155; looting defined, 165
police intelligence, 72
policy instruments, overview, 21
policymakers, academic research and, 248–49
policy responses, 239–44; coercive, 239–40; exemplary, 240; financial, 240; rhetorical, 240
political agendas: Afghanistan, 213; Colombian guerrillas, 182; motivations for conflicts, 252–53; predatory behavior, 2; rebel movements, 2
political economy of civil wars, 4, 204
political economy of conflict, 3, 252
political economy perspective, 237–39
political elites: DRC, 148; Sierra Leone, 92, 104
political entrepreneurs, 266–67, 272–74; identity factor, 272–73, 273–74
political exclusion, 60
political ideologies: Lebanon, 46; Shining Path (Peru), 54, 83
political repression, 5, 269
political structures: Afghanistan, 231, 231*n*; DRC, 142; Lebanon, 48, 49, 50; Sierra Leone, 111–12; spoil politics, 111–12

Popular Movement for the Liberation of Angola. *See* MPLA
Popular Movement for the Total Independence of Angola. *See* UNITA
Portuguese colonialism in Angola, 108, 113, 123–24
potato production, 57
poverty: Afghanistan, 227; conflict related, 258; rebellion and, 265; relative deprivation vs., 6; social dislocation and, 151, 157; state incapacity and, 266
praetorianism, 212
predatory accumulation, 85–86, 95–96
predatory behavior: political agendas, 2; UNITA, 128
presidential rule, Angola, 117–19
Pretoria agreement (2003), 173
prevention, 279–81
preventive intervention, 280–81
primary commodity exports: access to value chain, 110; coca in Peru, 14; coca production as, 14, 192; coffee in Colombia, 180, 184–88; conflicts characterized, 110; export booms, 186*n*; as lootable resources, 5, 96; as main motivation, 109; role in conflict, 7–8
primary school students, 88
private sector: policy response, 240, 243–44; in situations of conflict, 251
private-sector actors, compact, 243–44
privatization: Angola, 118; minerals and mining sector, 161; Peru, 74–75; of political space, 155–57
ProDev, 130*n*
proneness, 261
propositions, in case studies, 261

Qualitoles, 166–67

Rally for Congolese Democracy (RCD), 149
Ramírez, Fabián, 201–2
Ramírez Durand, Oscar Alberto (Feliciano), 70, 71, 79
Reagan, Ronald, 130

real estate, Lebanon, 39, 40, 40*n*

rebellions: capture of resources, 5; causes of, 203–4; motivations, 4–5; natural resource dependence, 260; objective of, 6; poverty and, 265; state collapse and, 276

rebel movements, 2; economic motives and objectives, 9; outcomes, 283; resource availability and, 9

Reconciliation Commission (Sierra Leone), 94

reconstruction: Afghanistan, 218, 225, 227; business of, 49; DRC, 150–51; international organizations, 151; Lebanon, 27, 49; Taliban view, 228

recovery, Afghani challenges, 210

reggae musicians, 88–89

regional conflicts: Afghanistan, 209, 211–13, 221–25, 232; regulatory efforts, 250–51; Sierra Leone, 16

regulatory instruments, 21

relative deprivation: Colombia, 271; Davies-Gurr theory, 263; deprivation, theories of, 265; Lebanon, 271; poverty vs., 6, 110–11, 258. *See also* need, creed, and greed argument

relief delivery, 228

religious conflicts: among Lebanese diaspora, 44; Lebanese militia groups, 35

rents, concept of, 6*n*

repentance (plea-bargaining) law, 70, 73, 74

reprisals, fear of, 106

Republic of the Congo, 116

resource dependence, 110

resource exploitation, 109

resource income: conflict's intractability, 12; market curbed, 10; opportunity creation, 12; role of, 3; role in political movements, 182

resource looting, 165–72

resource mobilization, 204

resource rents, 17, 110, 132

resources: availability of, 264; conceptualizing, 264; research on, 3; source of genuine grievances, 253; stages of conflict, 268–69

resource school of analysis, 262

resource wars, 252

revolutionary left: Lebanon, 46

Revolutionary Liberal Movement (Colombia), 190

Revolutionary United Front (RUF, Sierra Leone), 15; beneficiaries of conflict, 99–106; characterizing, 84–85; lumpen composition, 91–92; populist rhetoric, 91; rebellion criminalized, 99, 106; recruiting by, 97–98, 98*n*; student vanguardism, 88–92

rice dealing, 103, 104

Rindle, Fred, 101

rising expectations, 263, 265, 278

Rojas Pinilla, Gustavo, 191, 191*n*

rondas campesinas (peasant self-defense units), 15, 69, 71, 72

RUF. *See* Revolutionary United Front (RUF, Sierra Leone)

rule of law: breakdown in Lebanon, 24; DRC, 157

Rumsfeld, Donald, 206

Russia, 241

Rwanda: coltan trade, 170; DRC invaded, 140–41, 166; genocide, 144, 146; immigration from, 145–46; militia, 146; mining sector, 165, 166, 169; motives in Congolese war, 18; strategic agenda, 147–48; UNITA routes, 127

Salazar, Antonio, 113

sanction-monitoring mechanisms, 136

sanctions: Angola, 116, 134, 139; as policy response, 240, 246–48; reform of, 246

sanctions busting, 136, 246–47

Sankoh, Foday, 86, 91, 95, 99–100, 101*n*

Saudi Arabia, 226

Savimbi, Jonas: background, 119–20; Compaoré tie, 102; death of, 17, 108, 120, 123, 125, 239*n*; diamond earnings, 17, 138; electoral defeat, 115, 115*n*; grievances, 121–22; ideology, 120; as political entrepreneur, 119–23; South Africa tie, 120; support for,

Savimbi, Jonas (*continued*)
121–22; UNITA, 113, 114; on UN sanctions, 132
secondary sanctions, 134
secondary school students, 88
sectarianism in Ottoman era, 38
sectarian nationalism, 36
security forces, policy responses, 244
Sendero Luminoso (Shining Path): advance/challenging state, 54, 60–68; Artemio faction, 79; cultlike, 53, 55; decimation, 54, 68–77; described, 52–53; doctrinal development, 59; ethnic issue, 14; factions, 79–80; four stages summarized, 53–54; growth, reasons for, 55; Guzmán's capture, 68; ideology, 14, 58–60, 65–66; image, 65, 69; initiation, 53–54, 55–60; lifestyle, 63, 68; membership, 53; militants arrested, 70; origins, 13; overview, 13–15; Proseguir faction, 79–80; reasons for joining, 66–68; recent, 77, 78–79; resurgence attempt, 54, 77–83, 275; "strategic defeat," 14–15, 68–71, 74. *See also* Peru
Sendero Rojo (Red Sendero), 71
Sesay, Issa, 95
Shaba wars, 142*n*
shadow state, 9; as conflict actor, 9; defining, 9*n*; DRC, 154, 157
Shihab, Fuad, 30
Shiite Muslims: Afghanistan, 214; Lebanon, 25, 30, 31, 38, 45*n*, 47
Shining Path. *See* Sendero Luminoso (Shining Path)
Sierra Leone: child soldiers, 87, 97–98, 99; as collapsed state, 270; grievances, 92; political entrepreneurs, 272; regional aspects, 16; RUF origins and character, 15–16; system of profit and power, 238; university students, 85, 87–92; youth identity, 273. *See also* Revolutionary United Front (RUF, Sierra Leone)
Sierra Leone People's Party (SLPP), 92, 93
Sindicato Único de Trabajadores de la Educación Peruana (SUPTEP), 81–82

sobelization, 86
sobels, 86
social class: Congo, 17–18; identity appeals, 267; Lebanon, 26, 46; Peru, 14, 59; Sierra Leone, 15–16
social hierarchies, 176
social inequalities: Lebanon, 26
socially responsible policies, 243, 245–46
social mobility: DRC, 147; economic vulnerability and, 110; Peru, 58, 64; Sierra Leone, 93, 96, 97
social programs: Angola, 118; Peru, 15, 75
Solidere real estate project, 39, 40*n*
Somalia, 238
Sominki mining company, 164
sorcery, 176
South Africa: Angola policy, 124, 124*n*, 126; frontline state policy, 108; heterogenite, 172*n*; mining sector, 160, 174; UNITA ally, 114
Soviet Union, former USSR, 124
Special Security Division (Sierra Leone), 90
speculation: exchange-rate, 166–67; global economy and, 159
speculative real estate, Lebanon, 13
spoil politics, 111–12
squatters, Lebanon, 39, 39*n*
stalemates, 269, 274, 275
Starpoint Goldfields, 173*n*
state: as conflict actor, 9; core functions, 10
state absence, Colombia, 19
state collapse, 152, 265–66, 265*n*; cases of, 270–71; causes of, 279; compared, 284; DRC, 155; Mobutu regime, 17–18; prolonged conflict, 269; rebellion and, 276
state failure, 265, 265*n*; Afghanistan, 206, 217–21, 232; drug-trade related, 219; overcoming, 279–80
state-in-society model, 49*n*
state revenues, mining in DRC, 18
state terror, 243
Stevens, Siaka, 88, 93
street children, 151
structure of opportunity, 142–44

student expulsions, 89–90
student union government, 89–90
student vanguardism, 88–92
Sudan, 244–45
Sunni Muslims, Afghanistan, 214
Switzerland, 245, 246
Syria, 24*n*, 25; border regions, 30, 30*n*; drug activities in Lebanon, 33; Lebanese cease-fire, 49

Taif agreement, 23–24, 24*n*, 45, 45*n*, 49, 50
Tajikistan, 224
Taliban, 215–16; central Asia, 223; characterizing era, 226; ethnic appeals, 273–74; foreign aid, 228; links, 211; poppies banned, 220, 229–30, 229*n*; removed by Coalition, 19, 207–8; support for, 226
Talisman oil company, 244–45
tantalite. *See* coltan
Tanzania, 161
tax collection: Colombian guerrillas, 197, 197*n*; reforms, 136
Taylor, Charles, 16; as beneficiary, 100–101; Bockarie link, 100; Compaoré tie, 102; Côte d'Ivoire, 102; diamond proceeds, 100; role in Sierra Leone, 86, 87, 99
Taylor, Charles, Jr., 101
teachers' unions, Peru, 81–82
Tell ez-Zaatar refugee camp, 38
terrorist organizations: Afghanistan, 208; financing, 210–11
threat, discourse of, 36
timber industry, 241
time, concept of, 28–29, 46
Togo, 127
Toledo, Alejandro, 78, 79, 80, 82–83
toxic wastes, 40*n*
transaction commissions, 131*n*
treason against the mother country, 74
Tripoli militia, 33
Turkmenistan, 224

Uganda: DRC invaded, 140–41, 166; mining sector, 165, 166, 169; MLC,

149; motives in Congolese war, 18; strategic agenda, 147–48
Ukraine, 247
UNAVEM, 116
UN Convention against Transnational Organized Crime (2000), 242
UN Global Compact, 243–44
UN International Convention for the Suppression of the Financing of Terrorism, 242–43
UNITA (Popular Movement for the Total Independence of Angola): Cold War and, 16; control, 117; creation, 113; criticisms of, 139; diamond access, 108, 133; diamond windfall, 125–29, 138; ethnic conflict, 273; foreign allies, 120; Global Witness report, 235–36; guerrilla activities, 125, 128; history, 119–20; negotiations stance, 115; notion of power, 132; rule through fear, 122; status and survival, 120–21; support for, 139; UN sanctions, 134, 246–47
UNITA Renovada, 119, 123
United Kingdom, 147, 235–36, 235*n*, 236; financial sector regulation, 245–46; security force regulation, 244
United Nations, role of, 255
United Nations Counter-Terrorism Committee, 243
United Nations Mission in Sierra Leone (UNAMSIL), 104, 105
United Nations Mission in the Congo, 151
United Self-Defense Forces of Colombia (AUC), 275
United States: Afghan policy, 226, 229; Angola policy, 124, 126; central Africa policy, 147; Colombia policy, 190; food aid, 75; military aid, 190; missionary plane shot down, 76; narcotics diplomacy, 229; oil in Colombia, 194; Savimbi ally, 114; security force regulation, 244. *See also* U.S. Drug Enforcement Administration; war on drugs
University of Sierra Leone, 87

university students: Peru, 58, 64; political recruiting in Peru, 77, 81; Sierra Leone, 85, 87–92
UN Panel of Experts on the Illegal Exploitation of Natural Resources and Other Forms of Wealth of the Democratic Republic of the Congo, 175
UN panel on Liberia, 136*n*
UN Sanctions Committee, 134
UN Secretariat, 246
UN Security Council, 109, 134, 246; Permanent Monitoring Mechanism, 247–48
UN Security Council Resolution 1373, 243
Upper Huallaga River Valley, 195; coca fungus, 77; guerrilla income, 13; Senderista faction, 79; Shining Path, 60, 61
urban guerrillas: cells in Peru, 15; in Colombia, 199–200
U.S. Drug Enforcement Administration: Colombia, 202; Lebanon, 33–34; Pakistan, 214; Peru, 62. *See also* war on drugs
Uzbekistan, 208, 224

Velasco, Juan, 56
violence: economic vulnerability and, 110; extraction/production of resources, 111; functions of, 4; resource allocation, 110; Senderista, 65
La Violencia, 178, 181, 184–88, 188*f*
violent conflict: explanations, 2
Voluntary Principles on Security and Human Rights, 244

war, continuation as self-enrichment, 11
war crimes, 100
war of cultures, 24, 26, 50

war on drugs: U.S. policy in Colombia, 179, 195–96; U.S. programs in Peru, 61–62, 80. *See also* U.S. Drug Enforcement Administration
war economy: Afghanistan, 19–20; DRC, 158; elements of, 2; globalization as context, 254; greed associated with, 35; of "new wars," 2; regional dimensions of, 251; regulatory framework for, 135–37; strategies and calculations, 8
war expenses, 29
warlords: Afghanistan, 20, 21, 210, 218, 227; Angola, 239*n*; economic agendas, 8; Lebanon, 32*n*
war profiteering, 21; military officers, 103; open markets, 22
Warsaw Pact (former) nations, 129
war system, 47
weak states, 2, 278–79
weapons, guerrilla purchases, 63
Weber, Max, 28
web of meanings, 28
Western Europe, 229
white-collar crime, 21, 250
white list, 242
witches, 13*n*, 122
World Bank, 131, 173; political causes for conflict, 259, 259*n*

young men, proportion in society, 5; in DRC, 143; as grievance, 143*n*; in Sierra Leone, 16, 97

Zaire, 124, 126, 270, 272, 273
Zambia, 127, 160, 172*n*, 173
Zimbabwe, 147, 148, 165; diamond concession, 167
Zollman, David, 127
zoning laws, 40